Intimate**Strangers**

Also by Bill Zehme

Lost in the Funhouse:
The Life and Mind of Andy Kaufman

IntimateStrangers

Comic Profiles
and Indiscretions of
the Very Famous

BILL ZEHME

Delta Trade Paperbacks

A DELTA BOOK

Published by
Dell Publishing
a division of
Random House, Inc.
1540 Broadway
New York, New York 10036

Library of Congress Cataloging-in-Publication Data
Zehme, Bill.
Intimate strangers : comic profiles and indiscretions of the very famous / Bill Zehme.
p.   cm.
ISBN 0-385-33374-9
1. Entertainers—United States—Anecdotes. 2. Celebrities—United States—Anecdotes. I. Title.
PN2285.Z44 2002
791'.092'273—dc21   2002025982

Printed in the United States of America

Published simultaneously in Canada

December 2002

10 9 8 7 6 5 4 3 2 1

BVG

For Suzanne Clemensen Zehme,

whose heart is never far

A Few Words About the Great Bill Zehme
by Cameron Crowe

He is, of course, the King of the First Sentence. And with the first sentence, you're inside his head. Like a great tour guide, he beckons you into the inner sanctum, whispering in your ear with a comic and sometimes poignant voice that says this is just between us. He has slipped past the personal barricades of many a generation-defining icon. And he does it by bringing something new to the game—himself.

As an interviewer, and more important as a writer, Bill Zehme has what the great director Billy Wilder once called the essential ingredient to anything that is memorable in life—"a little bit of magic." Zehme can communicate great truths in a joke, the casual observation, the quick turn. (He once described veteran *Tonight Show* producer Fred De Cordova as possessing an "Acapulcan tan.") He is the poser of the great question. (To David Letterman: "How would you explain your work to foreigners?") He reigns by bestowing nobility upon those who don't often get it. (On Ed McMahon: "To be near him is to feel your power magnified exponentially.") And to anyone who thinks Zehme is, as he once simply described himself, "a humorous impressionist of popular culture," you know that great truths are right there, flashing powerfully in between the jokes. (Again on Letterman, for whom Zehme remains the definitive chronicler: "Fear has never left the back of his mind, I will tell you. Because, along with his father's face, he always suspected—no, he was always

convinced—that inside of his lank thorax there beats his workaholic father's selfsame genetically cursed, fatally flawed, big and fragile rumpus-
loving heart.")

This collection is essential. These pieces are still talked about, and in a
shocking turn of events, they're even revered by that most jealous group
of judges—fellow writers.

Hell, they gave him some shit, but incredibly never even held it against
him that he actually got naked with profile subject Sharon Stone. (Her
suggestion.) Zehme's near twenty-year relationship with Letterman and
Jay Leno, assembled here in total, is a beyond-candid look at these very
private men, no longer on speaking terms, and Zehme's own service as a
sort of go-between and documentarian. Witness the moment when Leno,
about to ascend to Carson's position at *The Tonight Show,* takes Zehme
onto Carson's empty set to show the Pall Mall cigarette burns on the carpet behind Johnny's desk. ("The King is just a man" began the resulting
piece.) There is a candid glimpse of a lovestruck Hugh Hefner, about to
lose his grip on a wife he truly loved. And my own favorites, the flurry of
pieces in which Zehme found post-modern cool in Regis Philbin, Barry
Manilow, and (gasp) David Copperfield. But it was one profile that
makes all this praise somewhat of an understatement.

Warren Beatty.

For many years, Hollywood's golden producer/seducer/star was the interview subject no journalist could crack. It was Beatty who understood
the film game best. But the road to Beatty was littered with the maimed
bodies of journalists still clutching their notepads and cassette recorders.
Beatty was the Holy Grail, a man so in command of media encounters
that he would often simply stop speaking and journalists wouldn't even
notice. Only later, at the quiet of their desks, did those who interviewed
Beatty realize what they had—an up-close audience with charisma. And a
lot of tape of the interviewer himself talking while Beatty listened. And
bravo for Beatty, by the way. Mystique these days is rarer than Afghani
oil. (In my own quest to interview Beatty, I once held what I thought was
a sterling phone conversation. We made loose plans for a free-ranging,
in-depth conversation. I never heard from him again.) Yes, for decades,
Warren Beatty was the great untold story in the world of movies, never to
be captured. . . .

Until Zehme. And, damn it, he made it look easy. He wove a tapestry
out of the silences, and even timed the length of Beatty's pauses. That
lasting portrait is pure poetry. Never mean-spirited, always allowing the
reader a front-row seat, and never returning with anything less than a real
and lasting truth. That's Bill Zehme. As a writer, he's also a dancer. Follow

his personal jig through many a mine-field created by publicists and time restraints thrown up by wary and ultimately trusting subjects. Zehme's voice remains clear and hilarious. Think of Johnny Carson's stylishly subversive dazzle, and you're on the right track. (Many have long thought Zehme should host late-night himself. His account of an attempt to play second-banana to Charles Grodin, included here, is worth the price of admission.) For any aspiring reporter, or lover of pop culture, here is the manual on how it's done. So read these reports, and you'll find the klieg lights shine a little differently across the landscape of art and stardom once you've walked in Zehme's shoes. Those are the facts, that's the drum-roll. As we once spoke of Frank Sinatra, another subject of a unprecedented dialogue with Zehme—it's Bill's world. We're just livin' in it. Or as an editor friend of mine recently cried out, "Where can I find another Bill Zehme?" He knew the answer even as he asked the question. There's only one, brother. And this is some of his best.

An Introduction

So here it is: My charge in this racket has long been to find new ways to write about people who get written about way too often. I expect nothing less of me, either; I threw this gauntlet at my own big damned feet. I did so, most probably, in order to live with myself, since I seem to occupy space in a journalistic subdivision where residency has become more embarrassing with each passing year. This would be the noisy and overcrowded province of celebrity appraisal. (Lately, it's just plain clangorous here.) Stargazing-and-appraising, however, is endemic to our big-dream culture of hope and hopeless envy, and has been for at least nine decades (although never quite like during the last couple of them, when *infotainment* actually became a word *Webster's* defined). In times calm or trying, tales of spotlit lives have happily distracted our wishful masses and, more important (in terms of my participation therein), sold copies of magazines. It has been, at once, a pursuit both essential and ridiculous, but also the thing that has provided me a fine enough living for just over twenty years—because I believed it could be done differently. And quirkily. And comically. Even irreverently, whenever possible. It had seemed to me that not very many writers in this peculiar realm (not that there aren't a good few) were thinking much about such objectives, much less about writing. And writing, I suppose, is all that any of this has ever meant to me.

I do not believe in celebrity, by the way. The truth is, I have never written about a celebrity. I have always written about humans, replete with human traits and foibles and issues, who also happen to be famous. I aim always to de-celebrify them, to reveal odd minutiae of their humanity observed during our temporarily orchestrated intimacies, to tell you how they smell, if they smell. It is essential never to be in awe of iconic subjects (although, in the case of Frank Sinatra or Johnny Carson, the challenge was Herculean and insurmountable). In order to elicit the richest personal color, their star-power and wattage must be ignored completely. I have seen them all as my equal, despite the fact that they are multimillionaires with grand estates and publicists, whereas I am not. (*Damn.*) However, when familiarity bred a sense of genuine friendship with these people, I always recalled this useful axiom: *Never forget why you walk in their halls.* I did not write about them so as to become pals for life; I was permitted to write about them, for the most part, so that some professional project of theirs could be promoted on glossy paper stock beside fabulous photos by Herb Ritts et al. Still, most of the subjects in this collection claimed to enjoy how I teased and reconsidered them in print. At least, their publicists continue to take my calls, for whatever that is worth.

My prose, it has been groaningly said, issues forth in IV drip mode— and I owe a national debt of gratitude to every editor who ever withstood me. Nothing here arrived on or before deadline, ever. That's both my fault and my cursed signature. (I have confessed to countless editors that I care too much about sentences; the best ones correctly responded that one can never care enough.) I always felt that magazine writing demanded a greater sense of permanence, that it was less disposable than newspaper work and would sit around for a long time, as it does (in appalling stacks and piles) in my home—and has since boyhood. This, of course, was why I forced my way into the magazine game in the first place. I had written columns and features for my high school and college newspapers—I was, incidentally, one of those amorphous "communications" majors, at Loyola University of Chicago, an institution best known for producing doctors, theologians and, well, Bob Newhart (an accounting major). The campus I attended was located on North Michigan Avenue, three blocks south of the Playboy Building. My goal, of course, was to traverse those three blocks and secure my first big national break, which happened within a few years of graduation, thanks to the benevolence of a *Playboy* editor named John Rezek. Seeing my own prose in famous typeface on famous pages registered an indescribable thrill that has persisted over two decades. It is this little thrill that still reminds me why I do what I do.

The pieces collected in this book canvas all corners of the business of fame. With each one, I tried to create an unexpected—and hopefully entertaining—approach (or conceit) to explore the subject at hand. Because there inevitably were stories behind the making of each profile, I have written new mini-introductions that spill secrets and offer insights to lend perspective into the whole surreal experience of celebrity coverage. I've also reinstated a good deal of material previously unseen, lost to space constrictions in original form. And then there is one other particularly enlightening addition to this volume: the revelation of my "show business feud" with illusionist David Copperfield, who has kindly allowed me to reproduce the fine, angry letter he wrote after reading my *Esquire* profile of him. I trust that journalism professors everywhere will have their day with that colorful episode.

B. Z.
March 2002
Chicago

Intimate**Strangers**

Part One
GODS AND **PLAYBOYS**

Frank Sinatra, Dean Martin,
Sammy Davis Jr. ★
Hugh Hefner ★ Warren Beatty

Francis Albert Sinatra had long given up consorting with the media—in print or otherwise—when I began a unique correspondence with him in 1994. For decades, insecure men on bar stools had asked themselves the eternal drunken question: "What would Frank do?" They asked themselves this because Sinatra, for certain, famously swaggered with uncompromised bravado and a personal code of style unmatched anywhere. Here was a man who knew and attacked life like no other. It occurred to me, however, that nobody had ever specifically asked Frank to impart his life wisdom. So I tried to do just that and was thrilled that he didn't seem to mind at all. Subsequently, at his invitation, I also began asking his friends, associates, and relatives about the way he did things, large and little, as only he could. When Dean Martin died on Christmas 1995 (two weeks after Sinatra turned eighty), it seemed that the moment had come for me to share some of my findings and give due to an era in final eclipse. After the piece was published, I continued to seek out quirky minutiae about Sinatra style, which I assembled the following year in a book called *The*

Way You Wear Your Hat: Frank Sinatra and the Lost Art of Livin'. (I was told that he loved that title and was tickled to see that so many of his favorite drinking tales and personal policies had been memorialized.) His own death came on May 14, 1998. The piece that follows stands as his final interview experience.

And Then There Was One:
Sinatra Bequeaths
His Rules of Order

Esquire, March 1996

In black tie, Dean sleeps forever. He lounges in his marble vault, behind the bank in Westwood, draped in midnight attire, in the uniform, crimson hanky peeking from breast pocket. He was the beautiful one. Always did know how to dress. The Leader liked that. Sam was another story. He was the youngest, the wild card. Onstage, 1963: "What are you doing in that cockamamie street suit!" Frank admonished, emerging godlike from the wings of the Sands, Dean by his side. "And what is this, with the tie down and the collar open? Where the hell did you learn that? Now, go up to your room and get yourself into a little ol' tuxedo!" This happened nightly. Sam: "What're you, *Esquire* magazine? Let's get one thing straight, Frank! I'm thirty-seven years old! I will change my clothes when I get good and ready!" Frank: "Are you ready?" Sam: "Yes, Frank." Sam was a pussycat in his tiny tux, Frank always said. Right now he's up on that Forest Lawn hilltop, wearing one of his English toy suits—over a red shirt. (Red—the color of Bojangles's eyes!) On his wrist is the enormous gold Cartier watch he so treasured. "Laid on me by my man, Francis," he'd tell those who asked, before the end. "It goes with me." Frank gave it to him on the reunion tour, the last time the three of them tried to do it all over again. Recapture the old mothery gas—that, of course, was Frank's idea. Dean told him, "Why don't we find a good bar instead."

Wrecked, the Leader sat amid the leftover antipasti Christmas night. Dag was dead since before dawn. They called each other Dag (pronounced *daig*), for no one else could, would dare. He was not surprised by the bad news, but the sorrow was pounding him in slow waves. "Don't worry," he said softly to a few intimates, "I'm not going anyplace for a *long* time." And he picked at his food. The mantle of style would now be his alone, although of course it always had been. It was just nice to have some company, *their* company, those two bums in particular. He embodied the code to which all freethinking men aspired, but only two truly understood how it was done, no lessons needed, sang and swung to boot. Thirty-five years after it started—all that rehearsed spontaneity in the Copa Room at the Sands Hotel—only the oldest survives; the freshly minted octogenarian, he persists. His force wanes not at all, keeping younger men of close acquaintance up all hours while he belts his Jack Daniel's and explains history as he knows it. He does not let go.

"You've got to love livin', baby! Because dyin' is a pain in the ass!" That was what he always told them, never stopped telling them. Sam paid heed until he couldn't any more. Dean didn't, hadn't for years. His gorgeous indifference, which Frank quietly revered, finally withered him, which Frank detested witnessing. "How can you eat that motherfucking shit?" Frank goaded him from across the table last June. Together, they sat at Dean's booth, next to the bar, at Da Vinci in Beverly Hills. It was the final Summit. Dean had just turned seventy-eight, and Frank never missed a birthday. Frank missed nothing, never has, even now. So he saw what he saw and his heart broke and, hating it, he fought. (*"Fight, fight, fight!"* he whispers inside his head every day, staving off that rat-bastard, Time.) He wanted a rise out of gentle Dag, so he poked at the pasta and needled like a hero. He tore off bread and pelted his frail *paisan,* a ritual of theirs since always. Dean only smiled. Frank stayed feisty. They sipped their separate amber and talked as best they could. After an hour or so, Frank got up to leave, said he had to go to New York tomorrow. "Good," Dean said. "Don't come back." Such was the love between the largest of men.

In the beginning, there was only Sinatra. He lent out the hubris, covered every ass, cleared the forest, rigged the tempo, made the rules. His battle cry: "Fun with everything, and I mean *fun!*" Born an only child, he did not like to be alone. So he handpicked his pallies with care, shunned all the hapless clydes who wanted in, and held court till the sun shone.

Nineteen sixty: By day, they made their first film opus, *Ocean's Eleven*, playing war vets out to rob five Vegas casinos; by night, they kept on playing, onstage, on the Strip, on the loose, moving in a pack, like, well, never mind. In Frank's hands, hanging out turned to art, daubed with a palette of twinkle and menace. His good side was the side to stay on. He once said, "Trouble just seems to come my way—unbidden, unwelcome, unneeded." Above all, he was about fearlessness and good grooming. He bought his first jet in 1959, sang about it onstage: "When I'm up there wingin', I'm really ring-a-ring-a-ding-dingin'...." Like so, he reinvented language and instructed eager pupils. From the third Sammy Davis Jr. autobiography, *Why Me?*: "A young cat with two wild-looking chicks walked by and Frank raised his eyebrows. *'Cuff links.'*"

What man would not like to be near that man? Even Camelot came to the Sands. The young senator from Massachusetts became known as Chicky-Baby, as christened by the Leader, who shared all guilty pleasures guiltlessly. His men slept warm and strayed not far. The comedian Tom Dreesen, who spent thirteen years opening for and traveling with Sinatra, told me this story: "They were all in Las Vegas shooting *Ocean's Eleven* and one morning the actor Norman Fell woke up and looked outside of his hotel window. He saw Dean and Sammy and Peter Lawford running past the pool, running *fast*. So he stuck his head out and yelled, 'Hey, where are you guys going?' And Sammy said, *'Frank's up!'* So the day begins. You have to understand that when you are with Frank Sinatra, it's his world and you are living in it. If you revolve around his energy, you benefit. With Frank, you can never learn enough."

Only because somebody asked, he once said: "I think my real ambition is to pass on to others what I know. It took me a long, long time to learn what I now know, and I don't want that to die with me. I'd like to pass that on to younger people." He wasn't talking about song artistry; he meant life nuance, how-to stuff, the business of comporting one's self— all of that which he has suggested only through music or private example. Two years ago, it occurred to me that he had not made good on his promise. Men had gone soft and needed help, needed a Leader, needed Frank Sinatra. So I wrote to him and appealed on behalf of manhood and mankind. I wanted to ask him essential questions, the kind that could save a guy's life. I wanted what might approximate Frank's rules of order. He took the clarion call and instructed his publicist, Susan Reynolds, to gather my questions as they came and bring them along on the road. He would sit on his plane, Jack in hand, and do what he could as an oracle, when he found the patience, a virtue he has never claimed to possess. (He was, in the end, either charmed by or merely tolerant of this exercise. "It helps me pass the time," he said with kindly forbearance.) The process took many months. Later, I was encouraged to debrief his closest confidants, who further detailed the minutiae of his ways, both then and now. (To complete the style spectrum, I did the same with intimates of Dean Martin and Sammy Davis Jr.) Supplemented as such, there emerged a composite of how the role of Sinatra is played in everyday life, whatever the circumstance. "To be like Frank Sinatra," says his friend, producer George Schlatter, "you've got to be able to give a punch and take a punch. You've got to have a stomach like a still. You've got to be early for everything except bed. He'll make you eat salami at three in the morning with chocolate cake and pasta. You go, 'Oh no, Frank!' It doesn't matter. Frank is just like you. Just like me. Only bigger."

Q: What should a man never do in the presence of a woman?
A: Yawn.

Few mortals have seen him yawn. Yawning promotes sleep, which he does not. Sleep: dullsville, numbsville, weakness. He won't even do it on airplanes. Awake, he is aware, which is all. *Be aware,* he always told Nancy Jr., had the words inscribed on her St. Christopher medal, on her first key chain. "It's the number-one priority," she says. He dims only when horizons brighten. He favors the tint of sky he calls Five O'Clock Vegas Blue. "I tell him he's the last of the Italian vampires," says Steve Lawrence, who has greeted too many dawns at his side, where scores of men have slumped. They cannot hit hay until he does, and they must drink apace with him to the finish. Hank Cattaneo, his longtime road manager, addresses the subject with dread: "By four or five in the morning, I've had enough Jack Daniel's, so I get the bartender to color Coca-Cola with water so he thinks I'm still with him." Begin to nod off, he will say, *"Hey! What are you doing! Wake up!"* Rise from the table, he will say, "Where the hell are *you* going!" Only excuse: "To the bathroom." Mountainous Jilly Rizzo, Frank's late number one, would use it as his exit line and disappear. Others who sneak away are summoned back. "He doesn't like Do Not Disturb signs," says Lawrence. "God help you if he knows what room you're in," says Cattaneo. "Frank himself will light firecrackers outside your door."

Only Dean could leave. At the Sands, after a show, he'd stay for one drink, two, tops, then lie to Frank and say, "I've got a girl in my room." Dean fell under nobody's sway. He loved to sleep, then hit the morning links, nursing his glorious six handicap. Frank knew. *"He likes golfball-thumpin' like I like humpin'—to each his own!"* the Leader sang when the Friars roasted pally. Once, he gave a broad a grand to wait naked in Dean's bed. Dean gave her two grand to go back and tell Frank he was fabulous. Even Sam, after a couple and a half decades of merry nocturnes, after having finally seized sobriety, could no longer take it, but hung in. Sitting with his main man at 4 A.M. in the Golden Nugget lounge, all he could think was *Bed, oh bed. Bed, bed, bed, soft bed.*

How Frank does it: "He gets a lot out of a catnap," Barbara Sinatra told me. "He's like that little rabbit on television who keeps going and going and going."

Q: What kind of behavior will you never tolerate?
A: How much time do you have? Next question.

Q: What is worthy of a fair fight?
A: When I grew up, there was a lot of pushing, shoving, and occasional punching. But today we live in such a violent world that you must do everything you can to avoid any kind of brawl or fight. I never really was a street fighter—I never fought one street. My fights *became* street fights. They started in the saloons and then we went out into the street.

Q: What are your rules for drinking? Your most dependable cure for a hangover?
A: Don't drink to begin with. Dean and I did a lot of jokes about drinking. But let's face it: If we had actually drunk as much as people said we did, do you think we could have made movies all day and done shows at night, which we did? I would not recommend that anyone else live life that way. You have to know what you can handle.

Hangovers fear him. His metabolism knows no such thing. "He doesn't get hangovers—he *gives* them," says Schlatter. "He's a carrier." Only Sam saw him suffer, and that was just once!—after the night Frank wanted to punch out John Wayne. The Duke had briefly come over to Frank's table at a party and hovered uncomfortably close. "You're *leaning* on me!" Frank complained. Duke grinned and beat it, and an hour later Frank, who'd uncharacteristically gotten himself "about ten sheets to the wind" (per Sam), decided to settle the score. He confronted the big guy, who just lifted the Leader and set him aside. Sam went to the house the next day, he recalled, and "out of the back came Frank, staggering to the bar. He said, *'I gotta get a Ramos gin fizz.'* " (Cure—hissing hair of the dog!)

He is particular about that which he hates. "I won't tolerate certain things, like being crowded into corners and not enough ice in the drink," he once said. If he hears the word *nigger,* he explodes or walks away. "You don't berate another human being in front of Frank," says Dreesen. "If you harm a child, you are his archenemy. He's offended by foulmouthed women or any man who uses abusive language around women. Also, if you compliment him, he will change the subject." He cannot be pushed. "Don't tell me—*suggest,*" he suggested to Lauren Bacall. (She's the one who started that damned rodent phrase he hates—Rat Pack—back in 1955, when she was Mrs. Humphrey Bogart. After many sodden Vegas nights orchestrated by Frank, she gazed at the hungover carnage of Bogie and his drinking chums—the usual suspects such as David Niven, Judy Garland, and the writer Nathaniel Benchley—and groaned, "You look like a goddamned rat pack!" Bogie's was the *real* Rat Pack; how he and Dean and Sam and company later got stuck with it, he'll never understand. And their earliest moniker, the Clan, stank, too. His preference was always the Summit.)

"Frank takes things seriously; I don't," said Dean. Once, in a moment of contrition, the Leader confessed, "I'm too much of a volatile man." Like the time at the hotel in Pebble Beach when the two of them wanted room service after midnight and found the kitchen closed. Frank got the manager on the horn, hollered, got the guy up to the room, and punches flew, while Dean sat watching television. "Hey," said Dag finally, "can you guys fight a little to the left? I'm having trouble seeing the picture." But Frank was the master of extremes: "We cut the top of our thumbs and we became blood brothers," Dean would recall. "He wanted to cut the wrist. I said, 'What, are you *crazy*? No, *here's* good enough.' "

It was never that big of a secret: "Do you know that I spill more than he drinks?" Frank would say. "That's an actuality." At the Sands, Dean wheeled a booze cart across the stage every night, bottles clinking. "Hey, I better mix me another salad!" he'd say. His license plate read DRUNKY, but it was a sham. Dean mostly sipped and pretended. Onstage, it was apple juice; you could tell by his timing, even more physically precise than that of the beloved monkey, the former partner, Jerry. (Straight men work harder—support beams cannot fail.) Only with Dean did Frank truly loosen his coil. Perfect evidence, perhaps their most majestic moment: an eleven-minute duet medley on Dean's 1967 NBC Christmas show, during which neither man would ever look happier. Mimicking Dean's producer, Greg Garrison, who gyrated just off-camera, they jogged in place (Frank: "What, are we training? *For what?*"), skipped invisible rope, *played as men,* and swung like winking gods through a slice of American songbook. "It's still the best medley that's ever been done in show business," says Mort Viner, Dean's agent, who has seen everything. "One take, right straight through," says Garrison, awed to this day. "That was the peak."

"No one has ever seen me drunk," he told Oriana Fallaci that same year. When Dean drank, it was J&B scotch. Toward the end, he would measure out three tablespoons of club soda as mixer. The ritual was meticulous, unhurried. I watched him do it countless times in Beverly Hills, first at La Famiglia, which finally closed, then at Da Vinci. He always wore large black-framed glasses, a blue windbreaker, a powder-blue shirt, and the pinky ring Frank gave him. (In his final months, he kept his teeth in his pocket.) Each night, delivered in his white Rolls-Royce, he would be in his booth by seven-thirty, usually alone, blissfully alone— unless Viner or Garrison or his ex-wife Jeannie dropped by for a drink. At both places, his albums played in the background and sometimes he would quietly sing along with himself. Though enfeebled, there was something heroic about him, a bittersweet remove. His biographer, Nick Tosches, identified it as "that wall of *lontananza* between the self and the world." The death of his son, Dean Paul, in 1987 had fortified the wall. Yet he would smile and shake anyone's hand, kiss any woman, rise to any occasion. Jerry Lewis brought his young wife, Sam, over to the table one night to introduce her. "Sam, huh?" Dean said softly. "I always knew you'd end up a fag."

Frank learned to drink Jack Daniel's from Jackie Gleason. "Mr. Gleason introduced me to a lot," he says, as proof that swagger can in fact be taught. For his product devotion, the distillery rewarded him with his own acre of Lynchburg, Tennessee, ground—one of his proudest possessions, the soil on which the ambrosia cooks. Steve Lawrence calls him Jack's Original Test Pilot. Any man who drinks it is his friend. Sammy did, with Coke—a desecration, the Leader thought, but in the right ballpark, at least. For ongoing replenishment, he likes the bottle in front of him, on a silver tray, with a rocks glass, a bowl of ice, and branch water for splashing. His first drink is always preceded by the tapping of glasses in toast. If inebriation comes, it rarely shows; he has never been one to stumble or slur words. (At worst, he gets hotheaded.) "There've been

times, certainly, when he's feeling no pain," says Cattaneo, "but he's always lucid, always knows what he's doing. The Italian word is *la figura,*
the figure—one must always maintain the appearance." He once told
Nancy Jr. the trick he employs at parties: "You take a couple of sips and
you put it down in one corner and you walk away and they give you another drink and they think you're drinking a lot. They think you're as relaxed as they are."

Q: How do you know when a hat looks right on you?
A: When no one laughs. My favorite was the one in *Pal Joey.* And I
    was so crazy about that suit from the movie, I didn't want to wear
    the coat over it—and that's why I put it over my shoulder. I have
    no idea where the hat or the suit is now.

Q: How do you know when you've picked the right barber?
A: When you leave the shop and no one hands you a hat, you're okay.

Q: What details should never be overlooked when dressing in black
    tie?
A: For me, a tuxedo is a way of life. When an invitation says black tie
    optional, it is always safer to wear black tie. My basic rules are to
    have shirt cuffs extended half an inch from the jacket sleeve.
    Trousers should break just above the shoe. Try not to sit down, be-
    cause it wrinkles the pants. If you have to sit, don't cross your legs.
    Pocket handkerchiefs are optional, but I always wear one, usually
    orange, since orange is my favorite color. Shine your Mary Janes
    on the underside of a couch cushion.

"Cleanliness was paramount to Dean and Frank," wrote Shirley
MacLaine, distaff mascot to the fellas, in her recent memoir. "I'd sit in
their hotel suite, fascinated at the spectacle of them primping for a night
out." Sam was the same, if a tad more extravagant. He liked to luxuriate
in a bath of Lactopine, Hermès, and Eau Sauvage, then splash on Aramis
afterward. Dean and Frank were shower guys and electric shavers and
smelled of Fabergé Woodhue and lavender, respectively. "Strong colognes
drive me out of the room," Sinatra once said, which further evinces his
love for Sam. (Today, when thusly offended, he will inquire, "What's that
shit you're wearing?") If there was a Summit clubhouse, it was the steam
room at the Sands, where they met daily at five to clear the mucus of the
previous night and plot ahead. There, they ate hog dogs, blew cherry
bombs, gave grief to Joey Bishop and Peter Lawford, and all wore mono-

grammed robes. Frank's was FAS; Dean's was DAG; Sam's was SMOKEY. Don Rickles gained induction by being tossed out into the pool area, naked. His robe said RHINO. "Frank thought that was funny," he says. Standard Sinatra steam-room greeting: "How's your bird?" His concern was anatomical. Variation: "How's your Bell & Howell?"

"In a tuxedo, I'm a star," Dean always said. "In regular clothes, I'm nobody." Onstage, he never wore the same pair of socks twice. He had a fetish for shoplifting socks from haberdashers he patronized. "Everyone has a little bit of larceny in him, a little bit of original sin," Dag confessed. Nowadays, Frank will amuse himself by surreptitiously pocketing silverware, utensil by utensil, from swank restaurants, then letting his heist clatter to the floor on the way out. "I never go anywhere that I don't steal something," he says impishly. On late flights, he stuffs Tootsie Rolls into the shoes of sleeping friends. Years ago, when he disapproved of any pally's shoes—scuffed or white or, worst of all, *brown*—he would insert lit firecrackers. (He made sure they got new and better replacements.) He once accosted his longtime pianist, Bill Miller, for wearing a brown suit. Miller: "What's wrong with dark brown?" Frank: "It's nighttime. You wear dark gray or you wear black. Besides, it doesn't match your eyes." Moreover, none of the Chairman's men are to be caught in his midst without coat and tie, nor are they to open their collars until he does and decrees, "Hey, loosen up!" He has never performed without top button fastened unless in recording studios, and never recorded before eight o'clock in the evening. "The voice is more relaxed then," he said.

"The only guy can hurt you is yourself," he has lectured. On one bitch of a night in the sixties, he sat forlorn in a Burbank TV studio, the voice but a croak, lamenting that which had gone down the night before: "Drink, drink, drink. Smoke, smoke, smoke. Schmuck, schmuck, schmuck." The lungs of Dean and Sam were charred ruins when their cabs came. Frank called Sam Smokey with both affection and disdain—he smoked too goddamned much. Frank never inhaled, saving the reed while maintaining *la figura,* cupping them like Bogie did. Now he is down to three or four a day, always the unfiltered Camels. "He never smokes in the house," says his wife. "He always goes outdoors." Three puffs, then out. He keeps them loose from the pack, in a side coat pocket, extracting each with effortless sleight of hand.

"I was always fascinated by the pockets," says Nancy Jr., who has produced two books about her father. "Everything has its own little home, neat and tidy. The white linen handkerchief in the inside pocket. The little mints. The individually folded tissues. Sometimes a single key on a fob. And the money clip. In the old days, it was just a regular pointed paper clip. Now it's gold." (He has never had loose change—except dimes for the pay phones of yore, ten at a time—and he especially loathes pennies, which he often throws away.) Inside the clip, which resides in the pants pocket, are hundred-dollar bills, folded into small squares, so as to be discreetly pressed into hungry palms. In the realm of tipping—or *duking,* as Frank calls it—his legend towers. True lore: Parking attendant brings around Frank's Dual Ghia, Frank asks him what his biggest tip ever was, kid says a hundred bucks, Frank dukes him two hundred, then asks who it was that gave him the hundred. "You did, sir, last week."

That was nothing. The men of Sinatra must carry C-notes by the wad to peel in his behalf. "He'll always say, 'Duke this guy a hundred!' " says Cattaneo. "And then two minutes later: 'Did you duke him a hundred?' I say yeah. 'Well, duke him again!' He gets a crowd of waiters and waitresses real quick. It's not unusual for us to end up giving one or two girls five hundred dollars in an evening. I'll say, 'Frank, enough, *enough*!' "

Q: How do you get over a broken heart?
A: You don't. I think being jilted is one of life's most painful experiences. It takes a long time to heal a broken heart. It's happened to all of us and never gets any easier. I understand, however, that playing one of my albums can help.

Q: What is the most important thing to look for in a woman?
A: A sense of humor. When looking *for* a woman, it always helps to find a woman who is also looking. Make her feel appreciated, make her feel beautiful. If you practice long enough you'll know when you get it. And, by the way, "look but don't touch." You can't get into trouble window-shopping.

Q: What do you do when a woman cries?
A: I usually cry with her.

"What is this thing called love?" he'd begun singing, when Dean interrupted: "Frank, if you don't know, then we're all dead." No one loves like the Leader, ever has, ever could. It is his epic blessing and curse, that which informs his phrasing in song, that which delivers him unto zenith and nadir. "Having lived a life of violent emotional contradictions, I have perhaps an overacute capacity for sadness as well as elation," he once put it rather delicately. Random polarities: He told a young Shirley

MacLaine, "Oh, I just wish someone would hurt you so I could kill them for you." (And they were just friends.) Nancy crushed a mosquito in front of him not long ago. He winced. "I'm trying not to kill anything anymore," he said mournfully. "If anyone hits you, let me know," he instructed Sam on the first day they met. He is a sucker for stray dogs and for buying the ugliest Christmas tree on the lot. "He always feels sorry for it," says Nancy. He has raised billions for charity, but hates to admit it. Barbara Sinatra, his bride of twenty years, ponders the phenomenon: "It's a generosity of love that goes beyond anything. He can be very sweet and playful and docile, but you feel that he's like an army. I feel like I have a whole army behind me."

Love and marriage: Upon waking, "he'll go out into the yard to stretch, pick a flower, and present it to me," says his wife. "Every morning. One day we didn't have any blooms out there, so he brought me a little tree branch instead." When courting her, he would call, quickly say "*I love you,*" then hang up. "There'd be no further conversation," she says. She found her engagement ring at the bottom of a champagne glass: "I thought it was an ice cube." He stands when any woman approaches him, observes all chivalrous etiquette—holding chairs and coats, opening doors, ladies first always. "These are habits I could never break nor would I want to," he wrote to me. "We can be in the middle of a huge party," says the missus, "and he'll come whisper the most sexy things in my ear, then walk away." He is famous for calling to her from across crowded rooms, raising his glass, bellowing, "I drink to you, my darling, because *I adore you!*" She says, "He doesn't care who hears it or sees it."

He always preferred crying alone. "It's kind of a—it's a personal and an embarrassing moment, I think, particularly in a man, you know," he stammered after his mother died. (Dag was a pallbearer.) Now tears come too easily; audiences made him cry before he finally got off the road. "I miss Sam," he has muttered in the wee small during recent years. Sam called him the umbrella. "The patch is dramatic as hell," Frank said, smiling, when Sam lost the eye in the car wreck. All the pallies wore eye patches in the steam room afterward. Frank took him onto the golf course, made him hit balls, regain equilibrium. "Don't despair," he taught them all, no matter what. Then Sam got into the cocaine in the seventies and the Leader dropped him hard. "Frank didn't want to be an enabler," says Tracey Davis, Smokey's daughter. Three icy years passed, until a confrontation: "Sam, I'm so fuckin' disappointed in you, with that shit," Frank said. "Dump it. You're breaking your friends' hearts, Sam." That was all it took. When the throat cancer came, he lay in bed, taking Frank's calls: "There were times when he and Dad would be on the phone," says Tracey, "and they didn't talk. They just held on. They really didn't have to say anything."

Dean organized the order of their deaths twenty years ago: "Take Frank first. Then Sammy. Then Bing. Then come back for me. Maybe I just might be ready then." Dag changed his mind when son Dino, beautiful kid, crashed his jet into the same mountain that took the life of Frank's mother. (She had been flying to Vegas to see her boy.) Never had he cared less about living. Frank hatched a plan within months (*fight, fight, fight*)—the Together Again Tour, twenty-nine cities all through 1988, the Pack back in excelsior, gray and swinging, there but for the sake of Dag. It lasted one week. Onstage at the Chicago Theater, hours before Dean flew home for good: "Frank, as far as we're concerned," said Sam, "you're still the Chairman of the Board." Dean, holding glass: "Yeah, you're still Chairman and I'm still bored." It didn't smell like apple juice anymore, and he was tired, too tired to pretend it was still 1960. Mostly, he just watched television for the next seven years.

The funeral was after dark—always their time—in the little Westwood cemetery behind the bank. His records played, just like at the restaurants. Barbara went and so did Nancy Jr., but the Leader could not. "He just didn't want to face it," his spokeswoman, Susan Reynolds, told me. "He didn't want to grieve in front of others." At home, he felt the breeze blow through the windows and hurt. Decades ago, on some charity tour, a little blind girl asked him, "What color is the wind?" He had tears in his eyes then, too. "No one knows," he softly told her, "because the wind moves too fast."

Growing up in Chicago during the sixties, I loved listening to my grandfather, a devoted *Playboy* subscriber, tell me stories about Hugh Hefner. This homegrown Midas of sex lived on the Near North Side in a big Gothic house full of gadgets and gidgets, spun on a round bed, and lived the fantasy life that his magazine espoused without ever getting out of his pajamas. In college and soon thereafter—by which time Hefner had permanently gone west to Los Angeles—I found ways to get into that old house on North State Parkway and look around for nude ghosts. Once, a maintenance man actually let me ride on the rotating bed, whose panels were still stocked with bottles of Johnson's Baby Oil—just in case Hef suddenly returned. *Playboy*, as it happened, gave me my first big-time national writing exposure, employing me in various ways. Once I was even called upon to write words under Hefner's own byline. (It was, I think, a personal appreciation of Marilyn Monroe, his first cover girl; he wrote the lead paragraph and I wrote the rest.) At least a year before I began work on the following piece, some friends at *Playboy* had told me about a house Hefner bought for his Playmate wife, located next door to

Playboy Mansion West, an oddity that signaled marital trouble. Then, in January 1998, the Hefners announced their separation. By February, Hef, ever the notorious homebody, was being regularly spotted out on the town. And that is where I came in on the saga. For this profile, I aimed to crawl under his skin and explore his unfathomable heart, which seemed freshly bruised in that uncertain moment. Inadvertently, the piece also announced his return to the limelight, where he would soon begin controversial public dalliances with twins who had rhyming names and, later, a posse of seven blondes. He happily blamed me for getting all the action started.

Of Hef and Heartbreak:
The Man Who Loved Women

Esquire, August 1998

So now he leaves the property. It cannot be—but is! Now he is out among us—his children, his *children's* children—at the Opium Den, the Garden of Eden, the Whisky Bar, the Coconut Club, the Viper Room. He's actually been sighted at raves—historic! He never even went to his own clubs when he had them. But now! Here is the mack-daddiest of them all, making the scene, spoiling for action, cruising the spots, lamping the ladies, surveying that which he wrought by never going anywhere! "What the hell was it I was supposed to go out for?" he once said, quite rhetorically, and you knew exactly what he meant therein. That was Hef: Forty years indoors, housebound Dionysus, man of Mansions, pajama-clad, swigging the Pepsi, clenching the pipe, making Philosophy, making chicks, telling us to go out and play and not worry about it, while he stayed home on his Round Rotating Bed and had more fun anyway.

Look at him now! Hermetically unsealed, emerged from the gates, charting the new real world, night after night—he is wearing *suits,* for God's sake! He flashes the rabbit-head cuff links and shifts his long pointy jaw above the open white collar. It's *him,* in a Very Real Sense, as he would say. He even looks like him, especially when he's dancing. He can't stop dancing! That would be the Hefdance, as seen on his various television specials—a strange gyration all his own, slippery shuffles and twists, elbows pumping but fast; a Caucasian disco inferno, burning, burning. The girls keep pace somehow. Never mind his age, for he never has. But still—a *septuagenarian* swinger, indeed the chairman emeritus of sex American style, known today on his company website as "the reigning king of the cocktail nation and one of the towering figures of the 20th century." But of course. And the Gen-Xers know it certainly. They bow, they flock tableside: *"You're the man!" "You're the god!" "You rule!"* Hef just beams, amazed that they remember, although how could they not? He sips his Jack Daniel's and, *ugh,* Diet Coke—it is, alas, a Pepsiless cocktail nation. But he complains not at all: "With Jack in it, you don't really notice," he assures. Then: "Get these ladies some more champagne!" Blondes in rubber garments flank and squeal and bop. "Go, Hef! Go, Hef!" they chant. Oh, yes, the Party is back on! The Party is everywhere! It is a happening most groovy, let me tell you. Etcetera, as he would say.

Welcome to Hef's Epilogue, in which Hugh Marston Hefner, the most famous magazine editor in the history of the world, reclaims youth and reminds himself of whom he was before lately. "Everything old is new again," he keeps saying, over and over, by which he could, and does, mean himself. "It's part of the whole retro thing, etcetera. . . ." Which is to say: We, as a culture, have gotten back in touch with our Hefnerian impulses. It's part of a whole gratification thing. Thus, the ceaseless slope into hedonism redux, into this bachelor-pad hi-fi martini-olive cool-jazz swizzle-stick after-dark girl-crazy smoking-lounge whatever-world, wherein even the American president gets to fool around and almost nobody cares as long as it hurts no one. ("I just wish he had better taste," Hef sighs.) Forty-five years ago, he saw the future and then it came and then it went, but it is here again, fortified by youth, and so is he— although he didn't plan it this way.

Hef, you see, never guessed that he would be out painting Los Angeles scarlet. In truth, he has been *pried* loose from his legendary paradisiacal bastion, from his beloved Playboy Mansion West, by friends who seek only to distract him. Hef, you see, is experiencing that which other men know all too well, but never suspected that Hugh Hefner could. He is feeling the quiet pang that binds victims of love torn asunder. Hef has heartache. His wife has moved out on him, with their two young sons. She has moved into the house that he bought for them on the adjacent property, right over the large stone wall. The implications resonate in dark poetry. There is no getting around it: Hef, like never before, is hung up on the girl next door.

"Here I am again at a kind of crossroad," he says with a small shrug, and that is where I find him, at his crossroad, in black satin pajamas, one Tuesday afternoon in late February. I have come to Holmby Hills, to the Mansion, to Hef, to assess his heart, to document his moment of torment, to get in on the Party. The task, I knew, would be arduous and require months of personal attention. But societal benefit loomed large: However Hugh Hefner withstood marital discord would, no doubt, serve as an example to mankind for future generations. He quickly saw the importance of the endeavor: "My first reaction was, maybe this is the wrong time—let's wait. And then I realized, almost as an afterthought a day or two later, *No, this is the right time!*" He is a man legendarily unafraid of being chronicled, a man who understands his place in history and is ever ready to share it with others. "I'm an open book," he says brightly, "with illustrations!" Indeed, in the upper reaches of the house, locked away in a small room, there are nearly twelve hundred elaborately bound, museum-quality scrapbooks of his Life So Far. He meticulously oversees the compilation of each volume, writes captions himself, does not skip over any parts, dark or light. "They are the footprints in the sand," he says wistfully, significantly. They exist to tell him where he has been and to suggest where he might go. Now he needs the chapter covering what he confesses to be "this rather difficult emotional time" and I have been permitted to take the notes.

Hef Healing Night, One: He knows the scene already. He has been out for, what, a month already, looking for, what, hope again maybe. Pictures have turned up in tabloids. Most visible frolic to date: The January night at the Garden of Eden, a pajama party celebrating the fifteenth anniversary of the Playboy Channel; there was Hef, surrounded by Playmates inserting fingers and tongues into his mouth and ears while camera strobes flashed. This was the first public sign of trouble in paradise. Playboy Enterprises would, within days, on January 20, issue the statement of his separation from Kimberley Conrad Hefner, Miss January 1988, Playmate of the Year 1989, whom he shocked the world by marrying that same year, whereupon she became known as his Playmate for a Lifetime and, more intimately, as his Kimberella. She bore him two sons, Marston Glenn, now eight, and Cooper Bradford, now six, both of whom possess a remarkable angular, wiry resemblance to their father. The separation announcement cited "differing interests" and, as preemptive caveat, "no third-party involvement on either side." With Hef, randy speculation comes necessarily. But, in fact, he had been a one-woman Hef through-out all ten years with Kimberley—his first-ever monogamous love, no less. Even so, his beautiful blond wife had begun leaving the marriage long before the world heard. Seven years earlier, Hef had acquired a Malibu beach house for her as a refuge from the corporate hurly-burly of the Playboy Mansion. "This is not a home in the usual sense," he will allow. "It's like living in a resort. And, you know, she's a very private person." Then, two summers ago, he bought her the house next door to the Mansion, for $7 million, on their seventh wedding anniversary; she had taken up full-time occupancy by late last year. "I just started thinkin', if she wanted to have a place with a little privacy, let's make it adjacent. And if we do indeed separate, it would be a separation that will be least hurtful to all concerned, especially the children. We cut a hole in the wall so that they can come back and forth."

But now for tonight, a Tuesday: Cabaret virtuoso Bobby Short is opening in Hollywood. I get the call from Hefner's wry and indomitable executive assistant, Mary O'Connor, in whose Mansion office Hef squats on the floor most weekdays, doing magazine business—seat of the empire, Mary's carpet; or, otherwise, her couch. (He always did work on the floor or on the Bed, always hunched over strewn papers and photos; now the residual lower back pain requires an occasional elastic brace, the only thing he ever wears under his pajamas.) I am asked to meet him after ten at the Catalina Bar & Grill. Mary says Playmates will be present; it is unspoken, but implicit, that Hef should be seen with beautiful women whenever out. It is like a built-in dating service. At the club, Hef alights from his long black Mercedes limo with the HMH 1 plates. His entourage includes his personal doctor and friend, Mark Saginor (who briefly moved into the Mansion when Hef suffered a stroke in 1985, from which he miraculously recovered within two weeks), plus two blondes, a brunette, and a security guy. Hef introduces the women to me: "These, of course, are Dr. Saginor's nurses." Much laughter. One dusky blonde is Karen McDougal, 1998 Playmate of the Year; she sits beside Hef in our round booth. I suggest how it is remarkable to be Out With Hef, since he is famous for never doing such. Miss McDougal looks at me like I am an idiot, says with incredulity: "He never goes out?" Hefnerian lore is new to her.

He is courtly and debonair with the women; also paternalistic and instructive. Never is he brash or slick in the Guccionesque sense. He tells them that Bobby Short performed on both of his memorable television shows, *Playboy's Penthouse* (in the sixties) and *Playboy After Dark* (in the seventies), and also in the Playboy Clubs of old. They nod. Hef sings quietly along with Short on many standard tunes: "Just diiiiii-rect your feet!

To the sun-nnnyyyy side of the street!" On raucous numbers, Hef and the women raise their arms, sway, snap fingers; he is happy. Learning that Short was born in Danville, Illinois, he brightens and softly tells me: "I first got laid in Danville! Millie and I went there." Millie Williams was his first wife, mother of Playboy chairman and CEO Christie and individualistic David, a computer whiz; Millie now works in Playboy corporate human resources in Chicago. "Danville had a reputation as a kind of wild place at the time," he continues. "That's probably why we went there." It happened at the Wolford Hotel in the spring of 1948; Hef was twenty-two; he and Millie, both students at the University of Illinois, posed for pictures in front of the hotel. The pictures can be found in Volume 41 of the Scrapbooks. Hef and Millie have not been as close as they were before he married Kimberley. Not his choice, he says a little sadly.

All present buzz about a party being planned in Hef's honor for Saturday night. It is to take place at the estate of a friend. Dr. Saginor, a warm-hearted rogue bachelor, mid-fifties, has been inviting as many beautiful women as he can find; he is quite excited. Hef sighs, says with bemused patience: "They're calling it a *pre*birthday party." Dr. Saginor has prescribed it; he has seen the heartache Hef tries to hide; he hates it. Of Kimberley's final exit and its effect on Hef, the doctor whispers to me: "He was squashed like a june bug."

Not that he shows it. Not even to his friends will he show it. How can he? (Never mind that they can tell anyway.) He feels a solemn responsibility to all men: We need Hef to be the happiest of hepcats. While we may toil in dreary lives of drudgery, we envision him doing whatever he wants, because he can, usually in the vicinity of naked women. He is a comfort that way. He is the dream of our collective inner adolescent; fantasy is his life. "I'm still that boy who dreamed the dreams," he loves to say, full of wonder, as self-aware as any grown boy alive. And he made sure it would be so: "If we're smart enough, we start taking hold of our own lives and kind of reinventing ourselves in the way we'd like to be," he once said. "I think I've been doing that all my life. The most dramatic reinvention, of course, came with *Playboy.*" With *Playboy,* in 1953, he created a magazine that created him. The repressed midwestern Methodist became the living symbol of sybaritic engorgement and a millionaire because of it—today, his personal fortune is said to approach $400 million. (The Playboy corporate empire, meanwhile, is worth roughly a strong $375 million.) Soon, he who never thought to masturbate before turning nineteen would go on to have fabulous guilt-free consensual sex with a thousand women, per his own modest estimate. He unshackled sex from shame and made horniness healthy for all, himself especially. "Am I happy?" he said in 1962. "I wouldn't trade places with anyone else in the world." Men have wanted to trade places with him ever since. Until now maybe.

All things considered, however, Hefner looks good. He is a most chipper customer. He greets whomever he encounters with an inimitable *"Howdy-howdy-howdy!"* There is spring in his every velvet-slippered step. "I couldn't be in a better place," he assures me, after he has glided down his Gothic staircase into the Great Hall, turned left into the Living Room, then settled onto his striped baronial sofa in the Mansion Library beyond. (In the Hef hemisphere, formal capitalization is a way of life. You get used to it.) His face is smooth and pink and in no real need of the tucking he has been secretly pondering of late. ("The only thing that might keep him from doing it is that he absolutely *hates* pain," one of his friends tells me.) His seventy-second birthday, impossibly, is still several weeks away, but he appears to be no more than late-fiftyish. Moreover, his mind is quick as ever and only occasionally forgetful; he terms such lapses as "senior moments"—and then only among cronies. He is never not busy—at his magazine's Chicago headquarters, he is known with fond aggravation as the World's Wealthiest Copy Editor—and he is never not hopeful. He sees romance in life's every fillip. No jaded mogul, he is a chronic rhapsodizer; he slips into reverie whenever considering his considerable lot. *Lucky man!* he thinks when he thinks of himself—and that is not seldom.

"Even during this transitional time, I just feel...fortunate," he is saying, while alternating slugs of Diet Pepsi and Evian water. "It's also, you know, a *revitalizing* time, too. I think of it, in a very real sense, more as a new beginning than an ending because...I'm not sure there is going to be any ending. My comment when I got married was, 'Now I have the final chapter for my book—the marriage, the continuity of children, the toys scattered in the Great Hall, the Children at Play signs on the property.' Who knew that not only would there be a final chapter, but now also an epilogue? F. Scott Fitzgerald said there are no second acts in American lives. Well, we know that's not true! Not if you play it right. It's a miniseries!"

From Volume 1137 of Hugh Hefner's Scrapbooks:
    MEMO FROM HMH TO DAVID WOLPER, 9/12/95
    SUBJECT: THE HUGH HEFNER STORY
    PROLOGUE: THE WEDDING—THE CULMINATION OF ALL MY DREAMS

    As previously suggested, I think our story should begin with the wedding, here among the lush surroundings of the Playboy

Mansion West: the rolling hills, redwood forest, fountains, and waterfalls, with peacocks, flamingos, and crested cranes strutting the lawn. Friends and family have gathered for the Marriage of the Decade: Mr. Playboy is about to marry his Playmate for a Lifetime. The wedding will occur on the front lawn by the Wishing Well, where Hefner proposed....

It *is* a miniseries! Or it will be one day. Hef's miniseries—his magnum opus of self-mythography—now temporarily languishes in preproduction quagmire. Plus, life got complicated. The memo to his Hollywood producing partner Wolper runs sixty-nine (!) pages. (Among epic memo writers, the Hefner legend towers, as his minions would woefully attest.) Hef did not like any of the scripts submitted, so he dictated his life *dramatis,* point by point, as a screenplay compass. He has long seen his earthbound existence as a movie anyway, albeit one in which most of the action, wedding aside, is interior. It comes up a lot: "My life has been rather like a movie for a number of years...," he began one sentence in a memo circulated among *Playboy* editors in early 1988, providing groundwork for an internally infamous article called "The Great Palimony Caper." This was to be Hefner's indignant reaction to a misbegotten, quickly dropped palimony suit filed by Carrie Leigh, his omnisexual hellcat chatelaine, or Special Lady, of five years. Anyway, once Miss Leigh stormed out of his life in January of 1988, Kimberley Conrad—Playmate of that very Month—would within two weeks capture his fancy, love would bloom, and this, Hef insisted, would make for a happy ending to an otherwise fairly sordid magazine piece. As such, his palimony-story memo continued: "...but there has never been a more magic night than the first one Kimberley and I spent together. If this had really been a movie, that night there would have been strings, and perhaps a little Bobby Hackett horn."

The one who culminated his dreams, who became his most special Special Lady, who is now his Special Neighbor Lady—and who has, most certainly, screwed up Hef's whole miniseries prologue idea—was twenty-four when Cupid drew bow. Also, per Playmate Data Sheet, she was 36–24–36, five foot nine, 122 pounds, and aspired "to be financially self-sufficient, do a cover for *Playboy,* and travel the world"; turnoffs included "gossip, pretentious people, and early morning phone calls." Hef suggested this characterization of her, in a palimony memo: "From out of the northland came an Alabama-born, Vancouver-bred angel to turn all the stress and pain into sunshine and happiness." (Hey, he's a romantic guy!)

Here, then, was Kimberley, already known around the house as the kind of woman who could siphon oxygen from male lungs, one way or another. "I'd seen guys go down in flames trying to get her attention," says Hef now. "Which impressed me. There was an aloofness. She wasn't an easy lady." Back from Canada, she was boarding at the Mansion, in the guest cottage where most Playmates stay, working with Helmut Newton on a motorcycle pictorial. Hef was screening a pair of Yves Montand films for friends over two nights in the Living Room; each night he stopped her in the Great Hall and asked her to join him; she declined both entreaties. "I was afraid," she later recounted in her Playmate of the Year video. "Plus, I'm not the type of person you have a one-night stand with." After the second film ended, he approached her again: "I told her that I was really interested in her and would like to spend some time with her. And she said, 'Well, I really don't know you.' And I said, 'How are you going to get to know me if we don't spend some time together?'" (*Hef's Line!*) "And that line—the simple logic of that—from that moment on, everything changed! We spent that evening together." They repaired upstairs to his quarters, "just talking until four in the morning," she said, "and laughing about everything." This was their Falling in Love scene: Fate and chemistry had intermingled! They had loved each other from afar all along and didn't know it! Now they knew! She found him "very nice, very genuine, very sensitive.... He really wanted to get to know me. It wasn't just a fling." She moved in for good shortly thereafter, bringing two dogs and a cat. Hef recalls: "Within a relatively few months, I was thinking the unthinkable."

MEMO TO ATTORNEY TONY GLASSMAN, 2/17/88
SUBJECT: MY COMMENTS ON PALIMONY COMPLAINT

... Throughout the 1960s, 1970s and 1980s I have had a series of serious romantic, live-in relationships ... All of these women knew full well that there was little or no possibility that I would ever consider marrying again. These relationships included Cynthia Maddox, 1961–1963; Mary Warren, 1963–1967; Barbi Benton, 1969–1976; Sondra Theodore, 1976–1981; Shannon Tweed, 1981–1983; and Carrie Leigh, 1983–January 1988.

When he goes out, he goes out late. His early evenings are ritualistic events of socialization, carved in rock, immovably scheduled. Monday night is Manly Night, whereupon he bonds with male cohorts, who eat turkey dinner in front of him while he drinks Jack-and-Pepsi. (Hefner never dines with guests; his last meal of the day is consumed after midnight, usually in the Master Bedroom.) Wednesday is Card Night; more men, gin rummy. (During the seventies, before his world settled, Wednesday was allegedly known as Orgy Night.) Tuesday and Thursday are Family Nights, in which he and Kim and Marston and Cooper gather in nuclear fashion, often to watch TV or movies. (These have not been happening so much of late; she cancels regularly. Fretting for the boys, Hef keeps telling her, "They want to see us *together*.") Friday and Saturday are Classic Movie Nights—old movies preceded by cocktails and open buffet for his Closely Knit Family of Friends, also known as the Gang. Sunday is First-Run Movie Night, a longtime staple at both the fabled original Chicago Mansion and at Mansion West; the Gang and various drop-in Hollywood types drink and graze again and save eight dollars apiece on going to actual movie theaters.

Nevertheless, when you inform people that you have spent time at the Playboy Mansion, the reaction is uniformly the same: Eyes widen, pupils dilate. You are asked about the naked Bunnies and Playmates. Winking and nudging occur. If only. It is not like that. Hasn't been since the arrival of Kimberley and especially since the boys were born. Bunnies no longer exist, since neither do Playboy Clubs. And Playmates are a vaporous presence; they inconspicuously take meals in a breakfast area called the Mediterranean Room, off the Dining Room, and tend to hover slightly apart from the Gang. The Gang, meanwhile, is made up of a few dozen very pleasant, low-key people—many of them couples—ranging in age from fortyish to seventyish, almost none of whom work for Playboy, but several of whom have familiar faces, albeit somewhat more matured than in memory. (Tony Curtis. Bob Culp. Robert Blake. Dick Van Patten. Fred Dryer. Johnny Crawford. Larry Gelbart. Don Adams. And Playmates of rare and wondrous vintage.) It is not unlike being around friends of your parents', really. They move easily about Hef's Shangri-la. Their names are kept on the Gang List, permitting them access to the house at any time, although they mostly come when expected. Before they became later-life family guys, you would often see Nicholson and Beatty and Eastwood and Jimmy Caan. "They all came by because the chicks were here," Hef says. Now the big boys tend to show up only when live heavyweight prizefights are beamed in. (Kimberley further pruned from the List an assortment of ne'er-do-wells and freeloaders whose presence her husband had long tolerated, if not ignored. "He has a sometimes unbalanced sense of loyalty toward a lot of people," acknowledges Mary O'Connor.)

As the Gang Leader, he presides passively and stands out among his crew only because everyone else wears clothes whereas he wears pajamas and a smoking jacket. He is not one to hold court; he sort of wafts above and through the group. At the Chicago Mansion, he was known to throw epic bacchanals that began after midnight and didn't end for days, during which time he never emerged from his bedroom. Mailer likened him, in that way, to Gatsby, a reference Hef prized. But he is a born host, therefore an uncomfortable guest. "Even in grade school, my house was where the little coterie of friends in the neighborhood came," he says significantly. Still, he needs these people; in their midst, he is more relaxed, less restless, more grounded; he is no good alone. Of his hospitality and largesse, he will confess, "I do it for a very selfish reason: Everything is more enjoyable simply because it's shared." It is understood by all that there is nothing much anyone in the Gang can do for him except be there. So they come.

She appears behind him. He is seated, as is his custom, at the head of the Dining Room table, chatting with Gang members, who are eating dinner. It is Friday night, ten minutes before the regular seven o'clock screening. (He is a stickler for rolling film precisely on time.) Tonight it's John Huston's *Moby Dick*. But now she is here, without warning, back among his friends, who are also hers. She has come through the wall, from her adjacent property, accompanied by a dog the size of a pony. She taps his shoulder and he looks up. "Hi!" she says brightly. You can tell much about a man's heart at such moments; it is in the eyes. His glow; they sparkle like some faceted mineral; his countenance is more alive than I have seen it. *"Kimber!"* he says, and rockets to his feet, and flings his robed arms around her, and plants a long kiss on her cheekbone. He has got it bad. But he can only engage her for a few minutes. He must fetch the production notes he has prepared on *Moby Dick,* which he will read to the assemblage before he waves down the lights in the Living Room. (He works on notes for the Friday classic films only, usually that afternoon, scrawling odd errata on yellow legal paper; it is his thrill.) She goes to the buffet table and fills a plate for herself. He wanders through the house to collect his guests, summoning them, as is his custom, with a low singsong call: *"It's moooovie-tiiiime!"* She sits down to eat with an old friend, while the rest of the Gang files out. His hands, which grip the film notes, tremble a little more noticeably than usual, as he sits on the arm of his deep leather couch and waxes eloquent about Ahab and the big white sperm whale. When the lights go down, he watches the movie nestled in the corner of his enormous couch, and there is no one next to him. I am told that there has been no one next to him for nearly eight years.

The only woman he ever left was his first wife. Since then, they have all left him, largely because they could not make him theirs alone. And yet he loved falling in love with each and every one of them. "For me, being in love is the very essence of being alive," he has said, convinced as others would think not likely. But It's true—he is happiest swooning, being the blithe love-goon, stomach aflutter. By all accounts, his purest previous love was Barbi Benton, a privileged California beauty who was Barbara Klein before he renamed her in his magazine. "Barbi became a kind of Hollywood version of the teenage romance that I never really had when I was in high school," he says. Because Hollywood and high school are the most sacrosanct touchstones of his idealized life—one friend calls him High School Harry—Hef is saying that Barbi was an Extra Special Lady. It was Barbi who, in 1971, found Mansion West for him, who helped oversee its Hefnerian domestication, who cross-stitched the pattern that hung in the Library—Be It Ever So Humble, There's No Place Like Home. (In contrast, the brass door plaque at the Chicago house announced: *Si Non Oscillas Noli Tintinnare,* translated If You Don't Swing, Don't Ring.) It was Barbi who also got him to do things he did not like to do, like travel around the world. They would hop on his all-black Big Bunny jet, replete with Round Bed, shower, and disco—now gutted and flying commercially in Mexico—and go places. He has been loath to go anywhere ever since. "There's, you know, a lot of *inconvenience* in travel," he says a little grumpily.

Love could always transport him, anyway, and he never even had to leave the house. So he loved Kimberley Conrad: "Despite the age disparity, we enjoy the same kind of life," he was seen professing in her *Playmate for a Lifetime* video. She was seated beside him in the Library, as their love was being documented for eternity and also for sales in the U.S. and abroad; he was giddy and she was both giggly and weepy. "She enjoys spending her evenings here with me and with friends and watching old movies and playing games and just being together." And so it was on the night of July 23, 1988—six months after their first Big Night—that he led her out of the Game House, where she had just beaten him at Foosball, and over to the Wishing Well, where he did what he had not done since 1948, with Millie. He begged her hand in marriage. And Kim said,

"Do I have to answer now?" And his jaw dropped. "Well, no," he said. But she recovered within seconds and said, "Of course I'll marry you!" The following July first, they returned to the Well and pledged troth before friends and family. "You're *here*!" the pastor said to Hef; mock surprise, big joke, laughs all around. But the groom was serene and Kimberella cried throughout and he brushed her tears repeatedly and sighed dreamily each time he did so. The wedding pictures—shot by presidential photographer David Hume Kennerly—appeared in *People,* on whose cover the new husband and wife smiled beneath the incredulous banner headline, "HOLY MATRIMONY!" From the subhead: "The bride wore white. Hey, she wore *clothes*! Next week: Hell freezes over." They danced their first dance to "As Time Goes By" from his favorite movie, *Casablanca.* He has always seen himself as Rick Blaine, waiting at the Paris train depot, waiting for Ilsa Lund, who never comes, reading her farewell letter in the rain, which blurs the ink. He has always seen himself as the guy left standing in the rain. "We've all been there," he tells me one afternoon in the Library, exactly where he had cooed to his fiancée on videotape. "We've all had our punches in the gut."

All that is new again is not necessarily old: His progeny are sleeping over. These princes who will someday rule the rabbit, if they choose—they have invited a few little buddies to spend the weekend at their Other House, the one where their father lives. It is early Saturday evening, which means all of these old people are hanging around waiting to watch some black-and-white movie. Butlers wearing white shirts and black vests and black pants are running around with trays. Usually, the Hefner boys don't talk much to any of the older people at their father's house. Cooper, who is six, will give them a smile and a few polite words. Marston, who is two years older, kind of keeps to himself, would really rather not say anything, even when they ask him things. Tonight, however, the boys have an idea, which even their dad thinks is pretty funny. They've got this trick wallet tied to a long transparent string and Dad gave them a twenty-dollar bill to stick out of the wallet like bait. When nobody's looking, they put the wallet on the floor of the Great Hall, scene of all of those ancient disco parties that stopped after they were born. They drop the wallet, then run back up the stairs to the second floor, where Marston holds the string. First, a butler sees the wallet and bends over to fetch it—and, *zzzzppp,* Marston yanks the string and the wallet flies and the butler almost drops his tray and the boys laugh their heads off. And their father, standing there in his pajama outfit, is watching and chuckling, and he thinks this is great, too. He urges them to try it again and sends another butler into the Hall. "Somebody dropped a wallet!" the boys yell from upstairs and this other butler reaches down and—*zzzpppp*! This is just hilarious. And Dad, he keeps laughing, too. Then he starts telling everybody that it's time to come watch his movie and so all of the people wander into the Hall and now this older lady sees the wallet and she bends down. She was holding a glass of red wine when she screamed and—anyway, the butlers got it all cleaned up before anyone else noticed.

Hef Healing Night, Two: The Saturday movie, poetically enough, is *Harvey*: "The relationship between a man and a big bunny—could be the story of my life," Hef tells the Gang. He adds that next week he will show them *The Bachelor and the Bobby-Soxer,* "which could also be the story of my life!" Oh, yes, sir! He is *game* tonight, perfectly primed for his Prebirthday Party, which a financier friend named Len Ross is hosting at his nearby Coldwater Canyon estate—itself the former love nest of William Randolph Hearst and Marion Davies. Hearst died in bed there; JFK and Jackie spent part of their honeymoon there; now Hef is, more or less, redeclaring his enforced singlehood there. Dr. Saginor has stocked the pond like a champion—at least one hundred extraordinary women have been invited, mostly by him. On Friday night rounds with Hef, I had watched the dedicated doctor spread the word among lovelies—at Merv Griffin's swing-dance boîte, the Coconut Club, where Hef jitterbugged up a storm; at the Brazilian techno-rap club Mamagaya, where Hef grooved in a leopard-lined booth and studied talent from afar; at the tony Millennium, where he graciously withstood the advances of Playmates, previous and potential, all of whom somehow knew he would be there. By two in the morning, most of the city's club pulchritude had been installed on the guest list. Dr. Saginor felt triumphant; his patient felt tired, but reflective. "When I went to parties in college," Hef told me, "the ratio of men to women was seven to one. After that, I made the pledge to reverse that ratio at any party I ever threw." His pupils have learned well.

After *Harvey,* he trots upstairs to put on a suit and splash on cologne; he enters his limo in a cloud of Lagerfeld spice, carrying a traveler cocktail. He is most buoyant and a little nervous. (He is actually always a little nervous.) After wending up Ross's endless driveway, he steps directly into his past and also into his present. The women! Like an infestation, they are aswarm, cinched breathless in tiny dresses; it could be a silicone repository, so pneumatic is the faux-cleavage collective. (Hef, for the record, prefers God-given, but the world has changed and he does adapt.) "This brings back great feelings of nostalgia," he says repeatedly, invoking memories of his long-gone infamous Midsummer Night's Dream parties. "Except," he says, "if this were Midsummer Night's Dream, all these girls would be walkin' around in lingerie."

The house where they teem is all Spanish Mission palazzo—sprawling terraces perched above the Olympic-length pool, which is flanked by grand white colonnades. (In *The Godfather*, the place was used as the home of the studio chief who woke up in bed with the horse's head.) Hef says it was one of six houses he considered buying, before finding the Mansion. He thought it too formal: "My place was so wonderfully natural, with all the birds and flowers etcetera and the naked ladies around the pool. I can't imagine that here." Plus, he was concerned about the Hearst connection: " 'Citizen Hef' I don't need."

Bambini quickly set upon him. On the terrace, a gaggle moves forward to ask for a picture with him; they wish him a happy birthday and he says that his birthday is still weeks away. "Then what kind of party is this?" one asks. "It's a coming-out party," he says. "Coming out of what?" "Coming out of a *marriage*!" Well, then. He slips away and tries to open a glass door that is locked and, from the inside, an exotic woman comes to the glass and places her full lips against it and Hef leans forward and returns the gesture. Such flirtation, innocent in kind, consumes the night. An extravagant buffet is served and the host makes a heartfelt toast to "a person who has done more to shape this century in freedom of press, in freedom of speech, in standing up for what you believe in, than anybody! He's the reason we're all here living the good life!" Hef toasts, in return, to the future, which is taken to mean more of the same, and the celebrants cheer lustily.

Afterward, downstairs in the host's private discotheque, Hef dances and dances with a young woman he had met the night before at Millennium. Her name is Jaime Bergman; her blond hair is in a bun; her body is unfathomably proportioned and barely harnessed in a little red number. He is besotted with her; she will soon be a Playmate, month indeterminate; also she will be his own personal immediate future. He dances on, exhilarated, which seems to represent something larger to the assembled crowd—perhaps the hope of all hedonism foretold. "You should have seen this man a month ago," Dr. Saginor says, watching his friend. "He couldn't move. He was in the bushes. And the minute she comes back, he'll be right back in the bushes. He runs like a whipped puppy whenever she crooks a finger or bats an eyelash." He refers, of course, to the missus.

·   ·   ·

She is a strong one, wily and wise, and she knows him all too well, knows him better than she knows herself in ways, which isn't always the greatest thing for a marriage. He told me in our first conversation, "I don't think I will ever love anyone again as I love her, then and now." When I inform her of this, she says, "*Really?* You're kidding! Did he tell you that?" Her shock seems to mix validation and insecurity, as though she does not believe in herself enough to entirely believe him. Still, she is a woman who walked into a notorious lifestyle not of her own design and reordered it. She remade a pleasure dome into a functional family dwelling. In the Mansion's butler's pantry, there continues to hang a small placard that genially intimidates all staff—When Momma Ain't Happy, Ain't Nobody Happy. By all accounts, it was a battle—the rank and file were accustomed only to the unchanging whims of Big Daddy—but she had mostly prevailed through sheer will and, some say, political maneuver before she abandoned the project. To find her, one must still call the Mansion, where the butlers expeditiously put her on the line, connecting to the House Next Door—as it is somewhat ominously known.

The estranged Mrs. Hefner can be as warm and as chill as her translucent sapphire eyes portend. For instance, I first take an empathy tack and allow as to how life has probably gotten more difficult lately. "It has?" she says. "For who? For you? Are you asking me questions or are you assuming or are you trying to get something out of me?" Then she laughs. Then she says she has no comment. And then she tells me everything. (All of our very friendly chats would begin this way.) But she knows exactly what she is doing, just as she knows everything her husband is doing, often before he does it—his nightlife revels in particular. (On the day of his Pre-birthday Party, she blithely warned me, "Oh, you'll see a lot of the *old style* there. Listen, stay outta trouble, okay?") For his part, Hef tends to keep her honorably apprised of his outings. He has told me: "There are no secrets. She asks me questions, I give her answers. But there are no secrets *anyway*! Everything I do, she knows! I don't know how she knows, but she knows."

Most certainly, there is perceptiveness and credence in her version of events, the essence of which deserves to be presented. Thus, a random sampling: "Our interests, I would say, are still very similar. But it was the *same thing* every night for ten years. Sometimes I wanted for us not to have plans. Once in a while, it would've been nice for him to say, 'Let's just call and tell everyone not to come on Friday night and have a quiet dinner together and go to a piano bar or something.' But it was always, 'Well, I can do that after the movie.' . . . It wasn't that he didn't want to go out. It was that I wanted to go to bed at a reasonable hour. I get up early to work out. The truth of it became how I fit into *his* life. But what about *my* life? And I was lonely. But I don't want to sound like Poor Me. Because it wasn't Poor Me. I was having a nice time . . . I was twenty-four when I met him, and it may be unfair to say, but it's like Lady Di. She also married young to a famous man set in his ways. You think, or hope at least, that you can change him. But sometimes it's impossible. . . . You know, he's reliving his youth, and I think that's a good thing. What's wonderful is that we have remained friends. He's a good boy and I'm not his baby-sitter and I love him . . . He goes out on these dates, or whatever, with eighteen-year-old girls, then he comes home and he calls me, or I see him later. And he tells me, 'The whole time I'm with them, all I could hear was *blahblahblah*. All I could think of was you.' . . . You know what? I'm not ready to date. I could date if I want. I have been asked out by some very nice men. But I'm happy with my boys. They're all the men I need."

Anger is there, certainly. It is one inch below the gloss of rationale and benevolence. It is understandable. She married and subdued a Legendary Life that, nevertheless, needed to retain its odd quirks of routine as well as its fundamental history. He is who he is and his past cannot go away, because it keeps coming up, as in the two-hour A&E *Biography*, which did not pretend that there never was a Barbi Benton, which caused no small injury. Things do come up, always have and will. So there would be anger and then the instinct to flee and then flight itself and then more anger over having had to flee.

They have, of course, been seeing a marriage counselor. He has been all for it. In fact, the very next Friday, they were in session together when she said something and he said something and she stormed out of the room and called her attorney and instructed that divorce papers be drawn up and "irreconcilable differences" be used as the complaint. The attorney obediently filed the petition at the Los Angeles County Courthouse that afternoon. Somehow, she neglected to tell her husband about this; he learned of it from a Playboy publicity executive the next Monday, after a weekend during which he and Kimberley had made amends. She also forgot to tell the lawyer to rescind the papers. Then the media got wind of the filing. Together, the Hefners instantly issued a statement: "This filing took place in a moment of misunderstanding. We are still exploring a reconciliation and neither of us wants a divorce." The incident would soon become known around the Mansion as The Miscommunication. (Mary O'Connor: "What happened? Nothing happened. It's the same as before—the same bullets, the same ducking, the same kissy-kiss—nothing's changed. He's okay.") The following week, the missus bolted town for New York and was photographed at the Knicks game seated beside Donald Trump. She had confessed earlier to me that Trump—who apparently smelled blood in the water—started calling her from the moment the separation news hit in January. "Hey, listen," she assured me, "I know exactly what The Donald is all about!" The tabloids, one imagines, reacted just as Trump may have wished. (The *National Enquirer:* "Duck, Donald!! Hugh Hefner's Hot & Wants His Wife Back.") After returning to Los Angeles, she assumed a sly pose and told me, "I don't wanna say anything, I can't. But I would really appreciate it if you could get it in somewhere that I am definitely *not* in love with The Donald. That would be good." She added that Trump had also taken her to see *Phantom of the Opera* on another night, completely eluding the press. Hef, meanwhile, was not "hot" so much as exasperated. He would explain his wife's public assignation thusly: "Her decision to go off with *The Donald*"—there is disdain in the italics—"came about because she got pissed at me. But she got pissed at me for nothing, just because I went out the night before and ran into a Playmate that she has a particular thing about." But he was slightly shaken. "Well, she didn't *make it* with him!" he told his Wednesday card cronies when they asked. He also told them that her jaunt wasn't the worst thing that could have happened: "It just takes the heat off of me."

Never mind that it is now his seventy-second birthday. Never mind the lengthening-shadows-of-December bullshit. He may not want to fight with his wife—and he won't—but he will continue to fight that bastard Mortality. (What have all the young women in his life been but proof of that?) Mortality: "Why go quietly?" he says. "I think we should all go kicking and screaming." When he does go, he will sleep forever with Marilyn Monroe, right next to her, in his drawer at the Westwood Memorial mausoleum. He bought the space a few years ago, could not resist: At long last, he could recline with his magazine's first cover girl and centerfold, the one whose nude calendar pictures he discovered and bought for a song, begetting all romantic adventures to come. "I love those kinds of symbolic pieces fitting together," he says. Likewise, he loves that his son Marston, like himself, was born on April ninth and, moreover, he also loves that Cooper, born September fourth, is the numerical calendar inverse—4/9 and 9/4. "Magic!" says Hef.

No, his birthday is about *rejuvenation.* Before the day is over he will receive the gift of Viagra and know rejuvenation like never before. It is the Thursday before Easter weekend—Symbolic! Bunnies! More magic!—and he has opened the Mansion for a lunchtime reunion of actual Playboy Bunnies to celebrate the publication of *The Bunny Years,* a smart oral history of the original women who wore ears and tails for him. "What a wonderful way to start a birthday!" he announces. Media prowls and Hefner is aglow, proud as the peacocks patrolling his lawn; the ladies, aged forty to sixtyish, fawn all over him. He has dated most of them, slept with several—many had living quarters in the old Chicago house—and it is clear that they loved him then and still do. "We can open up a new Bunny Dorm!" he says pluckily. *"All right! We're movin' in!"* they squeal. Hef: "Works for me! Always did!"

That night, before screening a long film retrospective of highlights from previous birthdays, he tells the Gang that he will show *Saturday Night Fever* on Saturday night—to be followed by an authentic Playboy Mansion disco party, his first since, well, *whenever*! The group whoops, claps, cheers. "The old days," he promises them, "are returning!" Indeed, tonight he is not alone on his massive couch, nor would he be all weekend—Jaime Bergman snuggles beside him. He shares his specially hand-popped popcorn with her—*sharing*—and nuzzles her neck intermittently. Many former Playmates are present as well, reliving Mansion memories from the retrospective. Ex–Special Lady Shannon Tweed is here—"I wanted to see this part; this was before my time"—with her companion, Gene Simmons of the rock group KISS. Jessica Hahn, who once lived here, tells me in the Great Hall: "He gave me my life."

They would all say as much, these ladies; it is genuine love that brings them back to Hefner. "Some people still don't get that," he will say, putting it mildly. For these women, he would forever provide safe harbor; he would be love unconditional, sponsor, and support beam. They disrobed for the world on his behalf and he would forever cloak them, with gratitude, with concern. A dozen of them wander out to the terrace after the film and the champagne and the caviar, after the Gang has serenaded the birthday boy and Bob Culp has reprised his exultant Manly Night toast ("Gentlemen, gentlemen, be of good cheer, for they are out there, and we are in here!"). They sit outdoors at tables, these beautiful women, and talk and smoke and drink for an hour before Hef finally strolls out. He is feeling fine and mischievous: "Are you girls waiting to use the Jacuzzi?" And they peal with delight. He sits with them for a while. And then some of them aren't sitting there anymore and neither is he. They are gone. It is, after all, his birthday.

•   •   •

"The original idea was to hold a little family thing yesterday," he tells me on the day after his birthday. "But, at the last minute, it conflicted with Kimberley's plans." Because it was also Marston's birthday, she took the kids and their favorite cousins to Knott's Berry Farm. So there was no family birthday thing, about which he is stoic, as he must be—at least, he was able to attend Marston's laser tag party the evening before their birthday. (Hef firing a laser gun! He felt like Buck Rogers!) He says they will try to regroup again later this afternoon. He also says he cannot count on it, that she changes plans every hour. They were also supposed to be together a few nights earlier. "She bowed out. We didn't do it. But that's not a surprise to me. Every day is different. I only believe it when it happens." His tone is not angry, but matter-of-fact. We are in the Library and he is missing her and he is missing them and, in moments such as this, he would rather have that life back because it took him so long to get there and to get them. But he cannot say that exactly. He says, "I just don't want it to go back to the way it was before. Living two lives." He says he has never favored his friends over his family, which is her belief, which he calls a fantasy. He says it would be useless to cancel his movie nights for her: "If you understand the nature of the full psychological implications of her wanting that, you'll understand part of the problem. Which is that *that* isn't love. That isn't even wanting to spend time with a person. That's a *power play.* The reality is, *I wouldn't be spending time with her anyway.* I'd be *alone.* She would be busy doing her own things." He says this because he knows this. He has been alone and he never was any good at it. He hadn't been alone for a long time until he got married. Very quietly, he says, "It's the opposite of a real commitment." And then the phone on the desk rings and it is she, returning his call, and he says: "Kimber? Hi, darlin'! Hiya! Wanna get together today? Oh. Oh. I'm sorry. . . . What time do you have to do that? Oh. Okay. Well, we can—oh. All right. Around twelve tomorrow? . . . Okay. All right, darling. That would be fine. Okay."

Hef Healing Night, Three: He always preferred it this way. It works better this way. He went out and saw their world; now they have come to see his. They have come in great masses, beautiful women and young famous people, and they intermingle with the wide-eyed Gang. Disco music throbs in the Great Hall, whose walls melt and swirl with colored lights. If they want retro, he will show them retro. He wears his white Armani suit and dances with lovely ladies whose faces are flecked in glitter, who drape boas around his neck and shimmy before him. And here is Leonardo DiCaprio, all agog, acting as though he were shaking hands with the real king of the world: "Mr. Hefner, I couldn't be happier to meet you and to be in your house!" Leonardo's dream, he tells his host, is to be in the Grotto, in the Jacuzzi, at 3 A.M. Leonardo understands where he is. Hef nods and tells him, "If those rocks could talk..." Leonardo goes out to the pool and stares reverentially into the Grotto, while women stare, in kind, at him. But now here is Billy Zane, also of *Titanic*. And Tori Spelling, Jon Lovitz, Pauly Shore, and God knows who else— they're all so young! And, one by one, they all go out to the pool and stare into the Grotto like it was the cave from which Christ emerged nearly two thousand years ago this very morning. But nobody gets in the water. And Hef does not stop dancing until well after two. And when he climbs the stairs, he is not alone. He is lousy at alone.

This is one of the pieces that continually comes back to haunt me—*Rolling Stone* would anthologize it in both a commemorative anniversary issue and in the book *The Best of Rolling Stone: 25 Years of Journalism on the Edge*, for which I would write this introduction:

There are nights I dream of him, and it is still horrible. We are sitting there, and, of course, he says nothing. He begins to say something, and then he stops. He pauses that pause of his: The Pause! Like eternity is The Pause. I feel my hair fall out in clumps. I feel my teeth rot. At once I have aged—what?—forty, fifty years. Waiting for him to finish. To say something. But what can he say? We have both forgotten the question. He tries to respond, anyway. Blinking at me, smiling, shrugging, ageless in hesitation. There is no sound, nothing, just him, knowing what he knows and keeping it to himself. Somewhere a clock ticks as The Pause expands. . . .

   Then I awaken and remember that it was all true—it had really happened! I remember those Pauses the way other men remember mortar fire. And yet, because survival has a way of breeding nostalgia, I often find myself missing the Reticent One.

Warren Beatty is the Reticent One. It is art, the way he withholds! To this day, I remember everything he never told me. Many people read our published conversations and summarily proclaimed Warren Beatty to be the ultimate Impossible Interview. I pity those people. Tragically, they missed everything. After all, it is not what Warren Beatty says, but how he doesn't say it.

This had been Warren's first serious print interview in twelve years, and he had stored up a wealth of topics not to speak about. He had even once been quoted as saying, "I'd rather ride down the street on a camel nude . . . in a snowstorm . . . backwards than give what is sometimes called an in-depth interview." This was to change in the spring of 1990. Perhaps fearing (correctly) that a new generation of filmgoers had no idea who he was, Warren agreed to end his silence as best he could. He would sit for interviews on behalf of his forthcoming auteur project, *Dick Tracy,* in which he was to star opposite his newest love interest, Madonna.

As is customary, a tremendous fight erupted over which magazine would get Warren's first definitive interview. I am told that many people lost their lives in that battle, and certain movie publicists were forced to enter witness-relocation programs. But what matters is that Warren chose *Rolling Stone* to be his forum, a decision that may have forever altered the course of his life.

Warren has seen everything and done everything, especially with actresses. More than just a fabled Lothario, he is a Movie Star in a time when there are no more Movie Stars. He is a repository of Hollywood history, an icon who knew the icons that came before him. (He played cards with Marilyn Monroe the night before she died.) His knowledge of women, all by itself, could only be encyclopedic. He would seem, then, to be a fellow who could tell you a thing or two. Someone who could bend your ear and give you something to think about.

To Warren, however, such matters are trifling. More impressive than any knowledge are his skills as a brilliant diplomat, and I would eventually learn that few things equal the sheer entertainment value of listening to a diplomat circumnavigate truth. To ensure that none of his nuance would be misrepresented in print, Warren always had a tape recorder of his own running next to mine. "It's for your safety," he assured me. I returned this gesture of friendship by often letting him "borrow" my extra blank tapes. Sometimes we would both run out of tape simultaneously, and those, I think, were some of our best times together.

Warren did share my concern about the seemingly futile quality of our conversations. I remember how we would pace around his swimming pool, fretting together. "Let's keep moving around from subject to subject," he told me, "and maybe I'll not be boring on something." Often I would try to engage him by sharing tidbits from my personal life. I told him how an actress had recently wreaked havoc on my heart. He asked her name, then said, by way of consolation, "I never dated her." He then imparted staggering wisdom on the inherent perils of dating actors and actresses, but this was during an off-the-record break. I asked him to repeat himself when the tape was going, but all he said after a long silence was "I don't know what you're talking about." That always struck me as one of his finest moments.

Now, about those Pauses: Never had I encountered silence to match the breadth and scope of Warren's silences. Historically, silence, like odorlessness, is difficult to portray in print, which is understandable, since there is not a lot you can really say about it. Still, I could not in good faith cheat readers out of Warren's astonishing silences. You needed to in some way experience them to fully appreciate their richness. But how? A wise colleague at the magazine, Jeffrey Ressner, suggested a solution to me shortly before I was boarding a flight to Chicago. Upon deplaning at O'Hare, I called my transcription service back in Burbank, where a team of typists was about to begin work on the interview tapes. "Time them," I said. "Time what?" said the chief transcriber. "The Pauses," I said. And so a roomful of women in headphones set about clicking stopwatches on and off, measuring one man's reluctance.

I took the hard numbers and salted them throughout the published article. Readers could endure Warren as authentically as I did by simply consulting the second hand of any timepiece. Hubbub ensued. *USA*

TODAY reported that Warren's longest Pause was fifty-seven seconds. (There were, in fact, longer ones, but these preceded responses so bland they were unpublishable.) VJ Martha Quinn did dramatic readings from the piece on MTV. When Madonna was handed the magazine in a limousine, she reportedly recited the story aloud, repeating favorite comic passages over and over. She then included a tribute to Warren's Pauses in at least one of her Blond Ambition concerts. (She would ask a leering question of a dancer dressed as Dick Tracy, then turn to the audience and announce, "Pause: twenty-seven seconds.") Several weeks later, she expressed her glee over the piece by giving me the high five at a beach party for photographer Herb Ritts. Clearly, she was grateful that I had shown readers the Warren she knew so well. But when I asked her where he was that night, she said a tad bitterly, "Who knows?" Such is love's mercurial way.

As for Warren, I was told he read the piece on a flight to New York and appeared to be unmoved. "I don't hate it," he told his travel companion, "and I don't like it." (Always the diplomat!) Soon thereafter, he began work on another film, the splendid *Bugsy*, and fell in love with his costar, Annette Bening, herself a woman of great reticence. Next, news came that she was expecting Warren's baby. They married. When it was time to promote *Bugsy*, a different Warren emerged in media interviews, a Warren who actually spoke sentences of discernible color and merit, of self-revelation and candor. He hardly even Paused! Then his daughter, Kathlyn, was born, and he got awards for *Bugsy*. Warren had stopped running away from truth, and suddenly he had much to show for it.

Warren and Me:
A (Pause) Love Story

Rolling Stone, May 1990

He is a ghost. He is human ectoplasm. He is here, and then he is gone, and then you aren't sure he was ever here to begin with. He has had sex with everyone, or at least tried. He has had sex with someone you know or someone who knows someone you know or someone you wish you knew, or at least tried. He is famous for sex, he is famous for having sex with the famous, he is famous. He makes mostly good films when he makes films, which is mostly not often. He has had sex with most of his leading ladies. He befriends all women and many politicians and whispers advice to them on the telephone in the dead of night. Or else he does not speak at all to anyone ever, except to those who know him best, if anyone can really know him. He is an adamant enigma, elusive for the sake of elusiveness, which makes him desirable, although for what, no one completely understands. He is much smarter than you think but perhaps not as smart as he thinks, if only because he thinks too much about being smart. He admits to none of this. He admits to nothing much. He denies little. And so his legend grows.

You hear Warren Beatty stories. They get around as he gets around. What you hear is carnal lore, possibly embellished, certainly superfluous.

Warren Beatty, you hear, is gentle and respectful and never pushy, but he would not mind having sex right now, right this very microsecond. He loves women profoundly. Unsolicited, women tell me this and men corroborate. When Warren first meets a woman, he says, [*befuddled*] "Now, I forget your name." Or, [*bedazzled*] "You're the most beautiful woman I've ever met who's not an actress or model." Or, [*beholden*] "Your grandmother—she was one of the sexiest women I ever knew." (One of his old opening lines—"What's new, pussycat?"—later became a movie written by Woody Allen, who once said he wished to be reincarnated as Warren Beatty's fingertips.)

Warren says many things, always chivalrously; he gives books to women as gifts; he offers to carry their camera equipment if they are film students. One very famous director remembers having a conversation with him during which Warren, the director says, "had his hand up a woman! She didn't seem to mind, and he acted as though it seemed a perfectly natural thing to do." Another scenario: Warren calls an actress late on a Saturday night. Her husband answers the phone. She gets on the line, and Warren invites her up to his house right away to read for a movie role widely reported as already cast. She puts him off but takes his home number anyway. Next to the number, her husband notices, she mistakenly writes, "Warren Beauty." Many notepads have likely known this error.

Madonna has his number. She may have his number as others have not. He told someone at lunch last year, "Sometimes I look at myself in the mirror and say, *'I'm with Madonna!'*" He is reborn in love, restored to public persona. For we only see Warren when he loves deeply (we just *hear* about him when he prowls). From the sixties onward, we saw him most clearly (but never too well) with Joan Collins, Natalie Wood, Leslie Caron, Michelle Phillips, Julie Christie, Diane Keaton, Isabelle Adjani. Madonna is more famous than any of them; she is more famous than he is; she is more famous than everyone, more or less. By loving him, she makes him more famous than he was before. Theirs is a sort of vampire love: She needs his credibility; he needs her youth. He is fifty-three, and she is thirty-one, and they are evenly matched legends; hers is louder, his is longer. It works out.

When I first see him, I see him with her.

Warren is breathless, winded. Madonna wears a big hat and smokes. They have come, the satyr and the siren, some forty minutes late to see a rough cut of *Without You I'm Nothing,* the performance film by their friend Sandra Bernhard. They have sped down from their respective hilltop dwellings to this tiny Burbank, California, screening room, where

Bernhard and a dozen or so people fidget, waiting for them. Madonna enters, proffers no excuses, and jabbers. Warren parks the car, then scurries in, flustered, ashamed, apologetic. "I'm sorry, I'm sorry," he says, and collapses into a seat. When the movie begins, they laugh in the same places—mostly fitfully at a saucy monologue in which Bernhard conjures a sex romp with a mopey Warren, whom she instructs to don two condoms. "Oh, baby," she coos on-screen, "it's no reflection on how much I care about you. We all know you've been around." Postscreening, Madonna curls onto his lap, as is her wont, while Warren soberly discourses on directorial minutiae, as is his wont. They are cozy together in a prickly sort of way. Their pet names for each other are Old Man and Buzzbomb.

It is a comic-strip romance. She is, in this regard, Breathless Mahoney, the torchy moll who leads his Dick Tracy into temptation in *Dick Tracy*, the new Warren Beatty film—his first directing job since *Reds* nine years ago. (In between, he appeared only in the loopy $40 million stinker epic *Ishtar*, which he costarred in with Dustin Hoffman and produced.) *Dick Tracy* will be his resurrection, his last best hope, his first Disney picture. It is a florid cartoon of a movie (to be released in tandem with a new Roger Rabbit short), blazing with gats and gunsels and deformed villains with names like Pruneface, Flattop, and Itchy. Dustin Hoffman is Mumbles. Al Pacino is Big Boy. Bad guys have gooey faces. Madonna wears red and sings Sondheim. Beatty, as Tracy, wears yellow and fights evil. Often he talks to his wristwatch. Whereas *Batman* brooded, *Dick Tracy* sparkles—a $26 million thirties-era thrill ride done in seven Sunday-funny colors. It is nothing like other Warren Beatty movies, which tend to be bittersweet melancholies about vain bandits (*Bonnie and Clyde*), oversexed hairdressers (*Shampoo*), reincarnated quarterbacks (*Heaven Can Wait*), and dead Communists (*Reds*). Not that the incongruity of *Dick Tracy* counts for much; most of the younger, hard-core moviegoers have no idea who Warren Beatty is anyway.

Warren Beatty is paranoid. He is an occluded Hollywood god, one who shuts up and off and imagines himself invisible. Afraid of being misunderstood, he says nothing and is more misunderstood. He likes it that way. Unlike, say, Brando's silence, Beatty's silence is showy. Puckish and smooth, he phones up journalists to inform them *at length* and with sly humor that he doesn't cooperate with the media. He would rather eat worms. In a dozen years, he has said nothing. Maybe a few hollow words in behalf of *Ishtar*. Maybe a futile endorsement now and again for his crony, the presidential infidel Gary Hart. It was Warren who nudged him back into the election, post–Donna Rice. Otherwise, Warren has been so mum, he has all but evaporated. *Reds* did limp business, theory goes, because Warren gave no interviews. If *Dick Tracy* dies, so too might his career. Posturing has its limitations.

And so he has talked. And talked. For days, I have listened to him talk. I have listened to him listen to himself talk. I have probed and pelted and listened some more. For days. He speaks slowly, fearfully, cautiously, editing every syllable, slicing off personal color and spontaneous wit, steering away from opinion, introspection, humanness. He is mostly evasive. His pauses are elephantine. Broadway musicals could be mounted during his pauses. He *works* at this. Ultimately, he renders himself blank. In *Dick Tracy,* he battles a mysterious foe called the Blank. In life, he is Blank doing battle with himself. It is a fascinating showdown, exhilarating to behold.

To interview Warren Beatty is to want to kill him.

It is also to become fond of him. He seduces anything that is not mineral. He is impossible, but charming. Jack Nicholson, his neighbor on altitudinal Mulholland Drive, calls him the Pro. Meaning Warren knows what he's doing. I am invited one Friday night to watch him score. (*See Beatty score! Not unlike seeing Picasso draw, Astaire twirl, DiMaggio swing!*) Alas, there are musicians present; he is supervising *Tracy's* musical score on an old MGM orchestra stage in Culver City.

"I told you never to meet me here," Warren says, meeting me for the first time. (An opening line.) He looks tousled, untucked, an aging boy barely aging, with drooped shirttails and sweet comportment. He is at once good and bad and will do anything to make up for it. He fusses—dithers, really—eager to get me a chair, to get me liquids and solids, to get me. He settles onto a milk crate—"It makes me feel puritanical and worthy," he says—and chitchats. He appraises his young publicist in her long skirt and says approvingly, "You look like . . . *the president of Vassar.*" He feigns horror to hear Vassar is now coed. *"No!"* he says, stricken. The orchestra has been laying music behind a scene in which Mahoney puts the make on Tracy; on a screen high above us, she glimmers in freeze-frame, propped on all fours, crawling across his desk. Warren studies this contortion for a moment. "I think I knew someone who had a coffee table that looked like that," he says. "The only thing missing is the glass on top."

One week later, on the night of his fifty-third birthday, the interrogations begin. Feeling celebratory, he orders in Big Macs and El Pollo Loco chicken ("Hang the expense!"). There is much for him to avoid discussing. We hole up for the first session in a Hollywood sound-mixing studio, where he's been toiling on *Tracy.* Further conversations take place in his home, that bestilled sanctuary on his private Olympus, and on the phone, his instrument of choice. Because what he doesn't say is often more revealing than what he does, this interview will frequently pause (as will Warren), so that necessary detail, commentary, and homicidal impulses can be noted.

Let's get to what everyone wants to hear: Do you lambada? It's the forbidden dance, you know.

Lambada. At the moment, I don't, but I rule out nothing.

Do you vogue? [Note: This is, of course, a veiled attempt to broach the subject of his relationship with Madonna—"Vogue" being her current pop hit— a subject his publicists warned me against raising.]

I neither lambada nor vogue. I certainly *think* vogue. As a matter of fact, I also think lambada.

Okay, you and Madonna—the truth!

Art is truth.

That's all? You want to go with that?

[*grins*] Okay by me.

Describe the qualities that she possesses that convinced you to cast her as the sexpot temptress Breathless Mahoney in Dick Tracy. *How does she qualify?*

Madonna is [21-second pause] simultaneously touching and more fun than a barrel of monkeys. [*11 seconds*] She's funny and she's [*21 seconds*] gifted in so many arenas and has the kind of energy as a performer that can't help but make you engaged.

You mean sexual energy?

[*47 seconds*] Um, she has it all.

What's the sexiest thing she does on-screen?

She's funny. She's a wonderful comedienne. Is that sexy? Oh, I dunno. Everybody has their own criteria.

You two sing a duet, "I'm Following You," on her new album. How did you avoid upstaging her?

Upstaging her? I do as I'm told.

Warren, I would learn, has a habit of going off the record, and when he is off the record, he is almost like a person. At these times, one gets a greater sense of his playfulness. The lines blur occasionally. At one point, when we are neither on nor off the record, just sort of pacing around, he suggests that we depants his publicist, the Vassar president. He thinks it might ease tension. It is during his off-the-record spates, however, that the answer to the Big Question (Is It Over with You and Madonna?) fuzzily emerges: apparently not. They are just tremendously busy people—what with her preparing a world tour and him polishing off *Tracy*— and so what if he went to the Oscars with Jack Nicholson and his date? So what if he dined a few times with old flame Isabelle Adjani? The night after his birthday, Madonna tosses Warren a tiny party at his house, someone tells me. The following week, Warren attends the final run-through of her Blond Ambition stage show and gives me a rhapsodic review. "Oh, I wish you could have seen it!" he gushes (for attribution). "I really defy anyone not to succumb to it. Nonstop energy! It fulfills my name for her." Buzzbomb? "Buzzbomb."

Do you think your reluctance to give interviews has inflated your personal mythology?

I can't accept your flattering premise of me. To do so is unattractive or self-serving. It's hard to misquote someone who doesn't say anything. There's almost nothing that hasn't been said about me. But there's an awful lot that I haven't said. I don't talk about private things.

You don't talk about anything. Not even your movies, really. That's just bad business, isn't it?

I don't think it's helpful, in general, to get out there in the front of a film. By attracting attention to yourself, you distract people from the movie. Ideally, you like a movie to speak for itself. You don't describe a song before you sing it or tell about a painting before you show it. You don't reveal a recipe before you serve the dish. You taste it. That's why I stopped doing [interviews]. I didn't see any particular gain in personal publicity.

What's the most ridiculous rumor you've read about you?

Really an adroit question, because if I repeat a ridiculous rumor here, it gives fifty percent credence to the rumor, whatever it is. [*57 seconds*] If I tell you I saw an item that said I was actually born on Pluto, fifty percent of the people will say, "I *wonder. . . .*" It's a sin, you know, starting a rumor. You'll notice I picked a really outlandish one. I had to think for a minute.

All things considered, it could be true.

[*smiles*] You know I wasn't born on Pluto. I'd get much more attention had I been.

Why do you think there are so many rumors about you?

I could say something self-serving here, but I won't.

Maybe it's because you don't say they're not true.

Yeah, but if I say I do not beat my wife, I've lost on two counts.

Wife? Wait, is there something we don't know about?

No. But there is something in the spirit of [the rumormongering] that seems to be an unfortunate manifestation of the egalitarianism of our society: If I read that you are not so fine, I might feel a little bit better about myself. It cuts you down to my size. So I'll buy that.

I've experienced more than my fair share of egalitarianism lately. So it's probably better to go ahead and talk a little bit here and I'll sure be... um, boring.

But isn't there a germ of truth in every tabloid story?

That germ theory is bullshit, I can tell you. I had a little research done on it, insofar as I'm concerned. What I found is that eight or nine out of ten things printed are not true. Out of those eight or nine untrue things, four or five might even be positive or flattering. Half make you look bad, half make you look good. All of them aren't true.

Even when they take pictures?

Well, two out of ten are true. I'm not saying it's all lies.

"Fuck and suck" is Warren's pet term for scurrilous articles written about his sexual profile. He asks me if I know about any such pieces that may be currently in the works. The prospect seems to neither disgust nor please him. He is resigned to his reputation. He has never sued for libel and, moreover, feels there should be no libel laws: "Since the public is vaguely aware that there is some recourse in court, they figure what is printed about you must be sort of true." For instance, there is a tony British catalog of celebrity sex partners called *Who's Had Who,* in which Beatty's long section is billed thusly: "Fasten Your Seat Belts, and Hold Your Hats— This Is the Big One!!!" Among the alleged conquests listed: Britt Ekland, Goldie Hawn, Kate Jackson, Brigitte Bardot, Diana Ross, Liv Ullmann, Candice Bergen, Carly Simon. (Diane Sawyer is one notable omission.) Also quoted in the book is his sister, reincarnated actress Shirley MacLaine, who says she wishes she could do a love scene with Warren. "Then," she states, "I could see what all the shouting was about."

Your friend Jack Nicholson always looks like he enjoys fame. I wonder if you do.

[*34 seconds*] Well, I can't speak for other people. I don't know whether they do or they don't. Dustin used to say that I've been famous longer than I've been a person. His theory being you're a person in the years when you're not famous. Because I got lucky with the first picture I made

[*Splendor in the Grass,* in 1961], I had something like a ten-year jump on Jack and Dustin. So I haven't really dealt with being well-known as if I had an alternative to it. Although I guess there is. I could go someplace where nobody knew me at all.

Do you think you're eccentric?

Anybody who becomes a movie star when they're twenty-two, or whatever I was, is going to be eccentric. It's an eccentric situation. You become rich and famous out of proportion to that which is anticipated. Quite a candy store there.

Anything you want, within reason.

More without reason. Within reason, you're just another guy. The task is to stay within reason. I've tried. If I've been able to save myself, it has to do with my interest in art and politics, not in wealth.

You make movies slowly. You speak slowly. What do you do fast?

Prevaricate. [Note: Defined by *Webster's* as "to evade the truth... to lie."]

What else?

I can dial a telephone number faster than anybody you know. [*He demonstrates—his hand falls onto a Touch-Tone panel, his fingers perform instant symphony, he passes me the receiver, an operator answers at the Beverly Wilshire Hotel, where he kept a suite for many years. Dialing time: exactly one second.*] Want me to do it again? Want to see it again? [*He dials once more, full of swagger.*] That was quick, wasn't it?

That was breathtaking.

Thank you.

Do you drive fast?

I've been trying to drive at a sane speed. The other day I was driving along Mulholland and thinking about how sedately I was driving. Then around the turn came two cars side by side, and it's a two-lane road. On my right was a cliff, a steep drop. Straight ahead I faced a head-on collision. I didn't have time to fear for my life. It was a moment of realizing that there's going to be a very serious choice to make. So I tried to split the difference. Fortunately, the guy on the left slowed down, and the car passing him swerved and hit [my car] just behind my head.

This put me in a temporary state of manic elation. I got out of my car, and this kid who had hit me leapt out of his car and started to berate himself. I put my arms around him and said, "Don't worry, nobody's hurt." Then the people in the other cars came over and they were all from Italy and Switzerland. They all had portable phones, and when they saw me, they called their mothers in Switzerland and wherever. So they put me on the phone with these lovely women, who were fans of mine. I stood there taking transatlantic calls—how did I get into this?

If there is a moral here, it is this: Not only does Warren Beatty know how to cheat death, he gets to talk on the phone afterward to Swiss women. The telephone, of course, is Warren's second most legendary appendage. Rarely is he phoneless. It is said that he will make and take calls even while engaged in animal rapture. His mind swirls with phone numbers, memorized for ages. His phone voice is a mellifluous purr, instantly conspiratorial. He is at home in the ear. He has been inside all the best ears. On Easter, I call and ask, among other things, if he has been hunting eggs. "Just laying them," he replies, a bit luridly.

What's wrong with the film industry?
Nothing. It's making a lot of money. However, our attention span has become progressively curtailed. I like jokes that I get fast. But I like other things, too. We've placed too many restrictions on ourselves: A movie has to have a happy ending and be two hours or less in length. You've got to understand the premise from the top, so it's too often obvious. And that's too bad. Movies must be quickly understood and quickly assimilated. So that when you make a three-and-a-half-hour movie, as I did with *Reds,* some people tell you that it's *long. "It's long,"* they say. "Yes," you say "it *is* long. Three and a half hours long, yes. *Long.*"
In the spirit of speed, how would you pitch Reds *as a high concept, in one sentence?*
It would have been a pretty low high concept: a three-and-a-half-hour movie about a Communist who dies at the end, not having been happy.
After he wormed his way through the script, Charlie Bludhorn, who ran Paramount [which bankrolled *Reds*], said, "I don't understand why you're doing this." Then he said, "Do me a favor. Take twenty-five million. Go to Mexico, go to Peru. Spend a million on a movie. Keep the twenty-four million for yourself. *Just don't make this movie!*" I said, "Well, I'm sorry, Charlie. I really am gonna have to do this. It's worthwhile." There was something very moving in the idealism of the American Left from 1915 to 1920—particularly poignant in the life of John Reed [the journalist hero of *Reds*]. Plus I don't believe anybody ever made an American movie with a Communist hero before.
How did you interpret your switch from John Reed to Dick Tracy? You're obviously going for easy assimilation this time.

Well, there's something about *Dick Tracy* that gives me permission to be outlandishly heroic and clear-cut in dealing with good and evil, with love versus duty, with the wish for family. Tracy is completely good. What gives me the right to say this? The match of his yellow hat and yellow raincoat. The bright, twinkling stars you see behind his head. And the moon. The music tells me he's good. It affords me the chance to be naïve in a way that somehow doesn't embarrass me.

Where's Tracy's famous pointy nose and chin? How come you make the actors who play criminals wear doughy makeup and yet you've done nothing to alter your face?

See, it was the literal interpretation of the Tracy face that kept me from playing the part for a while. But when I began to realize that no one has that face, I felt I would be as good as anybody else. Even so, I tried prosthetics and makeup to approximate the nose and chin. And I didn't look like Tracy. And you know what? Nobody does. I just looked silly. I would be afraid of offending various nationalities if I said what I thought I looked like.

How do you imagine Tracy's sex life?

Let's just say very direct. Very straightforward. Unimaginably straightforward. I try not to think about it.

What does he do with his free time?

Oh, he might read military history.

What about Tracy merchandising? Is this the first time you've been made into a doll?

I think I've been made into dolls, but they had pins in them. That was not a kick.

Do you own Dick Tracy handcuffs?

[*ponders*] Let's see. Are my handcuffs Dick Tracy? Hmmm . . .

Warren's fact file—here are some things Warren won't discuss: Himself (in emotional terms). Where he keeps his Oscar (Best Director for *Reds*). How to successfully date an actress. The most fun he can have with his clothes on. Misconceptions about him. ("I can't talk about public perceptions of me. I have no idea how to focus on that.") The irony of his having produced *The Pick-up Artist* (a dreadful Robert Downey Jr. film). Warren Beatty jokes. Accomplishments of, attractions to, relationships (of any sort) with other human beings. For instance, on fatherhood (as in, Would he like to have done it? Would he want kids?), he says, "Um, to address this subject, by implication, I might be talking to some other people that I've known who may not want to be talked about." On what he sees when he looks in the mirror: "Why don't you get a little tougher, rather than ask me this open-ended kind of stuff, which I really can't do. I'm not gonna be the kind of guy who rambles on, particularly in the areas where the subject of the interview is left to muster up and exhibit a high level of personal narcissism."

It was Warren's wish, incidentally, to do the interview in the question-and-answer format. He felt it would protect him from misquotation. "Getting tougher," for Warren, involves asking him questions whenever possible that can be answered with a yes or no. "If it's not entertaining," he says, "we can do some more later."

Can you hear the word Ishtar *without feeling physically ill?*

Well, sure. *Ishtar* is kind of a funny little movie. But it cost too much. It was an ironic situation, because when Dustin and I realized what it was going to cost [$40 million], we went to the studio and suggested that we not take the money, that we'd take it on the other end. Columbia refused, based on a cable deal. We said, "Well, this is an inappropriate price for this film, and when people seem so obsessed with the cost of the thing, it'll make it hard to laugh." They said they'd be sure to keep the cost very quiet. Then they were replaced by new management, who seemed to want to make an example of *Ishtar*'s high cost. Just in the business sense, it didn't seem the most fiscally responsible way for them to behave.

You've said that every movie you make feels like a comeback. What takes so long?

I've never seen the point of just dishing it out there. I don't know that I take so long to *make* movies—I take a long time to *decide* to do one. I take much too long. And I think that's self-indulgent on my part, and I ought to try to get over it. Sometimes I think that I put off making movies just long enough so that I can't put it off any longer, for various reasons. Then I go make the movie.

Maybe you just don't like making movies.

No, I actually like making movies. I just don't like to make them all the time. There's so much inertia to overcome to make a really good movie. I felt that if I made a lot of movies, I wouldn't make the ones that were really tough, like *Shampoo* or *Reds*. Others are different from me.

Robert Towne, with whom you wrote Shampoo, *says you are "a man who is deeply embarrassed by acting." True?*

[*puzzled*] He said that about me? I'm very embarrassed by my own *bad* acting.

Could you, at this point, still act in other people's movies?

Oh, sure. I would prefer to be directed by someone else. It's almost impossible to act and direct at the same time. We pretend to do it. But in fact, when you're acting, you ideally are out of control. In control of being out of control. And when you are directing, you should be in control. Somewhat out of control of being in control. But in control. And if you're trying to be out of control and somewhat in control of being out of control but out of control and, at the same time, in control but somewhat out of control of being in control but still in control, it makes you crazy. [*beams stupidly*]

Well, then. Let's talk politics. You pushed your friend Gary Hart back into the presidential race after he dropped out over his entanglement with Donna Rice. Why? How did you expect the public to respond?

[*26 seconds*] I felt that he should not have gotten out. And I felt that if there was any way to combat this preoccupation people have with trivia and irrelevant matters—or let's say *less relevant* matters—in government, that it should be done. I get very irritated with people who are so condescending about political candidates. Gary Hart is a sensitive man with a high level of love and concern for his family. He didn't want them to be subjected to any more of that kind of humiliation, and it [*27 seconds*] was a tragic event for the country. It was not only a terrible thing to happen to him, but it deprived the country of its leading conceptualist presidential candidate at a time when that kind of detailed thinking was urgent. And I felt that if he and the family could take any more of it, that [getting back in] was the right thing to do.

You were a key member of his brain trust. What exactly did you do for him? I heard you actually wrote speeches for him.

Well, here's the way I participate in politics: I respect politics. And I respect the privacy of the people in politics with whom I am involved. I don't kiss and tell.

Didn't Ronald Reagan tell you that he wished Reds *had a happier ending after you showed him the film at the White House?*

[*startled*] Where did you hear that? I wouldn't want to...um, well, you know he has a great sense of humor. He's a funny guy. [*21 seconds*] I guess I have a lot of feelings about Reagan that I am not articulating. He is an actor and a very, very likable man. But I guess you know I'm not a conservative Republican.

Reagan did, in fact, wish for a happy ending. Warren tells many colorful Reagan stories, none of them for attribution. My favorite has to do with the former president lecturing him about the marble of meat, but I can reveal no more. Warren will, however, talk hard-core politics until eyelids calcify and plummet. Much of it he will say for the record and with great insight and invective. In fact, he would prefer we spoke of nothing else in this interview. But Warren is, with all due respect, an actor, and an actor filibustering on politics is a little like a plumber dispensing Buddhist dogma. Noble, to be sure; but who really cares?

Instead, I will describe his house: It is stark and Bauhausian, sprawling and all white, with no pictures on the walls of the main rooms, just lots of windows peering down on the basins of Los Angeles. His floors are all polished oak, which give the sanctum its echo. On tables: big flower arrangements and piles of books about communism and comic strips. Very tidy: Toilet paper is always folded to a point. Piano (he can play quite decently) in the living room. Unseen, down a long corridor, is the Bedroom, where he frequently retreats to take lengthy calls. He mostly holds forth in an electronically glassed-in room, just off the pool, where the sun bears down. Here, a young British fellow appears every fifteen minutes with phone messages. Handsome meals are impeccably served by the young woman who is paid to prepare them. Warren will occasionally lope into the kitchen, foraging for custards. One day an actor friend of Warren's named Marshall Bell emerges from the gym downstairs, and mildly lascivious chatter erupts. It is only then that one gets the irrefutable impression that this is, indeed, the home of the right Warren Beatty.

How old do you feel?

Eleven.

How so?

I guess I'm not fond of schedules, and I don't see any point in keeping to some fictitious schedule of [life].

Have you had a midlife crisis yet?

Many, I'm sure. They started when I was about eighteen. Ultimately, I learned that the secret to overcoming them is to not see them as crises. But I suppose the real answer to your question is, I don't know what you're talking about.

Has your sister, Shirley MacLaine, ever suggested how you might have spent former lives?

I don't remember her doing that, but she might have. No, I don't think she has. Shirley's not really pushy with me about that. I do think reincarnation is maybe the most appealing thing in life. It's just hard for me to rationally and scientifically deal with the subject. I wish it well.

Did you see her call David Letterman an asshole on his show?

Yes, I was curious and got a tape of it. I thought it was a standoff. And I felt that it's best not to have a standoff with a person in his own constituency.

How often has she called you an asshole?

Never.

How did your father's death a few years ago affect you? What kind of man was he?

Death always makes you aware of the limits of time and causes you to cherish relationships. My mother and father each come into my consciousness at least once a day. And I can always count on thinking of my father at the same time each day: when I shave. He recommended a new shaving cream to me before he died, and he turned out to be right.

We had a chance to get closer before he died. He seemed pleased with what I'd accomplished in life. My father was a very reasonable man. Cerebral. A teacher. Sentimental. Outwardly jovial much of the time, in a way that concealed a basic Baptist puritanism. Let's just say he wasn't overconfident. Or materialistic. [*ponders a while*] He was married once.

What does your mother think of you?

She has boundless faith in me. If I told her I was going to move Cleveland to a small island in the Bahamas, she would simply say, "I'm sure you can do that, and try not to lose too much of it in the ocean." She thinks I'm okay. I keep in touch with her all the time.

What does she want for you? Marriage?

Well, not just for the sake of being married. Marriage is a worthy thing to aspire to.

Do you aspire to marriage?

I have never bristled at the notion.

Would you have limitations as a husband?

No. I haven't been in a bubble. I've had very close relationships with people that have lasted longer than my friends' marriages that existed at the same time.

What's the most important thing to know about women?

[*21 seconds*] That they're not very different from men.

What do you mean?

That's eight pages.

Eight classic pages. What do you mean?

[*14 seconds*] Well, I'm lucky that I grew up in an atmosphere in which I was taught to treat women as respectfully as I would treat men. I don't differentiate. Sometimes people don't treat themselves very seriously, but that might happen more often when this business of sexual attraction rears its head and we all get a little giddy.

Are you a better friend to women than you are to men?

I hope not. I'm probably guilty of giving more women the benefit of the doubt than men. And I think there are probably more women that give me the benefit of the doubt than men do. But I'm not even sure of that.

Describe what love feels like to you.

Do unto others.

Romantic love.

Define romantic love.

When you're in love.

Well, as soon as you use the word *romantic,* then the word *fiction* begins to peep around the corner, or the word *bullshit* begins to lurk in the shadow. But if you say *sexual love,* which I think is not bullshit and not fictitious, that's something else. But I think there's a certain amount of do unto others even in that.

How do you know you're in love? What incites your love?

I don't know if you ever figure that out. If you're smart, you don't figure it out. Of course, you always try to figure it out. But if you're smart, you know you can't. I take great pride in my stupidity in this area. I have no clear way of being able to define at what point [*21 seconds*] passion for loyalty has overcome me.

Has your heart been broken?

Sure.

How many times?

[*laughs richly, then 17-second pause*] I'm sure I've reached my quota. I'm not at liberty to disclose my quota. But then you'd have to define *break* and *heart.*

How do you mend yours? Give advice.

To the lovelorn? There is no away. Nobody goes away. Except the Big Away, and there's nothing you can do about it. If you really love someone [*17 seconds*] and they're healthy and happy . . . you ought to be able to live with that.

Can you always be that philosophical?

[*24 seconds*] Pretty close.

A musical question. As per legend: "You're So Vain"—did you think the song was about you?

[*laughs, then 15-second pause*] Who wrote that?

•   •   •

Helicopter attack! Right over Warren's glass room, right when he is trying
to avoid the subject of Carly Simon's pop wrath, a helicopter dive-bombs
us! "Press!" Warren announces, both panicked and thrilled. This is a game
he's played before. He runs for cover, ducking into the living room. "Let's
see if they're taking pictures," he hollers above the prop wash, and moves
intrepidly from window to window, his gaze arched skyward. The British
assistant runs up from his office below and watches with us. "I don't think
it's press," the assistant says after a while. Warren is uncertain but says, "I
don't see a guy hanging out of his helicopter with a camera. That's usually
the tip-off." "No," says the Brit, "it must be something else." Both seem a
tad disappointed. They conclude that it's probably some local law-
enforcement mission. Perhaps to cheer himself, Warren then performs for
me his impersonation of Walter Lippmann, the great political journalist,
reacting to being interviewed by Warren himself (while doing *Reds* research). Warren leans forward and pushes his face very close to mine.
"Ask me a question," he says. "Can you cook?" I ask. He simply grins a
reproachful grin. And stares into my eyes. And keeps grinning. And says
nothing. Which is Warren's canny way of saying that he knows the feeling. He knows.

Do you think you're shy?
    Shyness is really a form of vanity.
    Describe the perfect woman for you.
    [*24 seconds*] I'm thinking of three or four punch lines, none that I'll
share.
    What's sexier: smell or sound?
    Sound.
    Long skirt or short skirt?
    Irrelevant.
    Long hair or short hair?
    Irrelevant.
    Kneecaps or ankles?
    Irrelevant.
    Mathis or Sinatra?
    In all deference to both gentlemen, Peggy Lee. And Mabel Mercer.
    *Here's something Robert Downey Jr. said about you: "Beatty is really
knowledgeable in a lot of areas, especially fucking." Did you have any idea
people talk about you in this manner?*

[*smiles*] Yes.

How do you feel about that?

Irrelevant.

How would you characterize yourself?

As someone who would prefer not to characterize himself.

What's the most paranoid thing you do?

Did I say I was paranoid? Hmmm. Gore Vidal said something like "A man without paranoia is a man not in full possession of the facts." That seems reasonable enough to me.

What do you suspect we've accomplished?

To tell you the truth, I feel as though we are just beginning.

Part Two:
BIG **SCREEN**

Sharon Stone * Arnold Schwarzenegger *
Johnny Depp * Tom Hanks * Cameron Diaz

I am ever humbled and mortified that people will not let me forget this bit of work. Since Sharon Stone had made many films in which, at various turns, she wore nothing, and since many people had made much of this fact, and since—to my utter surprise (and no, not glee, I promise)—she spontaneously made me get naked with her during this reconnaissance time together, there was only one way to effectively write the following comic portrait. Three years earlier, I had written a *Rolling Stone* cover profile of Miss Stone, after which we had not lost touch. (Things she had done to torment me during that experience and thereafter were revealed at last in this *Esquire* story.) I like to think of her as a throwback, as the last female movie star who enjoys being a female movie star. To wit, I found this passage, which I originally cut from the published piece and which seems less extraneous in preface:

Had she lived in another time, Sharon Stone would now be older or possibly dead. Still, she dreams of living in the thirties, likes to imagine herself having the career of Bette Davis or Carole Lombard. "I feel like I'm out of the time loop," she said wistfully. Had she made movies in the forties, she said, "I'd probably be in trouble, dating a gangster." And, more important, moviegoers would never have known how she looked naked.

Naked With
Sharon Stone

Esquire, March 1995

When nude, Sharon Stone usually wears nothing. As a naked woman, she is known for her ability to have sex or, at least, portray a naked woman having sex while filmed by a camera crew. Sometimes when naked, however, she has no sex at all. For instance, she likes to bathe without clothes of any kind. Also, she has conducted telephone conversations while nude without telling the person on the other end that she wasn't wearing anything. When visiting steam rooms, she will boldly walk around—or even sit contemplatively—without apology in that birthday suit of hers. Unfortunately, she tells me that she likes to sleep in men's clothing, but underneath said layering she manages to be completely unclad. Of course, certain men have had naked sex with her. I do not know how many, but suffice it to say that there have probably been a number. I do not think, however, that she has had naked sex with any women. ("It don't mean a thing if it ain't got that *schwing*!" she once said with enough conviction to quash speculation.) As for me, I have lain naked with her, only because she insisted, only because other people were present, only because I could tell you about it.

Fully clothed, we first ate lunch. Up until this time, it should be noted, we had had many meetings over the years, in which both of us had dressed in garments. Because Sharon Stone is the only female movie star left who knows how to be a movie star, she always wore very good things and looked very good while wearing them. She has a knack for not looking bad. She is said to be beautiful while sleeping and also upon waking up, although she maintains that she often drools when unconscious, thus finding her pillowcases dampened with saliva on many mornings. Some mornings she will rise and don a bathrobe. I saw her wear a bathrobe decorated with little cows, and she looked fine in it. In general, she dislikes awakening, especially awakening early to go make movies. "I like a good, solid twelve hours sleep—up at the crack of noon," she says. "My commitment to this industry is most noteworthy by the fact that I will get my ass out of bed before dawn. Oh, I hate it. I mean, like, *hate it.*" Still, she allows herself no caffeine in the morning, or ever. She does this for the safety of those around her. "I wouldn't give me coffee," she says ominously. "I wouldn't enhance *any* of my moods. You'd have to peel me off ceilings. There would be damage. Most of the time I need, like, Tranquilax."

Coffee spilled, and I spilled it, while rising to greet Sharon Stone, who pretended not to notice, obviously accustomed to such reflexes in men. She wore scruffy attire and no makeup and told me not to tell anyone. It was a Las Vegas afternoon, the kind you get if you're in Las Vegas, which we were. "I don't go out much here in the Devil's Summer Home," she said, meaning Vegas, where she was now in her fifth month of enforced residence, making the film *Casino* for director Martin Scorsese, playing the tortured wife of Robert De Niro. She has known De Niro for years, ever since she tested for a part in *Once Upon a Time in America.* "It was a part for which you were supposed to have no breasts," she said. "They told me I couldn't have it because I had too much breasts. Isn't that funny?" Nowadays, of course, her breasts bother no one, especially when seen naked. Inside a large sweater, she had joined me at a Dutch coffee shop of her own choosing ("They were voted the number-one diner," she said helpfully). "I'm just much more comfortable having a grumpy waitress shove a cup of decaf at me than having seven obsequious waiters with foreign accents fluttering around the table," she said wearily. " *'Oh, Miss Stone, would you like to move to another table?'* It's like, please, I wanna *eat*!"

Unsurprisingly, she is a carnivore, a woman who likes chewing flesh. Sitting before me, she weighed the notion of a hamburger against that of a rasher of bacon with eggs, settling on the pork product. "That's right—I'm a meat-eater," she announced defiantly. "Is that politically incorrect, too?" Recently, *Time* magazine inquired as to whether she wore fur. "I called my publicist back," she said, "and told her that I was Consuela, the black, underpaid, abused, illegal alien maid of Sharon Stone. I said Sharon couldn't come to the phone because she had a mouthful of veal and was drinking a Diet Coke out of a Styrofoam cup on a zebra rug in front of a fireplace burning Duraflame logs and that the cellular phone I was using was giving me a brain tumor as we spoke." She believes there are greater problems in the world, like homelessness and bad pantsuits and men who act like weasels.

Men fear her, and justifiably so. She is feral and forthright, quick and cunning. Often, she appears simply nuts. Conversely, she can turn to ice in a split second. She does not lose arguments and has no truck at all with arrogant fools. "If I get with someone who is bullshitting me, I *grind* 'em—right into the dirt," she said. I told her that Hollywood executives now call her Sharon Stones. "Because I have the biggest balls in Hollywood?" she surmised correctly. "Still scarin' 'em, huh? That's good. The longer they stay scared, the longer I get a job." Nevertheless, she clearly enjoys tormenting men. I am humiliated now to admit that she once made me hold her hand and skip blithely down a mountain trail, not unlike Dorothy and the Scarecrow. It was horrible. Naturally, she thrilled to my mortification. Another day, I had occasion to interview her at a nail salon, whereupon she slyly bribed a pedicurist to force off my shoes and file down my feet. "Let me ask you something," she said, grabbing the tape recorder. "Do you think pedicures are a test of homophobia? Many men in prison would share this sentiment. Look at those nasty calluses! You know what they say—big feet, big shoes!" She then wafted around me, singing, "I Feel Pretty." Except for how nicely my feet turned out, I briefly wished that I were dead.

That I would submit to further testing was inevitable. That disrobing would be involved I did not guess. At the coffee shop, she promised, "Afterward, you'll come to my house for a *treat*. We're going to spend the day there...doing *things*." Her eyes were filled with madness. She chortled huskily. She said, "Am I scaring you yet?"

"Take off your clothes and lie down," she said, welcoming me to her Las Vegas home. Actually, her only real home—besides the one in Meadville, Pennsylvania, where her parents raised her—is nestled high in the Hollywood Hills, tucked off perilous Mulholland Drive. I went there once for a potluck dinner and remember it as a big, open space crowded with many guests, including comedians Dennis Miller and Richard Lewis, actress Faye Dunaway, and Sharon Stone's mother and father, who were in town visiting and who are nothing if not solid, decent, no-nonsense, regular people. It was her father, a die maker, who first showed her how to use a gun. "I grew up shooting beer bottles off of tree stumps," she once told me. In her forthcoming western film, *The Quick and the Dead,* she shoots several men with bad teeth and also Gene Hackman. She looks good holding guns and is fond of holding them. She keeps two loaded shotguns always at the ready in her home. "I have one under my bed," she told me soberly. "Because if someone comes into my house, I'm going to shoot him."

She pulled no gun in the foyer of her Las Vegas town house. Instead, she gestured toward two foreboding women standing in the living room—a mother-and-daughter team of masseuses, a trap. Our flesh, she decided, was to be pummeled in unison, on twin tables erected between the sofa grouping. "You will like this," she said evilly, directing me to a bathroom to undress and return wrapped in a towel. Sadly, I could not protest, so immovable is her force of will. I would be made to watch her body be kneaded and caressed by large, muscular hands—not unlike those of Sylvester Stallone in her recent film *The Specialist,* except that they did it standing up in the shower. Together, we would be nude, on separate slabs, beneath thin bedsheets. There would be oils and lotions applied. "Think of it as the sauna room at the Vegas Friars Club," she said. "I'll be Don Rickles and you can be Alan King."

There are reasons, no doubt, why my table collapsed the instant I climbed atop it, crashing me to the floor in a loud naked heap. I may never know those reasons, but fortunately the women had left the room when it happened. Just the house cat, Octavio Boxer, witnessed the incident, suffering only minor nervous trauma. He has known worse, especially recently, when neutered on orders from Sharon Stone. "For revenge, he shit on my bed, on me, and in my suitcase," she said. Historically, the male species has had similar experience with her, although no greater revenge. Since first meeting her prior to the release of *Basic Instinct,* the film that made her famous, I have seen men come and go in her life. At that time, there was some investment banker, followed briefly by musician Dwight Yoakam, followed by a lean period, followed by a young fellow named Chris Peters, son of mogul Jon Peters and actress Lesley Ann Warren. Of the last, she now says, "I made a mistake leaving Christopher. He was the nicest, sweetest, kindest...a dear and sincere friend to me. I don't think he was my life partner, but he was certainly a healthier choice than what I did next." What came next cemented her reputation as a professional femme fatale, perhaps undeservedly. Still, it recalled the great, golden days of Hollywood decadence, when sexual roundelays were commonplace and stars were more memorable for them.

"Oh, I really got sucked into some kind of black hole," she will often lament upon reflection. It all began with *Sliver,* a bad film about voyeurism and nakedness, during the making of which she fell into the thrall of one of the producers, a man named Bill MacDonald, who had just married a woman named Naomi Baka, with whom he had lived for many years. With much haste, Bill left Naomi to be with Sharon, who would not be with Bill unless he left Naomi. Naomi Baka MacDonald then took to tabloid airwaves and accused Sharon of home-wrecking. In short order: Bill gave Sharon an antique ring that belonged to his mother as an engagement token. Screenwriter Joe Eszterhas, who had written both *Basic Instinct* and *Sliver,* and who had introduced Bill to Sharon, took it upon himself to console Naomi, eventually impregnating her, then left his own wife of twenty-four years and married Naomi. Meanwhile, Bill and Sharon traveled the world together, met with the president, looked glamorous always. I saw them backstage at the Letterman show and noticed that MacDonald was wearing leopard loafers and learned that he liked pedicures. I saw them again, in formal wear, posing for paparazzi with Cindy Crawford at the MTV Music Video Awards. "Bill, you're the luckiest man in the world!" the photographers shouted. "Did you dress Bill tonight?" Cindy asked Sharon, who smiled. "This man suffers!" quipped Sharon, whose bare arm he clenched solicitously. Months later, they went to Tucson to shoot *The Quick and the Dead,* and there it ended swiftly and he was gone. His belongings were removed from her Los Angeles home and his antique ring was returned via Federal Express to his mother, who later stood on her own lawn and ranted to reporters, repeatedly calling Sharon Stone "the slut."

She survived, of course, just as she survived *Action Jackson* and *Intersection.* She is that strong. (Also, do not forget that she made *two* movies with Richard Chamberlain.) Characteristically, she laughs last and laughs well, except when weeping inconsolably. Deep in massage, facedown upon her sturdy table, she now sorted through love rubble. Sighing, she told me, "I think of that period as like driving too fast and taking your hands off the wheel." (On a good day, it should be noted, that is exactly how she does drive; I have ridden in the passenger seat.) Disoriented by stardom, the huntress saw herself become the prey: "I didn't know him at all when I got involved with him. I got involved with an idea. About six weeks in, I knew I was in *serious* hot water, and told him so. I recognized how dangerous he was, like a whirling dervish of destruction. I explained to him that it was just going to have to stop. And that was about the time we got engaged—which was his attempt to be legitimate and make me legitimate." A boneheaded solution, perhaps? "So I made a mistake," she said, "and if you haven't, throw a rock at me."

Having taken a drubbing for having taken someone else's husband, she took no responsibility in public, until now: "I *should* have been attacked for getting myself into such a bad situation. I knew that I had to find my way out. I mean, from the moment some of my girlfriends laid eyes on him, they *hated* him. One used to say that I had Patty Hearst syndrome—that I was like a kidnap victim. He was constantly working on me psychologically to make me feel like I was always in danger, and weak, and that without him constantly there, I was vulnerable. So at a certain point, I had a very, very, very complex cohabitation agreement drawn up. After that, it still took me six months to get out of it."

I called Bill MacDonald, who did not call back, even though it has been rumored in publishing circles that he wishes to sell his version of the story. "Does he have one?" said Sharon, upon hearing this. "I hope he does sell it and makes billions of dollars on that story, because there's a confidentiality clause in our agreement. So it will be all mine!" She could have cackled here, but instead her blue eyes narrowed into sapphire slits. Plus, she was nude.

"Oh, look! It's your butt!" She meant mine. The daughter masseuse had instructed me to turn over, which I did, under my sheet, ostensibly protected. *"Heee-heee-heee,"* said Sharon, "I saw your butt!" "You did not," I said. "I did so," she said. The masseuse protested, "I don't know how she could have." *"Heeeeee-heeeeee,"* said Sharon. Thinking fast, I said that I've seen hers, too. "Who hasn't?" she said. "Anybody with seven bucks can see my ass, buddy. What's your excuse?" Her victory hung in the air, much like aromatherapy, unless it actually was aromatherapy—it's difficult to know. "Actually," she went on, "it doesn't feel like they've seen *my* butt. That butt belongs to fictional characters, you know?" Such self-delusion is key to the life of an actress. Earlier in the day, for instance, a girl approached her in the coffee shop and asked whether she was Sharon Stone. "Uh-uh, no," Sharon told her, adding kindly, "I get it all the time, but thank you." The girl retreated. Whereupon Sharon confided, "I'm not allowed to say I'm me when I'm out alone. Rules for sanity, so I don't get trapped and can't get out. And, anyway, sometimes I'm really just not her."

Having been her for thirty-seven years, she still wrestles with her identity, losing often. "I don't look like the thing that I am," she told me thoughtfully. "I never did. I do more so now, though, as I'm growing into myself. They say the first half of your life you get the face you're born with, and then the second half of your life you get the face you deserve. I'm getting there, I guess." In Las Vegas, I noted, her face was frequently covered with bruises, but that is largely because, in Martin Scorsese's *Casino,* she gets hit a lot. Naturally, however, she hits back. Nevertheless she is less keen on her face than she is on other body parts. The loci of her greatest sexual appeal, she feels, are the backs of her knees. "You know, the soft spots," she explained. "I like creases—the back of the neck, inside of the elbow. Those creases, *mmmmmmmmmm.*"

Breasts also interest her greatly. She claimed to be eager to see the film *Disclosure,* in which Michael Douglas has sex with Demi Moore this time instead of her, because "I'm told she suddenly has very large bosoms. Actually," she added a tad imperiously, "that's the only thing I've heard about the movie." Because hers is a lonely lot as a cinema sex-bomb, she is always happy to see contemporaries exhibit raw sensuality, just to have some company. She mentioned a recent magazine photo of Jodie Foster and crowed, "Babeland, I thought! She's become a babe! I'm very thrilled to see her blossoming in that realm. I just think it's bullshit to cover it up. I don't want to experience my power by emulating male behavior. That's where feminism went awry." While filming *Basic Instinct,* for instance, she brought her gun to the set and threatened the cameraman's life, so as to ensure that she would appear suitably luscious on film. "If I see one ounce of cellulite on the screen," she told him, "you're a dead man."

It is perhaps in this way, among others, that obvious similarities can be drawn between Sharon Stone and Madonna—but also many differences. Madonna, for example, possesses no redemptive self-irony. Stone, on the other hand, has no pierced nostrils. Still, the two women share a like bravado as well as a dark fascination with each other. Stone once told David Letterman about how foolish she felt while singing on a stage with James Brown: "Now I know how Madonna feels when she goes on a movie set." Madonna, meanwhile, seemed to dedicate every nuance of her naked-dominatrix performance in the unwatchable film *Body of Evidence* entirely to Stone. Interestingly, their paths have yet to cross, although last year there was a close call, at a Miami Heat basketball game. Madonna had shown up with actor James Woods and sat across court from Stone, who was told by Woods the next day that the singer "said she wanted to come over and give me a big French kiss." Here the actress shuddered. "Not in this lifetime," she said. "Christ, why? Because I'm the only one left she hasn't done it to? Like, 'Excuse me, Madonna, could you please take that salami out of my face!' Hell, it's just unfathomable to me."

Skin rubbed pink, she rose, slipped into her cow robe, smiled a mischievous smile, and made me go get dressed. She then handed me an apron and asked me to bake with her. "I'm one hell of a baker," she announced, and men who have known her know this to be true. Often when inquiring after her, they first ask, "Is she still baking?" Martin Scorsese covets her banana bread. At the camps for homeless children she visits, she is simply called the Cookie Lady. Together, we would now mount the task of macadamia-nut-white-and-dark-chocolate-chip cookies. "For Marty and the crew," she said. To set the mood, she put on some Miles Davis. "You have to chop the nuts," she told me. "That's a boy job." Wasn't that her specialty? I said. "Yuk, yuk, yuk," she said, handing me cutlery. I began chopping in a manner she disliked. "You're chopping them too big!" she said, snatching back the knife. "Make your nuts smaller!" she ordered, demonstrating how it is done, while cradling a telephone to her face. Into the receiver, she cooed, "He's doing your nut-chopping for you, honey." On the other end was the man she has now loved for just over a year, who entered her life in Tucson, once MacDonald had been run out of town on a rail. Among his job responsibilities as a production assistant on *The Quick and the Dead*, Bob Wagner, of Buffalo Grove, Illinois, was to drive Stone to the set every morning. Some days, they were very late.

To be her fellow, of course, requires a certain stamina and mettle. Last year, an episode of HBO's *The Larry Sanders Show* was devoted to this very subject. Titled "Mr. Sharon Stone," it featured perhaps the actress's finest work to date, in which she played herself. (Besides nudity, her greatest gifts lie in comedy, which Hollywood foolishly overlooks.) In the story, she begins dating talk-show host Sanders, as played by Garry Shandling, who quickly recognizes problems therein. "If you're in a show business relationship with a woman more famous than you are," Sanders is told by his producer, "she's the one with the dick. Your ego is gonna get the living shit kicked out of you, pal." (One scene had her straddling Sanders on his bed, happily telling him, "I could crush you!") Years ago, ironically, she and Shandling were similarly involved, although this was never reported when the show aired. "He really tried to keep it out of the press," she told me. "I thought it was funny that he didn't want anyone to know. Our relationship was not unlike what you saw. We would go out and people would laugh at my jokes—only because he's brilliant at being the straight man. But I don't think that was the best thing that could have happened." (Equally frustrating are her TV visits with David Letterman, who is forever flummoxed by her presence: "I could have a ton of fun with him if he would come out and play," she said. "But he wants to be mean with me—it's compulsive. David reacts like I'm there to do something to him, like he's leaping right out of his skin to defend himself. And I have no desire to hurt him. I'm actually kind of getting bored of trying with him.")

When Bob Wagner, who is roughly a decade her junior, finally watched a tape of "Mr. Sharon Stone," she hid in the next room, behind a closed door. She emerged only after she'd heard much laughter. "Bob's not so interested in the limelight," she had told me. Indeed, he is a hard-working guylike guy, with stubbly facial hair and a friendly air, whose sweaters she wears while sleeping in the bed they share. Calling from the set of *Casino,* on which he serves as an assistant director, he was not thrilled to learn of the massages but was not surprised it had happened. She put me on the phone with him so that we could commiserate. "I have met my match," she said afterward. "He's just as nuts as I am. We both have kind of feverish personalities, which gives us a lot of compassion for each other." For instance, early in their relationship, she told me, "I used to go through fits in the night, and kick him and punch him in my sleep." Thusly conditioned, he has by now mastered effective handling techniques. "Sometimes we get going on these screaming torture improvs," she explained, "and say mean things to each other and we laugh till we cry till we laugh again. It's pretty funny."

Such domestication has lately suited her, no matter that it took hold in Las Vegas. Before hanging up the phone, she softly told her man, "I'm sorry that you're having such a nightmare of a day...I love you, too." Likewise, around the kitchen, and affixed to the refrigerator, there were various I-love-you notes, from him to her and her to him, on display. They appear to excel at reciprocation: She will do his laundry and he will let her command the remote control. For Christmas, she gave him vintage movie-poster-art from Brigitte Bardot's *Sexy Girl.* "I'm like Cantonese food," she confessed, deep in cookie dough. "Sour on the outside, and sweet and gooey in the middle." Pouring melted butter into the mix ("I'm an artist with butter!"), she beckoned me to help squeeze her wet dough. She then rolled small cookie balls and smashed them flat onto aluminum sheets, frequently shooing away the cat, who hovered hungrily but accepted rejection well. "He doesn't care, as long as he eventually gets some," she said, quickly adding, *"How like a man!"*

One can safely assume that I tasted her cookies. They were warm and rich and very moist. I told all of my friends. She let me keep my apron as a memento, probably because I washed her pots and pans. "Few men have ever gotten an apron off me," she grudgingly acknowledged. Today I have that apron hidden in a drawer, and occasionally I look at it and think of her and tremble with fear. Of course, she would not understand this because she does not understand fear, except where spiders are concerned. "I'm a person who doesn't panic," she said when asked. "People don't really scare me. If someone pointed a gun at me, it wouldn't scare me as much as just being home alone, up too late, with a gun of my own. Do you know what I mean? I'm more scared of myself. Like someone once told me, I have a mind that's kind of like a bad neighborhood—I shouldn't go in there alone."

Once, long ago, a man did hold a gun to her head, in a Beverly Hills supermarket. He wore a ski mask. He grabbed her in the checkout line and screamed, "Anybody move and I'll blow her fucking brains out!" She was unfazed. Another man happened into the store for groceries, oblivious to the mayhem, and frightened the gunman, who dropped her and collared him. She carefully withdrew from the checkout line. "I sort of drop-rolled into the aisle and hid behind the Jiffy Pop display," she said. She then crawled to the back of the store, all the way into the meat locker, where she picked up a phone and called the cops, who told her not to leave. "I'm like 'Oh yeah, right, let me stay here and wait for the accomplice to come in the back door.'" So she did what only she would or could do in that situation: She put the cops on hold and left through the alley. "I took a powder," she said, grinning. That day she bought her food someplace else. That night she lost no sleep. Possibly, she slept nude.

I t is easy to get nowhere when spending time with Arnold Schwarzenegger. Our first meetings were quite worthless— one in a hotel room (always a horribly impersonal and unhelpful interview experience), another in an outdoor Euro café in Beverly Hills where he spoke German to people at other tables throughout. I recall that he only wished to speak on the record about his new film, *Terminator 2,* and not about himself. So I playfully asked him this: If the Terminator had sex, would anyone die in the process? "You shame your magazine with such questions," he told me very indignantly. He also objected to my asking whether or not he believed he could bench-press Sylvester Stallone. "Why should I vant to?" He tried to stop all further interviews but changed his mind when I appealed to him at the premiere of the film. He said, I swear: "I'm a funny guy, and I can take a joke [pronounced *choke*], but you waste fifteen minutes on the Terminator's rod!" He then brought over his wife, Maria Shriver, and said, "Maria, tell him how to ask good questions!" We got on fine after that and he had much fun ridiculing me at his gym the next morning. With this profile, I teased him back in kind, while striving to make the most of a fairly futile exercise in reportage. According to the *Boston Globe,* the following piece "explains Arnold's universal appeal with a put-down style so low-key that the Terminator could no doubt take it as a compliment." Yeah, well, I got no flowers afterward.

The Importance
of Being Arnold

Rolling Stone, August 1991

1. Men are in crisis, whereas he is not. He does not know the meaning of crisis. Or perhaps he does, but he pretends otherwise. He is Austrian, after all, and some things do not translate easily between cultures. (Lederhosen, for instance.) Throughout the world, he is called Arnold, but that is because there are too many letters in Schwarzenegger. By now, everyone has come to know that the literal meaning of Schwarzenegger is "black ploughman," and like many black ploughmen before him, Arnold knows exactly what it feels like when a horse falls on top of him. There is much pain, yes, but pain means little to Arnold, especially when there are stuntmen available. Anyway, Arnold is never in crisis. For this reason, it is imperative that Arnold be Arnold, so that others may learn. And, from what society tells us, there has never been a more crucial epoch in history for Arnold to be alive, which is, at the very least, pretty convenient.

2. It is a woeful time to be a man. It is a time when men gather to bemoan all that has become of them. Men, experts believe, went soft somewhere. Now, to correct matters, hordes of them retreat to the woods for strange rituals in which they strut about in loincloths and howl at trees, trying desperately to find the Wild Man within themselves, previously lost for generations. Men, alas, have forgotten how to be men. Arnold himself once said, "If I am not me, then who da hell am I?" Of course, he said this in the film *Total Recall,* while wearing a wet towel on his head, so who can tell whether his heart was in it? (Lest we forget, Arnold is an actor, first and foremost.) Still, it is a good question, applicable to most men, but certainly not to any man whose name is Arnold Schwarzenegger, for he is a man who knows exactly who he is: the biggest star in the world, a strong and hand-some man of forty-four possessing a Germanic accent, who likes his cigars expensive, his motorcycles purple, and his dialogue sparse.

Arnold is a formidable fellow, difficult to know personally, although easy to tell apart from Erich von Stroheim. (Arnold would be the one who is not dead.) He is protective of his time, which he prefers devoting to the accumulation of untold fortunes in outside business ventures. Luckily, however, understanding Arnold takes little time and effort, which is why he's become the enormous star that he is today. In fact, it is precisely this quality that earned him $12 million for his work in the colossal hit film *Terminator 2: Judgment Day,* in which he gives what is perhaps his finest performance ever as a cyborg. We live in complicated times, and complicated times demand uncomplicated heroes. Among those who are uncomplicated, Arnold stands without peer. (Even the ti-tles of each of his fifteen films are blissfully primal, a small sampling of which includes *Commando, Predator, Raw Deal, The Running Man, Stay Hungry, Conan the Barbarian,* and *Conan the Destroyer.* You can almost smell blood on the italics.)

"Arnold is a kind of role model, and some might say a dark role model, in a sense," says James Cameron, who directed Arnold in both *Terminator* films. "He's never gonna play a character where he sits around in an office and wrings his hands. He is about *direct action.* He's about being decisive. He's about knowing what you want and going for it. He's very clear." John Milius, who directed Arnold in *Conan the Barbarian,* and who is himself a celebrated man among men, attests to this theory. "Arnold is the embodiment of the Superior Man," he says. "Arnold is the Nietzschean man. There's something wonderfully primeval about him, harkening back to the real basic foundational stuff: steel and strength and will. And that's what Arnold's about."

"I don't ask for too much," Arnold says, as if to explain why he reigns in a world where failure prevails. "I don't ask for anything impossible."

3.   Understanding Arnold the Man—a selective dossier: Arnold is not aware of the fact that American men are in crisis, but explains that he was recently in Japan for a week, so he is behind in his reading. When Arnold wants to pay a man a compliment, he says of the man, "He's in control." There is no higher praise than this. When Arnold is greatly amused, he is the type of man who will toss back his head, clap his hands, laugh heartily, and announce to anyone present, *"I love it!"* He favors tan pants, wears them whenever appropriate, for he knows he looks good in them. "I always wear tan pants," he says. He is happiest when gazing at the color purple. He says he has no idea whether the Terminator is capable of having sex. Arnold owns guns but has never hunted. He fancies himself a decent dancer, but adds, "I wouldn't say that I'm going to show the kids so they could see what dancing is all about." He plays Strauss every day for his tiny daughter Katharine and waltzes her around in his arms. He characterizes his singing voice as "the worst," and claims to do no impressions of famous people. He can subsist on three to five hours of sleep per night. He will nod off in most any chair, if he is tired enough. If he finds something extraordinary, he will invariably exclaim, "It's wild, I tell you!" Of his wife, NBC correspondent Maria Shriver, he says, "She is a jewel," pronouncing it *choo-well*. When asked if he, like Kevin Costner in *Robin Hood,* used a butt-double for his *Terminator 2* nude scene, he says, "I don't know, it's for you to find out. You be the judge."

4.   Arnold drives a Humvee, which is basically a tank with wheels. It is a military vehicle, a massive war wagon, devoid of frills (gun turret is optional), painted the color of sand, and recently used to great effect in the Persian Gulf. Arnold is the first civilian to own a Humvee; it was handmade for him by AM General and stenciled with lettering that reads TERMINATOR. (Lesser mortals must wait another year for assembly-line models.) Arnold already has a regular Jeep, but found it offensively luxurious and streamlined. "It's beautiful," he says of the Jeep, sneering. "But there is a tremendous demand out there for something that looks a little ballsier, something that is a statement, you know?" He saw his first Humvee in a military procession, while in Oregon shooting *Kindergarten Cop,* and fell in love. It reminded him of his youth, when he served for a year in the Austrian Army and drove tanks frequently. How he had thrilled in those days to their demonstrations of strength and power!

"Isn't it wild?" he says to his friends, showing off the Humvee the morning after its delivery. He has just steered his leviathan into the parking structure of World Gym in Venice, California, where he begins most days of his life. (His parking space is demarked by a slab of terrazzo marble on which his name is emblazoned; often women leave roses there to honor him.) Men now encircle the Humvee, staring in disbelief. They listen to the engine, whose roar is deafening, like a Boeing's. They inspect the tires, which are enormous and clearly impervious to harm. They stroke its body covetously. "I just thought it was unusual," says Arnold of his acquisition with a shrug, yet beaming proudly. "There's still a few little stupid things wrong with it," he adds, not wishing to seem overly self-satisfied. "Like the turn signal doesn't shut off by itself, so I drove around yesterday for an hour with the left signal on."

There are many important reasons why Arnold requires a Humvee, and he makes no secret of them. Here, however, is the principal one: "I don't like the ordinary," he says. "We all want to have a look that is our own. The whole thing is a game. It's all nonsense. This is the equivalent to a Harley-Davidson. It's that simple. We all know it's craziness, that it's all about the little trips we go through. But why not? Why not?"

What is interesting is that none of his comrades attempt to ask for a ride in the Humvee this morning, nor does Arnold extend any offers, even after his workout is completed. Instead, he climbs behind the wheel and rumbles off toward breakfast, a small caravan of vehicles following his lead, as is customary.

5.   Arnold shames all men. Shame, he knows, is an excellent motivational tool. It is said that his father used it on Arnold when he was young and impressionable—and look at the result! Today, especially in his role as chairman of the President's Council on Physical Fitness, Arnold goads others on to personal greatness. He shames both by example and by taunt. "What's the matter with you?" he once asked his distant relatives, muscle men Hans and Franz, on *Saturday Night Live.* "I send you over here from Austria to become real hard-core Terminators and look at what you are! Little *termites*!" Conceded Hans, greatly humbled, "Ahnold, you could easily flick us with your littlest finger and send us flying across the room until we landed in our own baby poop." Even now, Arnold enjoys telling friends and acquaintances, "Look at the love handles! You could pull 'em over your neck and use your body like a shopping bag!" At World Gym, he introduces a man with long hair like so: "This is Alan—or as we call her, *Alice.* Isn't that right, Alice?" On the set of *Kindergarten Cop,* he spotted a little girl who was crying over a skinned knee. "Why are you crying?" he asked her. "Because my knee hurts," she said. "But this sounds like a little girl," he told her. "Real tough people don't cry. They fall on their knees, they look at it, maybe tears come to their eyes, but then they swallow and say, *'To hell with it!'* "

Arnold, on the other hand, can himself no longer be shamed. For instance, Patti Davis, the prodigal Reagan daughter, corners him in the

World Gym, where she too works out, and says, "I'm trying to think of what your car means in terms of penis envy. Isn't it sort of phallic gone mad?" Arnold grins and says, "I have no problems." He then accuses her of being a media addict. "She loves journalists," he says. "Shut up, Arnold," she says, laughing. "Media addict," he says. "*You* are!" she says. Moments later, two writers from a muscle magazine approach him. "Talk about being a media hound!" Davis yells. Arnold smiles a beatific smile and says, "Jealous bitch."

6.   The meaning of Arnold: John Milius, who among other acts of testosterone wrote the films *Dirty Harry* and *Apocalypse Now,* tells what is perhaps the quintessential Arnold tale:

"Arnold and I were coming back from skeet-shooting one day and we stopped at Tommy's Hamburgers in the Valley. We were sitting there and this motorcycle gang came up—the Hessian Motor Family or something. They surrounded the table and began chanting, 'CONAN! CONAN! CONAN!' It was real tense. Arnold looked up, and I don't remember what he said, but this guy called Road Pig sat down and said to him, 'Hey, man, I always wanted to arm-wrestle you, bro.' So Arnold said to this big guy, *'Look at this arm.'* Then he took his arm out of his sleeve, and it's faceted like a stone. He said, *'Have you ever seen such a beautiful arm? If I was to use this arm on you and I hurt it, how would I feel?'* And the guy, satisfied, claps him on the shoulder. Then the next guy says, 'Hey, man, would you fuck my old lady?' Arnold looked over, and the old lady was good-looking. He said, *'If I fucked her, how would she feel with you then afterward?'* Finally, to appease them, Arnold rode a couple of their motorcycles around the block. In the end, they wanted to give him their colors and make him an honorary member of the gang.

"I sat there amazed by it, because suddenly you realize that everybody owns Arnold. He is accessible to everyone. It works on every level. It works among the Kennedys and it works within this motorcycle gang. If Stallone were there, they'd have wanted to *challenge* him, they'd want to see how tough he is. But Arnold became theirs. No—ours."

7.   Arnold is an external man living an external life, from which he has benefited greatly. His body, and what he has made it do, gave him his fame—he is, of course, a seven-time Mr. Olympia and a five-time Mr. Universe—as well as the opportunity to appear in films with many firearms and, once, with Richard Dawson. Much is known of Arnold's physical being, a being that looks especially memorable in black leather jackets. But we know little of Arnold's interior life, largely because there doesn't seem to be much of one to know. Arnold's genius is that his brow does not often furrow. Unlike most men, he is never ambivalent. Life does not weigh upon him, and if it did he could bench-press it easily. Who, insofar as this quality alone, would not aspire to be in his place? As he would say, as only he can, "I was very lucky so far." Consider the calm in his face. "It's sort of Cro-Magnon or Neanderthal," says Milius appreciatively. "Arnold doesn't say a lot, but his face says everything." Meaning it says all it needs to say. It was Milius who first urged Arnold to capitalize on his face in film, during the making of *Conan.* "I said to him, 'Whenever you kill somebody, I want your face to have a Zen-like grace, always the hint of the smile.' And he's never forgotten that. He has an absolute serenity that gives a real power."

The Arnold face masks no confusion, for example, since he is never confused. "You have to understand that I'm looking at everything in a much clearer way," he says. "I see it very simple in front of me, so there are no complications. Other people look at everything in a twisted way maybe. It's very hard for me to relate to this and that's why I'm sometimes very hard on people. When I was young I had zero patience. As soon as someone complained about being depressed, I was outraged." Does *he* ever get depressed? "It maybe happens, but I would not even dwell on it. It's never held me back, that's for sure. I don't walk around with a sour face."

Indeed, a quick tour of Arnold's subconscious registers few bumps: He fears nothing, as far as he knows. He does not have a fanciful or dark imagination. Death does not cross his mind. "I haven't had those thoughts," he says. He recalls few dreams. "Some people train themselves to wake up and write them down," he says, incredulous. "Then what? What do you do with that information?" There is only one recurring dream he remembers: "Before I start shooting a film, I sometimes have dreams where you're out there lying totally naked in a forest and you have no clothes and you hear somewhere, *'In two minutes we roll.'* All of a sudden, the lights come on and you say, 'Wait a minute, what scene are we doing now? Why am I lying out here, and where's the clothes? What are the lines?' I'm caught totally off-guard, like I wasn't prepared."

Might this be the effect of having huge budgets, like the purported $100 million spent on *Terminator 2,* riding squarely on his shoulders? "Consciously," he says, "I am not aware of it. I never feel the pressure at all, consciously. I never go to the set and say, *'My God, it's a lot of pressure!'* "

8. Arnold never answers telephones, an exercise in abstinence that he feels would cure most societal ills. When a phone rings in his Pacific Palisades home, he ignores it. He chooses not to be bothered; either an assistant or his wife reaches for it. "To me, the phone doesn't mean anything," he explains. "It's more difficult for Maria, because she was brought up with the phone. I wasn't, so it doesn't mean anything. If the phone rings, it goes in one ear and out my other. What's it gonna be? Schmoozing? I schmooze at the gym every morning. Or later at lunch. If there's anyone I want to talk to, then I would call. And I never come to the phone for business at night when I'm with the family. Whoever answers will say I'm not there."

In this way, Arnold strives toward making ours (and his) an uncluttered world. He believes in the Structured Life, where there is less phoning and speaking, in general. Thinking, he says, must also be curbed. "The mind cannot relax otherwise," he says. "The key thing is to let the mind, like the body, float. And then when you need to hit hard, you're ready with all of your energy. That's why I always say to people, *'Don't think!'* That doesn't mean you shouldn't have a brain, but there's a part of us that likes to go through life instinctively and not make decisions. You free yourself and don't analyze everything and *interpret* or *misinterpret*." It is difficult to describe the disdain with which he pronounces those words. "This way you get rid of all the garbage that bogs you down and loads you up. So my whole approach is, I would say, simpler."

9.   Some men imitate Arnold, as well they should. Arnold understands the lure. "I play the characters that they would like to be," he says. On this day, he has arrived at a *Terminator 2: Judgment Day* convention, being held at the Stouffer Hotel near Los Angeles International Airport. Here, among nearly one thousand fervid delegates with more free time than other people, a group of young men have come to participate in a Terminator look-alike contest. They wear much black leather and shaded eyewear, and do so with great conviction, never breaking into knowing grins, even as they casually wander the hotel. Arnold's appearance will close the day of festivities, when he will judge those who best emulate his character. Cash prizes will be awarded.

"Everyone would like to be a Terminator," Arnold has been known to say. "Everyone would like to be a person who can take care of the job. Whoever makes you mad, you can get even. There's a tremendous amount of frustration in human beings, and I think this is a way of fantasizing to get rid of those frustrations. To think, *I can do this too.* It's a release, especially when you throw in a few cool lines of dialogue that always signal that you're not even concerned about the danger. You make fun of danger, like John Wayne. You never heard John Wayne talk hectic, even when bombs went off around him. You think, *Wow, how can he be so cool? This guy is standing in the middle of a bombing and* he's in control."

Onstage in the Stouffer ballroom, after sufficient buildup, Arnold emerges from a cloud of pink fog. He is in full Terminator dress. *Terminator* sound-track music pounds and pulsates. Conventioneers grow hysterical. Arnold, expressionless, stalks the stage, then elects to perform the twist. Finally, he silences the mob and addresses them, somberly, as befitting a cyborg. "In the first movie," he says, "I told you, *'Fuck you, asshole.'*" Crowd roars. "But I also told you, *'I'll be back!'*" More roaring. Arnold says, "The main man is back!!" Delirium has taken hold. Love grips all. People are on their feet. Someone shouts, "Down in front!" Arnold glares, as only he can. *"Fuck you, asshole!"* he says. His legion thunders with approval. (Jim Cameron has said of Arnold's Terminator, "What is enjoyable about him is that he's kind of the ultimate rude guy.") Arnold speaks a bit about the new film's merits, then announces: "Jim Cameron and I have just decided backstage that we're going to do another *Terminator* after this one. The title will be *The Sperminator: 'I'LL COME AGAIN!'*" Thunder.

A moderator intercedes in an attempt to begin the look-alike proceedings. Arnold halts him. "Remember one thing," he tells the fellow. "Whenever I talk, *never interrupt!*" This, of course, is just the sort of humiliation lesser men yearn to dispense. Naturally, it receives a well-deserved ovation among the conventioneers. At last, five contestants march out to stand before the man who represents all they dream of becoming. Arnold stares them down slowly, then taps one particularly sullen finalist as his choice. He pulls the lucky youth, named Scott, away from the pack. He deposits a leaden arm across Scott's shoulders.

"Congratulations, Scott," he says slowly. *"You look cool."* Scott shuffles modestly. Arnold continues his appraisal. "I like those sexy lips of yours," he says with uncomfortable sincerity. Scott smiles wanly. "It's true, Scott. They're driving me *wild,* I tell you!"

Everyone, of course, laughs. Everyone except Arnold, whose eyes dance behind his shades. He will be gone in an instant, out through the loading dock to a waiting car, taking with him yet another memory of his effect on mankind as we know it. For now he must rest. There is, after all, a world full of broken men left to fix.

Johnny Depp, who has since proven himself to be an actor of astonishing good taste, had just completed only his second starring role in a film, after having acted on a mediocre television show for four years. Here, then, was a young man, scheduled to appear on his first *RS* cover, who really hadn't accomplished all that much to date, other than fall in love a lot. (At the time, his romance with Winona Ryder—alas, doomed—was in full flower.) But he was a terrific subject—greatly uninhibited and game—and it was his fine esoteric spirit that freed me to write perhaps the most loopily aggrandizing mock–celebrity profile I had thus far attempted.

Johnny Depp
Smokes With Christ

Rolling Stone, January 1991

He was born Depp. He has always been Depp. As a boy, he was ridiculed for it. On the schoolyard, he was called Dipp. Or Deppity Dawg. Later, he was called Johnny Deeper, this based upon a popular adolescent joke he barely remembers: "Something about some guy having sex with some girl who kept saying, 'Johnny, *deeper*!' " He conjures this dark memory with visible embarrassment. Being Depp, you see, has never been easy.

Depp came into my life during his Hollywood years, a time when the Depp name had begun to really stand for something. The day we met, he extended his hand to shake mine, except that his hand was not a hand so much as it was weaponry. In place of fingers, there were blades. This was the sort of unpredictability I would later come to expect from Depp. At the moment, however, we were on a Twentieth Century Fox soundstage where he was making *Edward Scissorhands,* his second major film, in which he portrayed the man-made boy with scissors for fingers. He laughed quietly at his own comic gesture and then introduced me to his attorneys, who hovered nearby. (Depp is a master of the ironic nuance.) Soon, he was asking me what I knew of Al Capone and doing his impersonation of Warren Beatty blinking. Such is the irrepressible spirit of Depp.

Now I will reveal all that I know of Johnny Depp. I will tell of our adventures together: The time we found Jesus, or a guy who said he was Jesus, on Santa Monica Boulevard, and Depp gave him cigarettes. The time we ate eggs with his movie star fiancée, Winona Ryder, whom he loves profoundly. The time we trespassed on Harry Houdini's abandoned property in the Hollywood Hills and got yelled at. I will describe his tattoos, his problem facial hair, his recurring nightmares, which feature the Skipper from *Gilligan's Island.* Clearly, earlier biographers have never gotten much of the real Depp, focusing instead on the surface Depp. This, then, is an all-new Depp—a man who lives hard, loves hard, but most of all thinks hard.

The days I knew Depp best came and went quickly. There were three of them in all. They were November days, as I recall. The first one began in a coffee shop, as so many things do in the life of John Christopher Depp II. Winona had left him that day. Left him at the coffee shop. Then she drove off to do some errands. So he was very much alone. He was smoking too much and drinking too much coffee, but who could blame him? He said he was enslaved by caffeine and nicotine, and didn't sound proud of it. "I like to be pumped up and hacking phlegm at the same time," he said wryly. "Couple tequila worms flying out here and there," he said, but he was joking about that. He hadn't touched the hard stuff for a solid month, maybe longer. Depp was as dry as he'd ever been in all of his twenty-seven years.

Nobody recognized Depp in public places, not when I was with him. He is a man of the people and therefore doesn't stand out much. Yes, he continues to be a teen idol and a heartthrob ("a throbbing thing," he calls himself), but frankly he looks like someone else. Director John Waters, who cast Depp as a delinquent greaseball in the film *Cry-Baby,* used to imagine him as "the best-looking gas station attendant who ever lived." Or, as Waters later told me appreciatively, "Johnny could play a wonderfully sexy mass murderer. I mean, it's a part *made* for him." Which is to say, there is shadiness to Depp. He looks attractively unwashed. ("Nobody looks better in rags," said Waters of the basic Depp sartorial statement.) Like so, he does not possess the burden of great presence. He speaks and moves with quiet dignity. You hardly know he is there. It is easy to sit in silence with him, although ultimately—and I think he would agree here—not very interesting.

•   •   •

If Depp is anything, he is interesting. He takes the big risks. Tom Cruise, the rumor goes, wanted to play the tragic, disfigured role of Edward Scissorhands—but only if he got to have a cosmetically restored face by picture's end. Not Depp. He wore Edward's scars like medals. And he wore the unwieldy, imposing hand shears with brio, recognizing the lyric poetry in Edward's fateful curse. (Edward, who can touch nothing without slashing it, is a metaphor for the outsider in all of us, including Depp, who knows what it's like to be mocked for being a little different. He is, after all, a teen idol.) "He certainly was closest to the image of the character," said Tim Burton, who directed Depp in *Edward* and Nicholson in *Batman* and Keaton in *Beetlejuice* and Herman in *Pee-wee's Big Adventure,* as well as many other actors in those same movies. "Like Edward, Johnny really is perceived as something he is not. Before we met, I'd certainly read about him as the Difficult Heartthrob. But you look at him and you get a feeling. There is a lot of pain and humor and darkness and light. I think for him [the role] is probably very personal. It's just a very strong internal feeling of loneliness. It's not something he talks about or even can talk about, because it's *sad,* ya know? What are you gonna do?"

If you are Depp, you do what you can. Indeed, so devoted to Edward's metaphorical millstone was he that, while smoking off-camera, Depp stoically learned to hold his cigarettes between the scissors' blades. During shooting days in Florida, when temperatures soared above 110 degrees, he stayed trussed up in Edward's black leather bodysuit without complaint. "I would freak out," said Winona, who played Edward's dream girl in the film, "just thinking of how he must feel, like if he had an itch or if he had to go to the bathroom. . . ." But Depp, being Depp, simply suffered in silence and dramatically cut down on his coffee intake. He learned to ignore his bladder and thus diminish the likelihood of horrible self-inflicted wounds. It is no wonder, really, that his performance demonstrated such admirable restraint. "I had to just sort of deal with it," he would say later, a better man for having endured for his craft.

"If there's any movie in the history of the entire world, and even in the history of any literature," he said triumphantly, "this was the movie I would want to do. And I fuckin' did it. When I first saw it I was scared, because I kept thinking, *God, I just can't believe I did this fucking movie.*"

But then Depp is an impassioned, if unlikely, aesthete, a bedraggled *literateur* of sorts. He is a high-school dropout with a lust for first editions.

Once, I saw him pay $75 for a rare Hemingway as if it were a pack of Marlboros, and I noticed the swagger in his stride when he carried the book off. He cites Jack Kerouac and J. D. Salinger, two idols, with staggering frequency. His most prized possession—and one that cost him a good portion of his burgeoning fortune—is a book on black culture in whose margins Kerouac had scribbled and doodled. "It's a piece of history," he told me reverently. "I look at it every day."

And then there is fine art:

"Gacy!" Depp said excitedly, in reference to imprisoned mass murderer John Wayne Gacy. There, in our coffee shop, I had handed him an order form listing Gacy's latest oil paintings, knowing that Depp was the owner of a Gacy clown portrait. (Depp, incidentally, lives in mortal fear of clowns.) *"The Hi Ho Series!"* he exclaimed, impressed. "Shit!" He perused the form, shuddered, then told me that he'd gotten rid of his Gacy canvas. "When I got it, I heard the money was going to the families of the victims," he said, but later he suspected otherwise. "The paintings are really scary and weird and great, but I don't want to contribute to something as evil as that."

We went walking that evening. Depp likes to walk. "It's good butt exercise," he told me. "It's good for the rump." Depp, it turns out, has no car. He does have a broken truck. And motorcycles in storage. For a long time, he had no home. He and Winona moved from hotel to hotel until they recently got a place in Beverly Hills. They did share a loft in New York for a brief time, but they tired of the East. So they came west, where no one walks except Depp (whenever Winona is using their rental car, that is). But even on foot, Depp is like a dedicated motorist, ever vigilant of traffic minutiae: "Your seat belt! Your seat belt!" he hollered that evening into the snarl of Beverly Boulevard as we trod along. Depp had spotted a man driving with his seat belt dragging out on the pavement and could not bear to think of the consequences. The startled driver now owes his life to Depp. Likewise, Depp spotted a woman driving with her door ajar. "Your door!" he yelled. "Your door is open!" No doubt, that very woman is now living a rich and productive life, thanks to the selfless instincts of a certain movie actor who is currently looking carefully for his next big project.

Once, when he was very young, Depp harbored an irrational fear of John Davidson, the great musical entertainer. Today, Depp has conquered that fear and, in fact, even appeared in a major motion picture with Davidson. (In *Edward Scissorhands,* Davidson convincingly played a talk-show host who interviews Edward.) "He was a really sweet guy," said Depp magnanimously. "I felt bad for ever being scared of him." So imagine Depp's reaction when we purchased a map to the stars' homes from a street peddler, and the very first address he saw was Davidson's. *"Oooooh, John Davidson!"* he crowed, reading off the numbers and displaying no residue of unexorcised terror. This was one cured customer. (Of course, we never went to Davidson's house. We didn't go to anyone's house—not to Peter Falk's or Sandy Koufax's or Phyllis Diller's or Anna Maria Alberghetti's. We were, after all, on foot.)

Instead, we wandered aimlessly, and he spoke of his darkest visions. "The most disturbing dream I ever had," he said, "and I hope this is taken the right way, because I'm sure he was a very sweet man, was one where Alan Hale Jr., the Skipper [on *Gilligan's Island*], was chasing me. He was in his wardrobe from the show—the white cap and white pants and everything—and I was running from him. He got on a bicycle and chased me into this weird little apartment, really small, very low-rent. I looked over to my right, and there was an elderly woman, ethnic-looking, squatting. She raised up her muumuu and took a piss. I got the fuck out of there immediately, because she was very evil. Then I remember diving over the bushes, where the Skipper was trying to get me, and then I woke up."

By now, the origins of Depp are familiar to most functioning Americans: Born in Owensboro, Kentucky, the self-styled Barbecue Capital of the World, Depp was the fourth child of John Depp, a city administrator, and his wife, Betty Sue, a waitress at many fine coffee shops. (Her famous son would later have her name tattooed above his left bicep, so as to balance the Indian chief tattooed on his right one, a talisman of his partial Cherokee bloodline.) Depp was a small boy, so early on he learned to rely on his fists, especially when fighting. Eventually, his family settled in Miramar, Florida, and Depp, seven at the time, elected to go with them.

Rebellious in school, he was once suspended for mooning a gym teacher. He learned to smoke by age twelve and then drink and finally take drugs. By fourteen, however, he is said to have sworn off drugs forever. Two years later, his parents divorced, and soon after, Depp quit high school to join a rock band called the Kids, who became a local sensation and opening act for the likes of the Talking Heads, the B-52's, and Iggy Pop. (He remembers that his first words to Iggy Pop, one of his heroes and later a friend, were inexplicably "Fuck you, fuck you, fuck you." In response, a perplexed Pop called him a "little turd.")

At twenty, he married Lori Anne Allison, a twenty-five-year-old musician and sister of a band mate, and together (band included) they left Florida for Hollywood, where the Kids broke up and so did Depp and Lori. Alone and starving, Depp turned to acting and made his screen debut in the original *Nightmare on Elm Street* as a guy swallowed by a bed. (Grateful to this day for that break, Depp will graciously appear in the next *Elm Street* sequel as a cameo murder victim.) Then came *Platoon,* in which Depp played an interpreter who dies off-camera. But his movie career would have to wait: Depp next became, for four years, America's favorite boy detective, undercover high-school cop Tom Hanson, on Fox's *21 Jump Street,* a television series Depp hated and saw only six episodes of. Still, it transformed him into the major show business figure he is today, and, better yet, the babes loved him. Beautiful actresses flocked to his side. Before it was over, there were two failed engagements: to Sherilyn (*Twin Peaks*) Fenn and to Jennifer (*Dirty Dancing*) Grey. Then the TV show was canceled. But by now John Waters had hired him to star as the misunderstood hood Cry-Baby Walker—his first big screen lead role!—in the troubled-teen musical *Cry-Baby,* released last April. And it was during this time that he met Winona Ryder, the girl who would change his life forever.

On my second day with Depp, Winona showed up. She is nineteen and all pluck, the thinking man's actress for her generation. Depp is the thinking man who thinks of her most. He swells in her presence. When they hug, they hug fiercely, in focused silence; their squeeze keeps regrouping. They are lost in each other. She smokes his cigarettes, and she is not a smoker. ("You're on the filter, babe," he will coach her.)

Hands locked, they descended upon Barney's Beanery, a frequent haunt, for caffeine, which they now took in desperate helpings. She wore a Tom Waits T-shirt and Depp's engagement ring. She was saying, "I'd never seen anyone get a tattoo before, so I was pretty squeamish, I guess." Depp chuckled and said, "She kept taking the bandage off and staring at it afterward." They were speaking of WINONA FOREVER, the third and final (for now) Depp tattoo, eternally etched onto his epidermis: locus, right shoulder. (Depp told me he plans to have his tattoos pickled after his death as keepsakes for his children, should there be any.) This one was carved on at a nearby tattoo parlor, as Winona watched with awe. "I sort of was in shock," she said. "I kept thinking it was going to wash off or something. I couldn't believe it was real." Her eyes widened. "I mean, it's a big thing, because *it's so permanent!*"

"It ain't goin' nowhere," he said, and by this I knew he meant business. Over hash and eggs, they then traced the history of their romance for me: He knew her work (*Beetlejuice, Heathers*), and she knew his, but they did not know each other. At the premiere of *Great Balls of Fire,* a film in which she played Jerry Lee Lewis's child bride, they spotted each other from across the lobby. "I was getting a Coke," she said. "It was a classic glance," he said, "like the zoom lenses in *West Side Story,* and everything else gets foggy." She said, "It wasn't a long moment, but it was suspended." He said, "I knew then." They did not meet that night. Months later, a mutual friend dragged her to Depp's hotel room at the Chateau Marmont, where Belushi last drew breath, and this is where they began. "I thought maybe he would be a jerk," she said. "I didn't know. But he was really, really shy." They knew it was love when they both professed deep feelings for Salinger and the sound track of the film *The Mission.* Their first date, a few weeks later, was a party at the Hollywood Hills home of counterculture guru Dr. Timothy Leary, who is her godfather. "We were kinda blessed," said Depp, a Beat disciple. As it happens, Winona's father is an esteemed Beat bookseller in Petaluma, California, where she and Depp weekend often. "My parents really love him a lot," she told me. Depp said: "It could have been easy not to like me. Other people might have just seen tattoos."

Tim Burton calls them "kind of an evil version of Tracy and Hepburn." Which is to say, as celebrity couples go, these two are dark, spunky, glamorous, and resilient, all requisite traits in this cynical age. And so they must be: Tabloid photographers terrorize them at airports and tabloid reporters regularly report imaginary squalls and breakups. So he gets angry, and she gets incredulous. Winona: "They try to *trip* me at airports!" Depp: "What's shitty about it is they feel like you *owe* them! That you should stop dead in your tracks and let them piss on you!" Winona: "I will say that there *are* some really nice ones." Depp: "A couple of them are real nice." Winona: "But aren't we allowed to be in a bad mood sometimes? Everybody else is."

We found Jesus after lunch. Winona left (took the car again), and Depp and I stepped out into daylight, where we saw a miracle. There, on Santa Monica Boulevard, in front of the Beanery, stood a man who looked very much like the Son of God—in pictures, at least. He was swaddled in robes, his face was serene, his eyes were benevolent, his hair was long, his beard was crisp, he wore tattered Reeboks and a decent tan. He even seemed sort of divine, in an approachable street person sort of way. I do not know if Depp is a praying man, but he is, evidently, a closet theologian, if one is to judge by the adroitness with which he interviewed this hallowed figure. First, perhaps to put the holy man at ease, Depp complimented him on his clothing (was Depp considering a dirty-linen motif for himself?).

"I have always dressed like this," said the man in a soft, commanding voice. What, Depp inquired, was his name? "Jesus," the man said, although he used the Hispanic pronunciation (*Hay-zoos*). Where had he come from? "Oh, I don't know," he replied. "Heaven." His age? "Over forty." Why had he come to Los Angeles? "I'm here for a special occasion." What was the occasion? "I like it here." Where did he like it best? "Beverly Hills." At which point, Depp whispered to me, "Apocalypse. Second Coming. Armageddon." Suddenly, a Hollywood climber—short, with a noisy sport coat, on his way to lunch—accosted Jesus from the side. "Hey, I just wrote a story treatment about a guy who dresses like Christ and wanders the streets," the Hollywood guy said, seeming as earnest as one of his ilk can seem. "Do you have a phone number where you can be reached, in case a deal happens?" he asked. (He did not notice Depp, who looked properly mortified.) Jesus regarded the pitch artist wordlessly, but his message was clear: idiot. Defeated, the guy slunk away. Said Jesus, "He was different, huh?"

"You want a cigarette for the road?" Depp asked him. Jesus assented, and together the robed one and the young actor smoked for a while. "Take the pack," Depp told him. "I can buy some more." Afterward, Depp seemed thrilled. "I smoked with Christ!" he said, not a little boastfully. "Jesus is a Marlboro man!"

Perhaps it was the brush with Jesus that did it, but Depp spoke to me from his heart that night. He seemed somehow inspired by the divine fellow. "I wish I could grow more facial hair," he said, bemoaning the wispiness of his whiskers. "I can only get an Oriental sort of beard." Spooning up corn chowder in a tiny restaurant, he was openly penitent about his "younger, hellion, hitting-the-sauce kind of days." He owned up to his short fuse: "I've got a bit of a temper." He spoke of a tussle or two and of the circumstances surrounding his arrest in Vancouver during his *21 Jump Street* tenure. Apparently, he was trying to visit some friends late one night in their hotel, where Depp himself had once lived, and a security guard would have none of it. "The guy had a boner for me," Depp recounted. "He had a wild hair up his ass, and he got real mouthy with me, saying, 'I know who you are, but you can't come up unless you're a guest here.' The mistake he eventually made was to put his hands on me. I pushed him back, and then we sort of wrestled around a bit and I ended up spittin' in his face."

The police didn't want to hear Depp's story. He was jailed for a night, fingerprinted, posed for mug shots ("I wish I could have them"), and in the morning he walked.

But the most beloved legends of Depp are not violent legends. Hardly. For Depp is a name synonymous with great romance. In his young life, he has asked for the troth of four separate women. Whereas other actors are elusive Lotharios, Depp is the marrying kind, unintimidated by the notion of connubial permanence. (Is he trying to succeed where his parents did not?) "I knew this was gonna come up," he said, looking stricken. But Depp is nothing if not courageous. So, for the first time ever in recorded media, he offered these assorted insights into his mythic ardor: "I've never been one of those guys who goes out and screws everything that's in front of him. . . . When you're growing up you go through a series of misjudgments. Not bad choices, but wrong choices. . . . You know, people make mistakes. We all fuck up. . . . I was really young for the longest time. We were young. . . . [My relationships] weren't as heavy as people think they were. . . . I don't know what it is. Possibly I was trying to rectify my family's situation or I was just madly in love. . . . You're the first person that I've talked to about this kind of stuff. And I'm being really honest with you when I say that there's been nothing ever throughout my twenty-seven years that's comparable to the feeling I have with Winona. . . . It's like this weird, bounding atom or something. . . . You can think something is the real thing, but it's different when you feel it. The truth is very powerful. Now I know. . . . Believe me, this WINONA FOREVER tattoo is not something I took lightly. . . . Her eyes kill me."

He then said this about his engagement to Winona: "People don't realize this, but we've been together almost a year and a half. Out of any, whatever, *thing* I've been through before, it hasn't been this long. It wasn't like 'Hi, nice to meet you, here's a ring.' It was about five months [before we got engaged]. They thought we ran away to Las Vegas and got married." When will their nuptials actually transpire? "The wedding thing?" he said. "We're just gonna do it when we both have time, because we both know we're gonna end up working in the next couple of months. And we want to be able to do it when we can get hitched and then go away for a few months. Leave the country, just go wandering around, and be on a beach somewhere with tropical drinks.

"I've never actually come out and said this," he added portentously, "but the one claim to fame I'm most proud of is that I'm responsible for having John Waters ordained. I sent in to the Universal Life Church and had him ordained by mail. He's now Reverend John Waters, and we want John to perform the ceremony. Who better? You know what I mean? John is a stand-up guy. And Winona loves the idea."

(From the sanctum of Pastor Waters: "I told them I wouldn't do it without their parents' blessings. I mean, I've *met* her parents! They've eaten dinner here! I'm not gonna just horrify them. And of course, I always counsel Johnny and Winona—*too young*! I tell them to *wait, wait, wait*! But I'd be thrilled to perform the ceremony—I'd feel like the pope!")

My last day with Depp went like this: I picked him up at home, which wasn't really home, but a small bungalow he and Winona were briefly renting. (Their new house was not yet inhabitable.) Depp was on the kitchen phone, pacing furiously, caffeine wiring his arteries. Heaps of laundry and luggage and books cluttered the living room floor. A stray cat was loose in the house. Winona was out. Mail was strewn about. Depp told me about his fan mail, unique in its female pubic hair content—"I've gotten some weird pubes" is how he put it. We got into my car and drove. We passed a slatternly pedestrian. "That," said Depp, "was a man in drag." Depp cannot be fooled. We passed a coffee shop adorned with a giant rooster. "I have one of those," he said, meaning the rooster. "I have a nine-foot rooster. I have the biggest cock in Los Angeles. My large cock is in storage."

This was the old Depp, spry and antic as ever. He saw a dog and said that he based Edward Scissorhands on a dog. "He had this unconditional love," said Depp, who will probably cherish that role above any other in the Depp repertoire. "He was this totally pure, completely open character, the sweetest thing in the world, whose appearance is incredibly dangerous—until you get a look at his eyes." He then said, "I missed Edward when I was done. I really miss him."

We drove to Harry Houdini's house, which wasn't really a house, but a scattering of ruins perched above Laurel Canyon. Houdini's ruins, they say, are haunted. Depp read from a guidebook, " 'Nearby Canyon residents tell of strange happenings on the hilltop site.' " Depp, incidentally, believes that he was once Houdini. "I often think I might have been Houdini at one time," he said. So we dropped over to see if anything looked familiar to him. We scaled a steep hill and found a crumbling staircase and little else. "There's no house," said Depp, disappointed. He was now obviously soured on the whole endeavor. "I bet this was a really romantic place at night," he added dreamily. Then a German woman emerged from a nearby house and, apparently mistaking us for urban archaeologists, chased us off. "Yes, ma'am," said Depp politely as we fled.

Here is how I will remember Depp best: After the Houdini incident, he grew more and more quixotic, thirsting for the wondrous possibilities that lay before him. We snaked through the Hollywood Hills, whose lore endlessly enchants Depp. "I would love to buy Bela Lugosi's old house," he said. "Or Errol Flynn's. Or Charlie Chaplin's. I want some old, depressing history to call my own. Plus, I love the idea of a view." He sat in silent reverie, but within moments was overtaken with purpose. "I think I just have to make a lot of cash," he said calmly. "I also think I want to be a sheik. I want to be the Sheik of Hollywood. What do you have to do to become a sheik, anyway? I wonder if it just takes cash. . . ."

Before any further grandiosity could delude him, however, Depp made me stop the car. "Something's wrong with that mailbox!" he said, pointing to a blue corner mailbox, which seemed to have exploded. "I'll go see what happened." With that, he hurried to assist a U.S. postal worker hunched over the damaged box. I cannot be certain of how Depp managed to help. But now, whenever mail is delivered safely and on time anywhere in this great land, I don't think it would be presumptuous to say that one American actor did his part.

I wrote the following profile at the moment wherein Tom Hanks indisputably became a bona fide blue-chip movie star—almost the man of range and reason and Oscar recognition that we know today. In the nine films he had made up until then, he'd largely played the blithe wiseacre, but that was about to change forever. We came together on the eve of his marriage to Rita Wilson—which provided an opportunity to lampoon his very embarrassing early film, *Bachelor Party*, in the lead. Elegantly enough, he called me after he'd read the piece and enthused that what pleased him most was that I'd actually written exactly what happened, exactly the way it happened—a first for him, I gathered. Our paths would cross again, most significantly thirteen years hence for a piece celebrating his rise to iconography in the interim.

Tom Hanks
Gets Big

Rolling Stone, June 1988

Oh Bacchanalia! Tom Hanks is about to divulge details of his very recent bachelor party.

"You saw the film," he says. "Now live the reality."

So let's hear it. "I was on a sailboat with a bunch of guys," he says coyly, but not without promise. "We sailed to Catalina Island for the weekend. Seven guys on a boat. We left early Friday evening and got into Catalina by midnight. For two days, we just drifted around, ate a lot, jumped in the water, caught fish, and got very, very *stanky*. We didn't shower or shave in seventy-two hours. It was a manly thing."

Yes. Fine. But what about the debauchery? Girls in the baked goods. Donkeys in the lingerie. Your basic fraternal ripsnorting and cavorting. Like in the movie.

"Shamefully," he says, "there was no debauchery whatsoever. I'm not a real debauched kind of guy. I had a few beers. That was about it. Call the cops."

Long pause. He sighs guiltily, then caves in.

"We did smoke cigars."

Uh-huh. Anything else?

"Well, you know, funny thing..." Yes, yes? "As soon as we got out there on the island, we all envisioned ourselves as pirates." He smiles. "*Arrghh, matey!* You know, old men and the sea, grand adventurers who braved the twenty-six miles to Catalina. It was fun."

Fun.

"I even got to steer."

Tom Hanks is still a single man when I meet him. Within two weeks, he will pledge his connubial troth, and that will be that. For the moment, however, freedom prevails. Possibility is at hand. There is still time to indulge whims, to tempt fate, to fly in the face of responsibility. He suggests that we play golf. "Wanna go tap the Titleist, whack the Wilson, spank the Spalding?" he asks, but it is all for naught, since rain douses the City of Angels even as we deliberate. I propose that we do what he normally does, but what he normally does is drink coffee, read newspapers, and yammer on the phone (as he is inordinately fond of pointing out). He mentions something about going to the car wash, but, damn, the rain again. We decide at last to see a movie. On a lark, I suggest we take in a switch flick, one of those yarns wherein a gawky adolescent mysteriously finds himself trapped in the body of Dudley Moore or Judge Reinhold or George Burns. Hanks contorts his face at the notion.

In *Big,* the latest Tom Hanks film, a gawky adolescent wishes he were bigger, older, and more formidable—and he wakes up the next morning as Tom Hanks. ("Maybe this has happened all over America," Reinhold says in *Vice Versa.* "Invasion of the body switchers!") It is the quixotic allegory for our fast times: a wistful fable about fleeting innocence, about growing up too quickly, about the inalienable right to act geeky. I asked Hanks what he would call the genre. "Planet of the Apes," he says. "Well, that's what *I* heard."

He has steadfastly avoided seeing the other films. "No real point to it," he says, resigned to the glut, his work done. But, to be fair, *Big* was the archetypal property, reputedly in the works long before the formula fell into the craven clutches of Hollywood cloning engineers. Moreover, in this film bodies aren't truly switched—a kid simply grows up overnight. The situation is explored gently; extraneous high jinks are eschewed. "What I dug about it was there was no car chase, no bad guys, no guns," Hanks says. "A massive amount of the movie is just two people sitting around talking." Says the film's coproducer, *Broadcast News* director

James L. Brooks, "It was our conscious decision not to rush and try to beat everybody, but to just do our movie like the others weren't happening."

Hank's performance in *Big* transcends the film's premise. This is a controlled, sustained, sensitive, sweet piece of business. He is vulnerable. He is uncoordinated. He plays puberty as though his body hair sprouted yesterday. It is his finest work to date. And never once in the film can he be accused of being a smart-ass, his trademark attitude. "I was a little worried about that," says Penny Marshall, who directed *Big*. "His fans like him to be irreverent on-screen; most of his parts have been very sarcastic. But this is an actor's part, and he's an actor."

He is certainly no wisenheimer, this Hanks. I expect arrogance, smugness, glibness. I expect rapier retorts and high-voltage banter. Instead he is courteous and sincere. His liquid eyes, with their almost Asian set, are even a bit melancholy. They are never quite mirthful. Yes, he's funny, but almost never frenetically so. His laugh is an old guy's laugh, a slow, lumbering, fogyish sort of *huh-huh-huh*. And yet at thirty-one he has a childlike enthusiasm about him. He drives a Dodge Caravan, he says, because "I like sitting up high; it's nice to see what's causing the traffic jam." Whenever he spies an accident on the road, he lurches with excitement: "*Whoa!* What happened here?" When he stumbles upon a good parking spot, he crows: "Look at this! *Beeyooteeful!*" Even weather sparks him: "This rain is *crackin' me up!*"

Hanks wants to see *Stand and Deliver* (alas, a film utterly devoid of body-switching), so we head over to Westwood, a community that doubles as a multiplex Cinerama. It is early afternoon, and since he hasn't eaten anything today (he does not believe in breakfast), we first duck into one of his favorite Mexican haunts, a simple, cafeteria-style cantina, where the food, he insists, is "is all very, very fresh and healthy." He orders himself a chicken burrito, black beans, rice, and a grapefruit soda, then plunks down his tray on a wobbly table beneath a photograph of Pancho Villa. As he devours his burrito, a gangly guy in a business suit approaches tentatively.

"Tom, right?" says the suit guy, screwing up his courage. "Can I just shake your hand?"

"Sure," says Hanks, warmly offering his grip.

"Just so I can say I've shaken your hand," says the guy.

"You did," says Hanks with a tolerant grin.

"Really appreciate your movies," says the guy. Hanks graciously thanks him. The guy then says, "I saw you over here and thought, *Wow, he looks like an old friend of mine.*"

"And," says Hanks, chuckling, "you thought, *Who the hell is that guy?*"

Self-deprecation aside, Hanks has raised a salient issue here. *Just who the hell is this guy?* "I guess I come off in the movies as a guy who you wouldn't mind hanging around with," he says, not exactly answering the question. Of course, in movies he's our old friend, the life of the party, the king of quippery. But that's entertainment. The guy sitting across the table from me just spilled his grapefruit fizz all over and didn't even joke about it. Invariably, he is portrayed by the press as nerve-deadeningly normal, but that doesn't seem quite accurate, either. As Peter Scolari, his former partner in drag in the gender-bending sitcom *Bosom Buddies,* says, "There's nothing normal about the guy. He is an imaginative, eccentric individual. He's a very quirky, very unusual young man."

According to Sally Field, Hank's costar in the forthcoming *Punchline* (in which Hanks plays an angry ace stand-up comic), "It would be one thing if he was just this great, goofy guy. But that lasts for about thirty seconds, and then you want to meet somebody real. The reason he's a movie star and is going to stay one is that he's much more complicated than that.

"Yes, he's very entertaining and funny and easy to be around. But you know there's somebody else underneath, somebody dark. There's a sad side, a dark side. And that's what makes him so compelling on the screen."

Just don't try to pin him down on matters dark, sad, or angry. He won't hold still long enough to allow for scrutiny. He bops and jostles through conversations and changes subjects so adroitly that hours and days pass before you realize that he has done so.

"Did you ever watch the TV show *Then Came Bronson* in the sixties?" he asks in a rare revelatory moment. "Michael Parks as Jim Bronson— now that guy I honestly wanted to emulate. I wanted to be a friendly guy on a motorcycle who gave everybody a fair shake and yet always rode out of town at the end of the hour."

"What kind of reporter's notebook do you use?" he asks me, pulling out his own. It's true: Tom Hanks keeps on his person at all times an authentic reporter's notebook! He flips open the narrow pad (Stationers Model 801) and shows me that it is crammed with jottings, phone numbers, reminders. "I have a whole boxful of them at home," he says. "They're perfect for just keeping track of regular stuff."

We are now drinking coffee at a pizzeria, killing time before the movie. So I ask him about regular stuff, like his impending wedding to actress

Rita Wilson, who costarred with him in *Volunteers* and now shares his living quarters. Hanks blanches slightly; talk of personal details, no matter how mundane, makes him nervous. He takes privacy seriously. For this reason, he politely refuses to let reporters visit his Brentwood residence. He won't tell me who sailed on his bachelor-party cruise ("*Naaah,* just some friends") or even the identity of his best man ("*Naaah,* his name wouldn't mean anything to you"). I innocently ask whether he'll be married at home, but he stiffens and says, pleasantly enough, "No, it will take place at a location whose whereabouts will remain under lock and key."

Rita Wilson will be his second wife. He entered his twenties under the freight of early wedlock and fatherhood. It's a subject fraught with peril. He has been known to turn surly in deflecting discussion of his first marriage, to actor-producer Samantha Lewes, a union that gave him a son, now ten, and a daughter, five. The divorce was finalized within the last two years; he remains deeply devoted to his children and keeps their visits frequent and regular—"like clockwork."

He will say this much about the approaching wedding: "It's a wonderful thing to do—such a neat, optimistic, good-feeling, cleansing separation between an old life and a new life." I asked him what he values most about his relationship with Rita. "We say what's on our minds without worrying about any repercussions," he says after a moment of consideration. "Just very open communication, good news and bad news. As well as being able to laugh. We have laughed an awful lot. You need that. The person you're gonna marry is somebody you're gonna probably talk to every day for the rest of your life. You're gonna have to want to do that."

Earlier, I noticed on Hank's dashboard a greeting card propped open just enough to reveal a message from his bride-to-be—the words "I love you always, Rita" and a tiny hand-drawn heart.

She seems to stir in him an almost profound sense of gallantry. Last year, Hanks took Rita to the Oscar ball. At the boisterous party, he encountered a most unsettling trespass. "Bette Davis was sitting in my fiancée's chair," he says, still incredulous. "She just came over and sat down! Arlene Dahl, who was sitting at our table, said, 'Oh, go over and tell her to get out of your chair! Do it, she'll love it! Go tell her.' So I went over and said, 'Miss Davis, you're sitting in my girlfriend's seat, but if anyone can sit in her chair, you can.' She just looked at me and finally said, *'I can't hear a word you're saying.'* "

"Did I mention to you that this is a private screening?" he blusters as we step into the minitheater, which is virtually empty for the midafternoon showing of *Stand and Deliver.* "I bought out the house." He finds a seat and crumples into a comfortable slouch, then hollers, "Okay, Rocco, roll it!" The screen, of course, remains blank. A teenage couple straggles down the aisle. "Hey!" Hanks calls after them. "Hey! I think you folks are in the wrong theater! Hey!" The couple ignores him and plops down ahead of us. *"Damn,"* he says, grinning stupidly.

At last, a truly Hanksian display. Frankly, I had begun to worry. I had even proposed that we storm through some torpid business office where he could cast sly bon mots at hapless working stiffs, the way he did in the triumphant—and largely ad-libbed opening moments of *Nothing in Common.* Hanks brightens at any mention of that film, an underrated seriocomic exploration of strained father-son relations, in which Jackie Gleason portrayed his cranky old man. "It changed my desires about working in movies," he says of the experience. "Part of it was the nature of the material, what we were trying to say. But besides that, it focused on people's relationships. The story was about a guy and his father, unlike, say *The Money Pit,* where the story was really about a guy and his house."

The remainder of Hanks's oeuvre doesn't depart too radically from this sort of formula. Take, for instance, *Splash:* a guy and his fish. *Bachelor Party:* a guy and his libido. *The Man With One Red Shoe:* a guy and his footwear. *Volunteers:* a guy and the Peace Corps. *Dragnet:* a guy and his badge. *Every Time We Say Goodbye:* a guy and . . . um, has anyone actually seen or, for that matter, heard of this movie?

"I don't think I've ever gone back and repeated myself, though," he says. "There have been times when it was close. The guys I play all have a lot of flaws. Part of that is the confines of this face and this body. There's not a lot I can do to change it." Here he is just being cagey. As Penny Marshall says, "He has the handsomeness that isn't too beautiful. It's approachable. I think he's adorable."

Legions of women agree. They see him as a youthful avatar of romantic comedy, the rightful heir to Cary Grant. Last year a major men's magazine built an elaborate fashion spread on the concept, togging out our boy in all manner of debonair pastels. "Bad duds," he says. "I looked like a sleazy French golf pro."

Now Hanks just looks rested, which he rarely is. "*Big* is my tenth movie," he says wearily. "That's almost too many. I made *Splash* [his first film] in '83. In five years that's a lotta work. For a while there I made movies in an absolute flurry of activity. But the opportunity was there. And I had a great desire to be working. You do get those feelings that you're never ever going to work again." Last year alone, he made three films—*Dragnet, Punchline,* and *Big*—which left him so worn out that he caught pneumonia and had to spend a month recuperating.

So far he has taken this year off and has no concrete plans for his next project. He is laying low. "There are other things that are just more important than being a hotshot-celebrity movie actor," he says, uttering those last words a tad contemptuously. "I simply want to pay attention to those other things for a while, things like life and love and going to the bank and organizing your garage.

"When I'm on film sets, so much of life is completely put on hold. Eventually, you realize, *When the work is done, I have to go home to a place I've had so little personal investment in that it might as well be just another hotel room.* Which is just no way to live. And that's how actors get all fucked up. People tell them they're wonderful, and then they go sit alone in a hotel room or a very nice house, which has been decorated by somebody else, where the furniture has been placed by an *absolute stranger.* You have no connection to it!"

See Tom Hanks in his latest project: a guy and his priorities. Peter Scolari vouches for his old friend: "I hate to say this, but it's not easy being real successful in this town, particularly for a man of conscience. You get fed a steady diet of adulation. You get fed things that aren't necessarily bad or poisonous or toxic in any way. But they're not really on your meal plan. You have to stop and say, 'Wait a minute—I didn't order this.' You have to take your life by the horns. You have responsibilities that have nothing to do with being an actor. Tom Hanks has dealt with his success. I have never known him to be happier. And it's specifically not a career thing."

We visit Hanks's office the next day. Since November, his office has been located on the Disney Studios lot, in Burbank. To get there, you must take Mickey Avenue to the intersection of Dopey Drive and turn right, then clamber up into the Animation Building. There, through a glass doorway flanked by cartoon celluloids of Dumbo and Cinderella, is his sanctum. The decor is spartan, but there are *touches.* On the coffee table: crayons and a coloring book, plastic dancing raisins, a ball autographed by Hanks's beloved Cleveland Indians. Tacked to the bulletin board: an Indians T-shirt and a map of the United States. "I had that in my briefcase one day," he says of the map, "and decided to put it up so I can look at it and say, *'Here's our land!'* " Behind his desk: a motorized toy roller coaster and an at-a-glance chart of frozen-yogurt flavors available in the commissary. "What's today? Burgundy cherry. No, thank you."

Because he is so intuitively childlike in *Big,* I asked him earlier when he most feels like a kid. "I never feel like a kid," he said, "but yet I *always* feel like a kid." He is now playing with a Duncan yo-yo, so the subject resurfaces naturally enough. Childhood for Tom Hanks was a many-splintered thing. His parents divorced when he was five. He and his older sister and brother moved out with their father, while his younger brother stayed with his mother, who subsequently remarried three times. His father remarried twice and, due to a peripatetic career in the restaurant industry, continually uprooted Tom, his siblings, and their stepsiblings (of which, at various turns, there were scores) and lugged them all over California. "I moved about a milllon times," says Hanks sunnily. "I think we moved every six months of my life. The longest I ever stayed in one house was five years."

He steps up to his map and, jabbing his index finger at it, diagrams his youthful wanderings for me. Beginning at Concord, his birthplace, his finger thumps repeatedly at points up and down the Golden State, with a brief detour to Reno, Nevada. He taps meaningfully at Sacramento, where he attended Cal State for a year and a half, then his hand darts eastward all the way to Cleveland, where he interned for three seasons at the Great Lakes Shakespeare Festival (and discovered those Indians!). His finger flicks up to New York, where he stayed long enough to attend a cattle-call audition for a sitcom pilot called *Bosom Buddies,* and then whisks back to where it came from, landing approximately upon the spot we occupy this very moment.

But what kind of kid was he? "A geek, a spaz," he says. "I was horribly, painfully, terribly shy. At the same time, I was the guy who'd yell out funny captions during filmstrips. But I didn't get into trouble. I was always a real good kid and pretty responsible." Philosophical, too. He considers all of his early moving an excellent primer for the actor's life. "It made me flexible," he says. "It gave me a confidence to think I can be in any sort of social situation and know how to gracefully get out of it."

Like when I asked for phone numbers of relatives who might give me a good quote. "They won't tell you anything that I wouldn't," he says very sweetly. "Problem is," he adds, thinking aloud, "what you need is my own self-examination, which, well, I don't do." He shrugs helplessly. I ask him whether he thinks he's easy to know. "No, probably not. A guy with whom I once worked on a movie said somewhere that people on the set felt they knew me and yet nobody really knew me. And that's pretty much true. If I make people feel at ease, well, that's a wonderful thing. If they don't feel as though they're my best friend in the world, that's a wonderful thing, too."

He fetches a remote control gadget off the desktop. "Want to see something amazing?" he says excitedly, leading me toward the doorway. "Stand back. Watch this." I step into the outer office and, from inside, he aims the remote at the door. It automatically swings shut in my face. The symbolism is not lost on me.

"Here they are!" Penny Marshall says. Hanks and Rita have just arrived—fifteen minutes late—at the Zanuck Theater on the Twentieth Century Fox back lot, where five hundred people have been seated for a Sunday night test screening of *Big.* This will be Hanks's first viewing of the film. He and Rita, a spirited brunette in a billowy white windbreaker and leggings, race up the theater steps, where they are greeted by Marshall, Jim Brooks, and a handful of studio people. Hanks apologizes to them, explaining that he just drove his children to the airport (to send them back to their mother) and got stuck in traffic.

In Rita Wilson's company, he seems looser, livelier, more Hanksian, if you will. Elizabeth Perkins, who costars in *Big,* says of the couple, "They complement each other's energy. She bubbles over; she's so effusive. When the two of them are together there's just another force at work." Tonight they josh and laugh and eventually slip into the back row of the full, darkened theater. To prevent being discovered, Hanks keeps a Chicago White Sox cap tugged down across his brow.

He is pensive as he watches himself on-screen. He never laughs at his own funny moments, although they convulse Rita and the crowd. After a half hour, the film suddenly melts in the projector, and the picture dissolves into molten goop. "Hey," says Hanks, "great effect!" This happens again twice; each time it does, the houselights come on, and Hanks leans into his future bride, hiding himself. "What do you say we take in the midnight show of *Colors*?" she jokes.

At one point I ask whether she knew in advance that her fiancé would be so convincingly pubescent in the role. She looks at me incredulously and guffaws. "I *live* with this man!" She howls. "This is a man who plays hockey inside the house with a bag of Milano cookies!" Hanks protests: "Oh, stop it!"

Finally, the projector is fixed, and the film winds to its lovely, bittersweet conclusion. Hanks and Rita gallop out ahead of the throng, and it isn't until they are well away from the theater that I see that both are crying. He sweeps her up in his arms, pressing his face against her neck. "It was so sad," she says with an embarrassed laugh. "It's just a movie, hon," he tells her softly. "You'll get over it." He honks his nose and adds, "What a sweet movie. I didn't expect to cry."

They duck into Jim Brooks's production bungalow and split a beer while waiting for the crowd to disperse. "And here's Penny!" Hanks booms when Marshall enters. "She's a *genius,* a *genius.*" The director casts him a withering look. He chummily throws an arm around her and keeps jabbering. "I think we should keep the film breaks in! I think they work! Did they work for you? They worked for me! Wonderful film! Delightful! Much better than the other kids-switching-bodies-with-adults movies! What if we call it *13 Again?* Think about it."

When Hanks and Rita step outside a while later, a stray cat slinks past them. Hanks, who seems to be gaining buoyancy, affects a mock-showbizzy mien and announces, "Ah, one of the many studio cats here tonight!" Rita joins in the conceit and says, "He's the informer cat, the one who gives away the ideas to the other studios." Hanks snaps his fingers to a Vegas beat and actually begins to sing. Loudly. "He's a *stooooooooodio* cat," he croons. "He's a studio *caaaaaayaaaaat!*" Rita is now dancing around in the dark, meowing in accompaniment. Hanks giddily belts out another line: "He's a snotty-kooky-wacky-nutty-supah studio *caaaaaaaaattt!*"

Strangely enough, it is an exhilarating spectacle, a little bit of private lunacy they will forget by morning. He slips his hand into hers, and they saunter off across the empty movie lot, yowling exultantly into the night.

What follows became a minor footnote in American magazine history, if tragically so. This profile of actress Cameron Diaz, scheduled to be *Esquire*'s November 2001 issue cover story, was about to be shipped to the printers from the magazine's New York headquarters early on the morning of September 11. Whereupon terror struck, in devastating fashion. The dizzy comic tone of this piece suddenly felt inappropriate to me and to the editors, and so we shelved the story. (A new cover image of the crumbling World Trade Towers reflected in an eye's pupil served as the replacement.) Miss Diaz agreed that it was the correct move. Five months later, I would update the piece for *Esquire* readers in a new, less innocent world. I include it in original form here. As time and perspective intervened, the forthright humor seemed just fine for a zeitgeist on the mend. This was no time to cease with celebrity irony, after all.

Cameron Diaz
Before 911

Originally for *Esquire*, November 2001

She is the kind of girl who gets you thinking that you know exactly what kind of girl she is. She's like that, this one is. Like, for instance, one fellow that I know was thinking about her not long ago and he began telling me these things, even though he also claimed to know next to nothing about her: "She's a guy's girl," he started in. "She's a girl who would bait your hook for ya. She's a girl who would drive real fast. She's a girl who gets drunk and pees in the shower and smashes pumpkins and tears up traffic tickets, hopefully not all at once." She is the kind of girl who gets a fellow going just like that. She incites imagery and postulation that tilt toward game-spiritedness and fearless indulgence, toward Hell and Heaven stirred together. As for me, when I get to thinking about her, like I'm doing right now, I think about the first thing she ever said to me, which was: "I've gotta pee soooooooo bad!" She said that, by the way, in a loud whisper, and her crystalline eyes bulged, and then she ran to the john with her little blue flip-flops clip-clopping like thunder-hooves, but only after shaking my hand and telling me her name, even though I knew her name, but she isn't presumptuous about that sort of thing. Anyway, this happened at a place she doesn't want me to tell you about, because she thinks that you think you know all you need to know about who you think she is and what she does—like pee, for example—and where she goes when she does things. She is that kind of girl exactly, if not necessarily.

Like, for instance, a couple of hours after she introduced herself to me as Cameron, I asked her to tell me her middle name, insinuating that it could well be Danger, since she had by then given me sufficient reason to think as much. Instead, she told me it was McDonald. "Because," she said, "of all the French fries I ate when I was a child." Then she said: "No, my middle name is actually Yo Mama. Actually, it's Yo-Yo Mama. No, my middle name is Meet My Motherfuckin' Motherfuckin'. No, my middle name is Mismatched-Pair-of-Socks-If-You-Can't-Find-the-Other-One-Check-the-Dryer." I decided right about then that I didn't really need to know her middle name, because she's the kind of girl who probably shouldn't have one. Then she said: "I have to pee again."

So there we were, at this place, which she suggested I tell you was her home, which was not her home, because she doesn't want you to know anything about her home, and the fact is, she has long lived in a famous Hollywood Art Deco apartment building (not that she told me so), where it would be unlikely to have a lush green, sun-dappled patio restaurant dotted with hotel guests and an eager wait staff accustomed to her insouciant whims, as does this place and as do those who work here. John Belushi, meanwhile, died here. But the point is, she's the kind of girl who enjoys being a regular, or a habitué, or a steady customer. Therefore, they like to think that they know her here. In fact, if they were asked what Cameron Diaz was like, I'm sure they would just go on and on.

I will now say this without uncertainty: What she is like is the kind of girl who is like other girls similar to her. These would be girls men can drink and golf and wrestle and fish and cuss and spit and fart and shower with. These would also be girls who can do all those things and never not be easy on the eyes while doing them. At this moment in time, however, she would be the famous girl who's exactly like this—not that there haven't been other famous ones at other times. Like, for instance, Martin Scorsese, who directed her in his forthcoming epic *Gangs of New York,* told me that he thinks she is very much like Carole Lombard: "There's this look in her face, a lightness and also a toughness, but with humor." The *New York Times* last year also declared her to be like Lombard, as well as like Jean Arthur, Jane Russell, and Angie Dickinson—"an American type, a game, outdoorsy girl . . . with her sense of fun, camaraderie and forthright sexuality." Meanwhile, Bobby Farrelly, of the Farrelly Brothers, who co-directed the notorious 1998 comic outrage *There's Something About Mary*, in which she became more famous than she had been previously, due in part to an impulsive need for hair gel, has said: "Cameron's like Grace Kelly—but with gas."

To that end, as it were—and it's best to just get into this right away—she is the kind of girl who is very much at one with gas. She is not shy about it at all. Rather, she revels in all rumblings emitted from the body. "I love talking about it," she told me, quite happily, wherever we were at the time. "One of the biggest conversational pleasures I know is to indulge yourself in a little flatulent humor. There are no inhibitions here." Indeed, she has been known to catch whiffs of silent deadly ones released by friends and also by strangers, then compliment the perpetrators on their fine work. Among fond childhood memories are those of her father letting suddenly rip in the family car. Throughout the filming of *Charlie's Angels,* she and sister-Angels Drew Barrymore and Lucy Liu competed ferociously to produce the most offensive and reverberant fart sounds. (They used their mouths.) "We're now known for that," she proudly told me. She also possesses a remote control device that activates fart noises from beneath cushions in her home. "It's the best," she said of that device and the joy it brings to her. "It's like drugs. The first time you do it to somebody who's not expecting it—man, it's just the greatest high!" Then she added, "But you can never get away with it twice, so you have to move on to the next person." (I won't soon forget the sadness that tinged her voice when she said this.) Moreover, as millions of American youths will attest, she won the Celebrity Burp-Off at this year's Nickelodeon Kids' Choice Awards, handily defeating members of 'N Sync and the Backstreet Boys. Accepting the honor, she merely demurred: "It's not the best that I can do, but I will try to do better next time." Months afterward, she would tell me that she had purposely chugged a full can of Diet Coke scant moments before unleashing—"and it hurt, it was too soon, it was not right, it was really a forced burp. Twenty minutes later, as I was walking around backstage with the award, the real one erupted. An entire soft drink came swelling up, blasting out like a volcano." For this reason, in actual life, she is off the Diet Coke. About which I am thinking: *Damn.*

While you may not think so, she is the kind of twenty-nine-year-old girl who does not mind still being a girl, who has so far appeared in eighteen motion pictures, not including three more she has made since last year's

Charlie's Angels, two of which—Scorsese's *Gangs of New York* and Cameron Crowe's *Vanilla Sky*—are scheduled for December release and which will reveal her to be the kind of girl you had no idea she could be, except maybe you should have imagined as much. Those who have seen early cuts of *Vanilla Sky* are said to be stunned by her work with Tom Cruise. "I'm kind of like the lover that was this close to being the one," she told me of the character she plays. "Kind of like the phone-call-in-the-middle-of-the-night girl, the good-time girl sort of reaching toward wanting more in the relationship and thinking that it was mutual and finding that it wasn't." (That's the kind of girl she will now make us think she is.) "Diaz is the one that you're not going to spot coming," says Crowe, who prefers not to give away details of what he means here. "She's sort of the secret weapon of the movie. She's really got the big range. It's wild."

Her range, of course, has expanded exponentially since her lustrous femme fatale debut in 1994's *The Mask,* starring Jim Carrey—the job for which she first decided to hyphenate herself into a model-turned-actress. (On the DVD commentary of *Mary,* one of the Farrellys memorably recounts initiating this playful exchange upon meeting her: "I asked her, 'Is it true that you had to fuck Jim Carrey to get into the business?' She said, 'No, I blew him.'") Anyway, after *The Mask,* her hyphens would all but disintegrate while she acted her way through smart oddball roles in such camera-obscura as *The Last Supper, Feeling Minnesota, Keys to Tulsa, Head Above Water,* and *She's the One.* When she resurfaced before the general public in 1997's *My Best Friend's Wedding,* her fragile bride-to-be character shone so brightly as to dim the wattage of Julia Roberts in the conniving-bitch role. Plus, she sang achingly bad karaoke in pink. Soon thereafter along came *Mary,* for which she embodied the eternal girl-that-got-away fought over by all men who meet her, arguably the most despicable of whom was portrayed by her then true-life boyfriend Matt Dillon, who, in the film, describes her as a "butt-plug." Mary, of course, is the kind of girl who is anything but butt-pluggish. This can also be said for Cameron Diaz, although she may wish to argue.

Cameron Diaz, also known to associates as Cam-ron D—as per the hip-hop parlance of the Destiny's Child/*Angels* sound-track hit "Independent Woman Part One"—wished to argue: "Let's argue," she said to me. "Let's fight. We can be angry at each other the whole time. And at the end you can say I'm a bitch. You can write, 'And that was the last time I ever saw that bitch!' I like it!" She is that way, apropos of nothing at all, really. Call it pluck, or dander, or piss. At the place that wasn't her home, where we sat outside for hours, where she consumed guacamole and a veggie-burger and slugged Dr. Tema's Natural Honey Cola—she pulled the bottle from her purse; said she owns a distributorship for the beverage; a waiter instantly brought her a glass of ice—she saw red whenever she looked at me. This, however, had much to do with the scarlet tint of the shades she wore over her translucent blue eyes, although she claimed it mostly just pinkened her world. "I don't like dark shades," she said, "because the darkness swallows me up. I can't adjust." Brightness, on the other hand, seemed to worry her as well, since she kept asking if I was getting too much sun and offering me her sunscreen (SPF 30) and finally rising to lug our wrought-iron table toward shade so that darkness could better swallow me up, not that I cared one way or the other, but you could tell that she's the kind of girl who likes moving heavy furniture around.

Anyway, she looked good outdoors, like she belonged there. Last year, she took a dare (along with *Angels* costars Barrymore and Liu) and went on a three-day survivalist mission to the Utah desert so as to prove her mettle amid starkest nature and let *Marie Claire* magazine publish her journal jottings. A brief excerpt: "If there were a million good reasons to hike fifteen miles over a day and two nights with no food or water or blankets, the number-one reason would be to get naked with no one else around and swim in the river," she wrote. "I couldn't have felt more free and safe." Mostly, however, she is a beach girl, having grown up in Long Beach, California, where her family continues to reside, and having whiled away countless Floridian summers since childhood with her grandparents along the Tampa shore. She told me she had just returned from another Florida family beach-holiday where she happily sat in the water for three hours at a time—"It's so healing and meditative and ooohhhhh... I wish I was there right now." About that, I did not doubt her, since she is the kind of girl who hates to sit around answering questions about herself for magazine profiles, although she at least got to romp on a beach—"half-naked, funnily enough"—near pelicans and seals while being photographed for this one. So it could have been worse.

For the record: I didn't want to hear about her love life at all, because what could be worse than listening to this kind of girl blather on and on about some fabulous guy like the deeply handsome actor Jared Leto, with whom she has been involved for a couple years and who has appeared in such films as *Requiem for a Dream* and *Girl, Interrupted* and the television series *My So-Called Life,* and whom Cameron Crowe told me "seems like a really good guy"—but she turns out to be the kind of girl who has completely given up talking in any media about her romantic pursuits. ("I don't want anyone to know anything about it," she said of the relationship, in the politest way. "It's not for them, it's for me.") So I think you can imagine my relief. I certainly know that she could.

It was the great Charlton Heston who once said of her: "I honestly believe that woman would eat her young." Actually, he said that in Oliver Stone's *Any Given Sunday,* referring to her ruthless, gonad-eviscerating character, the owner of the fictional Miami Sharks football franchise. (Like Heston, by the way, she works well with apes, as seen in *Being John Malkovich,* wherein she was locked in a cage with one and also never once resembled the kind of girl she truly is; she was a brunette in the film.) As for eating her young, this will clearly never be the case—i.e., she gave up eating pork two years ago, despite her proud pork-loving half-Cuban heritage, because she was told pigs share the same mental capacity as three-year-old children. "My niece was three at the time, which is a magical age," she said, horrified. "I thought, *Oh, my god, it's like eating my niece!*" This, then, also put an end to her preferred hangover cure: Egg McMuffins, with Canadian bacon, natch, and beer. (A grease-and-hair-of-the-dog girl!) Other things she has put an end to: caffeine ("I'm out of my mind on it, completely"), meat (for now), and cigarettes—she famously rolled her own, since it slowed her intake, plus she loved the ritual and the natural flavor. "It's delicious," she told me kind of wistfully. "You don't inhale on it every time. It was like a lovely meditation...I'm sure I'll take it up again sometime." In terms of inhaling, by the way, you should know that she is a girl who breathes through only one nostril, due to a broken nose. Because of this, she wakes regularly in the middle of the night with pulsing headaches. "I'm not a mouth-breather," she pointed out to me, which I probably would have guessed anyway.

"I'm a thieving whore," she will say, incidentally, when describing the kind of girl she plays in *Gangs of New York,* which was filmed in Rome so as to replicate the long-extinct notorious Five Points section of downtown Manhattan, circa 1860, where the bloody saga unfolds. For the role, she learned to pick pockets—"That was rad!"—an art she practiced constantly on the set during breaks, targeting crew members and costars Leonardo DiCaprio and Daniel Day-Lewis alike. "She was crazy, running around lifting things from everyone," says Scorsese, whose own pocket watch she repeatedly tried and failed to purloin. ("It was hooked onto his belt buckle," she told me, still frustrated, "and I just never could get it all the way off before he'd speed away.") What is ironic here is that one day last December after work, she returned to her room at the Grand Hotel de Russie only to discover a pair of nattily dressed Italians making off with *her* loot. "I was getting out of the elevator," she recalled for me, "and I saw them coming out of my door. And I was like 'That can't be my door—what would they be doing coming out of my room?' They were carrying shoes and big shopping bags, and I thought, *Those look like my bags.* I passed them in the hall and sped up to my room, opened the door, and saw everything dumped out and torn up. So I turned around and started screaming at them—'Heyyyyyyy! That's my shit!' "

[If I may momentarily interject here, what follows may possibly illustrate the kind of girl that she is, in case you were wondering.]

"So I started running after them, chasing them down these European stairwells, clomping down the stairs, screaming down after the mother-fuckers, who were looking up at me while they ran. It was like a scene in some police show. Finally, at the bottom, they dropped everything, because the stuff was heavy—they had busted the safe out of my closet, which had my passport and cash; they had my computer and my leather jackets. I ran all the way outside, but lost them. I was white from the adrenaline. The violation goes so deep. My family's house was robbed when I was young, and there was nothing you could do about it at the time. They took things I never saw again—which is heartbreaking. So this time, there was something I could do about it. I just wanted to fuck-ing kill them!"

Scorsese, still astonished, remembers: "I said to her, 'You chased them down the stairwell? Did you not think that there may have been weapons on them?' She said no—they ran, and her first and only impulse was to chase them all the way down the stairs!" Would he have had the same im-pulse? He chuckled wryly. "I don't think so. I'm a New Yorker."

Incidentally, when I questioned that impulse of hers after she told me the chase story, she shrugged and gave with the large, wide smile that she gives and said simply: "Hey, buddy, I'm a proactive kind of girl."

Being just exactly that kind of girl she is, she decided that we should meet a few days after we first met at that other place and that we should paint pottery at a pottery-painting store called Color Me Mine, in Larchmont Village, near Hollywood. She elected to surprise me with this plan, which I wouldn't have minded trying to nix in advance, thank you, but what are you going to do? She told me to meet her at a pizza joint down the block, where I found her sitting at an outdoor table, wearing shorts and a pink camisole under a big open white shirt, watching pedestrians through her red glasses. Then she led me over and into the painting store, where, by the way, I noticed no men and many children and many women, one of whom immediately exclaimed, "Cameron! How are you?" And this turned out to be the gamine Hispanic actress Salma Hayek, who was sponge-painting several place settings of dinner plates and salad plates and soup bowls and such. "It's my boyfriend's birthday," she said excitedly—by which she meant it was her boyfriend actor Edward Norton's birthday—"and I'm doing the whole-set-of-dishes thing for him and then I'm going to make the dinner to go on it. I have sooo many gifts for my boyfriend!" (This, I gathered, is the kind of girlfriend Salma Hayek is.) And Cameron said, "How perfect! That's so sweet!" (Later, Salma would compliment Cameron on her own excellent choice of boyfriend in Leto—"He's so good-lookingggg, and usually, you know, the good-looking ones are jerks, but he's great and he's so niiiiiiiice. . . ." To which Cameron perkily agreed: "He is so nice!" Not that I cared to hear any of this, by the way.)

Anyway, she chose to paint a salad plate and I chose a mermaid figurine, which looked like the kind of mermaid who might be blond and blue-eyed and could sit in the water three hours at a time and wish that she could be doing it right now, like some girl or other. So we went to work, perched on our stools. "It's fucking hard to paint," grumped Cameron at one point, having already started and rinsed off two different plate designs. She is, I will vouch, the kind of perfectionist who can be hard on herself like that. Like, for instance, she was telling me about how she has made movie after movie, year after year, without taking much time to reflect on her work, and this past year she made *Gangs* and *Vanilla Sky* largely simultaneously, then immediately made another movie called *The Sweetest Thing*, which she finished only weeks before now, whereupon she decided to take the next year off—"I've retired" is how she put it—but you could tell she was simmering in anxiety, since there are no new distractions from thinking about the most recent work she has done. "All I have now is time to reflect, and it's difficult," she said quietly, while painting her third plate design. "You hope you've given them what they need. I haven't slept all week. I'm going through that time when you have to be depressed. It's hard to let go of things. . . ." She regarded my blond mermaid, whose fins I was coating in shades of soft blue, then said sort of yearningly: "She's going to be such a nice pastelly fish out of water. She's like one big puddle of water, happy and holding no form." I think this was a compliment, as it seemed to be what she wished herself to be right about then. Her newest plate design, meanwhile, was boldly washed in olive green with an amorphous red dot in the center rimmed in black, and she seemed relatively at peace with it—"It shouldn't be perfect," she said, not entirely convincingly, then turned it over and painted a large red heart on the bottom. She is, by the way, the kind of girl who always signs things with big hearts. Salma Hayek, in the meantime, seemed to have painted everything else in the store.

Afterward, we walked back to her car—a little black Porsche given to her by Sony Pictures as a token for making *Charlie's Angels*—because she had dinner plans which she didn't want to tell me about. ("Where are you going?" I asked. "Italian," she said. "Of course," I said.) She then thought it would be fun to argue about this for a while—"You know what?" she said, ready to play. "You should just mind your own fucking business, basically. All these questions are starting to grate on my nerves!" Her eyes were dancing when she said all that, by the way. But I resisted the temptation and deposited her into the Porsche and watched her peel off, with those blond tresses blowing in the breeze. And that was the last time I ever saw that bitch.

Part Three:

IN **JEST**

Woody Allen * Seinfeld * Albert Brooks *
Eddie Murphy * The Simpsons

I entered Woody Allen's orbit two years after his tribulations with Mia Farrow exploded in public scandal. He had been quiet since that time, ever busily expanding his remarkable canon of work and making the best of a difficult visitation scenario with his son Satchel. This profile was, among other things, a portrait of a dedicated father deprived. In the years hence, he would marry Soon-Yi Previn and they would adopt two daughters, Bechet and Manzie Tio, whom he named after jazz musician heroes. But his son Satchel—whom Farrow renamed Seamus—was eventually worn down by his mother's enmity for his father and ceased to spend any time whatsoever with Allen. Which gives this piece an unfortunate added poignancy. Likewise, their adopted daughter Dylan—who was renamed Eliza—still does not see her father.

Woody Allen in Hell

Esquire, October 1994

He is not a man who looks good in hats. He wears them anyway, although never indoors, which would invite bad luck, of which he has had enough. In a hat, he looks like himself in a hat—only older and more foolish. Most days, his hat is the funniest thing about him.

There are three hats on the coatrack by the front door of his Fifth Avenue penthouse. He rarely leaves without taking one. Hats famously obscure him. Long ago, when he worried more, he also wore false mustaches. Mia Farrow once gave him a mustache comb as a love token. Life has changed, of course, but his hats have not. Every day, he walks the streets of New York beneath a low canvas brim of the sort favored by men who fish. "Oh, you see it as a fishing hat?" he says to me, surprised and bemused. "I don't know what you'd call it, but I started getting these hats years ago because they did the job."

He believes hats make him 50 percent less recognizable. "People say, 'Oh, *everybody* knows you from your hat,' but it isn't true," he says. So we test the hat principle on Lexington Avenue, strolling purposefully into pedestrian traffic. Passersby pass briskly, but many of them openly grin at the spectacle of the famous man in the foolish hat who looks downward as he walks. Only one person approaches, a large guy in shorts, fey and ebullient, who stammers, "*S-so,* you're the great Woody Allen?" There is a brief pause for consideration.

Then: "Well...I used to be."

From the canon (*Broadway Danny Rose*):

Tina Vitale: Guilty? What the hell is that? People see something better—they grab it. Who's got time for guilt?

Danny Rose: What are you talkin' about?...It's important to feel guilty. Otherwise you, you know, you're capable of do-ing *terrible things*!

Tina: I never feel guilty. I just think you gotta do what you gotta do. You know, life is short. You don't get any medals for being a Boy Scout.

His guiltiest pleasure is eating steak. "I don't have it more than once every six or eight weeks," he says, full of contrition. And, perhaps to temper enjoyment, he eats it only at Sparks Steak House, site of the infamous Paul Castellano mob hit. "But I sit in the nonshooting section," he says. Guilt also forces him to practice clarinet each day, even when he would rather do anything but. "If I don't, I'm riddled with guilt," he says. Otherwise, he is not a guilty man. He is encumbered by much, but not so much that he cannot function. His heart aches, but his conscience is clear—which is miraculous to many who damn him for indiscretions he cannot revoke. (He sees no crime in his misdemeanors.) He works prodigiously, as he always has. "Not as hard as it looks," he says evenly. He is less somber than he is serene, and I have often seen him smile and laugh, though such phenomena are rarely recorded. One day he tells me a joke to explain himself: "There's an old Jewish joke, you know, about the Jewish mother whose son goes into the Army. The mother is out there watching the troops train, and the son is marching badly, and finally she says, '*Look at 'em all—they're all out of step!*' And the truth of the matter, to me, is that the world is all out of step. From the start of this situation, I thought the whole thing was ridiculous, that they're all nuts. I haven't done anything. I mean, it's inevitable that the truth will come out."

And so I find Woody Allen trapped in Hell, where the food is fine, the scenery familiar, and the air-conditioning plentiful. In no small measure, he is relieved that death was not a prerequisite for taking up residence here, and that ordering new stationery was never necessary. "*Ohhh,* I *hate* change," he confesses, shuddering slightly. A creature of habit, he has not stopped rising with the sun and consuming his regular breakfast of prune juice—"I love it!"—and Cheerios topped with raisins and bananas. ("I'm such a dull eater," he laments.) Indeed, after two years in Hell—during which time he has made three films and written a fourth, plus finished a short play—he looks rested, fit, and pink. His red hair has not grayed, but merely fallen out, slowly and according to schedule and only at the crown. Soon, he will be fifty-nine, a juncture whereupon freckles and wattle have begun to coexist and little in life can surprise, even terrible things. What has happened has been terrible, of course, costing him a fortune in legal fees and, much worse, impugning his right to be a father, a role he finds vastly more rewarding than being America's preeminent comic genius.

Here, then, is a man flummoxed, persecuted for something he did as well as for something he did not do and now made to pay the price for both. Finally, he has created for himself the perfect existential nightmare, but unfortunately done it in real life, where people are less reasonable and frequently charge by the hour. "The real world," he has said, "is a place I've never felt comfortable in." Yet that is exactly where his troubles began.

Once, fifteen years ago, Woody Allen fell in love with the actress Mia Farrow, ex-wife of Frank Sinatra and Andre Previn. Celebrity love being what it is, much peculiarity ensued. For the next thirteen years—the span of their involvement—she would appear in his next thirteen films. During this period, she would continue adding to her brood of children, finally amassing thirteen, many of them adopted from the shores of blighted nations. Always the couple lived separately, directly across Central Park from each other, a detail that charmed those who idealized them. Thus, he was alone and she was swarmed and neither minded this terribly and eventually neither minded it at all.

They never married but, in 1987, produced a son, Satchel, and thereafter functioned together as parents, although never again as lovers. Woody focused further affection on two particular Farrow adoptees—a teenage boy with cerebral palsy, Moses, and a girl, Dylan, who arrived shortly after her birth in 1985. He legally became their father in December 1991, with Mia's blessing. By then, it had long been his ritual to awaken at five-thirty each morning in his own apartment and cross the park to be present when the children rose. Similarly, at night, he would rush over from film sets to tuck them in. Besides his own three children, however, he kept his interaction cursory with all else in the Farrow household, the chief exception being Mia, with whom he regularly worked and dined.

Another exception would emerge, though, and this was the second-eldest Farrow adoptee, Soon-Yi Previn. (Farrow had adopted Soon-Yi when she was seven; Allen came into the picture two years later.) By the end of 1991, at age twenty-one, Soon-Yi had entered into a secret entanglement with Allen. Thirteen days into 1992, Mia discovered nude Polaroids of Soon-Yi on Woody's mantelpiece, whereupon the portals of Hell opened. Wrath enveloped him. Then months of wrath followed, during which he persisted in his parental duties, under baleful watch, until the August day when Mia accused him of molesting Dylan in the attic of the Farrow Connecticut country house when no one was looking.

An avowed claustrophobic who assiduously avoided attics whenever possible ("In light-years I wouldn't go into an attic," he said), he saw transparent desperation in the charge and, in the tempestuous weeks that followed, publicly said as much. Also, he confirmed his love for Soon-Yi to the world: "The heart wants what it wants," he said, most memorably, in *Time*. Meanwhile, he claimed, Mia said, "You took my daughter, and now I'm taking yours." Woody openly questioned Mia's stability and sued for custody of his children but was denied, although the allegations of molestation were conclusively judged unfounded. Nevertheless, for two years now, he has been permitted to see Satchel only six hours per week, under court supervision, has not seen Moses and Dylan at all, and sees Mia only in court, where he cannot find empathy or justice. Furthermore, in an effort to reinvent life, Mia has decided that Dylan should henceforth be called Eliza and Satchel should be known as Seamus—although for several months he also answered to Harmon, until he tired of it. Woody Allen, meanwhile, answers to no one.

To keep busy, he has redecorated his apartment. He is, of course, an accomplished aesthete, and those who know him best have long marveled at his flair for interior design. He is a man who enjoys order and knows where everything goes. Over the last year, he has had walls knocked down, space opened up, solid antiques hauled in, and cozy textiles draped about. The feel of his penthouse duplex is one of country comfort—all oaken and overstuffed and incongruous with who dwells there. "This is as much of the country that I can tolerate," he confesses the day I first come calling. He is alone, as is customary, dressed in khakis and a white polo shirt. I bring him a basketball and he brings me a beverage, and we face each other on plump sofas below his mantel (*that* mantel) in the living room, where he most likes to plot his work and ponder life's vagaries. (He likes to write upstairs facedown on his bed, with pencil and legal pad.)

Photographs of his children line the walls, representing both loss and hope, and he invokes their names easily in conversation, although not their newly conceived names, which he finds absurd. "I thought this was the stupidest thing in the world," he says, groaning. "At least the names aren't legal, because if Mia tries to do it legally, I think I could fight it."

Hell has toughened him greatly. Nowadays, he lives to fight, having fought for two years and gotten used to the adrenaline. As a father denied, he has found unexpected bravado that is sometimes a thrill to behold. One year ago, for instance, on the day a Connecticut court dismissed child-abuse charges against him, he concluded a press conference with this message to Dylan: "I love you and I miss you, and don't worry, the dark forces will not prevail. Not second-rate police or publicity-hungry prosecutors, not judicial setbacks, not tabloid press nor those who perjure themselves nor all who rush to judgment, not the pious or hypocritic or the bigoted. I'm too tough for all of them put together, and I will never abandon you. . . ."

His pluck is eclipsed only by his incredulity, which I witness in repeated waves, punctuated with his slapping both palms to his cheeks, in the manner of Jack Benny, only more stricken. "From where I was sitting," he says, "it's all been absurd. You know, if for a moment you remove the element of the court's preventing me from seeing my children, the whole thing becomes almost completely comic. It was just so crazy. I mean, one Tuesday I say good-bye to Dylan, Satchel, and Moses. Dylan says to me, 'Daddy, don't forget, when you come back on Saturday bring this toy and this toy.' She had checked off things in a toy catalog, which I still have—it was a court exhibit. And I say, 'Okay, see you Saturday,' and I go. And that was the last I ever saw of her. I mean, I've always had a spectacular relationship with Dylan, as testified in court by her schoolteachers, her nanny, her doctor. There was never any strain between us after things ended with Mia, never anything but hugs, kisses, and affection."

To that end, if his love left room for misinterpretation, he cannot fathom where. Like a bloodhound possessed, he has occupied countless dark moments retracing his steps. "It wasn't even like I chucked her under the chin or tickled her anywhere," he says, emphatic. "You know, I played with her, people were there. Then I go home and get a call saying Mia has accused me of molesting her. And I think, *Well, this is laughable, this is a new low in tactics.* I figured three days later there'll be an apology or something. To me, it was hilarious, because within months a multimillion-dollar industry was built on it—I was on magazine covers all over the world; lawyers and detectives and doctors and experts were hired. I mean, you can't believe what happened. And the *most* hilarious part is that *nothing whatsoever ever happened at all*! A total zero, a total zero—you know, no event. But the thing was *enormous* all over the world."

Often he cites the conclusions of the Yale–New Haven Hospital Child Abuse Evaluation Clinic, an institution that has investigated over fifteen hundred such cases. According to Yale, Dylan's allegations, which had been videotaped by Mia, "were made up by an emotionally vulnerable child who was caught up in a disturbed family and who was responding to the stress in the family"; moreover, she was quite possibly "coached or influenced [to do so] by her mother." Nevertheless, his visitation privileges with her remain suspended indefinitely.

"The day that report came down," he says, "I should have been instantly allowed to see my daughter again. I felt we had an overwhelming case—not even a *close* case—but we were not able to dispel the image of Mia as this wonderful mother. You know, she is a good actress and a great-looking woman, but *not* a good mother. People just irresponsibly let her adopt children and no one says, 'Hey, can you really take care of so many children?' I mean, you can't. I've had to do and say a lot of things over the last couple of years that were very tactful, things that I don't necessarily believe, because my children are under her influence. It's a difficult situation to deal with, and you have to go very, very slowly. Just as it was frustrating when the hostages were held in Iran. You know, you *can't* rush in."

Lately, he has come to know much about space aliens. He can easily identify various intergalactic villains and understands the specific evil each can wreak. His son has taught him well. This is what they do when they are together, which is to say, they goof off magnificently. "When we're together he sees not what he hears at home—he sees that I'm *not* a monster," says Allen, who adds, laughing, "I know *all* about monsters."

Satchel Farrow's room in his father's home is called the Monster Room. I ask to see it and so Woody trots down a long corridor to light it properly. "Come right in," he says, opening the door a tad ominously. I am greeted by two eight-foot-tall grotesque replicas of Alien and Pumpkinhead in malevolent poses. A massive rubber spider (the size of a Buick, as the saying goes) sprawls across the bed. Shelves brim with *Predator* videos and plastic figures of unholy, gut-oozing demons, most of them assembled by father and son. *"Ohhhhh,"* says Allen woefully, "assembling things is the curse of my life. I'm too mentally lazy to follow instructions." (Friends love to recall the notorious incident of Woody and Satchel mixing cake batter and adding the frosting before baking.) We bend over toy bins, and he pulls out creature after creature: "This is the Queen Face Hugger, this is Deirdre, this is Carnage." He points to snapshots pinned to corkboard of himself with the blond, cherubic boy who delights in said horrors. "This is him," says Woody sweetly. "He's a cute kid. Fortunately, he takes after the Farrow family, 'cause they have the good genes."

What they do together they must do in weekly supervised six-hour increments—"a silly and niggling and destructively small amount of time for him," says Allen. To worsen matters, Mia has moved her flock to Connecticut fulltime, abdicating her Central Park West digs entirely, thus inflicting many commuting headaches. Since there is no leeway in time allotment (minutes of overtime are always subtracted from the next visit), Satchel cannot sleep in his Monster Room, nor can he bring home any of his treasures. (Also, he cannot see Soon-Yi, who remains estranged from her family.) "When he first used to come over, he would say, 'My mommy stuck my phone number in my pocket and said that I don't have to stay here if I don't want to,'" recalls Woody. "And I used to say, 'No, that's not true, you *do* have to.' Or, when I'd tell him I loved him, he'd say, 'I like you, but I'm not supposed to love you.' *Now* it's a pleasure— you know, all we do is have fun. And the reason we have supervision is the judge was afraid that *I* would poison him against the family! I only say to him the most supportive things about Mia. *He's* the one who gets poisoned."

From the canon (*Shadows and Fog*):

Dorry the prostitute: I know what's on your mind. Let's go up to the bedroom.

Max Kleinman: [*indignant*] I've never paid for sex.

Dorry: You just think you haven't.

A man must take some responsibility for his lot if he hopes to earn respect, and this is where Woody Allen waffles perilously. He is most beloved as a victim of fate, of others, of life. He looks good losing. Helplessness becomes him. It is a difficult persona to discard, especially since it made him rich and famous and powerful, but he has made attempts. From court transcripts: "I'm not saying my selection of Soon-Yi was a brilliant selection, a wise selection. . . . I fell in love with her, perhaps this was wrong. . . . And so this relationship began. I began it. I mean, it's my responsibility. . . . I did make a mistake, an error in judgment here. I do think that. But I think the response to it has been absolutely degrading and criminal."

Then, as always, comes the rationale, also from transcripts: "I was never for one scintilla of a second a father to her in any remote way. She was an older person—much, much older than the kids. . . . I did not perceive of this as a sister relationship between the kids. . . . I'm not saying that I'm right, [but] I did not perceive this as a traditional family." Moreover, in our conversations, he often reminds me that in thirteen years he never once slept in the Farrow apartment, that he and Mia always kept separate bedrooms in Connecticut or when traveling, that they were friendly mutual parents of three children and nothing more. "People have no idea," he says, exasperated. "They think that I was married to Mia and Soon-Yi was my daughter and I'm sleeping with my daughter. It's just incredible."

There is a refrain in his very funny new film, *Bullets Over Broadway,* that goes as follows: "An artist creates his own moral universe. You gotta do what you gotta do." Elsewhere in the film is the line "The heart obeys its own rules." Also, there is much gunplay. (We see an actress shot for being bad.) He has long protested the notion that autobiography bleeds into his work. Still, he tells me, "It's hard for me ever to experience anything that I don't think of as grist for the writer's mill."

Love is never rational in his films, nor has it been in his life, now especially. Now he loves Soon-Yi Previn and is seen with her at Knicks games, in restaurants, on walks. She does not live with him; as ever, he must live only with himself (except when Diane Keaton comes to town and needs a place to stay). Soon-Yi just turned twenty-four and is a senior at Drew University in New Jersey, studying art and social work and English; she has her own Upper East Side apartment in addition to a campus dorm room. "She locks herself away and can study endlessly, weekends at a time," says Woody proudly. "Her mother tried to say that she was retarded, which is absurd. And I said to people, 'Use your head—am I gonna go out with a girl who's mentally deficient?' I mean, she's made the dean's list every year. She's a wonderful person—you know, completely open and honest and direct and unspoiled. For the first seven years of her life, she was eating out of garbage pails, living in the streets. Then she was adopted into a very unhappy situation for her. But she's great—up and funny and has a wonderful sense of humor."

One day I ask him how he knows when he's in love. "The same way you've always known," he carefully replies. "It's who you are. I feel the exact same way now as I felt years ago, you know. You get a positive feeling about someone. I mean, I was never one of those guys that would go out on a date and then dance home in the rain with an umbrella. That's funny—leap in the air and click your heels together to one side. No, that's only in the movies. People think from *my* movies that I'm cynical about love, but I'm not. I would say that I'm realistic."

If it is Monday, he will make jazz. For more than two decades, he has done so, always on Monday night, at Michael's Pub on East Fifty-fifth Street, and it is such a well-known fact that it is widely forgotten. (Tourists remember best.) Amid scandal, he played; in its aftermath, he plays. He never speaks onstage, only blows clarinet, which he does very well, but not as well as he would like. "I'm truly a terrible musician," he says on the Monday I come to watch his band. His father, Martin Konigsberg, who is ninety-four, silver-haired, and dapper, is also present. Soon-Yi, he reports, is out eating ribs with friends. "She called me today and asked, 'How long has it been since I had meat?'" he says, smiling. He has slipped into the room alone and sat down at our table, where he regards his father for a moment. "My father forgot his lower teeth tonight," he notes happily. "He likes to come every week. My mother comes occasionally—not a lot. But he just loves to party. He's a little crazy and he can't hear, so don't worry. But with a full set of teeth, he looks great."

On clarinet, Woody Allen is a merry fellow. He bops and he swoons, neither of which he does a lot of offstage. Also, he wails plaintively, especially on his solo during "What a Friend I Have in Jesus." ("I could sit and play blues all day and be very, very happy," he says.) After the final peppy number, he solemnly packs up his horn and retreats, although not before a nervous man asks, "Woody, would you play at my funeral?" For an instant, he appears to consider the request, until hearing it would mean a trip to New Jersey. Outside, his Mercedes and driver await to dispatch him and his father to their respective doorsteps. I ride along and watch him peruse mash notes from audience members. "Actually," he says, "this is not a mash note. I don't get propositions so much as I get very, very antiseptic encouragement." We pull up at the Park Avenue portico of his parents' building, and Woody addresses his father loudly, so as to be audible. *"Okay—can you get upstairs? Do you know what apartment you live in?"* Whereupon a doorman comes out to retrieve Mr. Konigsberg, who tells his son, "Stay well! See you again next Monday!" He then totters off jauntily. Woody watches him go and marvels at his verve. "He's very fastidious, you know. He gets up and changes his clothes several times a day."

For perspective, I probe his state of consciousness and, over days, uncover these findings: He wonders why O. J. Simpson did not immediately proclaim his innocence. He worries that Frank Sinatra might have Alzheimer's. He has never met any of the New York Knicks, all of whom he worships. "It's nothing that I particularly want to do," he says. Suddenly, and ironically, he finds that he has more female friends than male friends. He loves the illusions of David Copperfield and Siegfried & Roy: "Their stuff is great!" He has never seen an Arnold Schwarzenegger film. Nor has he seen any of his own films after releasing them. He subscribes to *National Geographic*. He approved of Michael Jordan's retirement: "I thought it had a beautiful cleanliness to it, you know?" he says. "I'm hoping that he doesn't come back." Madonna impresses him: "She's a funny personality, in the way Mae West was. There's wit in her approach." He has never heard her music. He channel-surfs, mostly for sports, and is stunned by public-access sex programming: "Unbelievable! If you had told me when I was growing up that my mother and father could sit at home and watch two guys undressed, tied up, and chained to a wall, doing things to each other, *on regular television. . . .*" He is astonished that Fox is planning a miniseries about the life of Mia Farrow. "It's funny that someone will be playing me," he says. "I must call Tom Cruise and tell him that there's a job opening." He knows about *Seinfeld* and the late-night talk-show wars from what he's read. He missed Johnny Carson's retirement. "I go to sleep early," he says. Although he often substituted for Carson when *The Tonight Show* originated in New York, he says, "It never even occurred to me to host a talk show." Moreover, he found hosting pleasurable: "For me, it was a breeze and I got very, very good press on it." He has seen no more than an occasional few minutes of David Letterman. "As I'm brushing my teeth, I'll turn on the television set, and if Channel Two happens to be on, I certainly don't turn him off or anything," he says. "From what I've seen, he seems likable, amusing." He thinks Alvy Singer, were he not fictional, would today be a Letterman producer and also Annie Hall's husband. When he looks into a mirror he sees his parents, especially at night. He falls asleep less than one minute after turning out the light. "Once I get into my spot, *whack,* I'm out," he says. His only recurring dream: "There's a door and there's something unpleasant behind it and I don't want it to come in."

From the canon (*Annie Hall*):

Alvy Singer: I've a very pessimistic view of life. You should know this about me. . . . I feel that life is divided up into the horrible and the miserable. . . . The horrible would be like, uh, I don't know, terminal cases, you know? And blind people, crippled. . . . And the miserable is everyone else. That's all. So, when you go through life you should be grateful that you're miserable.

"I'm covering my eyes," he says, covering his eyes. "I don't want to get hit in the eye." Wandering his neighborhood, we have stumbled upon sidewalk construction, and workmen with jackhammers now pummel the pavement before us. Woody uses his hat to shield himself from flying gravel. Unafraid to be afraid, he scrambles to safety, and I cannot help but admire his instinct for self-preservation. Never is he not cautious, especially when faced with threat of bodily harm. Still, he would not trade the roar of jackhammers for anything. "I love it," he confesses with glee. "I miss that sound if I don't hear it. I used to try to go to sleep in Connecticut and I'd hear silence, an occasional cricket, and a bullfrog. It was awful. I like jackhammers and sirens." Even on this hot and foul Manhattan morning, he can find romance in his city—probably because he must soon leave it. Within days, he departs on a European holiday, and before that, he will spend the next two afternoons driving to Connecticut to visit his son, three hours at a time. "I wind up driving four hours to see him for three," he says unhappily. And because he is unwelcome on Farrow property, he must scour suburbia, looking for stimulation where he is certain none exists. This afternoon, he and Satchel will see *The Mask*, which is playing outside Danbury. ("It was a godsend," he tells me later.) Tomorrow, they will end up at the mall, buying toys, eating ice cream, killing time. In this fashion, he continues to work off his sentence.

There is, I have sensed, a newfound stoicism about him, and I tell him so. He brightens. "People think that I'm a hypochondriac, but I'm not," he says. "They fail to see the difference between a hypochondriac and an alarmist. I'm an alarmist. I never imagine I have an ailment when I don't have one. On the other hand, if I've got a hangnail, I think it's a brain tumor. I always cut to the worst possible conclusion. Unfortunately, the level of my panic is funny only in retrospect." Nevertheless, by preparing himself for doom, he is somehow able to stave it off. "For instance," he says, "I'm about to go to Europe, so I'm having my usual voyaging anxiety. I can have a nice time only if I pack all my various medicines. I never need them. I just pack them. And every day of my life, I carry around this pillbox." From his pants pocket, he pulls out a tiny silver container and opens it for inspection. "See, there's two Lomotil, a Compazine, a Librium, two Excedrin, a Donnazyme, and a Zantac. That's all I need! But I never take 'em. I'm not a pill person. I just like to know it's there, you know?"

From the canon (*Love and Death*):

Boris Grushenko: How I got into this predicament, I'll never know. Absolutely incredible. To be executed for a crime I never committed. Of course, isn't all mankind in the same boat? Isn't mankind ultimately executed for a crime it never committed? The difference is that all men go eventually...but I go six tomorrow morning.

Once he has left the country, I feel it is safe to bring up death. It is a subject that vexes him like no other, with the possible exception of court costs. "I don't want to achieve immortality through my work," he once said. "I want to achieve it through not dying." Still, each day he grows closer to the inevitable, and a man can only muster so much denial. So I phone him in London, where he is promoting *Bullets Over Broadway* and hiding from Fleet Street paparazzi. "We hit a slightly bad break at our hotel yesterday," he informs me. "Arnold Schwarzenegger and Jamie Lee Curtis checked in because their movie opened last night, so there are swarms of photographers." Undaunted, however, and equipped with his hat, he has made his rounds and managed to find a Forbidden Planet store, where he acquired a trove of new alien model kits for Satchel. "So now," he says, "I'm traveling through Europe with these big boxes of Face Huggers, Queen Face Huggers, and Chest Busters."

Risking morbidity, I put it to him. I ask him how he imagines he will die. He does not shirk the question. "I envision myself dying in my bed," he says slowly, "when I'm very old...looking out my windows at New York...surrounded by loved ones, by my children...and just quietly expiring...*or else,* one day, again at a *very, very* advanced age...you know, like my father's age...just slipping away in my sleep. I think sleep would be best. That's the nicest thing you could wish a person. You know, it's been said that I'm cynical about life. But if you think about it, what else can you be in a world where the kindest thing that you can say to someone is 'I hope you die in your sleep'?" Whereupon he laughs a little, which indicates progress.

Throughout the 1990s, *Seinfeld* reinvented the art of the urban television sitcom. Like the series itself, this piece was conceived as a celebration of Nothing, explored in quirky little beats. The surreal final section of the story—which deposited all four stars at a table with me outside a New York restaurant—is almost like a lost episode of the show, created on the spot by the participants. (Jerry Seinfeld himself thought it would make for an amusing public spectacle.) Somehow, at that dinner, I briefly became a member of the cast. Passersby who got a glimpse of this fiction-come-to-life have, no doubt, never forgotten the utter weirdness of it.

Nothing Doing:
In Search of Insignificance With
Jerry & George & Kramer & Elaine

It was a nothing that he knew too well. It was all a nothing. . . .
Some lived in it and never felt it but he knew it all was *nada y
pues nada y nada y pues nada.*
—Ernest Hemingway, "A Clean, Well-Lighted Place"

Rolling Stone, July 1993

Now dawns the age of Nothing. Once, not so long ago, people thought little of Nothing. They pretended Nothing ever happened when, in fact, Nothing was happening all around them. Back then, Meaning was everything, and people sought only larger truth. Those who dared to ponder the Meaning of Nothing could not expect to be taken seriously. Fortunately, one such man did not let this stop him. He spoke out fervently about not much of anything, about the implications of socks and cereal and pens and pockets—about Nothing, really—and always he was laughed at. Because this man was a comedian, he took the derision well. Eventually, he was given a television show on which to not do a lot. Like him, the show was called *Seinfeld,* and it dwelled on matters mundane. Every week, Nothing gloriously transpired as characters waited in lines, looked for parking space, smelled things, or tried not to masturbate. "Even Nothing is *something,*" Seinfeld himself would say during an episode in the show's fourth season. Soon thereafter, people began to invest new pride in how little they did. All of a sudden, you realized you couldn't even really *know* another person until you saw him or her do Nothing.

But what about these *Seinfeld* people? Yes, they do Nothing on television, do it in a way all others envy. But what about in life? To sate our curiosity, the four principal cast mates agreed to let themselves be watched not doing very much. By name and role, they are Michael Richards, as the peculiar neighbor Kramer; Jason Alexander, as the desperate friend George Costanza; Julia Louis-Dreyfus, as the platonic heroine Elaine Benes; and Jerry Seinfeld, as himself, more or less, the calm center around which all manner of Nothing revolves. What follows are details of how each of them rose to a pronounced lack of occasion.

IN THE NEIGHBORHOOD OF KRAMER

He greets the day fuzzily.

He leaves his bed to open the door, which he does slowly, unlike Kramer, who prefers his doors flung with velocity. Kramer makes entrances, explosive and erratic, for which no door is safe. There is dire purpose in his every intrusion. "You got any meat?" he said, for instance, upon his first *Seinfeld* entrance four years ago. Michael Richards, who is Kramer, has arisen this morning to open his door for movers. His daughter is moving out and into her first apartment, and men have come to take away her things. "I want to watch them," he says, "because this is comedy, you know." Richards watches for comedy everywhere, and always sees it. "Their van is parked on a bit of a hill," he says, "so it could easily roll backward, up the curb, over a flower bed and into a tree, and that could be kind of funny." This does not happen, but he sees it anyway. "I think those guys just fell over a hedge," he says next, peering out a window. They didn't. But that is how he sees.

The hair also rises.

"This is not the way I *amuse* myself," he recently said on *The Tonight Show*. "This is the way I *am*." Because he has become a national oddity, coffee mugs bear his likeness, with the legend I'M HUMAN IN MY WAY. Worshipful men gather about Richards in public places and chant: "*Kra-mer! Kra-mer!*" "If I could arm these people," he says, "I could take a country over." Women yearn to touch his hair, which stands tall, as does he, at six foot two, not counting hair. "It's electric," he says, meaning the hair. "It just goes *whoooom*! It's interesting. It just took its own shape. It's fascinating." For summer, the hair has been cut, although fresh out of bed, it looks spry as ever. "It *is* like a back-to-nature look, isn't it?"

• • •

We are locked out of the house.

"For a single man, it's fine," he says of his house, a large California ranch-style structure in Studio City, near where *Seinfeld* is filmed. At forty-three, Richards is genially divorced from his wife of eighteen years, who is, conveniently, a family therapist. "This place is basically just for me," he says, showing me ongoing renovations. "It's tranquil." But suddenly a gust of wind blows a door shut, and we are trapped in an unfinished addition. "Well, there we go again—to Kramerland," he says with a sigh, as though it were a familiar journey, and he begins knocking loudly to regain entry. He pounds for minutes and says nothing until a mover readmits us.

Kramer has a first name.

There is, in fact, an actual Kramer. That Kramer lived in New York, across the hall from Larry David, the writer who created *Seinfeld* with his friend Seinfeld. "He was a jack-of-all-trades—and he still is," says Richards of his prototype. "He's just a hustler." Kramer, it's said, was the sort of man who paid $400 rent on an $1,800 apartment. He lived by mysterious means. He had free access to Larry David's place. His first name, like his fictional counterpart's, is a secret. "We just never talk about it," says Larry Charles, *Seinfeld*'s supervising producer, who gave TV Kramer his unspoken name. "It's a funny name, too," teases Larry David. [Years hence, we learned it was Cosmo.] If Richards knows it, he doesn't say.

He steals fruit to throw at a guy.

"Hey, let's pick a tangerine," he says, plucking two of them from a tree belonging to his neighbor. "They're Dr. Joseph's," he says, tossing one over generously. "Have a Dr. Joseph tangerine." He spots a guy walking past his house. "See if you can hit that man over there with your tangerine," he says to me. "Come on, do it. I'll give you a hundred dollars. I swear. He's getting away." How to react if there is contact: "You just say that you didn't mean it," Richards says. "Don't even acknowledge it. Just hit him!" Meanwhile, he has already eaten his own purloined tangerine, which he found pleasantly sweet.

• • •

Kramer smells like eternity.

Calvin Klein said of Kramer, "His buttocks are sublime." This happened in the episode where Kramer creates a fragrance called The Beach, which recalls beach smell; Calvin Klein (played by an actor) appropriates the concept for a new scent called Ocean and repays Kramer by photographing him for an underwear ad. After the show aired, the real Klein shipped Richards vast supplies of Eternity for Men, which he has ever since splashed on before tapings—to further demark Kramer's presence. Says Richards, "I work very hard to make this character three-dimensional." Charles concurs: "He's not a simplistic character at all. Kramer is full of facets and contradictions; he's real and unreal; he's like an adult and a child; he's like neutered yet very sexual; he's very light yet very dark; he can be idiotic and yet very wise."

He teases a very old man wearing socks.

Across the street from Richards, there lives a shoeless octogenarian; he walks the streets in socks. We see him now padding along the pavement. "Hey, Captain!" Richards hollers after him. "He was a great psychiatrist and studied with Freud," he tells me. "He's crazy but brilliant." "My brother!" says the Captain, greeting Richards, kindred spirits enjoined. "I'm going to be eighty-five soon," says the Captain. "You look eighty-four and a half," says Richards, whom the Captain seems to be studying keenly, as though eyeing a lost specimen.

His body emits noise.

"You can hear my spine cracking," says Richards, settling into his Lexus, and he is right. Vertebrae pop audibly. "It twists," he says, "from yoga." He is a spiritual fellow, happiest on a mountainside, pondering Eastern religion and Greek myths. He and Kramer wear a crystal around their neck. Though he looks otherwise, he was born Californian, which might explain the above. "I am an eccentricity specialist," he will say of his work, and what he means is that he has always been physical and unusual. "He can break one second down into a hundred distinct parts," says Seinfeld, who enjoys watching him do anything. (Richards would rather do funny than say funny.) On *Fridays,* the bad early-eighties comedy show for which he was best known, Richards did things like burn plastic soldiers and wear dresses. As a boy, he feigned seizures in supermarkets. His heroes are Chaplin and Tati, and he aspires to make comic short-subject films in which he can frequently fall down: "I would love to do things in the area of Sellers." On-screen this summer, he will be the first human encountered by the Coneheads.

He works on his exits.

"We don't know too much about Kramer's personal life," he says, predicting the disclosure of a former Mrs. Kramer and offspring. Mostly, however, he wishes Kramer would leave more. "Exits are showstoppers," he says, knowing he has made the most of entrances. Later, at a nearby restaurant, he demonstrates various momentous departures, while customers gawk. Repeatedly, he crashes softly into a wall. Then he sits down and reaches for bread. "Eat the bread," he says. "Yeast is good for your hair."

GEORGE NEEDS BETTER EQUIPMENT

Woody Allen ate no yeast here.

This is where Alvy Singer lost Annie Hall forever, after ordering the plate of mashed yeast that never came. Moments later, he was arrested in the parking lot. This is the Source health-food restaurant, on Sunset Boulevard, where I find Jason Alexander, who is George Costanza, who is not unlike Woody Allen in character. George is beset and bespectacled. Alexander is neither, although he does squint. He is a younger man than George, who he figures is "pushing forty." Alexander is thirty-three, pink, and elfin, given at any time to sudden bursts of singing and dancing. He is a Tony Award–winning Broadway refugee now gone west, where both money and diets are more plentiful. "My first day of a new diet!" he has just announced, having explored his share. "This is the Maximum Metabolism diet." He extracts several tablets from a pillbox and swallows one at a time, saying, "This one kills your hunger pang, this one kills your sugar pang. . . ." Then he orders eggless tuna salad.

The difference between him and Fabio:

Fabio is sitting on the other side of the restaurant, and this is who he is: Fabio is the Perfect Man, impossibly attractive, whose long-haired, bare-chested likeness has appeared on the cover of hundreds of romance paperbacks. No woman can resist him. "He's a *very* handsome man," says

Alexander, appreciatively, blowing his nose. "Actually, he's a very good friend of mine, Fabio. I'm the one who said to him: 'Fabio, grow the hair! Let the hair grow.'" Regarding hair, Alexander himself has been balding since age seventeen. "I never had a good year," he moans. "I had nine years of orthodontia, and the day the braces came off, the hair started falling out. My father is eighty-three years old and has a full head of black hair!" He grows bitter and contemplative. "Maybe he's not my father."

Why George is also a sex symbol:

When George is seen with a woman, she is usually a remarkable woman. "George gets great women," says Alexander, eating tuna. "You know why that is? For the first three seasons, Jerry was very uncomfortable about being an actor. He didn't want to do anything he didn't feel comfortable doing, like getting angry or having a romantic scene. At that point, they didn't feel Kramer could be a secret weapon to women. So the only guy left was me. I got thrown all of Jerry's refuse." Of his own off-camera allure, he says, "I do well with the moms of babes." Long ago, however, he cohabited in New York with spitfire actress Holly Hunter, if only platonically. "I had a thing for Holly," he now confesses, "but nothing ever happened. I actually first dated my wife thinking it would make Holly jealous and kick-start something between us. It just backfired." Eleven years ago he married Daena Title, a writer, whom he instantly wanted upon that first date. Last year, they produced an in vitro son. "He was a test-tube baby," says Alexander, beaming. "He was spawned in a dish."

Somebody else plays George in real life.

On TV, George is the best friend of Jerry Seinfeld, who is Larry David's best friend off TV. David and Seinfeld modeled the series on their rapport: "We wanted the show to be about those idiotic conversations we have all the time," says David, meaning about Nothing. Thus, when we see George and Jerry discuss how the words *seltzer* and *salsa* might confuse a Mexican waiter, we see David and Seinfeld. "George is Larry David's id," says Larry Charles. "He embodies all the dark impulses that Larry David has occasionally acted upon." Alexander frets: "There are times when George walks the line of really being kind of hateful, but ultimately his heart's in the right place." Indeed, Seinfeld has said that a

George spin-off could only be titled *This Poor Man*. Even so, "George is not a loser," says Charles. "People inaccurately pigeonhole him. He's *struggling*, but he's definitely not a loser."

Nobody plays Jason Alexander in real life.

"Nobody drives like me," George once said proudly. "I'm doing things in this car you have no idea what's going on!" Inside Alexander's Toyota, we nudge perilously into traffic, sustaining honks from many sides. "I still think I'm on the motorcycle, that's my problem," he says nervously. Once he rode, but now he drives. The name on his California driver's license is Jay Greenspan, his name since birth, in New Jersey; Alexander is his father's first name. In Los Angeles, Jay Greenspan drives what he fondly calls "a 1988 piece of shit." "Jerry, God bless him, with his Porsches," he says, chuckling. "I would never spend money on an automobile! It means *nothing* to me."

He was caught, not alone, in a car.

An erotic man, Alexander is becoming known for irrepressible carnality. In the film *Pretty Woman* we saw him sexually molest Julia Roberts. "I was the Scumball of the United States," he says sheepishly. "I struck Julia Roberts." Later, as George, he found himself aroused during a massage given by a man. "It *moved*!" he said, panicked. Then, off-camera in the infamous episode "The Contest," George was caught by his mother masturbating to a copy of *Glamour*. Now Alexander confesses: "I did actually get caught. Not in a masturbation thing, but when I was eighteen, my girlfriend and I were pretty hot and heavy in the backseat of a car when a cop threw a light in there. That was no fun. I lost a little more hair that evening."

He buys $1,400 worth of telephones.

"I'm not a shopper," he says, but we are, nevertheless, shopping for multiline phones and fax machines at the Good Guys. "George!" says the salesman, by way of greeting. "Are your prices the best?" says Alexander, not waiting for a reply. Much merchandise is hastily acquired, as Alexander dances around the store, a spendthrift sprite. He noodles on keyboards, playing the show tunes he so loves. But something is obviously weighing on his mind, and it turns out to be Fabio. "I keep thinking about him," he says, agitated. "What bothers me about guys like that is they can walk into any clothing store, pick up a shirt, put it on, walk out—and it looks great!" He squints hard, stewing. *"That's never happened in my life!"*

LOOKING FOR STUFF WITH ELAINE

She breaks her fast with sour cherries.

Back in Manhattan, her cradle of origin, here is Julia Louis-Dreyfus, hyphenated, caffeinated, eating hot prunes she does not want. "Where are the sour cherries?" she asks, perplexed, in the dining room of the St. Regis Hotel, where she is a registered guest. "I don't like this one bit." She is a child of Park Avenue, now thirty-two, grown into a lustrous comedienne, sly and comely and regular. As Elaine Benes, former girlfriend of TV Jerry, she is a woman men want and women want to be. Meanwhile Louis-Dreyfus—*Louie*-Dreyfus for those who pronounce—wants this: cherries, not prunes, for breakfast. Even so, she eats three prunes until a waiter remembers that it is someone else who ordered them. "I just got three free prunes!" she says, exultant, once the error is corrected. Her sour cherries arrive, beneath a creamy glop of something beige. "What *is* that shit?" she says, mystified anew. "What the hell is going on here?"

Her husband speaks of her genitalia.

Previously on *Seinfeld,* Jerry said of Elaine: "She enjoys teasing animals; Ban-Lon; and seeing people running for their lives. She loves throwing garbage out the window, *yet* she's extremely dainty." Also, Elaine knows baseball, drinks scotch, and masturbates. Among men, she is treated like a man, albeit one with insight. "In return," Louis-Dreyfus has said, "I treat each of them as one of the girls." As one of the boys, Elaine is unprecedented on television. "It's not a gender-specific kind of comedy," she says, amid cherries. Here her husband, Brad Hall, who is breakfasting along, says this: "It doesn't matter whether or not Elaine's a woman—she has the same lusts and feelings that all guys have. The only woman-specific thing about her is her genitalia." This he says with great authority.

Elaine's sex life with Jerry, reconstructed:
Unlike Elaine, Louis-Dreyfus does not run with ex-boyfriends. (Lore

has it that Elaine is loosely based on Seinfeld's stand-up cohort Carol Leifer, whom he dated briefly in the late seventies.) As it is, the ranks of her old boyfriends are thin—the price paid for meeting her mate at age nineteen. She and Hall were yearlings together at Chicago's improvisational Practical Theater Company, after which they did hard time on *Saturday Night Live* during the laughless early eighties. Less is known about Elaine's beginnings with Jerry, or, for that matter, how it all went wrong. "There was a little problem with the physical chemistry," Jerry said in the second episode. Larry Charles disagrees: "They had a very good sexual history," he says, sounding less than certain. Recently TV Jerry recalled: "She likes talking during sex. . . . Just chitchat, movies, current events, regular stuff." On a whim, they had sex at the end of the show's second season, and never spoke of it again. "Evidently, it was a great reunion," says Louis-Dreyfus tentatively. "My theory is that Jerry and Elaine will get married one day, but she'll be forty-eight and he'll be fiftysomething. Then they'll get divorced six months later."

Roseanne called her a bitch on *Letterman.*

As widely reported last March, Louis-Dreyfus was instructed to park her car, for one day, where Tom Arnold usually parks his car, at the Studio City lot that is home to both parties. Thus inconvenienced, Arnold left her an obscene note; she confronted him; other notes followed (even after she parked elsewhere), plus a Polaroid of some unidentified buttocks and the word *cunt* soaped on her windshield. Roseanne Arnold, who is said to have done some of the soaping, later issued halfhearted apologies, then accused the *Seinfeld* gang of self-importance. "They think they're doing Samuel Beckett instead of a sitcom," she said. "I am willing to make a bet that she has never read anything Beckett ever wrote," says Jason Alexander, who would like to say more but won't because of a *Seinfeld* gag order on matters Arnold. Declares Michael Richards, "Julia is obviously being fucked with, and I want to expose the truth!" But he can't. (Otherwise eschewing comment, Louis-Dreyfus urges that the caption beneath the group cover photo read DON'T PARK IN OUR FUCKIN' SPACE! "That," she says, "would be the coolest.")

These buses are making her sleepy.

"I love the sound of a bus," she says wistfully. "I can't tell you how this takes me back!" Out on Fifth Avenue, we listen to buses go by but board none. Reared uptown (her father is a French-born capitalist and lawyer), she spent years sleeping to the low rumble of traffic. Now, away from the relative soundlessness of Los Angeles (where the Halls dwell with their baby son, Henry), she is reliving the din of her youth. "Oh, I'm so happy right now!" she says. But this could well be because we are walking toward Bergdorf Goodman, where she needs stuff. "Follow me," she says.

Her head is very big.

"It's nobody's business where I buy my shoes!" Elaine once ranted, shielding her Botticelli shoes from the clutches of envious women. Still, there is much to learn from a woman in a fine store. That she hates herself in gray, for instance: "Gray looks like shit on me," she says. "I'm a dog in gray." That she is easily lost: "How do we get off this floor?" That hats make her dizzy: "I can't wear one longer than an hour without my head spinning." That her head is larger than those of her coworkers: "The big head? It's gigantic! We measured the widths of our faces in rehearsal one day, and I came out ahead of the entire cast. I'm the shortest person with the widest face."

She thinks Elaine needs new friends.

"Definitely," she says, knowing that the truth is brutal. "The reality is that these four characters are a pathetic group, and they should disassemble promptly. I mean, if you stand back from it and look at what happens every week, they do *terrible* things to one another. And yet they continue to hang out. It's sociopathic. It's nuts! This is a sick group of people."

JERRY GETS A LIGHTBULB

The master is in his domain.

He is home, encased within his Fortress of Solitude, fifteen floors above Central Park West—the apartment where Nothing happens best. He has been called the Father of Nothing, but he is neither a father nor a husband. He is a hero bachelor, desired by thousands of women, entrapped by none. "You know what your problem is?" Elaine once said to him, or to the character with whom he shares a name. "Your standards are too *high*." Him [*defensive*]: "I went out with *you*!" Her: "That's because my standards are too low." (In what passes for real life, he insists,

"I disqualify no one.") At present, Jerry Seinfeld is thirty-nine, the eternal age of Jack Benny, whose memory he invokes by quietly filling the core of his own show. "He draws attention to himself without having to try," says Larry Charles. "He almost becomes the center by doing nothing." Which is what I have just found him doing—staring out of his corner windows at the lush acreage below. "It's great fun watching the seasons change from up here," he says, watching spring lengthen and doing it peerlessly.

He announces future cereal plans.

"I'm going to have cereal in about ten minutes," he says, checking his watch. Seinfeld is a man of organization, not fussy so much as disciplined. For instance, if there is to be midafternoon cereal, it will occur in midafternoon or not at all. "My hobby," he says, "is identifying little behavior difficulties and eliminating them. I'm constantly working on better breakfast systems and getting-dressed systems. Lately, I'm experimenting with putting my socks on while standing up. I have a large walk-in closet in my L.A. house, and there's no chair in there. To put the socks on sitting down, I would have to walk a long way out of the closet. So I'm experimenting with a new system." Because of such proficiency at problem solving, he has never seen fit to seek therapy. "There's nothing in life that I haven't thought about," he says, awash in self-knowledge.

There is no double crunch, but there is hope.

Both Jerrys were raised on Long Island and live in the same Manhattan neighborhood: the Upper West Side. His Real apartment, however, is nothing like his TV apartment, which is falsely rumored to resemble his previous Real apartment, two blocks away. "If I'd had an apartment that good, I'd probably still be there," he says. Anyway, Real Jerry dwells starkly, as per Zen, yet expensively, because he can. His is a swell black and gray place ("*alien tech,* I call it") whose door stays locked, thus foiling Krameresque pop-ins from fellow tenant Pierre Salinger. Also unlike TV: Seventeen cereal boxes do not line his shelves; there are just three (Cheerios, shredded wheat, Health Valley granola), kept cold, inside a near-barren refrigerator. "But I just got back to town," he says. "I haven't quite gotten up to speed." Cereal, of course, fuels his life force; he must have it and have it often. Ten minutes having elapsed, he says, "I'm going to make cereal now." How he does it: His bowl is enormous ("That's my

Jethro bowl!"). He mixes in up to four brands per serving; today, he lays a granola base, tops it with Cheerios, then adds pure maple syrup and skim milk. After consuming all cereal, he gulps down the liquid residue. "That," he states, "is the nectar of the gods." He is now ready to fight crime.

Why women want him:

He is elusive. He is self-sufficient. He parallel-parks flawlessly: "Girls love to see me pull in," he says. Mostly, he dallies with models, because they are safe. Still, his restraint is exemplary: In "The Contest," he tied with George in abstaining the longest from masturbating; in life, he discovered masturbation at college. "His image is that of the perfect catch," says Charles. "He's a nice Jewish boy, very content with what he has. He's not in a rush or desperate; he's like this placid lake whose surface is never broken. Onstage or off, he's never in character, or *on*—he's just *him*." Seinfeld attributes this to his discomfort with acting: "Actors love to extend themselves. As a comedian, I don't want to do anything. I'm like 'Can I just wear my own pants in this scene?'" Thus far, his greatest acting feat on the show was portraying his own penis in a chess game. "My motivation there was to *get more blood*," he says, recalling the technique. *"Must get more blood."*

He gets great quantities of Mulva.

Seinfeld fans are a scholarly lot, known to memorize dialogue and repeat it to each other. When out doing stand-up, Seinfeld constantly hears these catch phrases hurled forth. "I'm getting a lot of Mulva," he says, which refers to a character who hinted that her name rhymed with something anatomical. *"Are those the panties your mother laid out for you?"* TV Jerry once said to a woman, instantly repulsing her. "Is that the suit your mother laid out for you?" audiences now yell at him.

His life as the King of New York:

"I'm the King of New York," he says, out walking the streets, receiving his public with warmth and courtesy. Wholly accessible, he faults no one for thinking they know him personally: "They're in their homes seeing me play myself in *my* house." Around New York, Seinfeld sightings are among the most common of celebrity sightings, since he is not a reclu-

sive king. "The only time I'm truly content is when I'm here," he says
happily. True to legend, his secret powers allow him to find logic
shrouded in the chaos, order in the disorder. "He's almost like a child
who sees things with a whole different perception than you," says
Charles. "He sees universal wisdom in Bic pens." What he sees now are
lightbulbs, the objective of our mission. ("Think of it as a metaphor—
comedian looking for an idea," he suggests.) On Amsterdam Avenue, we
find a hardware store; miraculously, steps from the entrance is the bulb
display. It is clear that he is not unaccustomed to things going his way.
"I'm an instinctual guy," he says, shrugging. He pulls from his jacket the
bulb he has come to replace—"an obscure refrigerator lightbulb"—and
obtains a new one, plus a backup. "I won't be coming back here again
soon," he says, all swagger. Momentum gathered, he stops in at a nearby
locksmith and purchases a basic key ring—"That's a beauty!"—for
twenty-five cents. "This is my idea of utopia, doing things like this," he
says. "I could do this all day. In fact, if you can find something to do
that's less than this, my hat is off!"

He bestows his fortune upon a beautiful stranger.

We sit on a bench across from his building and see a stunning dark-
haired woman hail a cab. "She's very cute," he says, watching her speed
away. "Nice look." No woman escapes his gaze, and lately his gaze is more
intent than ever on finding a life mate. He lists among his obstacles
wardrobe considerations: "I have no dating wardrobe really. I'm one sport
jacket and a pair of brown loafers away from real commitment." But suddenly, the dark-haired woman reappears before us. "There she is again!"
he says as she lopes over. She has forced her cab to return so that she
could beg for an autograph, handing over a blank check for him to sign.
"We were admiring you," he says pluckily. "We were saying, 'Boy, that's
the perfect look!'" He inscribes her check and, under the amount, writes,
"Millions." After she leaves, he smiles broadly and says: "She's going to
make some guy very happy. She made *me* very happy. And my mother
says to me, 'How are you ever going to meet a girl?'"

FOUR CHARACTERS IN SEARCH OF AN ENDING

Scenes from an Italian restaurant:

They all converge, against the odds, to blur reality, to test spontaneity, to frighten other diners. It is a warm night on Columbus Avenue, where they now meet for late alfresco food and fellowship, at a place called Isabella's. (Seinfeld chose it.) They come as themselves, by themselves (except for Richards, who brings his daughter, Sophia), but they resemble their characters nevertheless. Seinfeld arrives first, followed by Louis-Dreyfus, then by Alexander, who has been waiting for fifteen minutes at the wrong restaurant across the street. Richards comes once the others have been seated at an outdoor table, where all pursuant Nothing takes place.

Jerry picks.

He selects the wine, white, and then says of the restaurant, "We referred to this place on a show one time as a place I was uncomfortable with. I thought it was too pretentious." Julia says, "I'd like to point out that he chose this restaurant for us to get together tonight. What does that tell you?" Oblivious, Richards urgently interjects, "You guys ready to order?"

They offer to get naked.

Alexander and Louis-Dreyfus are in New York to play husband and wife in the forthcoming Rob Reiner movie, *North.* They say their marital chemistry comes easily. Alexander says, "Actually, we play George and Elaine as if they were husband and wife—the bickering and the simmering sexuality." To which Seinfeld says, "Beneath the surface, we try to inject a simmering sexuality between all of the characters. Between me and Kramer, between Kramer and George—it's all simmering sex." And then:

Jason:	I've seen Julia naked.
Julia:	You did not. When?
Jason:	Our dressing rooms on the show are separated by a curtain.
Julia:	*And you peeked through?*
Jason:	[*shrugs*] I don't peek.
Julia:	Jason Alexander! Do you really?
Jason:	I get a pretty hard shadow on my curtain sometimes.
Julia:	I gotta tell you, I'd be happy to take my clothes off anytime, and we'll get it over with.
Jerry:	I'll take mine off! I'm in top shape.
Julia:	Well, I'd prefer if you didn't.

Michael: [*oblivious, noticing weather*] Ahh, this is lovely! This breeze! What a night!

Julia licks.

She asks for a bite of Seinfeld's bread. To be polite, he offers her the unbitten end. Taking this to be germ-consciousness, she proceeds to lick the bread on both sides. "There, now it's ruined!" she says to him. He inspects the bread and sticks it into his shirt pocket. "You couldn't be more wrong," he says covetously. Whereupon she says, "I'll lick anything."

How she licks:

Elaine once taunted Jerry on a show by leaving anonymous filthy messages on his tape recorder. "I'm going to slide my tongue around you like a snake," she said huskily. Now Louis-Dreyfus says, "That was nowhere near as dirty as I thought it should be." Seinfeld says, "I'll tell ya, the idea of a snake sliding around me is *not* appealing." She goes on: "To be honest, I would have gone so much farther." There is a long silence. *"Really?"* says Alexander, with great interest.

They are kissed by a drunken woman.

They are accosted suddenly by an unsteady woman in business attire, who announces: "You don't have to say anything—you just have to let people come up and kiss you, like this, so they can tell their friends the next day, *'I kissed Kramer.'"* (She kisses Richards's cheek.) *"'I kissed George.'"* (Now Alexander's.) "And *'I kissed Jerrrrr-reeeeeee!'"* (Here, she plants one upon Seinfeld with ferocity.) She sees Louis-Dreyfus. *"It's Elaine!"* she says, not kissing her. "Elaine, talk to me about men!" "You're very unique," Alexander tells her, not unkindly. Embarrassed, she says, "Now I'm leaving." Richards, charmed, says: "Wait, what's your name? You're fun."

They foresee their imminent deaths.

"Who would you say is least like their character?" Seinfeld asks, nominating Alexander. Louis-Dreyfus agrees, but thinks Richards is close.

Jerry:	Really? I wouldn't say that.
Julia:	Michael's not like Kramer.
Jerry:	I'm not saying in the *same way*. But he's off the beaten path equally. Equally distant.
Michael:	[*oblivious, keeping his eyes on the woman who kissed them, now out on the street*] I'm just watching that woman. She crossed the street, then she sat on a fire hydrant, now she's walking back.
Jason:	Watch, she's gonna come back with a gun and say, *"I shot Kramer!* And *I shot George!* And *I shot Jerrrrrrr-reeeeeeee!"*

Julia pulls a knife on Jerry.

The body of Louis-Dreyfus is once again in question. The men remark on how impressively she slenderized after giving birth last year. Chewing bread, Seinfeld posits the following theory:

Jerry:	I think you've got one of those bodies.
Julia:	No I don't.
Jerry:	You do.
Julia:	No I don't! I don't, Jerry!
Jerry:	Julia, you do.
Julia:	Damn it, *I don't!* [*She grasps cutlery, holds it near his throat.*]
Michael:	Can I have some bread?

They grow hungry and restless.

"I'd like to take this moment to apologize for the service we're getting in this restaurant," says Seinfeld, slightly perturbed.

Julia:	I will accept that apology reticently.
Jerry:	We are the kings and queen of New York. What's our waiter's name?
Julia:	I think someone just spit on me.
Waiter:	[*flustered*] Our computers crashed, so we're behind.
Jerry:	Do you think that happens to the chefs of France?
Michael:	[*confused*] My salad was made by a computer?
	Food arrives.
Jerry:	See, as soon as you complain . . .

Michael: [*distracted, staring at street*] Uh-oh! She walked three blocks up that way, and now she's coming back again.

Who would take a bullet for Jerry:

"Let me tell you something," says Alexander, consuming pasta. "If anything happens to Jerry, my life's not worth living! I'm a million and a half in debt right now. I'd take a bullet in a minute. Take my arm, go ahead! I'll give up an arm right here." Touched, Seinfeld assures him: "We'd still keep you on the show with one arm. Like that drummer in Def Leppard. Now, *that* guy has job security!"

Jerry goes to the bathroom and loses his seat.

"Okay, he's gone," says Louis-Dreyfus. "Let's reveal the truth!" Alexander wiggles his pinky finger. "He's hung like this," he says. Richards, oblivious, says he wants to wear his bathrobe on *Regis & Kathie Lee* the next morning. At which point *Seinfeld* executive producer Larry David shows up, having just been to a Knicks game. He takes Seinfeld's chair, knowing it will displease him. *"What is this?"* says Seinfeld, displeased, upon returning. Discussion ensues about how Seinfeld hates having his stuff touched, prompting an idea for an episode in which Jerry sublets his apartment.

Larry: You are the last person in the world who would ever sublet to another person.
Jerry: I'm annoyed already.
Larry: When his own mother comes to town, he takes her straight to a hotel.
Jerry: [*shrugs*] A friend was recently using my bathroom for number two and I objected. I said, "Do you have to do that in here?" He said, "It's a toilet!" I said, "Nevertheless."

George wins in the end.

Always it comes back to masturbation: There remains a major controversy, thus a need for resolution.

Jerry: People are still asking who won the contest? That won't go away.

Larry: I thought it was so clear that you and George tied.

Jerry: Nobody wants a tie.

Julia: Money should change hands.

Jerry: Nobody called the bet off officially.

Jason: [*inspired*] I should still be, you know, abstaining. I could say
four episodes into next season, "I'm still the Master of my Domain!" Jerry could say, "You're still doing *that*?"

Jerry: [*laughs*] I'd say, "What, are you kidding? It's *over*!"

Jason: "Nobody said anything to me! Where's the money?"

I had somewhat gotten to know the reclusive comic genius Albert Brooks through his friend, comedian Richard Lewis, and was always astonished by Albert's spontaneous brilliance. In the rare social scenarios in which he chose to appear, pure comedy flew from his fiber with every twitch. (I remember him doing ten amazing minutes in a friend's hotel room bathtub, empty at the time.) Moreover, I had been a devout fan since the moment I first saw his television stand-up work in the early seventies. I got my chance to write about him once he completed work on a new film, *Defending Your Life*. Today, he is a happily fulfilled family man, a most evolved husband and father. And he has made more funny films.

For this profile—which begins in the direct manner Albert himself often began his own work on record and film—I had asked him to briefly address the reader in a very personal way, breaking the third wall of print journalism. He complied, spontaneously (of course). Initially, his funny little pitch appeared just after the first paragraph—but, frankly, it didn't quite work there or anywhere else. So, for the first time ever, I share it now:

Hello, I'm Albert Brooks. Are you as tired of movies as I am? Do you leave the theater saying, "What the hell just happened?" And, "How did she do *that*?" Have you said to yourself, "I have a total of sixty-one kernels of popcorn here and I paid twenty-two dollars for them. How could they use this stuff as packing material if it costs so much?" Have you ever said to yourself, "I don't want this much Coca-Cola! I wanted a sip—I've got enough for a *team*!" If so, maybe you've been dissatisfied with your cinema experience. *Defending Your Life* will change all that! And if it doesn't, remember, I have absolutely nothing to do with the way your neighborhood cineplexes are operated. But I'm sure your theater managers will be happy to hear any comments and suggestions. Thank you and enjoy!

Albert Brooks Is the
Howard Hughes of Comedy

Rolling Stone, April 1991

Hello and welcome. You have begun to read something we like to call the Albert Brooks Celebrity Profile. This is an exciting opportunity for you to learn about Albert Brooks, a man most experts believe to be the funniest human being currently living. You say, If Albert Brooks is so funny, why haven't I seen more of him? The answer is not simple, but let me ask you this: Is it necessary to see more of someone in order to appreciate how funny he or she is? In fact, aren't most people actually funnier in retrospect than they are when you're with them? And what's funny, anyway? It's a foolish word, when you think about it. *Funny.* How would you like to be called *funny*? It's not exactly dignified, is it? Therefore, if people were running around calling you the *funniest man alive,* maybe you wouldn't be making a public spectacle of yourself. Maybe you'd like a little privacy and prefer to stay at home and watch a great deal of television and think about death. Well, that's what comedian-auteur Albert Brooks has done, and now he's ready to talk about it—just in time to coincide with the release of his fourth film in twelve years, *Defending Your Life,* in which he and Meryl Streep portray two very funny dead people.

•   •   •

Long ago, when life cost less, Albert Brooks roamed the earth. He had curly hair then, and his posture was rigid. Also, he wore much plaid. Even so, he was merciless. If he came upon houses, he would bring them down. If he came upon aisles, he would force people to roll in them. The great hosts of television—Sullivan, Griffin, Carson—loosed him upon their viewing herds, and always he left them laughing. They laughed when he left, you see, because if he had stayed, audience members might have died or possibly suffered internal bleeding. Years later he would say, "My biggest fear was of being *too* funny and murdering people by making them cough and winding up in a lawsuit."

And so he stopped.

He turned to film—not literally, of course, but as a career move. No longer would he speak before mobs or visit men with microphones on their desks. Immediacy bored him; he craved *delayed* response. He wondered, *If I created a humorous concept today, would people laugh when they experience it a year from now? What about three years?* The challenge was irresistible. First he made seven short films that aired on *Saturday Night Live,* a brand-new program for which he declined an offer to be the permanent host. (Such was his comic enormity.) In one film, Israel and Georgia traded places. In another, Albert ordered in broasted chicken. Then, in 1979, Paramount released his first feature, *Real Life,* an echo of the classic PBS documentary *An American Family,* in which he portrayed a comedian named Albert Brooks who spent months filming daily tedium in a Phoenix household until, desperate for action, he set it aflame. Two years later he unveiled *Modern Romance,* perhaps the finest film ever made about horrible behavior in love. In 1985 his third film, *Lost in America,* about a couple who give up everything to live in a Winnebago, succeeded in a way its predecessors did not: Many people saw it. But never was he more visible than in *Broadcast News,* the 1987 movie made not by Albert Brooks but by his friend James L. Brooks, in which Albert delivered an Oscar-nominated performance as a brilliant network correspondent who sweats prodigiously on-camera. (From *The Larry King Show,* on radio, last summer. Caller: "How did you get all the sweat to pour from your head?" Albert [*in a rare media appearance*]: "They read me the back-end deal that I made.")

Before that film, and in between all of the others, he was nowhere to be found, unless you went over to his house.

Albert Brooks reinvents comedy:

Albert: Knock, knock.
You: Who's there?
Albert: [*pauses, confused*] I don't—what do you mean?

I have never been to Albert Brooks's house, and he has never been to mine. And yet, we have both been to other people's homes. He is rigorously private and difficult to pin down without the help of several muscular men. Like many private persons, he has much to protect. One day, for instance, I ask him on the telephone to describe the contents of his refrigerator, since there would be no chance of me seeing for myself. He goes to look, then reports: "Chopped-up fruit. Melon and cantaloupe. Spinach in a bag, which, by the way, is a great delicacy. Nonfat milk. Six truffles, a layer cake, a wedding cake, and a human body."

He is known as Comedy's Recluse. Imprisoned by impossibly high standards, he has become a show business hermit. He is uncompromised, therefore unseen. As such, he lives a hermit's life, if hermits lived in the San Fernando Valley, had offices at Warners, drove a Mercedes, ate great quantities of sushi, and thrilled to the company of beautiful women. For the most part, however, he burrows in the handsome Sherman Oaks ranch home where he has dwelled for nine years. There, he will phone up friends and disguise his voice, pretending to be an angry neighbor or a law-enforcement officer. (Among those in his comically astute telephone circle: Richard Lewis, Carrie Fisher, and Rob Reiner.) Or he will watch television over the phone with many of these same friends, instructing them on which channel to tune in to. He then supplies detailed commentary on what he sees, often while impersonating famous people. (His repertoire of mimicry is vast, ranging from Bob Hope to CNN anchor Bernard Shaw.) For example, as Rex Reed: *"Jessica Llllllange, marry someone else! You're getting bad advice!"* As George Bush (his excellent Bush, friends point out, predated Dana Carvey's version): "Wanna *preserve* the right of the hunter. At the same time, *don't* like to see those children shot. Maybe there's a compromise. Maybe we can send *deer* to school."

And when he can be no one else, he will resort to being a forty-three-year-old Jewish man who is always worried and who never laughs harder than when he is being laughed at. Or with. Or something.

Why he lives where he lives:
"As long as I've been supporting myself, I've always lived in the Valley.

And I think about leaving all the time. But I look at it like this: I pretty much would be living the same life wherever I lived. I'm always afraid that if I get too far away from show business, I won't do it anymore. If I moved to a little cabin somewhere, I'm afraid I could sit and do nothing for too long. Here, at least, I can watch people zoom right past me."

You Are There: the wrap party for *Defending Your Life*, May 1990, downtown Los Angeles. Mr. Brooks has taken over the large, swell club Vertigo for a full evening of celebration. Everywhere there is bounty: ice sculptures, grand buffets, free liquor, two bands, laughs aplenty. Mr. Brooks elects to arrive late, perhaps ninety minutes late, with his lovely female companion, the one called Cathy, a production coordinator on the movie. Now he is coming over here, propelled by his extraordinarily purposeful gait. His hangdog face betrays great discomfort. Now he speaks to you. "I look around this room," he says, finally, "and all I can do is wonder how this money could have improved my life."

From "Albert Brooks's Famous School for Comedians," a 1971 parody article he created for *Esquire*:
Q: Is a life in comedy *always* fun?
A: No. But is anything *always* anything?

He is never on and he is never off. For this reason, he is considered less a comic, more an oracle. His name is spoken reverently by those who know comedy. To them he is Albert, simply Albert. As if to say, We are here, but he is Over There. His mind produces only pungent thought or, in essence, entertainment; there is no respite. Brain waves crash, pound, thunder, and permit him only three, maybe four hours' sleep—usually while the TV flickers in the darkness. "It's disturbing," he says. "Of the last thirty dreams I've had, I've been on that show *Amazing Discoveries* in twenty of them. It must be because it's on at three in the morning. Or maybe I really do have a product to wash your car better than anyone else."
Of mind and man:
"I don't think of him as being on the same way that comics are on," says nonrelative Jim Brooks, comedy impresario (*The Simpsons, Broadcast News*). "I just think it *bursts* out of him. It's his way of communicating. It's *him*. His mind questions itself and never locks in. Listen, the big deal is never can you find a moment that wasn't a moment of absolute

integrity. Never did he do something because the money was right. He's a comic *artist,* man. And he's one of the great comedy directors."

"Albert has always been one of the few people in my generation who has been taken seriously in comedy," says *Saturday Night Live* godfather Lorne Michaels (the very fellow to whom Albert reportedly suggested the concept of different weekly guest hosts, having refused the full-time gig himself). "He plays to the top of the audience and he's paid a price for it, but not too great a price. It's very hard to get integrity late in life, and he's had it from the beginning."

"He has a *huge* brain," says actress Kathryn Harrold, who was the object of Albert's affection in *Modern Romance* and, for a time thereafter, in life. "He's almost too smart for his own good."

Billy Crystal once told a *Playboy* interviewer the following story about a birthday party for Rob Reiner, boyhood chum of Albert Brooks's:

"Albert Brooks had bought Rob some books. One was *Stunts and Games.* And Albert said, 'Let me read you some of these things.' Then he started making them up and reading them as if they were in the book: 'This one's called National Football League. Get thirty of your friends together, have them donate five million dollars each to buy black people who can run and hit.' Or 'Kennedy Assassination: Pretend you see smoke coming only from the Texas Book Depository, ignoring the man with the rifle in the tree standing next to you.' I'd probably never seen anyone funnier in my whole life. In fact, it was so funny that he had to leave immediately afterward. I felt sad that Albert couldn't be a person; he had to leave."

Albert entertains a president:

"When we were in Washington doing *Broadcast News,*" he says, "a dinner was set up in a private house. There were five of us from the movie, plus Ronald Reagan and his wife and four other people. He had had prostate surgery a month earlier and was recovering. So I felt it was my patriotic duty to get a chuckle out of him. I really don't know that many jokes, but I had heard a joke about a month earlier and it made me laugh and it was the only joke I knew, so I told it to him privately as the others all walked in to dinner. I said, 'Come here for a minute.' He listened, and laughed, but later on, I thought, *Gee, that joke might've been taken the wrong way.* Here's the joke: An eighty-year-old Jewish man goes to a doctor in Miami and says 'There's something wrong with me, I'm not sure what it is.' And the doctor looks at him and says, 'All right, I'm gonna need a stool sample, a urine sample, and a semen sample.' And the Jewish guy says, 'Here, take my underwear.'

"I'll tell you, he laughed, but he didn't eat much dinner. He did eat a lot of cake, though, and he said to me, 'I love cake.' I said, 'Good.'"

Let us now ponder the Brooksian oeuvre, a small body of performances whose chief thematic link is desperation. Albert Brooks *is* the Desperate Man, a universally beset character crusading (mostly internally) for order and respect in a cold, capricious world. ("Wouldn't this be a great world," he asked in *Broadcast News,* "if insecurity and desperation made us more attractive?") Pauline Kael, who once admiringly likened Albert's curled hair to brains worn outside of his head, has correctly observed, "When he's at his most desperate, he's funniest." As with many desperate lives, his personal desperation was honed as a stand-up comic. But it was immortalized in the seventies with a legendary *Tonight Show* appearance, wherein he announced that he had completely run out of material and proceeded to smash eggs into his hair, drop his pants, squirt himself with seltzer, rub pound cake on his face, and storm offstage, bellowing the caveat, "This isn't the real me!"

Likewise, in his films, he dares to be pathologically, um, persistent. In *Real Life,* he fought to keep his documentary of an ordinary family from boring itself to death by asking the wife to have an on-camera affair with him. In *Modern Romance,* he ended his relationship with Kathryn Harrold in the first scene and fought for the rest of the film to reinstate it. ("Let me ask you something," his character, Robert Cole, said to Harrold's character, Mary Harvard, after waiting for her to return from a date with someone else. "If a person's not home, and you start driving around their house, and you drive around and around and around and around, and then you start driving around the city, and you're going ninety miles an hour, and you call 'em every four seconds, and you don't think about anything else, what is that? Is that not love?") In *Lost in America,* he was an adman who fought a lateral job transfer by dropping out of society to wander the country in a mobile home. Then, when his wife (played by Julie Hagerty) immediately lost their six-figure nest egg in a Las Vegas casino, he begged the pit boss to return their money as a public-relations gesture, suggesting as a campaign jingle: *The Desert Inn has heart! The Desert Inn has heart!"*

"What distinguishes Albert's work," says James L. Brooks, explaining the Essential Albert Truth, "is that he sees how painful life can be. He uses comedy to get further inside the pain."

Which brings us to *Defending Your Life,* whose title, even, is the apotheosis of desperation. In the opening moments, Albert drives into a bus and dies. He awakens in Judgment City, where he must wear strange linen gowns and account for his earthly lot by viewing tapes of terrible moments from his life (the perfect couch-potato fantasy!). If he proves that he faced up to his fears, he will "move forward" in the universe and become smarter. If not, he will be reincarnated on earth and try again. Meanwhile, he meets Meryl Streep and together they frolic and play miniature golf in the afterlife.

"Sure it's optimistic," says Albert one afternoon in his Burbank office. "None of it takes place here." And as far as death goes, all in all he'd rather be in Judgment City. "Nothing else ever made sense to me, and the only other thing I thought it might be was dirt, which I couldn't get financing for. Two hours of dirt—no one's gonna really put up much money. But my father died when I was twelve years old, which does start one out thinking, *Gee, where did Dad go?* If nothing else, it forces you. I wasn't looking for answers as much as ideas. And so I started to look at what are the few things that bind us: What would make me the same as somebody who lives in Brazil or Haiti or Ethiopia or London? And basically, all human beings are frightened."

From *A Star Is Bought,* his classic 1976 comedy album: [*Reading tip: Albert plays both roles.*]

Psychiatrist: Do you still feel like you can buy your friends with laughter?

Albert: [*angrily*] Let me tell you something, Doctor. I don't have to buy my friends with anything. I don't need friends. I shouldn't have friends.... You don't go into this business and expect friends. I am a loner—that's what an artist is!

Psychiatrist: You don't believe that.

Albert: [*deflated*] You're damned right I don't believe that. Help me, man, I'm sick.

He was born a joke.

His father named him Albert Einstein, and his mother did not stop his father from doing so. His father was Harry Einstein, a radio dialect comedian known as Parkyakarkus (as in *park-your-carcass*) who worked with

Eddie Cantor and Al Jolson. His mother is actress-singer Thelma Leeds. His older brothers were named Cliff (an adman) and Bob (a comic-actor also known as deadpan-daredevil Super Dave Osborne). Albert, however, was called Albert, a human punch line with no choice but to live up to the name. (He switched to Brooks when he started performing, since, he says, "it sounded great with Albert. I tried Finney, but I got sued. I tried Prince, but it was taken. I tried Salmi and actually used it for two years.") They were the Einsteins of Beverly Hills adjacent, and showbiz was their life. "Everybody was fighting for ten minutes at the dinner table," says Albert, "with the youngest having the roughest time."

"I think Albert's father's absence has been the largest event in his life in the forming of who he is today," says his friend, writer Paul Slansky. Indeed, Albert covets memories of his father, a wily, antic man, and shares them with zeal. We sat one morning in Art's Delicatessen, in Studio City, where he devoured matzo brei pancakes and regaled me with happy recollections. Like the time his family went to see the movie *Peyton Place,* and his father stood up at the end to loudly sing "Auld Lang Syne" with the cast. "I'm pulling him down, saying 'Dad, please!'" Then there was the ritual of announcing to crowded restaurants that his youngest son was not eating his vegetables. "He would take his knife and for ten seconds just hit on the water glass"—alas, here Albert demonstrates—"until everyone was quiet. Then he would say, *'Ladies and gentlemen, my little boy here...'* By then, I am not only eating the vegetables, I'm eating the farmer! I've gone back to the source. I'm eating all of *agriculture.*"

His father died a great show business death. He died onstage, at a Friars Club roast honoring Desi Arnaz and Lucille Ball. By this time, Harry Einstein was ill and semiretired but still an active Friar. "It was a dais of legendary performers," says Albert, "and my dad was on the dais and, the night before, I had helped him with his routine. He would talk very seriously and sincerely about the honorees and then miss their names: *'My closest friends in the world, Louise Bowls and Danny Amaz!'* I never saw it, but he got up, and he was brilliant. It was elegant, and they screamed, and he sat down and passed on. Right there. They stopped the dinner and took him backstage—the classic *'Is there a doctor in the house!'* They cut him open backstage, shocked him with a lamp cord.

"The interesting thing," he says hopefully, "is that he *finished.* That's what makes you believe in something. Whatever reason death comes, something is here to make us finish. He didn't die in the middle of a line, and that's something."

•   •   •

The Impossible Truth! Did you know that:

Albert and Woody Allen once appeared on the same *Merv Griffin Show*! Afterward, Woody told Albert, "You're a funny man, Brooks." They have not spoken since, even though Albert has tried calling.

Once, there were no young comedians! Sensing this, Albert gave up plans to become a young actor and embarked upon a life of young comedy. "As an actor at nineteen," he says, "I was one of a thousand. As a young comedian, I was one of two!" But first he completed three years at Carnegie Tech in Pittsburgh.

His first Comedy Bit was that of the World's Worst Ventriloquist, whose dummy gurgled when Albert sipped water. Other early favorites: *Albare* the French mime, who described his every movement (*"Now I am walking up ze stairs"*); Alberto the animal trainer, whose elephant was lost, forcing him to make do with a frog; and the impressionist whose every offering sounds like Ed Sullivan.

Albert is an accomplished pianist, owns a clown suit, and holds ticket No. 70 on Pan Am's first flight to the moon, should one be scheduled. "Hell, I'm only glad it's not on Eastern," he says.

Albert will proudly tell anyone, "I am one of the longest wearers of contact lenses in the country!"

Often Albert's friends haven't known the last names of the women he's dated—unless they were famous. Among these: Linda Ronstadt (they lived together), Candice Bergen, Julie Hagerty and Harrold, who fondly remembers Albert's penchant for talking to livestock when driving through farmland. "If he saw a cow," she says, "he would always pull over and say, 'Hi, how are ya?'"

Albert *has* acted in other people's movies: You may remember him as an annoying campaign aide in *Taxi Driver*; as Goldie Hawn's dead husband in *Private Benjamin*; as the guy Dan Aykroyd eats in *Twilight Zone: The Movie*; and as conductor Dudley Moore's manager in *Unfaithfully Yours*. On *The Simpsons* he was the voice of Marge's amorous bowling instructor, Jacques.

Albert gave Michael Dukakis comedy lessons during his presidential campaign and wrote many jokes for the small governor. Dukakis, a reticent pupil, used only one. "I was trying to get him to be a little self-deprecating," says Albert. "The joke was *'George Bush says it's time to give the country back to the little guy—here I am!'*"

"So I'm on trial for being afraid?" Albert says in *Defending Your Life*.

To overcome fear, he had to make a movie about overcoming fear. Fear has kept him hiding. Fear kept him from showing up in public as Albert Brooks, which kept America from remembering that there still is an Albert Brooks. His Carson appearances are now gauzy memory. Prior to this film, he had been a guest on the Letterman show exactly once. He last performed live in the days of the druids. Woody, at least, makes a movie every year, and is therefore difficult to forget. Steve Martin may never do stand-up again, but he sops media with aplomb. (Plus, unlike Albert, when Steve Martin is offstage, he is achingly sedate; a natural resource is not being wasted here.) Meanwhile, Albert's idea of exposure is to call Larry King in the dead of night and claim to be a black decathlon athlete. People begin to talk.

"There are people throughout Hollywood who for a long time have theorized that Albert is afraid of success," says comedian Harry Shearer, who coproduced *A Star Is Bought* and cowrote *Real Life*. "I don't think it's that simple. From a standpoint outside of his head, it's easy to say that Albert's too protective of himself. Because he's so good, you can bet that whatever it is that he's afraid of is clearly not going to happen. He's the comedian least likely to fail in a spontaneous situation, because he is so spontaneous. So it's sad that those explosively spontaneous gusts of comedy that Albert is more capable of coming up with than anybody aren't on public display. That side of him doesn't come through in his movies, where he's always extremely controlled. More than anybody else, he taught me the value of saying no in show business. But for my taste, he says it a little too often for his own good."

As cruel irony would have it, Albert once knew no fear. "I was abnormally fearless," he confesses, almost ashamedly. "I remember being offstage at *The Ed Sullivan Show,* talking to a friend on the telephone while I was being introduced! I wasn't even talking about the show—I was talking about *dinner.* My friend said, *'Hang up! You're on!'* I said *nonchalantly*: 'Oh, okay.' I didn't even think about it. I wish I could have gone through my whole life that way. But unfortunately, it caught up with me. One day I said, *'Jesus!'* I was like the Road Runner. I ran a half-mile off the mountain, and then one day I looked down and went, 'Oh my God!'

"Now, I don't think the object is to have *no* fear; it's to exist *with* fear. That seems healthy. To have no thought of fear isn't brave—it's a little crazy. Because when you finally do think of it, your equilibrium is thrown. The best combination is to say *'This is scary and here I go.'* "

So, then, could he ever perform again?

"I think it might be great fun to do it again," he says, as though he possibly believes this. "Especially since life doesn't hinge on it. I'm a director now, so I don't have to be funny. One of the terrible things stand-up comedy can lead to, if you're not careful, is that your life starts to hinge on your performances. If it doesn't go well, your life stinks. I'd rather measure my life by my movies. Maybe I'd film it. Be interesting to see."

He stops and smells his lack of conviction. "Edit this part out," he says, woeful and embarrassed. "That was all bullshit. It doesn't matter that I have another profession. It would still make me nervous. Because I'd still want it to be as good as it could be. And you couldn't convince me that it was all right not to be good, just because I had another job. You know? It's still the only game in town while you're doing it."

An epilogue: Because there is nowhere else to put it, he keeps some comedy to himself.

Above the desk in Albert Brooks's office there hangs a framed letter. Few visitors ever notice it, but that is inconsequential. Badly typed on New York Yankees stationery, the letter is dated August 5, 1928, and is addressed to a Dr. Herbert Stevens at Mount Sinai Hospital. It reads as follows:

Dear Dr. Stevens:

Last Sunday when I visited Tommy on the fourth floor, I promised him I would hit a home run. As you may have heard, I grounded out four times that day. I understand that little Tommy has since passed on. In the future, I won't promise anything specific to the children. I'll just do what I can.

My best,
Babe

Albert's secretary typed the letter exactly as he had dictated it to her.

She says that lately he has been asking her to find federal-prison stationery.

erhaps the most uninhibited interview subject I have ever debriefed, Eddie Murphy was, at this moment, America's undisputed box-office king. And, during our time together, there always seemed to be a royal cortege flanking his every movement. Regality, therefore, became the subtext for the piece. Some ironies in aftermath: His dim views about love and marriage, evidenced within, obviously were amended later; four years hence, he married Nicole Mitchell, who in fact was the unnamed woman described in the introduction. His remonstrations about ever doing a third *Beverly Hills Cop* film also proved premature. And then there was a bit of grim foreshadowing when he explained his penchant for driving through blighted neighborhoods and talking to prostitutes. He was arrested in 1997 while giving a ride to a working transvestite named Shalimar. I am convinced that he had been simply conducting an interview with said Shalimar, in order to sate his thoroughgoing sociological curiosity, as he described it.

Eddie Murphy:
Elvis in Ebony

Excerpted from the *Rolling Stone* Interview, August 1989

The king sleeps through earthquakes. There have been two already this morning, both sizable enough to bestir gasps of panic and alarm. But the door to the king's sanctum remains closed; the jolts have elicited no reaction from within. "Where's Eddie?" the king's manager demands, himself looking a bit ashen, a bit unsettled. "Sleeping," he is told by the king's men, an omnipresent coterie of employees whose business it is to know what Eddie Murphy is doing every moment of every day. *"Sleeping!"* says the manager, incredulous. But it is true: Eddie is asleep, he is out cold, he is snoozing through the peril. Nestled on the expansive ebony sofa in his vast ebony office, he naps and feels nothing, nary a rumble. When he emerges much later, all eyes in the room intently scan him to ascertain his condition. He groggily rubs his face. "What earthquake?" he says.

"Suits!" he hollers across the Paramount back lot later that day. Frank Mancuso, who is wearing a suit, sees trouble coming. Mancuso is chairman of Paramount Pictures, and he is presently loitering on the grounds, chatting with three studio executives, also in suits. Eddie Murphy, who's wearing black warm-ups, barrels up in his customized golf cart (festooned with ersatz Rolls-Royce grillwork) and bleats the horn. *Aaaoooooo-gaaaaah!*

"Hello, suits!" he says, at once warm and defiant. The big shots chuckle at this insouciance. (*Oh, that Eddie!*) They are, after all, his subjects: He is Paramount's billion-dollar box-office sovereign, currently the nation's foremost comic commodity. And the back lot is where he reigns most conspicuously. He briefly schmoozes the Mancuso gaggle, then tears off again in his buggy, chasing down and hooting at pretty secretaries who appear in his path. "Yo! Yo! Yo!" he calls. *Aaaoooooo-gaaaaah!*

His friends call him Money. He looks like money, like $40 million, if perchance one speculates. He looks crisp, controlled. He is twenty-eight yet not terribly youthful; he fancies himself much older, more world-weary. He stares straight ahead and seems to notice no one, but he sees all and hears even more. Unless he's erupting into his deft repertoire of character voices, his presence is shy, inscrutable. Usually he is sullen, almost somber—but this creates a quiet aura of power. You feel him before you see him; first you see his men. He is insulated by bodies, a cleaving pack of old friends and relations on the payroll. These are Eddie's Boys: Fed, Larry, Jerome, Rough House, Roy, Fruity, Lee, Ray-Ray, and several others. They attend to him, fortify him, whether back home at Bubble Hill— Eddie's palace in Englewood Cliffs, New Jersey—or here in the balm of Los Angeles. They ride shotgun in the Rolls cart; they motorcade along in separate buggies, racing with Eddie around the lot (and letting him win); they flank, defer, cajole, tease, adore, grumble, serve, laugh approvingly, and get beaten by him at chess ("Whaddya gonna do without no queen, you spineless fuck!" Eddie will say). Mainly, though, they just watch. Eddie makes his own ham sandwiches—his Boys just watch. Eddie falls into stride with passing female joggers—his Boys just watch. And crack up.

Because kings can do anything, Eddie does everything. He hyphenates recklessly. His astonishing talent gives him license. Since March, he's been directing his first film, *Harlem Nights,* on which he is cowriter, producer, and costar along with Richard Pryor (his idol), Redd Foxx (his foul-mouthed forefather), and Arsenio Hall (his close friend). It is a period con-game yarn—*The Sting* done black. The elders praise their nascent director. "It's turning out to be more pleasant than I expected," says Pryor. "He's wise enough to listen to people. I see him be very patient with his actors. It's not a lark to him. He's really serious." Foxx says, "He's on top of the world, and he's doing a hell of a job. He sure knows how to handle people with sensitivity. He'll come over to your side and give private direction—he never embarrasses anyone." Another thought from Pryor: "You walk around here and look at the people—have you ever in your life seen this many black people on a movie set? I haven't."

Because Eddie can do anything, he also sings. It is a comedian's disease, this unfortunate urge. Carson wishes he could, but he can't. Jerry Lewis did but shouldn't have. Eddie can, and he does. The first album, *How Could It Be,* came out four years ago and was timid fare. (The dance single produced by funkmeister Rick James, "Party All the Time," however, was a novelty hit.) A second album, called *So Happy,* just released, is more confident and musically impressive. He takes kidding pokes at pop (in songs like "Put Your Mouth on Me" and "Bubble Hill") and also manages to display craft in the process. The voice is strong and practically unrecognizable; only the subject matter—and the occasional trademark *eeeh-eeh-eeh* walruslike guffaw—betrays his identity. (Recurring lyrical themes include bondage, outdoor sex, and distrust of women.) Still, he worries about the record; he has deigned to promote it and agree to test his press paranoia one more time. Eddie takes care of business.

As such, Eddie is like Elvis. In many ways, he is like Elvis. He likes Elvis. "Are you going to butcher me?" he says, by way of salutation, to a reporter meeting him for the first time. He says this in Elvis Presley's voice, a voice he conjures up often. Between takes on the set of the "Put Your Mouth on Me" video, he becomes Elvis—strumming a guitar, sneering, muttering, singing.

"Heybabybossanovababy," he croons, Elvis-like. *"Thankyouthankyou-verrmuch."* His office is stocked with Elvis gold records, Elvis books, Elvis street signs, arcane Presleyana of all sorts. "Elvis looked like every hair was where it was supposed to be," explains Eddie, who is known throughout his household for interminable rituals spent each day before mirrors, combing and recombing his hair.

To interrogate Eddie Murphy, you must become one of his minions. You must join his court, ride along in the tiny Rolls, wait while he directs his movie or while he sleeps through earthquakes. Dedication warms him. In conversation, perhaps as a reward, he is jarringly candid. (Bathroom habits! Sexual proclivities! Threats of violence!) "Everybody has something about them that nobody knows," he says buoyantly. "Except for me. I'm straight up." What follows then is an amalgam of several talks held in his Paramount office during days of pursuit. To ensure intimacy, he would toss associates and his Boys out of the room. The single exception was an unnamed and very pretty young woman who was permitted to witness one chat—and then only from a remote corner. When her clanking earrings began to drown out Eddie's whisper-soft voice, however, he considerately instructed her, "Take 'em off! He's recording this. You're gonna fuck up the recording." She obliged. "That's what's gonna be in the article," he continued. " 'In the middle of the interview, a woman's earrings are clanking. Murphy demanded that she take them off.' Write it that way and you'll make me out like an idiot. *Eeeh-eeh-eeh.*"

How much money does a box-office king carry around in his wallet? Let's see your dough.

Right now I've got nothing on me. I don't carry a lot of money—no more than three hundred dollars in my wallet at a time. I'm a credit-card fiend. I'm not like Mike Tyson, who walks around with thirty grand. I'd come in beaten up every day, going: [*shrugs helplessly*] "They got me again!" *Eeeh-eeh-eeh.*

But where's your wallet? Don't you carry it yourself?

No, I never carry my wallet. There's a song on my album called "Until the Money's Gone" where I keep asking "Where's my wallet?" That, in fact, is the question I ask most. Fifteen times a day, every day.

You mean there's one person who's in charge of holding your wallet?

No, I'll give my wallet to anyone who works for me. Which at one point caused me to change my staff. With my old staff, I'd say, "Hold my wallet," and then when I'd get it back, I'd say, "Waitaminute, there's only seven dollars in here and it was full yesterday." They'd say, "Oh, you must spend a lot of money, Ed." I'd say, "I *know* I didn't spend ten thousand dollars yesterday." "Well, Ed, I don't know anything about it, but I gotta go. My limo's here."

Do you have an idea how much you're worth?

[*earnestly*] Oh, yeah. To the dime. Oh, absolutely. I'm completely on top of that. It's an obsession. One of my major fears has always been that I'd get that call: "Your accountant's gone with all your money!" That kind of shit is spooky. So I know where every dime of my money is, and no one but me can sign checks for me. Which is a job in itself. I get crazy with that.

People see the pack of friends that follows you around and wonder, What's the deal with those guys? *Does their presence allow you to move into unfamiliar territory and always feel comfortable?*

Maybe so. I came to the realization that if you're lucky, you'll have five to ten friends in your life. And my old friends, people who were around me in grammar school and high school, they're all around me still. They're all intelligent and all serve a purpose. The thing is, I know they're my true friends. They knew me before it was financially desirable to know me.

Do you ever like to be alone?

No, I'm uncomfortable alone, especially at home. The only time I go off by myself is when I hop in the car and just drive for a couple of hours.

Where do you go?

I'll just get on the freeway and go real fast. Or drive around in a fucked-up neighborhood, which can be really scenic. I like to see the hookers, the drug addicts, the bums, street fights, people getting arrested and shit. I do that a lot.

Is it some kind of reality check?

Maybe, but I just find it interesting. I once stopped and asked a prostitute, "Why are you out here?" I thought she would give me a heavy philosophical answer. But she just said, "Muthafucka, you wanna buy some pussy or not?!" *Eeeh-eeh-eeh.* I was anticipating this deep conversation about life and despair, and she said, "Do you want me to suck yo' dick?!" I said, [*sheepishly*] "Excuse me, I'm gonna leave now...."

Your first words to me were "Are you going to butcher me?" Why were you worried?

You know why I get paranoid about journalists? The first thing I hear about myself every day is some new shitty rumor. Something comes out in the *Enquirer,* and seven people who work for me all have a copy. Every time I walk into another room, I hear, "Hey, did you see this?" I've developed this low-down self-image because every day I hear something horrible about myself. It gets to be a drag, to say the least.

What kind of rumors do you hear?

I've heard everything about myself. The most ridiculous rumor was that I was a faggot. I don't know where that came from. I've never had a dick in my ass *or* in my mouth! Maybe it's because I've made fun of homosexuals. The reasoning being "He does a gay impression, so, well, he must be one." Then I've also heard I'm a notorious womanizer, which is sort of a contradiction in rumors. Another outlandish rumor is that I smoke crack, or that I do serious cocaine, or that I drink.

But you're in fact the picture of abstinence, right? Have you ever let liquor touch your lips?

I drank once. While making *Coming to America,* I had some weirdness with John Landis, who was directing the movie. We had a tussling confrontation, and when I went home, Arsenio gave me some alcohol to settle me down. I thought a drink might help, so I drank a whole quart of Absolut vodka. I won the Most Vomit Award. I was bent over the toilet for hours. That was the first and last time I'll ever drink.

•   •   •

You give the impression that women can't help but prey on you. Is it difficult to know who to trust?

I'm not a trusting person by nature. My first reaction is to be distrustful—especially of women. I'm a target. As shitty as it sounds, I'm sure there are women who have gone out with me only because I'm Eddie Murphy. On the other hand, a lot of women go so far out of their way to show me that they don't care who I am that they end up being disrespectful. They treat me worse than they would some guy who works at Arby's. They act aloof and bored and won't even look at me. The least they could do is smile.

What qualities do you require in women?

Honesty, man. I'd take a dumb, honest woman who has nothing on the ball, just honesty. I'd take her every time over a smart one.

In the concert film Raw, *you performed a lot of misogynistic stand-up material, especially about marriage and divorce. Did you hear from a lot of angry women afterward?*

Women got pissed off, but the truth pisses people off. Don't get me wrong: I love women, and I have nothing against marriage. But I'm afraid of divorce, and divorce is a reality. Why should I take a shot at getting married and risk losing so much? Steven Spielberg has to give up $95 million because he was married for four years, and that's not *fair.* Clint Eastwood wasn't even married to his woman, and he's gonna lose money on her. Carson supports an army of women. *Why should I get married?* Why? There's no reason. I can have children without being married. I can have a monogamous relationship without being married. Why risk a divorce and having to give up half your shit?

You'll never be married?

No, never. [*groans*] I'll never live with anybody, and I'll never get married. There's no marriage for me. I'll have children. I'll be the best father in the world but a horrible husband. Marriage has to be a give-and-take thing, but I'm a my-way-or-the-highway guy—that's Stallone's line I'm stealing. But I'm a realist; I don't kid myself. If I got married with my attitude, she'll eventually be out there on the highway with half of my things.

I think you should take care of your child and get a woman back on her feet, give her a pat on the ass, and go about your business. Just because you're rich and you married someone, this person doesn't have to be rich for the rest of her life if the marriage doesn't work. Lots of people scoff: "Oh, money isn't everything." Well, if you were making a lot of money, you'd see it differently. The idea of giving somebody Bubble Hill and twenty million dollars would fucking blow my mind, man. I'd have to kill somebody. *Eeeh-eeh-eeh.*

You seem more romantic than that. On your new album, you cowrote this lovely ballad called "With All I Know." That had to come from somewhere.

Isn't that a pretty song? I was *sooo* depressed when I wrote that song. Because I was singing about how I wanted to feel: hopeful about love. It's not going to happen for me.

You're discounting it?

Don't get me wrong—I could fall in love in a second. But all the shit in the movies, the running-in-slow-motion montage stuff that part doesn't ever happen to me. The only thing that'll get me married is when I feel life moving that slow and we're riding horses and the leaves are brown and I've got a sweater on—when shit like that starts happening, that's when I'll be married.

Redd Foxx thinks you'll be married within a year.

Eleven months, he says. He bet me a thousand dollars. He says: [*in Foxx's voice*] "She ain't even gonna be *fine*; she's gonna be a big, fat, ugly bitch with a big, fat, long jaw and you gonna love her." Richard [Pryor] says the same thing. He says: [*in Pryor's voice*] "Muthafucka, you gonna find somebody eventually. Her pussy's gonna fit and that'll be yo' ass." I say, "Not me." He says, "All right, you'll see...."

You seem depressed about this.

I get depressed a lot. I was depressed this morning. It's just natural; it's human. My depressions are even more frustrating because I think, *Why the fuck am I depressed?* But more entertainers are like that. Michael [Jackson] and Stallone tell me they feel the same way.

Wasn't Stallone supposedly jealous over your working relationship with his then wife, Brigitte Nielsen, on Beverly Hills Cop II*?*

I haven't talked to him since then. He thought I fucked his wife. He heard the rumor and believed it. He came after me and said, "YOU FUCKED MY WIFE!" I said, "*Down,* brother, I didn't fuck your wife!" We talked about it, but I guess somewhere in the back of his head, he'll never really know the truth. Sly and I liked each other, too, but after the weirdness with Brigitte, it was ruined. I didn't fuck her.

Did it ever cross your mind?

Did I ever want to fuck Gitte? No, she's not my type.

What, she's too leggy?

No, she was *married.* And married to somebody who was my friend. I'm not that kind of guy.

Didn't you once date Robin Givens? Was she your type?

I saw Robin on and off for a couple of years. We were children then. I was nineteen or twenty; she was seventeen. I remember she spoke like a white person, very mannered and aloof. Every sentence was an exercise in linguistic propriety. She was very bossy. A powerful girl. When she and Mike Tyson hooked up, I thought, *Shit, they're exact opposites!* I tried to pull Mike's cards on it, because he and I were close. I told him, "Mike, *please,* PLEASE!" Mike said "Hey, man, I don't give a shit 'bout no girl, I just want some pussy!" Next thing I knew, he was married! *Eeeh-eeh-eeh.* I guess he really wanted that pussy.

[*sighs*] Love is no punk, boy. Love will whip your ass. Because Mike was honestly head over heels in love with her and still is, I think. Love is not only blind—love is deaf, love is crippled, love is a quadriplegic. Mike used to come by all the time, but after he got married, I saw him maybe twice. They broke up a year later, and I know he had to pay her something. He could've just fucked her for a year and once it went sour, he could've just walked away. Instead, she just bought a two-million-dollar house with his money. If this love shit is as potent as they say it is, maybe his good memories outweigh the bad. Maybe it was worth it. But no marriage for me.

How does this translate to your music? Why do I get this feeling you'll never release an album of ballads?

I don't like singing ballads. I'm uncomfortable with it. I don't buy me singing a slow song about love. There is no love.

How do you see yourself positioned as a singer? You once said you wanted to project a pure masculine image.

It's not even a conscious effort. I'm masculine, and that's what I put across. I'm glad that androgynous shit is over. If I had kids, and my kid came downstairs wearing pumps and lipstick and lacy drawers, I'd be *mad.* You don't want your kid to look like that. Maybe if I had put some lipstick and pumps on for the cover of the first album, I'd have done some more business. *Eeeh-eeh-eeh.*

But your songs do have a raw sexual edge.

That's because I'm a sexual person. I write sexual stuff. I'm a freak.

You're a freak?

Actually, I'm not a freak at all. I'm very conservative. You'd be surprised at a lot of stuff I've never done: I've never fucked in a car. I've never gotten head in the back of a limo. None of that superstar shit. Never fucked anyone in my office or on my bus. In my house, I've only done it in the bedroom. I don't fuck all over the house. I'm very prudish, really. I'm a *clean* freak, if anything. In a day, I probably take three or four showers and wash my hands up to fifteen times.

What do you think that means?

I'm just worried. You don't know where people's hands have been. I shake a lot of hands.

Is it true that you won't use public bathrooms?

I won't take a dump in a public bathroom. I can pee anywhere. I can pee outside.

Bubble Hill, your house in Englewood Cliffs, New Jersey, has taken on mythic status now that you've put a song about it on your album. Describe a quiet night at home.

Bubble Hill is never quiet. I named it after the black expression *bubble*, which is slang for *party*. Translated: Party Hill. It goes deeper than the party, though. I really feel at home in that house. My lifestyle is very conservative. There's always a lot of swimming and Ping-Pong and listening to music and watching movies. There's not a bunch of fucking going on, because basically everybody's too afraid to catch herpes and AIDS and die. And if my guys do drugs, they don't do them in front of me. I'm not gonna say you won't go behind the house and find somebody smoking a joint every now and then. But there are no orgies and coke and stuff.

If Elvis was alive, would you take him in at Bubble Hill? It is your version of Graceland, after all.

I *love* Elvis. Funny you say that. Arsenio does this routine for me about how, if Elvis was alive and his career was in the toilet, he'd be trying to get into Bubble Hill. I'd be going [*sotto voce*] "Tell him I'm not here." And Elvis would be in the lobby going [*in Elvis's voice*] "Is Eddie there? Say, man, he *tol'* me to come over. Where's Fruity? Fuck y'all. Tell Eddie I'll call him later." Elvis pissed off in the lobby of Bubble Hill—it wouldn't happen, though. I'd hang out with Elvis constantly.

Explain your fascination with him.

His presence. He had the strongest presence of anyone ever in this business.

You must know you have a strong presence, too.

Yeah, but it's no fucking Elvis Presley presence. Maybe after I die. It didn't matter what he was singing—and after the fifties, his music got really weird—he was Elvis up there. He looked like he was in total control, even though he was totally out of control and had no idea where he was. This guy was a fucking recluse, doing drugs, fucking up his body and his diet. He had this terrible deal with his manager, who got maybe fifty percent of all his money, and he paid in the seventy percent tax bracket. It's lunatic, man.

Speaking of Elvis's manager, you once met Colonel Tom Parker, right?

Colonel Tom Parker rubbed my head in Vegas. A couple times he set me up in the Elvis Presley Suite on the top of the Hilton, and I would go play Elvis for a week, which was really cool. One night we were at the craps table together, and he rubbed my head for luck. I wanted to punch him in the face. But this guy is like eighty years old—too old to be taught the limits of racism. There was nothing I could do. What would it look like in the papers? "EDDIE MURPHY BEATS UP COLONEL PARKER!" To this day, he probably doesn't realize how horrible a thing that was to do. "Let me rub your head for luck, boy!" My blood was boiling, though. I wanted to choke him.

When was the worst moment in recent history to be black?

We lost our minds in the seventies. We had big, long Afros, big platform shoes, big lapels, big hats. That was two hundred years of oppression coming to a head. We'd been under so much pressure for so long—look how you made us dress!

Do you ever feel discrimination in Hollywood?

I'm aware of racism, although I don't feel overt racism toward me. What Hollywood doesn't do, however, is acknowledge your accomplishments as readily if you're black. For instance, Michael Jackson is never given enough credit for being the biggest thing in the world. Taking nothing away from Bruce Springsteen—I like him—but I attribute a lot of his popularity to the fact that there has to be a white counterpart: "Michael is the Thriller, but Bruce is the Boss!"

If you think about it, we get all-fucked-up nicknames. Bruce is the Boss, Sinatra is the Chairman of the Board, Elvis is the King, John Wayne is the Duke, Jackie Gleason is the Great One. Michael is the *Gloved One.* The Thriller! Fred Astaire: the Greatest Dancer Who Ever Lived; Bill Robinson could outdance anybody who ever existed right off of the planet and they called him Mr. *Fucking* Bojangles!

In retrospect, do you regret your comments during the Oscar ceremony last year about black artists being overlooked by the Academy?

Because of what I said, I will never, ever get nominated for an Oscar, much less win one. I said that only three Oscars have been given to black actors in sixty years. I was just stating a fact. You know what was interesting? Everybody who was white felt that it was the wrong timing, and everybody who was black gave me the right-on sign. Wrong timing! Where else can you say something like that? On the *Soul Train* awards? Nobody's gonna see it.

Would there be a Spike Lee if there wasn't an Eddie Murphy?

That's like saying there wouldn't be an Eddie Murphy if there wasn't a Richard Pryor. Spike just does a different type of film than I do. Spike is more of a politician than I am. I'm an entertainer. If I can get a message across through my entertaining, fine. I think *Coming to America* is a polit-ical movie without shoving a message down anybody's throat. It's a black love story, in which black people are seen being black people, and it made two hundred and fifty million dollars. And that's a political statement without having to run a Malcolm X quote at the ending [as in Lee's *Do the Right Thing*]. Not that there's anything wrong with that. You can be overt or covert—you make the choice. I don't hold anything against the brother for being overt.

How has it been directing Richard Pryor?

First of all, he doesn't need to be directed much, because he has such good instincts. Directing Richard is easier for me than it might be for someone else, because there's so much Richard in me. I know how bril-liant the man is. The thing I like most about this picture is that Richard's character is so laid-back. He's, like, acting in the movie. It's a real classy role, and he's laying it out.

Some people think you shouldn't have played Axel Foley more than once.

Do you know what's scary? *Beverly Hills Cop II* was probably the most successful mediocre picture in history. It made two hundred fifty million dollars worldwide, and it was a half-assed movie. *Cop II* was basically a re-hash of *Cop I,* but it wasn't as spontaneous and funny. But my pictures make their money back: No matter how I feel, for instance, about *The Golden Child*—which was a piece of shit—the movie made more than a hundred million dollars. So who am I to say it sucks?

Which means you'll do a Cop III*?*

There's no reason to do it: I don't need the money, and it's not gonna break any new ground. How often can you have Axel Foley talk fast and get into a place he doesn't belong? But these motherfuckers [at Para-mount] are developing scripts for it. They're in preproduction. The only reason to do a *Cop III* is to beat the bank, and Paramount ain't gonna write me no check as big as I want to do something like that. In fact, if I do a *Cop III,* you can safely say, "Oooh, he must have got a *lot* of money!" *Eeeh-eeh-eeh.* Because we're *whores.* Stallone said it best: We're whores. If you think about it, they take you, put makeup on you—I got makeup on my face right now—they dress you up how they want you to dress, and they tell you to go out there and make that money. They give you a little cut of it—if you're lucky, you get ten percent of what the movie makes. If you're lucky. And then when you get old and fucked up, they throw you out and bring in some new bitch.

You've put your stand-up comedy on hold. Do you miss it?

I've retired from stand-up. I'm the Sugar Ray Leonard of stand-up comedy. What do I have to gain from doing stand-up? That's the only time people really take potshots at me. You know, when I did the concert film *Delirious,* I got all this flak for my material being so filthy. The truth is, it's nowhere near as filthy as some of the stuff they're doing now. I'm feeling like an old fucking guy watching Sam Kinison or Andrew Dice Clay. Shit, I'm nowhere near that dirty. I just said *fuck* a lot. I mean, Kinison does this bit about homosexual necrophilia—fucking a dead man in the ass—which is hysterical. But that's pretty dirty, you know?

Would that be crossing the line for you?

No, if I'd thought of it, I would've done it. Absolutely. It's hysterical. My thing is, if you're funny, fuck it. If you're watching my show and nineteen thousand people are laughing, but you think there's too much cursing, then get the fuck out. Why'd you come in the first place?

When you get mad, how do you vent your anger?

I have no way of venting my anger, and I haven't blown up in ages. I walk around with a big, huge knot of tension in the back of my head. I very rarely lose my temper. I haven't screamed at anyone in four years. One of the luxuries of having a staff is that if somebody pissed me off, no matter who it is, with the exception of relatives, I say, "Excuse me," and walk out of the room, and someone comes in and tells that person, "You have to leave." And that's it.

I don't know if this is a blessing or a curse, but when someone's out of my life, I have the ability to wipe them out like they never existed. If somebody fucks me over—that person is gone. There's no sitting back and singing: [*as Elvis*] "Memories . . . pressed between the pages of my mind."

Have you ever been to a therapist to learn how to better deal with your anger?

Nah, I feel like if I went to an analyst, then I must be crazy. I don't talk to many people about personal shit, so I'd probably wind up liking it. But I don't know. I think crazy people go to therapists. I know that a lot of people who've had analysis will read this and say, "Fuck you, I'm not crazy." But *I* would feel crazy. Every now and then, though, I feel like losing it.

Losing your temper?

Losing my mind. But I haven't yet.

What's your secret to maintaining sanity?

The only way I keep my sanity is the realization that every problem I ever had in my life, no matter how huge, right up to this moment, has worked itself out. Think about it: That problem you thought you'd never get out of—it worked itself out. It's behind you now. It doesn't make any sense to worry about it. The only problem that you can't get out of is kicking. Dying.

How do you think you'll die?

I used to think about death all the time. I guess when things are going good for you, you just expect it. I'd like to die in my sleep when I'm very old, but who wouldn't? I've never heard of someone saying, [*in high, effeminate voice*] "I want to die very young, dancing!"

I don't think it's gonna be cancer or some lingering illness, though. I think I'm gonna go in some horrible crash. It'll be one of those stupid entertainer's deaths. Maybe it'll be a plane crash. They'll be showing the wreckage on the news and interviewing farmers who saw the explosion from three miles away. Fruity and Ray-Ray will be quoted saying "I told him not to get on that plane!" *Eeeh-eeh-eeh.*

You've probably heard this before, but you don't smile much for someone with such a famous smile.

People come up to me and ask me to smile all the time. The thing I hear most is "Yo, smile! Why aren't you smiling? *Smile.* Smile for me!" And it gets irritating. Sometimes in restaurants, I'll see people across the room pressing their fingers into the corners of their mouths, showing me how to smile. I kid you not. When I'm driving down the street, people pull up to me and ask why I'm not smiling. Never mind that if I was driving around with a big smile, then people would think I was a lunatic.

Maybe you're just shy.

That, and I've got a mouthful of fillings. I'm a sugar freak—that's my one indulgence—so I get a lot of cavities, and I have to go to the dentist more often than most.

So, the million-dollar smile is fake?

The million-dollar smile is hollow, actually. At any moment, the teeth could all fall out. It's the sad truth: The million-dollar smile is rotten. So, I'll fucking smile when I want! *Eeeh-eeh-eeh-eeh.*

The notion here was to invent a journalistic fantasy of what it would be like to insert myself into the animated world of the Simpson family so as to write about them as if they, well, existed. The series' creative brain trust of executive producers (Matt Groening, Jim Brooks, and Sam Simon) spent hours with me one day on the Fox lot to imagine—and give voices to—all the fanciful self-consciousness that follows. At the time of this writing, *The Simpsons* had established itself as the most important and successful series ever broadcast on the fresh-born Fox network. Twelve years hence, the same remains basically true.

At Home With
The Simpsons!

Rolling Stone, June 1990

The Simpsons exist! These people are orange. Their eyes are very large. They get by with eight fingers apiece. Their hair is, well, hair, although not in any recognizable sense. They are keen on pork chops. And their private lives have become popular entertainment. The Simpsons do not fully understand this. While they watch television incessantly, they do not know they have a show of their own. They know nothing of their cultural impact or their monumental importance to the Fox Broadcasting Company. They are unaware of the vast merchandise on sale bearing their curious likenesses—air fresheners, for instance—nor are they able to ponder the unsettling implication of this. "We keep hearing that there's some TV show based on us," says Homer Simpson, befuddled patriarch and doughnut enthusiast. "But I called all three networks and they said we weren't on." And further: "I mean, I haven't seen any checks."

As such, the Simpsons live in ignorance. They receive their mail there. And that is where I recently found them. I arrived by bus (Homer's suggestion). He met me at the depot. He could not fathom why *Rolling Stone* would wish to visit with his family. He himself tries to avoid doing so whenever possible. Still, he seemed to welcome the attention. Homer

Simpson is a man, it would turn out, who has spent his entire life being barely noticed. He feels this may be because he has never changed his shirt, but who can truly know for sure? At least there have been doughnuts to fill the void. His, then, is a world of honey-glazed despair.

Ah, Springfield! Now here is one redolent burg! Smell the burning tires! Smell the toxic waste! Everything you need, hemmed into a small parcel of nondescript acreage: mall, prison, dump site, nuclear power plant (where Homer works), Barney's New Bowlerama (where Homer plays). "Would you like to sleep in our house when you're in Springfield?" Homer asks me. "Because there's no room. So I don't know what we're gonna do if you want to sleep in our house."

Homer needs fortification, numbness, beer. We stop off at Moe's Bar. I order scotch. Homer looks stunned. "Let's get this straight," he says. "You want *not* beer?" He insists we quaff the local brew, Duff Beer (slogan: "You can't get enough of that wonderful Duff!"). It is fulsome and acrid, but foams nicely. To be sociable, Moe, the saloonkeep, sidles up and explains how his establishment got its name. "Moe's is *not* named after me," says Moe. "Everybody thinks that. I just thought 'Moe's' was a good name. But I didn't think of it because I'm named Moe." Homer quickly changes the subject, invoking what is clearly a favorite conundrum: dry beer. "How can you drink it if it's dry?" he cries, over and over, a tad giddily. Much laughter ensues, and coughing spasms. Eventually, he tires of this.

"Now that you've had a few," he says finally, with steely resignation in his voice, "we can go home."

Bartholomew J. Simpson, who is ten, whose conception forced his parents into wedlock, who speaks some French and at least one phrase in Spanish (*"Ay, caramba!"*), who has based his life on the teachings of Krusty the Klown, who excels at the game What's That Odor?, who has his mother's fortitude and his father's forehead, is at present (if not usually) imprisoned in his bedroom. At Springfield Elementary School, where he feigns interest daily, Bart is celebrated for his philosophical writings, which he inscribes repeatedly each afternoon on chalkboards at the behest of his superiors. A sampling of his work: "I will not draw naked ladies in class." "I did not see Elvis." "They are laughing at me, not with me." "I will not instigate revolution." "I will not waste chalk." On the day I meet him, he says he has just been detained (unjustly, he feels) to write out the pledge "I will not claim reporters are coming to see us."

The secret origin of "Don't have a cow, man!" (Bart's preferred expletive): "Oh, man!" he says, inimitably perturbed. "Don't have a *fish*. Don't have a *pig*. Don't have a *cow*. What would *you* say?"

From Bart's Rules of Unacceptable Behavior: "Make sure there are plenty of escape routes."

Lisa Simpson is all pearls and conscience, brains and blues. She is eight, a second grader of daunting intellect, a virtuoso on the saxophone. "I'm not precocious," she announces almost stridently. "*Precocious* is the word that adults chauvinistically use to diminish the fact that you're reasonably intelligent!" She is, in this regard, the opposite of her brother. "Oh, Bart," she will soulfully moan, "you're just like Chilly, the elf who cannot love." Or: "It's up to you whether you confess to Mom and Dad, but I just want you to know I'm going to tell them myself in six minutes." It is Lisa who greets us at the Simpson domicile, who regales us with insane, plaintive riffs on her sax. ("Are we wasting our money on lessons?" Homer says during Lisa's performance. "Is it worth all those blisters she gets on her lips?")

It is also Lisa who shows me her mother's novel in progress, a secret writing endeavor unearthed from a drawer of large hair nets, a historical opus based on the lives of Marge Simpson's own mother and grand-mother. It is a book about denial, servitude, and suffering. There are recipes, too. ("Recipes are the quilts for people without thread," Marge states.) The first sentence of her prose work: "She rises in the morning, concealing before her first breath the pain she feels for her children."

The book is titled simply *The Color Orange*.

Marge Simpson's Secret Pork Tenderizing Tip: "The extra ingredient is care."

"It's God's gift," Marge says demurely. "I can't take any credit for it." She speaks of her hair, that magnificent azure alp, a soaring monument to follicle power and genetics. It is the biggest of big hair, engineered with a single bobby pin and silent prayer. It looms. Maintenance time: one hour to shampoo, one half hour to comb out, six hours to dry. (For special occasions, she frequents three salons—Betty's Beehive, the Hair Apparent, and the Beauty Barn—each of which attends to a separate third of her coif. The process requires a full day, plus mileage.)

"Do you have to print that?" she asks me later, meaning her hair-care regimen. "It seems vain. I feel very strange. I'm sorry that I ever said it. I don't want people to think I'm that indulgent. Can you make sure they know that, at least?"

When Homer met Marge, a love story:

Marge: He wanted so much to make an impression on me, he painted this big fence. Then when he found out that it wasn't where I lived, he said the cutest thing. He said, "I'll paint the whole town! Then part of it has to be right!"

Homer: I remember our first kiss. Three guys pinned her arms and I kissed her. Right on the cheek! Hey, I was twelve!

Marge: Will you stop telling that story! He wrote me poems, too. Like this one: "Roses are red, violets are blue, sugar is sweet, and so are you." It's not original, but it *was* in his own handwriting.

Homer: There's a word to describe her; that word is *toasty*. Marge is the *toastiest* woman I know. Whooooopeeeee! Whenever I question whether we're a civilized society and not just beasts, I just think of how all men restrain themselves when they see my Marge!

Maggie Simpson suckles. That's about it. She pacifies famously. Few have seen her infant lips; always her mouth is corked, obscured by contentment. She sees everything, however, and perhaps understands more. "We let our children develop at their own pace," says her mother. "In many ways, she's very advanced."

"You hardly even know she's here," says her father, "unless…*stinky pants*! Let me tell ya, you hope they're burning tires over at the dump when she does that!"

•   •   •

I ask Bart, once he is liberated from confinement, to show me what's in his pockets.

He pulls out three hundred dollars.

In tens and twenties.

"Where did you get this money?!" says his father.

"I'm collecting for underprivileged kids," says Bart. "I only take a thirty percent cut; United Way takes forty. Call me a saint, man!"

Bartspeak—the issues:

On fingers: "I have four on each hand. Four. How many do you have? Is this the kind of great conversation you're looking for? How many toes ya got? How long can we do this? Come on, man! Ooooh, one head! That's interesting."

On education: "You want me to tell you about the damned school system?! Wanna hear something good for your story? Are you tired of the homespun crapola? Wanna get to it? *They hate children!*"

On what he reads: "Lisa's diary. I make notes in the margins. Mostly I read book reports of kids who've been in my grade before. Also, I once read the Boy Scout handbook. But, basically, I don't think anybody should willingly join an organization where there's a big guy with a whistle telling you what to do. Where the plus is that you learn to make knots!"

On women: "I don't like girls. They don't like me. Anybody who says different is gonna find something hot and smelly on their doorstep in the near future."

Bart catches. Homer pitches. They toss the old apple around. They unpeel the old onion. They fire the old aspirin tablet. It happens every evening, in the backyard, like classic Americana. A man and his progeny at play: "There's nothing sweeter," says Homer, winding up, "than being in your yard at the end of a long summer day, throwing the ball around with your own son, and really burning one in there and seeing him shake his mitt a little after you've stung the hell out of his hand! Oooops! Dig it out of the dirt, boy! Heh-heh-heh!"

Later, he expands on father-son philosophy:

"I guess I wish that no matter how old he gets, he always listens to me and does what I say. Even if I've got stuff coming out of my face and I'm bent over double and everything hurts—I just say one thing and he jumps to it! But I'm not going to get that wish. Parents don't get this wish. Your children forget. All those years you spent playing with 'em . . . My big wish is that he never gets into any *serious* trouble with the law. Ultimately, I guess I wish what all parents do—that he doesn't grow up. And who knows? Maybe I've got a shot."

Consider Homer Simpson, a man of thirty-five who looks fifty, a man at whom evolution has laughed, a man with three hairs. Perhaps he eats too much too loudly. Perhaps he is too prone to proneness, a sloth of fabled proportions. Homer understands his place on the sofa. He is comfortable in life. For instance, I ask about his baldness. "There's a saying," he says, " 'A good toupee looks like a good toupee.' And I can't afford one. Plus, for the kids' birthdays I always write their names on my head. You can't do that if you've got hair."

Homer bonds easily. He confides well. He has had private thoughts and remembers many of them. A sampling:

"Here's what women don't understand: Women don't understand how we, as men, need to be alone together for long periods of time. For instance, we left that bar an hour and a half ago, and I don't know about you, but I just want to sit on some dirty bar stool next to another slob. You know what I'm saying. . . ."

"Down at the plant, I'm doing a job. And when I die, somebody else will be doing this job. And when he dies, somebody else will do it. I dunno. Makes you feel great to be a part of something like that."

"Marge was very mad at me once. I'll never forget this. She went crazy. Sometimes you say things in fights you regret later, so you have to be careful. Some things never go away. And this is something I'll never forget: She called me a peckerhead. I still think of it. That's how much it stung. I wonder: Was it just anger or is this what she thinks every time she looks at me?"

An experiment in consumerism at its most crass: Say the Simpsons are given twenty-five dollars each to spend however they like. Say they are loosed upon the bounty that is the Springfield Mall, whose concourses bulge with acquisitive possibility: the Jerky Hut, the Ear Piercery, International House of Answering Machines, and so on. Here is what happens:

Marge takes a facial at Betty's Beehive. "All that squeezing!" she later reports, pleased and relaxed. "I didn't have to do a thing. I dozed off with music playing, and when I woke up there was a glow." ("That's because you realized you'd blown twenty-five bucks!" a rueful Homer says.)

Lisa heads to Ye Olde CD Shoppe, where she purchases cassettes by grizzled bluesmen (Muddy Waters, Howlin' Wolf, Cow Cow Davenport). For Maggie, Marge descends on Sweet 'n' Tinkly, a music box emporium, selecting one that plays the love theme from *An Officer and a Gentleman*. "It's my favorite song," says Marge a tad moonily.

Bart goes to the Carousel o' Violent Toys. He gets a BB gun. Homer: "Bart! You can put somebody's eye out with that thing!"

Bart: "I hope so, for twenty-five dollars!"

Homer buys doughnuts. Seventeen dozen doughnuts. "It's so silly," Marge complains, "to pay all that money for something that's just gone, with no lasting benefit!"

"You're forgetting *belching*," says Homer. "Mmmmmm, deeeelicious!"

Later, the authorities will discover that the window of the bus on which this reporter departed Springfield, U.S.A., was shattered by a small pellet, shot from a low-caliber weapon, possibly an air rifle.

From Bart's Rules: "Commit the following sentences to memory; you'll be surprised at how often they'll come in handy: 'I didn't do it.' 'Nobody saw me do it!' 'They can't prove anything!' "

Homer on the phone, two weeks hence: "I've never had anybody to talk to like this before. Was it just professional or are we friends? Do you play cards?"

AN ANIMATED EXPERIMENT EXPOSED

So we lied.

The Simpsons do not exist! Alas, they are paint. They are graphics. They are made, partly, in Korea. Three men, none of whom is orange, rule all that is Simpson. Foremost is Matt Groening—the cartoonist who created the Simpsons in his own family's image and has since been forgiven for doing so. Besides Groening, there reign James L. Brooks, comedy deity (*Broadcast News, The Mary Tyler Moore Show, Taxi, The Tracey Ullman Show*), and Sam Simon, ace sitcom scribe (*Taxi, Cheers*). These men, as executive producers of *The Simpsons,* conspire on the Twentieth Century Fox lot in Los Angeles, where they tend to an empire built on boorishness and prolific licensing (dolls! bubble gum! snow boots! beach towels! talking toothbrushes!). They are T-shirt magnates who write. Together, and abetted by a crack staff, they give Homer's family life, dyspepsia, dialogue.

Therefore, in order for *Rolling Stone* to interview the Simpsons, these men must convene in a room and speak in animated tongues. They must drink much coffee. They must wrestle with conceit, reality, and caprice. "It's Homer's point of view that nobody ever went wrong trusting a reporter," says Brooks, thus sardonically establishing the ground rules for the session. Having the Simpsons comprehend their TV stardom, it is decided, would ruin them. "I don't think it works to have them come in for a script conference," says Brooks.

"But," says Simon excitedly, "we should have them use language they wouldn't use on TV. Can Homer say *asshole*?" (He can but ultimately doesn't.) All three stress that the Simpsons are not Toons. "Although," says Groening, ruling out no possibility, "they could be in *Roger Rabbit 3!*"

Buckets of swell story ideas for future episodes emerge in the exercise. Among them: "Sexual Harassment at the Nuclear Plant." ("Mr. Burns [Homer's Boss] could enforce a dress code that all female employees wear halter tops!" says Brooks somewhat giddily.) "Bart Goes to Camp." ("Wow," says Brooks, "there's real rebellion opportunity!") "Homer Gets a Gun." ("I don't know," Brooks-Homer says, "it just makes me feel terrific to have my hand wrapped around it." Simon adds, laughing, "He should shoot the burglar!") And "The Repulsive Church Function," which hatches like so:

Groening: Cake auction! Marge bakes!
Simon: And she gets her hair stuck in the cake! Then the mayor buys it!
Brooks: Wow, that's great. Hey, even better—we put a real recipe on the screen. No, wait! A recipe book! We put out a recipe book! Pork chops! Pork chops!

The scent of merchandising can do odd things to a man.

Without Brooks, of course, it is doubtful Simpsonia would have gripped the land. He sponsored the Simpsons' rise by hiring Groening three years ago to contribute his incisive cartoonery to *The Tracey Ullman Show.* (Groening's semiunderground weekly comic strip, *Life in Hell,* featuring profane rabbits and gay twins in fezzes, is pure cult classicism, a decade old and thriving still.) Each week, the Simpsons, in skitlet form, bracketed Ullman's commercial breaks. Spun off last January into a half-hour show all their own, they've become the soul of Fox Broadcasting, dependably notching Top Twenty Nielsen ratings. (The Ullman show, which recently shut down forever, rarely got out of the bottom ten.) Roughly 150 animators—most of them from South Korea (to offset labor costs)—toil over six-month periods to complete single episodes, matching up imagery with the characters' voices, which are recorded beforehand. (Ullman alums Dan Castellaneta and Julie Kavner speak for Homer and Marge; Yeardley Smith is Lisa; Nancy Cartwright is Bart; and Harry Shearer is almost everybody else, although Albert Brooks and Penny Marshall, among others, have turned up in the occasional cameo voice.)

All of which makes Matt Groening, thirty-six, really rich.

He has, nevertheless, clung steadfastly to his wits. "It's pretty funny," he says. "I like it because [the Simpsons] are not glamorous. So much in our culture is designed to make you feel envious. The Simpsons definitely do not." Last year he named his firstborn Homer, but then Groening himself is a son of a Homer. And a Margaret. For sisters, he has a Lisa and a Maggie. There is no real Bart (anagram for *brat,* which rhymes with *Matt*). "Bart reminds a lot of people of their disgusting little brother," Groening says, "I mean, *nobody* I've ever met has ever said 'You know, I'm just like Bart Simpson.' "

Bart Simpson is a sociopath. He will, according to those who know him best, one day be arraigned. His will be a life of either happy crime or government espionage. "Bart is trapped in a world where everybody else is struggling to be normal," says Groening. "Bart's response to being normal is 'No way, man!' He is irreverent; he never learns his lesson and is never repentant. He is an outgrowth of those times when, as a boy, I was unfairly made to sit for hours in the principal's office, vowing to get revenge later in life for my punishment.

"The best part of all this," Groening says, "is seeing Bart Simpson graffiti on freeway underpasses. The worst part is seeing Bart Simpson graffiti on the side of my house. Somebody wrote HOME OF BART, which is a little unnerving. So I guess what I'm saying is, the best part is graffiti on *other people's* property."

And there is the sheer pleasure of being banned. Bart has lately been expelled from grade schools across the map—in the form of T-shirts. The prime contraband has been garments bearing the wily youth's countenance and the legend UNDERACHIEVER. AND PROUD OF IT, MAN!

Educators, it seems, frown upon such candor. In a prepared statement (read by Groening), Bart Simpson will only say "I have no comment, other than my folks taught me to respect elementary-school principals, even the ones who have nothing better to do than tell kids what to wear." He then asks, "Is it possible that grade-school principals have lost their sense of humor?"

"When people get mad about Bart," Groening says, mustering the correct perspective, "my response is, no one should take advice from any cartoon character—with the obvious exception of McGruff the Crime Dog."

Part Four:

FOR **SHOW**

Liberace * Madonna * Barry Manilow
David Copperfield

During the mid-eighties, Tina Brown appointed me *Vanity Fair's* Chicago Correspondent—a position that has not existed since we parted company. Frankly, there wasn't a lot of fabulousness—the magazine's then-sudden specialty—to write about in my sturdy no-nonsense hometown. Most often I was dispatched to write the magazine's last-page monthly feature, Out to Lunch, which detailed the patter dispersed while a celebrity ate lunch. Among those with whom I consumed lunch in Chicago were Christie Hefner, Siskel & Ebert, prima ballerina Maria Tallchief, and Pia Zadora (she was visiting). But during a stretch when I was working briefly out of the New York office, I convinced Tina to let me take Liberace to lunch. It was a long lunch, a fine lunch, and an expensive lunch, and he was exactly as one would have wanted him to be—a very irrepressible customer. And then he was dead of AIDS within two years. I had a lot of funny unused material left over from that afternoon in New York. So I composed this deeply loving homage-parody, laden with classically presumptuous showbiz platitudes, which *Spy* magazine gladly published.

Liberace, Requiescat in Pace:
Lee, We Hardly Knew Ye

Spy, April 1987

I remember Lee as he himself—were he able to remember anything now, God rest his soul—would have wanted to be remembered. Of this I am certain. Why, it was just two years ago when we huddled together in our booth at the Russian Tea Room, laughing and gossiping and slurping borscht, for what seemed like three and a half hours. Not that anyone was counting. When you were around Lee, time stood still. He was that way. "This is *faaabulous*," said Lee that day, as he probably said every day, in that very warm and special whine of his. But that's the kind of man he was. By *man,* of course, I mean *giant,* although I am sure he could wear a 40 Regular with negligible alterations. But I digress....

Lee, we hardly know ye. Though you're gone, I'll be seeing you in all the old familiar places that this heart of mine embraces all day through. Mostly, however, I'll be seeing you in the first scarlet banquette beyond the bar, nestled beneath—and looking very much like—the brass samovar and the tinsel garland and the flowers. And I say this with all due respect, because I know that it is exactly the way you would take it. That day was pure Lee, and by Lee, of course, I mean Mr. Showmanship, the grandfather of glitter, the sultan of schmaltz, Wisconsin's favorite son,

Wladziu Valentino Liberace. In that moment, the Russian Tea Room was abuzz, his name on everyone's lips. But then New York was his Easter egg that month, as he prepared for his second record-breaking Radio City concert series.

The Lee I knew looked as natty as a boulevardier, in a vanilla double-breasted sport coat with turquoise slacks, tie, and handkerchief. He had brought with him—because a man of this stature cannot just go out *alone,* you understand—a publicity yenta who kept talking about "killa Bloody Marys" and a sturdy, bronzed, and bejeweled young man with highlighted hair named Cary-James. Onstage, Cary occasionally played Lee's "chauffeur," the one who peeled off Lee's fabulous furs and, feigning a hernia, lugged them into the wings.

I remember once asking Lee—it was that very day, in fact—to name his favorite fur. Lee winked at me, as he was wont to do, and mewed, "*The newest one!* Always the newest one!" Oh, how we laughed. We also spoke of his rings and how he had to glue them to his fingers before performances. He did this to prevent fans from pulling the rings off when they shook his hand. "You'd be surprised how often they try," Lee told me, adding, "Even if they grabbed one and ran like hell, they'd never get out the door." Cary said, "But people think they *can* really get away with it, to have a piece of you." It was the publicity hen who then, I think, put it best: "One thing about, you, Lee, is that fans are not content to just see you across the room—they want to *touch* you." We all quietly contemplated that for a moment.

What an appetite for life that man had. But for now, let's limit it to food. "I'm eatin' bread like it's goin' out of style," he mused that afternoon. I will always remember the way he ate bread, and this is something I've never told anyone. So meticulous was he that after buttering his pumpernickel, he would take the greasy knife and use it to pick up every crumb from the tablecloth. He would then slather the crumbs back onto his bread and gobble it down, repeating the process throughout the meal. I remember thinking, *Here is a man who savors—who luxuriates, if you will.*

I can still hear him ordering his lunch: "Would hot borscht be considered an appetizer?" he asked one of the waiters, who nodded and suggested sour cream on the side. "I like it in the *middle*," Lee proclaimed. "Then, for an entrée, what am I gonna have? Oh! I *love* chicken Kiev. The butter oozes out?" he inquired. The waiter assured him that it was so. "All right, I'll have that! And how 'bout a little ratatouille too? Gee, I sound like a horn." Such was his playfulness with language.

And wasn't that exactly like Lee? I think it was. A restaurateur in his own right (his pasta palace, Tivoli Gardens, adjacent to his personal museum, is Las Vegas personified, if not more so), Lee was a man who knew his way around a griddle. "I'm an experimenter," he said to me in a sweet revelatory moment. "I take a basic recipe and I add to it." That could have been his philosophy of show business, but alas, we were still talking culinary commerce. Recipes for Liberace Lasagne and Liberace Sticky Buns were included in his book *The Wonderful Private World of Liberace,* and I don't mind telling you that both are *delish,* as Lee so often put it. As he himself wrote: "You should serve my sticky buns while they are still warm. . . . Believe me, there'll be none left over." How right he was.

It is no wonder that people were drawn to him, as if he were a shaman. And never were they rebuffed, even when they may have deserved it. There was the furtive approach of Joe Raposo, one of the legends of the business, who wrote songs for *Sesame Street.* "Oh yes, all that good stuff," said Lee, perhaps a little too patronizingly, or so I thought. "Mr. Liberace, you're the sweetest man in the world," Raposo said. "We have many friends in common, and they always speak of you with such love." "Aw," said Lee, which was typical of him, "that's nice."

Later, the incomparable Miss Eartha Kitt, in an orange turban, slithered over from another booth, and much hugging ensued. "This gentleman and I used to walk up and down Fifth Avenue at five o'clock in the morning," she purred, incomparably. "He pointed out the jewelry in the windows of Tiffany's and Cartier's and *never bought me a thing*!"

"Never!" echoed Lee. "But we were great lookers, weren't we? So how've you been? Whatcha doin', whatcha doin'? Tell me."

"Getting ready to go to Europe," she replied. "Where are all your jewels today?"

"I put 'em in the vault."

"I'm still waiting for you to buy me one of those things," Miss Kitt persisted, pointing to the lone opal ring he wore that day.

"I know," said Lee, sighing. "Cheapo, cheapo."

It should be noted that Lee's New York was really not all that different from your New York or my New York. He may have been holed up that month in a Trump Tower apartment, but Donald Trump was paying. He may have been enjoying an expensive lunch at the Russian Tea Room, but I was paying. No, Lee's pleasures were the simpler things—and isn't that so telling? "There are so many sights in New York that you could only see here," he would say profoundly. He rhapsodized over visiting the kitchen of Balducci's. "Everything I admired, I would end up with a carton of," he marveled. Of some hookers he'd seen soliciting outdoors, he crowed delightedly: "They wear *nothing*!" And so enamored was he of the Pathmark supermarket near Chinatown that he boasted of filling three shopping carts whenever he stopped in.

"You know, I found the cutest thing at Pathmark," he practically squealed at one point. "It's a rabbit holding a carrot, and when you squeeze the carrot, it plays 'Easter Parade.' *Soooo* cute. They're only eight ninety-nine, but they look like FAO Schwarz. I mean, they're *faaabulous.* I want to buy one for everybody, but they're completely out of stock. I told 'em to reorder." (I would later learn that he called such bestowals "happy-happys.")

The child in Lee, as you can see, was irrepressible. When I mentioned his turn as guest villain on the old *Batman* TV series, he grew euphoric. "Oh God, I loved that," he said. "I played a dual role, you know. Two brothers: One was the pianist Chandell, whom I did as an exaggerated Liberace, if that's possible. *Very* exaggerated. The twin was a gangster, so I played him as Edward G. Robinson. I'd be puffin' on cigars and using a gravelly voice." He growled a little here.

I would be remiss not to recall Lee's views on professional wrestling. By coincidence, that very week he was to climb into the ring at Madison Square Garden to dance with the Rockettes in *Wrestlemania*. The prospect made him giddy. Lee told me, "Forget Carnegie Hall, forget Radio City, forget the Royal Command Performance—if my mother were alive today, she would say, *'Son, you finally made it!'* She was such a wrestling fan, I can't tell you. This sweet lady who was so proper and so elegant and never said a nasty word in public would sit there in front of the TV and scream, *'Kill the bastard, the dirty son of a bitch!'* I'd say, '*Mom!* I've never heard those words come out of your mouth!' She'd grit her teeth and scratch at the upholstery and swear some more. I'd say, 'C'mon, Mom, it's all *fake*!' She'd holler, 'Don't you say that! Look at that blood—it's *real*!' Oh, if she could be here today."

None of this is meant to suggest that Lee and I didn't share serious times in the hours we knew each other. I remember how unsettled he looked when I asked whether he had ever been burned by wax drippings from his candelabra. "I was forced to go electric" was all he said, and I respected him for it. On the subject of overexposure, he became self-conscious and slightly abrupt. "In the late fifties, I was on TV ten times a week," he said gravely. "I got the hell out of the country and went to London and my career was like brand-new again. There is such a thing as staying too long at the fair, you know?"

For some reason—and I will forever be grateful for this—I got around to asking him about the afterlife. "Actually, I'm sort of in reverse," he confided. "I feel like I've lived before. Sometimes when I put on a period costume I seem to know just how to manipulate it, how to put it on. I favor those past eras, which some of my homes reflect. Like the Napoleonic time and the Victorian time. I love imagining I lived in those days." He added portentously, "The future is something that is less understandable."

What happened minutes later will remain perhaps my most haunting memory of Lee. Another aide arrived, bearing dozens of cards for him to sign that would be sent with flowers to friends. Lee wearily drew a long breath and began to write LIBERACE LOVE on every card. "I do have a life of my own," he softly grumped. "Nobody seems to know it but me. You know, it's in my contract that I'm allowed to go to the bathroom. I'm gonna get some of those Depends, so that when I have to go to the bathroom, I can sit still and let my shorts turn to jelly."

Then he laughed fabulously, and wondered aloud, "Say, who's payin' for all these flowers, anyway?" But that was Lee all over.

Madonna wore the best perfume of any celebrity I have ever encountered. If she ever told me its name, I have forgotten. It was because I was so aware of her smell that I asked her a very peculiar question about Prince, with whom she had recorded a song for her newest album, *Like a Prayer*. Also, because she smelled so good, I was especially embarrassed that the rental car in which I drove her home smelled so unbelievably gamy. It was a time—shortly after her marriage to Sean Penn unraveled—when the tabloid press stalked her unmercifully, which lent a special urgency to the tenor of the piece.

On the Lam
With Madonna

Excerpted from the *Rolling Stone* Interview, March 1989

"Do you see a black Jaguar?"

The voice, small and insistent, issues from the passenger seat, where the world's most famous woman burrows deep into the upholstery. She slumps and scrunches, lying decidedly low. Her rump is poised perilously above the floor mat. Her boots are propped against the dashboard. Her tresses are piled beneath a leather cap, and tiny dark specs pinch at her nose. Occasionally, her head bobs up, and she peers through the windshield in order to give navigational tips. Then, just as quickly, she ducks back into hiding. Madonna is on the lam. She is incognito. She is in my car. I am driving her home. It was her idea.

"The paparazzi won't recognize your car," she says, hatching her intrepid scheme after our first interview session. For her part, Madonna recognizes her most dogged pursuers. She knows what they drive. Every TV in her house is wired to the security system and transmits a continuous picture of the front gate and the street beyond. She sees those who park and lurk and obsess. She watches and remembers their movements. All of which might explain why she is cowering in my rented Chevy Corsica, fretting about a particular black Jaguar that is nowhere to be seen. "At this point," she says, sighing wearily, "I know them all."

Madonna has a new home—a sanctuary, really—nestled high in the Hollywood Hills. As it happens, an aerial photograph of the spread, snapped from a helicopter, was published in this morning's paper. The accompanying text: "The soon-to-be divorced Mrs. Sean Penn took title to the house Jan. 18. She paid $2,950,000." She had not yet seen the item when I showed it to her a few hours earlier. "They say how much I paid for it?" she asked, sounding surprised and violated. "'The house has seven bedrooms and six bathrooms'? *They are so misinformed!*" (Indeed, the next morning the same column reads, "A friend of Madonna's called to say we were incorrect to report... seven bedrooms. 'It has three bedrooms plus a maid's room,' said the caller.")

The point being, she is hounded. Her woes dangle like shredded pulp from the jaws of gossip carnivores. Among supermarket-literature queens, she is the ultimate checkout girl. Her reign currently rages, due to the noisy unraveling of her three-and-a-half-year marriage to actor-pugilist Sean Penn. Divorce papers were filed by her attorneys on January 5— thirteen months since the last time it happened (when she just as hastily rescinded the action). As before, "irreconcilable differences" were cited. But this recent connubial rupture was reportedly prompted by a mysterious postholiday altercation about which nothing is known for sure. Speculation abounds, however, and gallons of tabloid ink have been expended to document it. Why conserve now?

Rumors surrounding Madonna's "night of terror" (December 28, 1988): A drunken Sean explodes at Madonna in their Malibu estate because (a) having a baby in the near future does not jibe with her plans; (b) he is annoyed at her friendships with Warren Beatty and/or Sandra Bernhard. Sean demonstrates his displeasure by (a) roughing her up; (b) threatening to thrust her head into an oven; (c) hog-tying her with leather straps (and/or twine) to a chair and leaving her "trussed up like a turkey" (tabloid description) for nine hours. She persuades him to release her and/or escapes to the Malibu sheriff's office, where she swears out an assault complaint against her husband. (The complaint, which was actually filed, is withdrawn by her days later.) She then seeks refuge in the home of (a) photographer friend Herb Ritts; (b) her manager, Freddy DeMann. Meanwhile, Malibu police descend upon the Penn house and order Sean to come outside with his hands up. He does so but later denies abusing Madonna, claiming she trumped up the charges because she is jealous that he has been dating a stripper.

The veracity of any of the above is questionable. Maybe even superfluous. Throughout the ordeal, Madonna remained mum; by dropping charges, she implied that her marriage had been more than adequately scrutinized, that an ensuing trial would be a macabre circus. What is curious, however, is that she has chosen instead to bare her soul musically on the matter. On her forthcoming album, *Like a Prayer,* there is a jarringly urgent song titled "Till Death Do Us Part" that chronicles a violent and harrowing marriage: "He takes a drink, she goes inside / He starts to scream, the vases fly. . . . I wish that it would change, but it won't if you don't," she sings, her voice soulful and plaintive. The performance is arguably her finest artistic moment, and that in itself is a sadly ironic notion.

Similarly, *Like a Prayer* as a whole represents the maturation of Madonna Louise Veronica Ciccone. The ethereal title song itself seems to portend a personal spiritual purge. It is the debut of the philosophical Madonna, who, at thirty, seems to be making a public-policy changeover: Getting It On has been stoically supplanted by Getting On With It.

She arrives at the designated Hamburger Hamlet, alone and serene, and at once comports herself with cheerful confidence. Scruffily dressed in tattered chic, she slides into a back booth and pertly flags down a waitress. ("Yoo-hoo! Could we get some coffee?") She is discovered only once, by an archetypal young Hollywood hustler who presses into her hand a film script he hopes to direct. She endures his protracted schmoozy pitch with bemused graces. "Being rude doesn't get you anywhere," she tells me after the interloper says "Ciao" and disappears. "You end it quicker by being nice."

For the second session, I am summoned to the new hilltop hacienda— a white, stark, airy affair, replete with marble floors and important art. Among her collected *objets* is a painting by her idol Frida Kahlo, whose own marriage to Mexican muralist Diego Rivera was notoriously stormy. Also on display are a few framed photographs of Rivera's mistresses. Accordingly, when Madonna steps out of her bedroom, she has traded guises. Hair down, heels spiked, she radiates retro-glamour—a gossamer goddess in billowy black loungewear with matching brassiere showing through the gauzy décolleté. Even her bearing this time seems a tad regal as she flounces onto an overstuffed ocher satin divan and accepts inquiries. "Please," she wryly instructs a few chattering associates in the next room, "don't anyone bother me. I am being interviewed!" Throughout both conversations, however, she good-naturedly plumbs her feelings and, even in the matter of Sean, manages to comport herself with jaunty charm. Still, as an icebreaker, I brandish an early copy of the *Playboy* issue containing LaToya Jackson's nude pictures, thinking Madonna might enjoy the momentary reprieve of basking in another woman's scandal. And, of course, she does.

Have you seen LaToya? Perhaps you could share any spontaneous observations.

[*She lunges for the magazine.*] Give me that! No shit! [*She pores over the pages, amused.*] She had a tit job, for sure! This isn't bad. They're funny. But you see only tits? Major tit job! Well, LaToya, *this* is a *shocker.* Oooh! The Jackson family must be outraged. This is desperation. Well, maybe she'll get a job out of it.

Jumping from one kind of exposure to another, I suppose there's no tactful way to ask you about the dissolution of your marriage.

[*She smiles coyly.*] Inquiring minds want to know? Now you're gonna get all nosy, huh? Well, this is something incredibly close to me right now, and very painful. I have a difficult time talking about it. You can ask, but I can refuse to answer you.

Fair enough. You've said in the past, "I'd rather walk through fire than walk away from one." Are you attracted to flame?

Am I attracted to pain? Is that what you're trying to say? I'm attracted to obstacles I need to overcome. I'm interested in facing challenges, things that are going to be harder rather than easier.

The song "Till Death Do Us Part" on your album portrays a tormented, volatile, and dangerous marriage. The implication is autobiographical. How honest are the lyrics?

Like most of the songs on my album, it's very much drawn from my life, factually speaking, but it's fictionalized, too. "Till Death Do Us Part" is about the destructive relationship that is powerful and painful. In this song, however, it's a cycle that you can't get out of until you die. It's futile. I wanted the song to be very shocking, and I think it was. It's about a dysfunctional relationship, a sadomasochistic relationship that can't end. Now that's where the truth stops, because I would never want to continue a terrible relationship forever and ever and ever until I die.

Has Sean heard the song?

Yes. And he loves it, strangely enough. [*laughs*] But Sean is very, very keen on being brutally frank in his work. He's attracted to writers and artists who don't mince words.

Do you ever think you married too young?

No.

Do you think the odds were stacked against this marriage from the start? It seemed people defied it to succeed.

Oh, yes. I felt that no one wanted us to be together. They celebrated our union, and then they wanted us to be apart. There were rumors about us getting a divorce a week after the wedding. We fought that. And, yes, that is difficult. I don't know if anyone can do it [under these circumstances]. You have to be really, really strong and immune. Very sure of yourself.

In terms of your chemistry, you are two strong-willed individuals, volatile in your own ways.

Both passionate people. *Way* over the top. [*laughs*]

Did your marriage thrive on the friction?

Yes. I have an incredible fascination and attraction to it. Like I said about walking into the fire. Well, he's fire, that's for sure.

You almost seem like an old-fashioned girl in your enthusiasm for marriage.

I'm a *very* old-fashioned girl. Marriage is a great thing when it's right. And I did celebrate it and embrace it, and I wanted the whole world to know that this is the man I loved more than anything. But there's a price to pay for that, which is something that I now realize. Ever since I was in high school, when I was madly in love with someone, I was so proud of this person, I wanted the world to know that I loved him. But once you reveal it to the world—and you're in the public eye—you give it up, and it's not your own anymore. I began to realize how important it is to hold on to privacy and keep things to yourself as much as possible. It's like a runaway train afterward. So if you ask, Did I complicate things by being very public about [my feelings]? Yes, I did.

Are you a woman who loves too much?

No. I don't think you can ever love enough.

Your public persona is characterized by flirtatiousness, and Sean appeared to be a traditional guy, jealous of his woman's sharing herself so openly.

But I'm not immune to jealousy? We're both jealous.

Are you a challenge to live with?

Definitely! Do you think it could be any other way? Yes, I'm pretty headstrong. And stubbornness comes with that, a certain amount of inflexibility. In going after what I want, other things tend to fall by the wayside, things you should maybe pay more attention to. Most passionate people are headstrong. [We were] two fires rubbing up against each other. It's exciting and difficult.

How accurate are the tabloid tales of your night of terror—the nine hours in bondage?

Extremely inaccurate, as they usually are. They made it all up. But I expect it. They're always making shit up. I've completely reconciled myself to that fact.

So there wasn't one single breaking point?

It's been a slow breaking point all the way. I can't say there's anything specific that happened.

You've maintained in your music that dreams come true. What are your dreams like?

Most of my dreams are really violent. But then, obviously, my life is pretty crazy. I'm always in the public eye. People are always sort of chasing after me and imposing on my privacy, my area, my space. So I have those kinds of dreams, where people are chasing me or I'm naked—you know, exposed. Also, I dream of children a lot. Specifically, I see different people in my life as children. That may be because, in a way, I feel I take care of a lot of people. But, yes, dreams are an important part of my life.

You're an insomniac on top of it, right? What's your secret to falling asleep? Do you count sheep?

No, you know what I do? I remember the past when I can't go to sleep. I think of a very specific moment in my life, like when I was nine years old and I was the fourth-grade hall monitor, and everyone in class was all lined up to go to the bathroom. I remember every detail—what people were wearing, what I felt like, what I was wearing, the smell of the school. It works my mind and tires me out. Then I find myself drifting into sleep. Although I spend many a night not going to sleep at all.

Does the preponderance of Madonna clones blaring from the radio bother you? Who comes closest to the real thing?

When it first started happening, I kind of got pissed off. You know, if you create a sound, then you want to have dibs on it. But then I felt flattered. But it *is* confusing sometimes, because I'll hear a song on the radio and for a second I'll think it's me. It's uncanny sometimes. There's one girl in particular, a girl named Alisha, who's had a couple of songs that ripped off the chord progression of some of my songs. And her *voice* sounds so much like mine when I sing in a higher register. I was shocked! She's definitely one who stunned me. I think a lot of the imitators are black.

Do you ever feel black?

Oh, yes, all the time. That's a silly thing to say, though, isn't it? When I was a little girl, I wished I was black. All my girlfriends were black. I was living in Pontiac, Michigan, and I was definitely the minority in the neighborhood. White people were scarce there. All of my friends were black, and all the music I listened to was black. I was incredibly jealous of all my black girlfriends because they could have braids in their hair that stuck up everywhere. So I would go through this incredible ordeal of putting wire in my hair and braiding it so that I could make *my* hair stick up. I used to make cornrows and everything. But if being black is synonymous with having soul, then, yes, I feel that I am.

Whose voices blow you away?

Ella Fitzgerald has an incredible voice. She's the greatest. Joni Mitchell. Patsy Cline. Chaka Khan—I *love* her voice! I love all the old soul singers—Marvin Gaye, Frankie Lymon, Sam Cooke. I like really smooth voices like Belafonte and Mathis. My father had all their records. Then there are the gravelly voices—Joe Cocker. Tom Waits. And Prince— Prince has an incredible voice.

You wrote and recorded "Love Song" with Prince on your album. What surprises you about him? For instance, what does he smell like?

He does smell good! I'm really aware of people's smells. I love fragrances and perfumes. Ever since I've known Prince, I've attached a smell to him, which is lavender, and I don't know why. He reeks of it. And I'm sure he would probably disagree with me. He's very private, you know, and very shy. He's great when you get to know him. Charming and funny, in his own way. More than anything, he really comes alive when he's working.

You dedicated the album to your mother, who taught you to pray. When do you pray?

Constantly. I pray when I'm in trouble or when I'm happy. When I feel any sort of extreme. I pray when I feel so great that I'll think I need to check in with myself and recognize how good life is. I know that sounds silly. But when it seems there's so much bullshit around, it's important to just remind myself of the things I have to be grateful for. On the other hand, when I'm feeling really bad or sad, I pray to try to reassure myself. It's all kind of a rationalization. I can't describe the way I pray. It has nothing to do with religion.

You've forsaken your Catholicism?

Once you're a Catholic, you're always a Catholic—in terms of your feelings of guilt and remorse and whether you've sinned or not. Sometimes I'm racked with guilt when I needn't be, and that, to me, is left over from my Catholic upbringing. Because in Catholicism you are born a sinner and you are a sinner all of your life. No matter how you try to get away from it, the sin is within you all the time.

Would you raise a child a Catholic?

No, I don't think so. That's a tough question. I don't know what sort of information I would pass on to them in terms of God. Catholicism is not a soothing religion. It's a painful religion. We're all gluttons for punishment.

Do you ever think you missed your era in this town? I can imagine you running Hollywood as the Bombshell Queen of the forties and fifties.

How do you know I'm not running it right now? [*laughs richly*] But, yes, I do in a way feel it would have been great in those days. Hollywood was so different then. The studio system really nurtured and cared for you in a way it doesn't now. On the other hand, your life was not your own. Now you have more individual freedom, but you don't have anyone looking out for your career the way they did then.

The studios used to arrange dates between its stars. Who would you have wanted on your arm?

Oh, Jimmy Stewart! I love him so much. I would die to meet him! I can think of two incredibly favorite moments in his films that just melt me. In *It's a Wonderful Life,* there's that scene where he's standing with Donna Reed, who's talking on the phone, and he's telling her that he doesn't love her as he's kissing her, and he's crying. Clearly, he loves her so much. [*She swoons.*] *Ohhh!* And then the other moment is in *Rear Window* when he gives Grace Kelly this look. She's spending the night with him, and he turns and rests his chin on the back of a chair and looks at her so lovingly. I can't describe it, but that is the way I want someone to look at me when he loves me. It's the most pure look of love and adoration. Like surrender. It's devastating.

How do you think old-line Hollywood sees you?

I don't really think they understand me well enough to think of me in any way. A lot of them see me as a singer.

Do you consider yourself a movie star?

Yes, if I could be so immodest as to say so.

Do you want to become a mogul someday?

[*laughs*] I would rather own an art gallery than a movie studio. Or a museum. I would rather be Peggy Guggenheim than Harry Cohn.

But you do have a production company set up to find movies for yourself.

Yes, Siren Films. You know what a siren is, don't you? A woman who draws men to their death.

Is that how you see yourself?

Oh, I suppose I've had my moments of sirendom. [*laughs*]

•   •   •

Last year you took nine months to do the David Mamet play Speed-the-Plow *on Broadway. Yet, if we're to believe your crack on the David Letterman show last July, you hated the experience.*

Oh, but I loved it, too. I hated to love it, and I loved to hate it. It was just grueling, having to do the same thing every night, playing a character who is so unlike me. I didn't have a glamorous or flamboyant part; I was the scapegoat. That's one of the things that attracted me to it. Still, night after night, that character failed in the context of the play. [Madonna essayed the role of a manipulative, possibly altruistic, and ultimately beaten Hollywood secretary on the make.] To continue to fail each night and to walk off the stage crying, with my heart wrenched . . . it just got to me after a while. I was becoming as miserable as the character I played. So when I did the David Letterman show, it was very much toward the end of the run, and I really was marking off the days on the calendar!

Your character withstood epic verbal abuse from the Ron Silver and Joe Mantegna characters. Had you been playing yourself, wouldn't you have just punched their lights out?

Absolutely, I would have. So many times I wanted to smack Ron Silver. I wouldn't have taken their shit after two minutes in the office. I wouldn't have had a job, if it was me up there.

How're you getting along with your father these days? Do you understand each other?

Yes, we get along very well right now. I mean, it's been up and down. You know, my father is not an incredibly verbal man, and that's my frustration. He doesn't really express himself. And more than anything, I want my father's approval, whether I want to admit it or not. But he's always been very affectionate with me. I have a million different feelings about my father, but mostly I love him to death. What's difficult for my father is the idea that I don't need him. But I need him.

Has he been able to comfort you lately?

Yes, absolutely. I can confide in my father. It wasn't that I couldn't before, but I didn't want to. For years, I resented him. You see, when my mother died, I attached myself to my father. He was my only parent. So I felt in many ways that my stepmother stole him from me. I felt deserted. All my life I harbored that resentment. For five years after I left home, in fact, I barely spoke to him. But we've made our way back into each other's lives. Whenever I need him, he's there for me.

Do you think about death much?

Yes, but in spurts. Sometimes I just assume I'm going to live forever. I don't want to die. It's the ultimate unknown. I don't want to go to the dark beyond. I want to stay where I know where everything is.

Had she not died, what kind of role do you think your mother would have in your life right now?

If she were alive, I would be someone else. I would be a completely different person. I have to be careful sometimes. When someone dies and the years go by, you tend to make them into something they're not.

What kind of mother do you think you'll be?

Very affectionate, but probably domineering—maybe too domineering. And I'll have to acquire patience, but I think when you go through the nine months of pregnancy, you learn to be patient. I would love to have a child. But you've got to have a family first . . . can't do it by yourself. But it's definitely up high on the list of things to do.

Maybe you noticed this already, but a number of songs on the new album have sort of anti-male themes.

[*surprised*] Well, gee, I never thought of that. The album definitely does have a very strong feminine point of view. Hmmm. I've had some painful experiences with men in my life, just as I've had some incredible experiences. Maybe I'm representing more of the former than the latter. I certainly don't hate men. No, no, no! Couldn't live without them!

Are you a good women's friend?

Yes. I used to think I had more men friends than women friends, but over the last few years—especially since I got married—I've nurtured a lot more female relationships. My mother's death was the catalyst in this, because I didn't have any strong female role models as I was growing up. I was the oldest girl and kind of took care of everyone. So I thought I really didn't need women. I didn't really look for it and had no women that I confided in. I saw the world as a man's world for a long time. I discovered that it isn't, though.

Your Letterman appearance with your friend Sandra Bernhard was history-making television. I understand it was your idea that you two dress identically that night.

To dress alike? Definitely. Whenever we would meet up for dinner or whatever, we were constantly showing up in the same or very similar clothes. So then, when we decided that I'd go on the show with her, I just thought we should follow through with that. In retrospect, it was a little mysterious to me why that was so interesting to everyone. We were just having fun, which is what I always do with Sandra. She's a gas. I felt totally comfortable out there.

You stirred some controversy that night by suggesting you two hang out at a New York lesbian club called the Cubbyhole.

Well, yes, we threw that out there to confuse people. It was definitely an inside joke for people in New York. I mean, I've never been to the Cubbyhole. I just think it's hysterical.

At the moment, you're a brunette. How different does brown feel from blond?

I can't dwell on it too long because I have to dye my hair blond again for *Dick Tracy.* Being blond is definitely a different state of mind. I can't really put my finger on it, but the artifice of being blond has some incredible sort of sexual connotation. Men really respond to it. I love blond hair, but it really does something different to you. I feel more grounded when I have dark hair, and I feel more ethereal when I have light hair. It's unexplainable. I also feel more Italian when my hair is dark.

Speaking of your look, you were recently named to Mr. Blackwell's annual worst-dressed list. Is there any list on which you'd like to name him?

I'd put him on my list of men I'm least affected by. [*She grins mischievously.*] I think I always make the worst-dressed list. It's just silly. But it is kind of nice having something you can count on.

If you could change anything about the way you look, what would it be?

I always wanted to be taller. I have a little-person complex. People who are smaller are always trying to be bigger, I guess.

You seem mighty big.

Well, that's good, because I've been working on being big for so long. [*laughs*]

What of life can you see from behind tinted glass?

It looks even more inviting. If I'm in the hotel and I know there are paparazzi downstairs, I find myself looking out the window wistfully. Last summer, during the play, I would look out my window in the theater and see tons of people outside waiting for me every night. And I would find myself enviously watching some anonymous woman down the street, just slowly window-shopping and taking her time, with nobody bothering her. I envied her.

What becomes a legend most?

[*puzzled*] You mean like the fur you're wearing? Is that the question? I don't know. I think that's one of the great mysteries.

Do you make your own bed?

Yes, I do. The maid comes three days a week, so on the days she doesn't come, I make my bed. I've even been known to wash my own clothes.

Well, that ought to be worthy of legendary behavior. Confess your worst fault.

Impatience. I just can't stand waiting. I always want everything right away. Nothing comes as fast as I want it.

Over the years, you've jokingly called yourself a bitch. Do you think you're a bitch?

Oh, I can be. Deep down inside, I'm a really nice girl. But, certainly, I can be a bitch. I'm a perfectionist, and I'm under lots of pressure. Sometimes you have to be a bitch to get things done.

This is one of my favorite profiles—one that I felt needed to be written, one that nobody else had ever dared to attempt. I had long been fascinated with how most people I knew (and most people alive, for that matter) reflexively scoffed at any mention of Barry Manilow; uniformly, they were reticent to admit that they had ever liked even one of his songs. I wondered: *How, then, can he have sold so many millions and millions of records?* Clearly, his work inspired some magnificent secret shame, thus an epic-size closet fandom. He was either the ultimate Mocked Icon or else the guiltiest pleasure in music history. And so I also had to wonder: *What could it be like to be him? Rolling Stone* had rigorously and gleefully ignored his career. But, fortunately, music editor David Wild—who, like myself, could admit that the man had much talent and greatness—told me to go for it, with Jann Wenner's blessing.

I spent several months dipping in and out of Manilowland, wherein the stoic maestro's wisdom and humor amazed me. Jann exuberantly praised the resulting piece, which then went unpublished for eleven frustrating months. (Publishing this, much like saying Barry Manilow is a great entertainer, apparently required no small courage. A few years later, I would nevertheless proudly write liner notes for the Manilow compact disc boxed set.) There was one particularly poignant postscript to this profile: I learned that after Billy Joel read the piece—which briefly recounts a long-held misunderstanding between the two musicians— he called Manilow to apologize. That made me feel like the Henry Kissinger of pop music.

Barry Manilow:
The King of Pain

Rolling Stone, November 1990

When your name is a punch line, you live in Hell. Barry Manilow lives in Hell. There are worse hells than his. He gets to park wherever he wants, for instance. Also, he can shop recklessly and overtip in restaurants without concern. Perdition, however, must have more dire consequences. And, as such, being Barry Manilow is no frolicsome lot. Rather, it can be an existential nightmare. Example: Sincerity is commerce. Only he never knows when to trust it. He suspects compliments. He sifts them for snide subtext. Conditioning has taught him this. Bob Dylan stopped him at a party, embraced him warmly, told him: "Don't stop doing what you're doing, man. We're all inspired by you." This actually occurred. He knew not what to make of the encounter. One year hence, it haunts him still.

"Who knows?" he says, shrugging the shrug of one who has shrugged much. "It seems so odd that Bob Dylan would tell me this. I wasn't exactly sure what he meant. He may have been laughing out of the other side of his mouth while he said it, but it didn't *seem* like it. I mean, he looked me dead in the eye. But maybe he says that to everybody who walks by. He may have had one drink too many. You know, people give me jabs all the time—but not to my face. . . . I sort of left the party for a minute because I wasn't sure. I thought, *Well, maybe,* maybe. . . ."

When Barry Manilow tells a Barry Manilow joke, he usually tells this one: Record mogul announces to Ethiopian embassy that a collective of music stars is making a single to benefit the blighted country's starving masses. "Think of it!" mogul says. "Michael Jackson, Bruce Springsteen, Billy Joel, Barry Manilow—" Ethiopians cut him off. *"Barry Manilow?"* they say. "Hey, we're not *that* hungry!"

"It's my favorite joke," he says a tad giddily. "But every time I tell it, people go, 'Aw, I'm sorry.' It makes me look kind of pathetic, I guess."

Japes, like barnacles, cling to his career, impervious vessel that it is. He epitomizes grace under mockery. "I feel bad for Dan Quayle, let me tell you," he says, all largesse. "You want to talk about being the butt of jokes . . ." Nevertheless, he has withstood his share: nose jokes, clothes jokes, geek jokes, masculinity jokes (Barely ManEnough, alas). Not only does he know all the barbs, he actually *archives* them. In his home, he has festooned a prominent corridor with cartoon-strip razzings—from *Bloom County* to *Andy Capp* to *Popeye.* Simply, he curates a personal hall of shame, displays it in game defiance. He even has the artists sign the originals. "I know they hate doing this," he says, giggling mischievously, as he will.

He wore yellow. His coat, in this way, was like plumage. So there he sat, a canary icon, in a room full of peers—a little aloof, a little ignored. Around him, a large celebration swirled. His record company had taken over a ballroom at the Beverly Hills Hotel to showcase its most promising new acts. Onstage, much jamming took place. He watched this from a distance, applauding generously whenever appropriate. His presence was meant to confer support; he understood this. He sipped wine and softly rapped on the table to the staccato beat of the music—music that did not at all resemble his own. A fat crystal shimmered on his finger.

Because he was asked, he took one bow. This was requisite: No one in the room was more famous than he. Nor was there anyone on hand who had sold, or could likely ever sell, more records: so far, fifty million-plus, worldwide. Still, he rose from his seat warily—or, at least, with some embarrassment—as though he almost expected to be pelted. He got a nice hand. He looked relieved and slipped back onto his chair, his curious yellow aura handsomely aglow.

•   •   •

He has grown into his nose. So say his friends, and by this they mean two things: First, and few would quibble here, he looks better than he used to. He used to look, well, dorkier. Maturity has obliged him. Second, and some would quibble here, although they oughtn't, Barry Manilow has become formidable, extremely large, a legend even, in the show business sense. At age forty-four, after fifteen years of Top Forty toil and adult-contemporary lionization, he is irrevocably a giant among entertainers. He endures. He adapts. He persists. There is always a new album (twenty-two with the recent release of *Because It's Christmas;* the ninety-minute videocassette of his twenty-first, *Barry Manilow Live on Broadway,* reached number one on the *Billboard* charts this summer). And there is always a world tour. Most probably, he is *the* showman of Our Generation. He lives for production values, for rich staging, for catchy hooks and big finishes. He wants your gooseflesh. Musically, he is a populist nonpareil. Sinatra, it is said, once jabbed a finger at Manilow and portentously announced, "He's next."

Even so, he is beset with insecurity. He is an outcast, and has resigned himself to it. As his favorite joke suggests, he did not participate in the pop congress of "We Are the World"; he was not asked. And this was fine with him. "I'm not in that clique," he reasons. "I've never really been a group person. I've always been a loner." He realizes he has no other choice. He cannot fathom his place in the culture. He feels uncategorizable, adrift, a freak.

"I am a musical misfit," he will readily admit. "I've never been able to put myself into a musical slot. I don't consider myself a cohort of Billy Joel—he's more rock and roll. Kenny Rogers is more country. Barbra is a little older, more theatrical, actresslike. Neil Diamond is guitar-oriented, gruff. I don't know where I fit in. I think a lot of critics have always been uncomfortable with my life as a pop star; there was just nothing that they could grab on to. Nobody, including *me,* could figure out why my records were making it. I've got my one little slice of this pie. It's very small, but it's mine."

Some random Barry Manilow findings, gleaned from months of scrutiny:

He has recurring nightmares about concentration camps. He does not know why, but surmises, "It probably has to do with my feeling undeserving of any success, even though I work my ass off for it."

If he could be anyone else, he would be Sting. "He's on his own path," he says admiringly. "I wish that I could be as brave as he has been with his career and his life." Next choice: Tom Waits. "He sings from his *kishkas.*"

"Lite" radio stations, the kind that broadcast his own work, bore him. "I'm grateful that they play me, don't get me wrong," he says, "but I just can't get behind them. Pop radio has never challenged me." Mostly, he tunes in progressive rock or jazz.

If told tomorrow to forsake singing "Copacabana" (his biggest hit) and "I Can't Smile Without You" in concert, he would not sulk. Also, the lyrics of his signature anthem, "I Write the Songs," have always embarrassed him, at least in theory. Especially since somebody else wrote the song. He laments: "It will follow me for the rest of my life, I guess."

He feels his best work is unreleasable: an album of would-be standard tunes he composed to lyrics bequeathed him by the widow of legendary songwriter Johnny Mercer ("Moon River," "Skylark"). "These are old-fashioned pop melodies completely out of place in 1990," he says, grieving. "Maybe when I'm dead, they'll all come out."

He barely eats. And he would rather die than eat Parmesan cheese. He brushes his teeth every couple of hours. Touch his newspapers before he does and risk death. Same goes for magazines. He hates surprises and spiders. He loves Roger Rabbit and white gardenias. The mention of outdoor activities makes him apoplectic. "Jews don't camp," he will insist. Or "Jews don't ski." And so on. He drives a red Range Rover; large dice hang from the rearview mirror. He yearns to grow a beard, but would only do so in seclusion. He is almost never secluded.

This man has a driveway. It is a long driveway. It is a driveway that could be seventy or eighty driveways, arranged end to end, that snake and slope up toward a pristine Bel Air aerie. There, at the tip of his quarter-mile driveway, he meets me one afternoon. He wears stubble and enormous European eyeglasses and a baseball cap and a gray T-shirt and jeans and sandals. On him, scruffiness of this sort looks like an effort. Certainly it seems incongruous—as do reports that he likes to motor-scooter down to the front gate for newspapers at dawn, clad only in his underwear.

Barry Manilow at home is not much like Barry Manilow in concert. Wardrobe considerations aside, the lighting is all wrong. And, if the soaring driveway is paved with expectation, Manilow manor itself is kind of anticlimactic: a cozy ranch-style affair, busy with crystal, art, and fabulous views of Los Angeles below. Here, he dwells quietly, if not in solitary. "This is where Linda and I live," he announces, referring to Linda Allen, the woman with whom he has been most often linked throughout his celebrity. But Linda is not home; she decorates movie sets, usually in remote locations, and is therefore not home much at all. For that matter, neither is he, what with touring. Basically, then, his is a home where no one is home very much.

"Is it gonna be a campy thing?" he asks me, meaning this article, leery as always. He is simultaneously grateful for attention and incredulous that he would get any. Although his demeanor is unfailingly earnest, he does not know how to be taken seriously. He yearns for respect. Yet he frets that his demographic appeal may be askew. For this reason, whenever in my presence, he took to wryly imploring friends and associates: "Be hip. Please, just be hip."

He wanted to see Jody Watley in concert. So we went to the Universal Amphitheatre and saw her. For three songs, we stood at our seats and, like most of the audience, he danced and bopped to the music. After the third song, he nudged me and said, "Wanna go get some coffee?" We left the building. Outside in the parking lot, he said, with a tinge of exasperation: "I get it, I get it. Lots of bass drums. Big voice. Big earrings. Lot of energy. I mean, it's *loud*. I'm too old for this." Later, over coffee at a nearby restaurant, he added, "It looked like a bad Vegas act, but she *meant* it. So, you've got to give her credit. But she looked like Ann-Margret or something."

Billy Idol, it turned out, was sitting in the same restaurant with a group of people. Once he realized Barry Manilow was in his midst, he began to stare. Then he began making goofy mocking faces, in the manner of Harpo Marx. In this way, he amused himself thoroughly. Eventually, someone informed Barry, who had seen none of this, that Billy Idol was on the premises.

"Oh, God," he said, his sigh full of dread.

Here is how he once alienated Bruce Springsteen and Billy Joel:

Because life makes no sense, they were sitting together, the three of them, at a small table in a Philadelphia diner, circa 1974. Somehow, all three happened to be in town. So they convened, in casual assembly, at the behest of a local deejay named Ed Sciaky, who, with his wife, was also present. Bruce drank water, acted detached. Billy drank Black Russians, acted surly. Barry drank coffee and, to be friendly, made conversation. Much too much conversation, it seems.

"Sciaky reminds me that I made an asshole of myself then," Manilow says. "Apparently, at one point, I said, 'Out of all three of us, just watch,

I'm going to be the biggest star at this table.' Ed says he winced and his wife began to gag. I don't remember this, but if I said it at all, it was because, of the three of us, I was making the most blatantly commercial music. I respected their music more than my own and said [*cynically*], 'Hah! Just watch!' But it just came out wrong, and they never forgot it. To this day, Billy Joel gets pissed off when people mention my name—and I have always been such an incredible fan of his."

Feats: Twenty-five Barry Manilow singles have, in consecutive order, reached the Top Forty. To date, no one else has ever managed this. In 1978, five of his albums logged in at once on the charts—a record surpassed only by Sinatra and Mathis. In Great Britain, where he is uniformly adored, only he has received three platinum albums inside one twelve-month period—the Beatles never did. He owns an Emmy, a Tony, a Grammy (Best Pop Vocal Performance, Male, for "Copacabana"), accolades aplenty. He is revered—worshiped even—in Japan, in Germany, in Latin America, in many places where irony is incomprehensible.

Ultimately, he knows why he succeeds. In part, it is for the same reason he is also ridiculed:

"I'll tell you what you see," he says of his performance persona, eschewing all coyness. "You see *passion*. I read an article someplace that said the true artist is an artist that can convey his passion across the footlights. The quality doesn't even matter—just so that you displayed the passion. For instance, Springsteen is not my cup of tea, but I get it. I understand what he's doing. He gets me because he is so passionate. At the very least, what you could say about me is that I am trying to convey my passion and that's what's working. Not the fact that I sing so well, because I don't sing so well. Not the fact that I write so well, because Billy Joel writes better pop stuff than I do. Not the fact that I can perform well, either. It's that I believe in what I do, and you get it. Now, some people don't get it! But my guts go out there onstage, take it or leave it. And that's very uncomfortable for a lot of people to witness, especially to be coming from a man."

His heart has been broken three times. If this is significant, it is only because heartbreak is his racket. A master of mushcraft (because someone has to be), he gilds heartbreak, inlays it with bathos and life-shattering key changes. Onstage he will ruefully announce, "For a guy who makes his living singing romantic songs, my romantic life has been for shit." He will then lament his one-and-a-half-year marriage, which ended while he was in his early twenties, telling audiences, "I thought it was going to last forever." (This constitutes one heartbreak; the other two he never tells me about.) But, in truth, marriage gives him the willies. "I don't believe in marriage," he says, citing the rubble of his own divorce and that of his parents, who parted during his infancy (he's seen his father, a truck driver, only a few times since). "I haven't seen really happy [marriages]. Either people are together because they have to be or they're miserable together and cheating or whatever."

And, anyway, relationship-wise, he thinks he's defective merchandise. "I'm tough to live with, because I'm tough on myself," he says plaintively. "I was uncomfortable being married. As soon as I signed the papers, I thought, *Now I have to be here.* It's a good thing Linda is such a free spirit. We do live together—for five years now—but we're not tied together every night. We are lovers together, we're friends, and we're separate. And that's the way I like it. The few times I was ever really tied to someone, I was impossible to live with. I'm just not made to be committed to one person. I need independence. I need to have room, not clinging. If I know that I have a tender distance, then I'm all right. Maybe I'll get better at that, the more I get to like myself. . . ."

Like so—and not surprisingly—he speaks the lingo of shrinkage fluently. He is one well-therapized customer, one who gives excellent couch, a behemoth among codependents. That is, he aims to please all interplanetary life—which, as you might imagine, can at times be a tad futile if you happen to be Barry Manilow. So, like a mule driver, he Works on Himself. "I don't know who I am, but what I want to do is love him," he says. "I want to be able to say that I'm proud of this guy that I've become." Or "Wouldn't it be nice to trust yourself? To say 'This is it, this is me.' "

Indeed, the first time he trusted himself, he unspooled his greatest musical achievement—a truly stunning jazz album called *2:00 AM Paradise Café,* released in 1984. Lean, bluesy, and heartfelt, the record boasted a peerless supporting cast, including Mel Tormé, Sarah Vaughan, and Gerry Mulligan. "Come on, can you imagine?" he says, still aflutter with the memory. "I was a wreck. I can't even talk about it without getting emotional. I gave myself permission to not worry about where the thing was gonna land. I took away all the police that I have in my head that say 'Oh, no, that's not going to sell,' or 'No, all the people in Cleveland who love your pop stuff will not connect with that jazzy stuff.' As soon as I allowed myself to stop being attached to the results, I wrote *Paradise Café* in one week. It was the most thrilling thing I've ever done."

• • •

I saw him turn black one day. Since he is perhaps the whitest of white musicians who breathe, this seemed noteworthy. It happened, albeit briefly, in a Hollywood rehearsal studio, where he and his tour band—an extremely facile group of players and singers—were attempting a new, heavily gospel-flavored arrangement of his bouncy early hit "It's a Miracle." At the piano, he was released; he swayed, he soared, he became Andraé Crouch. It was as though a revival meeting had erupted, so exhilarating and soulful was this rendering. He had broken form entirely.

Afterward, he shook his head unhappily. "The only thing bothering me," he told everyone, "is that it feels like church. I don't want it to feel like church. It's dishonest. It's not me. I do like the excitement. But how could we do this in, like, Kansas City? Don't you think people in the audience will say, 'What the hell is he doing?' It's too broad. Maybe I can just square it up a little bit."

"Barry, it just shows another side of you," protested the keyboard player. "You shouldn't feel you can't surprise people."

Debra Byrd, his longtime backup singer, who also happens to be black, seconded this: "You know, if you believe it, they'll believe it," she said. "It's all in the approach. If you wanted to, you could put on a black bustier and writhe around in front of a black idol, too."

Unconvinced, he tamed the arrangement. "It didn't come from here," he later told me, pounding his chest for emphasis. "It just felt weird."

On meeting Madonna: "I saw her in the lobby at a Laura Nyro concert. She was with Warren Beatty and Sandra Bernhard. I told her I liked her latest song, 'Cherish,' a lot. And she said, [*nonplussed*] 'Not my favorite.' I said, 'Well, thanks.' She said, 'It just doesn't *say* anything.' I said, 'Well, I like it.' She said, 'Thank you.' She's an intriguing girl. I can see why she's a star. There'd be no place for her if she weren't a star. You can't picture Madonna working as a secretary. She has convinced me that she is talented."

"Have you ever seen a thousand naked men with party hats on? It was insane."

We now engage in some Manilore, shocking in substance: The preceding quote, excerpted from his 1987 (unghosted) memoir, *Sweet Life: Adventures on the Road to Paradise,* conjures his first impression of the seventies, his decade of emergence. Indeed, this would be his moment of epiphany. The night was New Year's Eve 1970, and the place was the Continental Baths, New York's then-notorious gay-sauna-replete-with-entertainment. Up to this point, Barry Manilow could be characterized as quite the singular nerd: a scrawny, numbingly self-conscious, Brooklyn-bred nascent lounge lizard who favored tight black suits and lugged a briefcase to gigs. He had just started doing weekend piano accompaniment at the Baths—a job from hunger—wherein he nervously played show tunes for guys in towels. On this particular evening, however, all that would change. On this night, he would finally embrace the rightful liberty that is afforded in show business.

Which is to say, he took off his clothes in public.

"All during the show, people kept passing drinks and joints up to me," he writes. (*Drinks! Joints!*) After midnight, nude men and women alike flounced in the house pool and, showing no regard for "my Jewish middle-class uptightness," beckoned him in. "I looked at myself, with my nice black suit still on," he continues. "I was thinking I'd love to lose my inhibitions and jump in with the rest of them, but it goes against everything in me."

But metaphor waits for no man: After a protracted inner dialogue, he shed the suit and, cheered on by a chorus chlorinated in sexual ambiguity, got wet. And so he writes: " 'Welcome to the seventies!' I yelled as I hit the water."

He looks at tapes of himself conducting the business of his life during said decade. Invariably, he blanches and mumbles, "Gee, somebody smack this guy." When flipping through old photographs of himself, he will ask aloud, "Who dressed this man?" He sees elevator shoes and fat bell-bottoms and constricting blouses ablaze in rhinestones. He sees fakery and goosery. He never knew who to be onstage; always, he chose to be someone else.

"You get up there with the lights and the sound and the makeup, and your first instinct is to be a phony," he says. "Have you ever seen those old TV specials? Come on—this is an idiot on television! This is just a jerk. But I thought this was the way I was supposed to be: campy, giggly, charming, cute, silly, entertaining, goofy. By the fourth special, I was convinced I was a sex symbol. Oh, boy, this was Manilow Run Amuck! It's very, very difficult when you've got millions of people applauding you and girls screaming nonstop. You say, 'Well, maybe *I should* wear tight pants.' But I'm telling you now—I shouldn't! I ain't got it. I look at this and I cringe."

He has the career he never wanted. He never wanted to be Liberace; he wanted to be Hoagy Carmichael. His is the soul of an old jazzbo. He fantasizes about wearing berets and noodling on battered uprights in smoky Parisian dives. His curse was his ear; he hears sweet. Sweet sells. It sells hamburgers and acne pads; so he became a jingle virtuoso, and he was assigned posterity by playing or singing or writing hummable odes for McDonald's and Stri-Dex and other various sundries. As an arranger, he packed resonance into microcosm, he stoked swoons into simple charts. At the Baths, it fell to him to refine the raw tumult of Bette Midler, then an unwieldy chanteuse of epic potential. She en-snared him, took him on the road; he gave her context, created her in a sense. Their union begat vinyl; he coproduced her first and best record-ings. Then he won his own contract from Bell Records, which soon be-came Arista, which released his first single, a song about a dog named Brandy that was retitled "Mandy," which quickly hit number one, which firmly established Manilow as a frontman, thereby shackling him with the career he never wanted.

"Being the overambitious Jew that I am—this overachieving Brooklyn guy—I went for it," he says now. "I said, 'Come on! Let's go!' I didn't like it, I didn't want it, I wasn't comfortable with it. But I figured, *Who can turn down this opportunity?* I knew that it was too much. That there was no build. That I had no hope. It exploded with such ferocity that I have spent the last ten years trying to pick up the pieces."

Terrified of where he found himself, he lost himself. He'd gotten too big for his sequins. Bad behavior surfaced. "I didn't know what to do to alleviate the agony of this pressure," he recalls. "At that point, most people turn to drugs, and I can understand it, believe me. Not that I ever considered it. Instead, I hollered. I was abusive: bratty, throwing tantrums, being selfish, temperamental, inconsiderate. I was pretty much of a total asshole. I really believed that I was better than others, but in my heart, I knew I wasn't. And the danger was that the people around you want to keep their jobs, so they indulge you. I could have gotten anything I wanted. I've watched the Anita Bakers and the—I don't want to men-tion names—but I see what they're going through. I've been there. All I can do is say a prayer for them and hope they get through this. My assholiness ran out after only a couple of years, thank God."

"Should Prince meet the Jewish Prince?"

He meant it as a joke, but the prospect of this apocalyptic confronta-tion brought me to Minnesota one chilly week. The Manilow contingent had set aground on purple soil. Paisley Park, seat of the lovesexy empire, had been commandeered by Manilow, who decided to shore up his huge stage show on Prince's huge soundstage—for a fee. Logistics dictated as much. His tour, then on hiatus, was to resume days later in nearby St. Paul. And so he infiltrated the mammoth white fortress, where doves fly in cages or are etched into stained glass windows. But, alas, the tiny host remained sealed in his upstairs lair.

"I think he should come and greet me," said Manilow with mock indignation. "It would be the hospitable thing to do: Prince meets the Jewish Prince."

During breaks, we wandered the corridors together, hoping for a glimpse. He is, it turns out, in awe of Prince. "I heard this place was in trouble," he said, meaning the vast studio complex. "Not a moneymaking enterprise, I heard." He reminisced about a Prince concert he'd seen in Los Angeles. "He was amazing," he said. "I remember asking a promoter who worked with him, 'What's Prince like?' She said, 'Never met him.' I said, 'Never met him?' She said, 'No, he came in a box.' He came to his shows in a box! They wheeled him off the truck and all the way to the stage in a box! Did the show, got back in the box, wheeled him back to the truck, and he was gone! Now *that's* a star! It never got that bad for me. I never had a box!"

Now and again, he will register at hotels under Elvis's old pseudonym, John Burrows. He hides only a little these days. Unlike Elvis, his fandemonium, while widespread and fervent, is not unmanageable. (Many of his most ardent fans, shamed by peers, keep their fealty secret—a prominent exception being Arsenio Hall, who defiantly gushes whenever Manilow visits his show.) Like Elvis, however, he is pursued by a sisterhood possessed. Women who live for Barry Manilow don't want hanks of his hair or bed linen tatters; they want *inspiration*. For them, he is an example. Says his friend and manager Garry Kief: "When you've had the shit kicked out of you for fifteen years and you can still breathe, maybe you finally start to believe that there is a God. People see that and respond to it."

He is, in effect, a patron saint of misfits and lonely hearts everywhere. "We're all lonely in our lives," Manilow says, not making too much of this. But his music evinces hope, urging the downtrodden that, like him, they too can Make It Through the Rain. Indeed, self-improvement is the nutmeat of his largely autobiographical stage show—which is more theater experience, less pop recital. One elaborate, leg-kicking production number called "God Bless the Other 99" celebrates the bravado of those in life who try and invariably fail: "I learned more from failure than I learned from success," he belts, a Busby Berkeley sage. Another tune— "Please Don't Be Scared"—is a stirring paean to survival instincts. He sprinkles concerts with cozy aphorisms like "You can give in, you can give out, but you can't give up." It is like a motivational workshop for the chronically intimidated—only with better choreography.

"We all need somebody to say these things," he states, accepting the mantle. "So if I've been chosen to do this, if that's what they want to hear—I'll do it. I'll tell 'em what I know so far. I've done everything else. I can't be doing it for the number one records anymore, ever again. It's not satisfying. *Nice,* but unsatisfying. I don't know—I feel better when I feel I'm giving to somebody. It's corny. But it's me."

Late one freezing night in St. Paul, a gaggle of women lingered outside the stage door of the Ordway Music Theatre, where they had just watched their shaman give a benefit performance. Most of them had seen the show several times before in various corners of the continent; this time they paid up to $250 apiece, mingling among Minnesotans in formal wear, to see it again. They'd come from parts unknown and, their teeth chattering in the nippiness, bore such gifts as Mylar balloons and ruggelach pastries. Upon exit, Barry hurried over to them, then took their cold hands and warmed them in his own. "Thank you for waiting out here," he told them, and fussed about their health. "You gotta get out of this wind!"

The next morning at a record signing in downtown Minneapolis, hundreds of women—and some self-conscious men—filed in serpentine fashion past a table where he was bestowing his signature upon anything placed before him. The ladies, aged mid-twenties to late forties, in varying physical contours, proffered mash notes and confessional platitudes. "I'm laid off right now, so 'Please Don't Be Scared' means a lot to me," said one. Another echoed this, mentioning her sister's several suicide attempts. "I work in a prison," yet another told him, "and you're my sanity."

Through all of this, he listened, served up perfunctory messages of goodwill, politely declined kiss requests (how to accommodate one and not incite a mob scene?), and kept on writing his name. "I love you, too," he would say to those who needed to hear it. He said it more than once that day.

•   •   •

"I think he's a sad guy," he was saying one night in his St. Paul hotel suite. Conversation had turned to Elton John, the only performer with whom Barry Manilow shared majority ownership of the seventies. "We didn't know each other back then," he continued. "He's not a friend or anything. I've since bumped into him at a party now and then, or backstage when he came to see me or I went to see him. He's a survivor, but all the interviews I've ever read about him are sad interviews. He seems sad. I wish the best for him. I wish he could pull himself together. He's a talented guy, a wonderful singer, a good songwriter, a fancy dresser. Snappy, dapper dresser! I just wish he was not sad. But I think he brings it on himself. It seems to me that some of these people, they can do it, they can help themselves, but they just..."

He stopped, tossed up his hands, and grinned stupidly. He sees pain the way others see carpet lint. It is what he does. He can't help himself.

"Here I am, being the self-help guru, again," he said, chuckling. "But what I'm learning is that you don't have to be a victim, you know? You can take your life into your hands and you can just change things if you open your eyes. I think Elton needs a little nudge, that's all."

He shrugged and smiled and shrugged some more.

It is what he does.

Not only was this my first *Esquire* profile, but it was also the first time a subject truly despised what I wrote and told me so in no uncertain terms. David Copperfield, perhaps the most innovative of illusionists, had somehow escaped the radar of any real major magazine coverage. Though his work had by then made him one of the richest entertainers alive, he had never experienced the admittedly odd phenomenon of having a writer enter his world and stay there for days and nights and weeks on end. He was deeply jittery about it, but also pleasantly excited. That he had begun dating Claudia Schiffer a few months earlier further stoked his wariness. In any case, I found him to be a funny, wry, likable guy, albeit one who worried greatly about what I would write. As I did not come to skewer him, but merely to get a load of his unique lifestyle, I did what a writer must do: I told him with great humor and friendly reassurance to relax, to be real, to tell me what was on the record and what was off, which I would honor completely. So he did just that and so did I, per the record.

Because editors David Hirshey and Ed Kosner had lured me to *Esquire* so that I could continue to make some gentle comic hay with our cultural idols, and because Copperfield was never not (purposely) amusing in my presence, I wrote what I hoped was an entertaining piece. My fax machine rattled shortly after publication, and an excoriating missive from the illusionist singed through. Someone at the magazine—not I, for sure—gave syndicated columnist Liz Smith the gist of his fury, and she wrote: "Word from the bowels of *Esquire* magazine—recent cover-man David Copperfield did not care at all for Bill Zehme's in-depth profile. In fact, Copperfield reportedly sent off a sizzling three-page letter, detailing his displeasure. Apparently, the illusionist didn't appreciate Zehme's emphasis on s-e-x, on other aspects of his personal life, and the attention given to his fiancée, Claudia Schiffer. Not enough stuff on his work as the world's foremost magician.

"Hmmmmm, well . . . I thought it was an excellent piece. It certainly told me more than I had ever known about Copperfield—but not so much that I felt his privacy had been invaded. Of course, reading about oneself is a very subjective matter, indeed. What strikes others as fascinating may make the subject's own skin crawl. . . ."

There would eventually be an interesting resolution to all of this. Copperfield's letter and my response to his ire follow just after this profile.

David Copperfield:
How Did He Do *That?*

Esquire, April 1994

Of Copperfield, let me begin by imparting the following: Nothing he does is real. He does not believe in magic. His greatest regret is that he cannot sing. He was born to dance. He is never tired. He touches no coffee and has never seen cocaine. He is, he claims, "seventy-five percent happy" at all times, except when preparing his annual CBS television special. At such times, he is fifty percent happy. He has never completely gotten through the Charles Dickens novel from which he took his name. "Even the Cliffs Notes aren't that interesting," he says. Neither did he care for the film version, starring Freddie Bartholomew. "It's kind of dark," he says. He revels in obscure facts and takes pride in knowing both theme songs to *Lost in Space,* which he will gladly hum on demand. He admires the packaging of Pringles potato chips. He is the tenth-wealthiest entertainer currently alive, having earned $26 million last year alone. He has no home, only a secret lair in a Las Vegas warehouse, which Bruce Wayne and Hugh Hefner would envy. While he is most famous for vanishing the Statue of Liberty, he has never actually performed in New York City, the world capital of cynicism. He gives more than five hundred performances a year everywhere else, however, and sleeps mostly on a bus.

He has no driver's license, automobiles, or motorcycles, despite his frequent poses on Harley-Davidsons. He likens his stage persona to that of Superman. "That's who I am now," he says. The gadgetry that allows him to "fly" onstage cost roughly $700,000. "I fly because there's a market for it," he says. He summarizes his touring show, *Beyond Imagination,* thusly: "The structure of the show is me posing, looking really cool, and having girls wrapped around me." He will never forget the night at Caesars Palace when a female audience volunteer reached into his pants, grabbed his genitals, and wouldn't let go. "That was very terrifying," he says, "and also maybe a little arousing." To his great delight and the dismay of most other men, thousands of women clamor for him. Only one woman, however, has made him her own, and she is arguably the most beautiful woman on the planet. This constitutes an accomplishment, in the minds of many, that eclipses every other feat he has managed, including escaping from a burning raft over Niagara Falls. Nevertheless, it is true: His girlfriend is the German supermodel Claudia Schiffer, and she has agreed to become his wife, and there is not a man alive who does not wonder exactly how he did it.

What I know of David Copperfield he pretty much told me. He is that kind of guy. Although he is professional deceiver, I feel he bared his soul in earnest and have no reason to doubt him. True, I was urged to sign a secrecy agreement before we met, but that was mostly to keep me from giving away how his tricks are done. Otherwise, he was an open book. For days, I rarely left his side, and when I did, he would ask people where I went. Regularly, we would hold forth well into predawn hours. Shortly thereafter, he would wake me on the phone and say things like "Let's go to work!" and "Time is wasting, man!" Such was his enthusiasm, which must be considered exemplary and is woefully lacking in the general ranks of profile subjects, most of whom have done far less with their miserable lives than has David Copperfield, master illusionist, age thirty-seven.

"The worst thing I can say about David Copperfield is that he puts shoulder pads in his straitjackets," Penn Jillette of Penn & Teller once told me. Considering the petty and vituperative lot that are magicians, this is high praise. Indeed, among those who conjure for a living, Copperfield is generally exalted, a presence akin to Elvis—the first pop idol of prestidigitation and, more significantly, Houdini's only logical heir. As he himself declared, in rap verse, on one of his TV specials: "I dress real cool, with an attitude; that's why I've lasted longer than that

Henning dude." Still, after sixteen years of celebrity, he must combat a certain stigma—a point he made evident a few years ago when I had occasion to briefly chat with him. "I'm not a Vegas act," he gently asserted, "and I'd appreciate you kind of not indicating that I was."

If anything, Copperfield belongs to the world. In Germany, for instance, he is known as sex wizard Coppi, breaker of all national box-office records and perhaps the greatest human being who has ever lived. (So revered is he that Munich newspapers recently devoted front-page headlines to his brief but valiant bout with diarrhea.) In China, whose Great Wall he passed through (effortlessly and without benefit of trick photography!), he is a serene mystical icon. In Florida, where I found him on tour, he is a nice Jewish boy who could do with putting on a few pounds. But moreover, you will see, he is also a magician in love, who was preparing for the trick of a lifetime. From Florida, I flew with him to New York, where I saw him frolic with the woman whose troth he would beg days later on the Caribbean isle of St. James. By the time we met again the following week, in Las Vegas (alas), he would shyly disclose her answer, long before others knew and could sputter enviously. "I have to admit it—he must be better than I thought," Penn Jillette said, once the news spread. "Because the other possibility is too horrific to contemplate."

As with most of his pursuits, Copperfield tans peerlessly. This he owes, in part, to his father, retired haberdasher Hyman Kotkin, who has long stressed the merit of personal tint. "We're both sun-worshipers," the elder will proudly announce to this day. "I love that!" Indeed, rarely a winter passed that the family Kotkin did not flee gray Metuchen, New Jersey, for golden Miami. It is a memory Copperfield lately invokes at the close of every performance, bemoaning a snow-deprived youth, before making it snow throughout the auditorium. Night after night, grown men cry when this happens. (Copperfield believes his work is not done unless throats lump.) Even Claudia Schiffer's father wept softly at the spectacle, when he witnessed it in Berlin. Clearly, he knew, his daughter had found a good and sentimental man.

I first saw the snows of Copperfield in Fort Myers, Florida, where much sniffling ensued. After the show, limp and flake-covered audience members queued up in the lobby to receive the magician's inscrutable signature—another unique Copperfield ritual!—and to look at him from behind rope. One especially overcome subject happened to be a fellow alum of Copperfield's from Metuchen High School, who approached with their 1974 yearbook. This greatly pleased the magician, who turned pages to find his own geek countenance. (Next to one photo, he now inscribed, *legibly*, "David 'Kotkin'"—quotation marks included.) During dinner break, he continued to thumb through the book, searching out faces of Metuchen girls who'd broken his young heart. "I remember this girl!" he crowed repeatedly. "She shot me down!" Eyeing the photo of one girl, he sighed. "It coulda been you," he muttered at it, "but instead I have to settle for Claudia."

Davino, boy magician, was born of sex. David Kotkin became Davino only to impress girls, for girls were his obsession. Before becoming Davino, he had been invisible to girls, a common curse among nascent great men. "I would always fall in love with the girl in the next seat, who would then ignore me and be in love with somebody else," he told me. "But I knew that somehow, someday, I would capture her attention." He knew he had to do something, so he did magic, which was all he could do. In this way, he learned to dominate girls and make them like it. Magic, he realized, taught him sex, before sex was an option. "Men enjoy seeing a woman controlled, say, with levitation," he later explained. "Women, on the other hand, see magic as an act of trust—especially if she's going to let a guy do horrible things like stick swords through her body." Thus, his life would be spent wreaking out sweet revenge, having his way with women by skewering, floating, vanishing, and resurrecting them. And, afterward, there would always be applause.

Like a Scud missile, he finds pulchritude in the darkest showrooms. If it is there, he sees it. In Fort Myers and Orlando, he pulled comely women of every variety from their seats and onto the stage to fool them and sometimes suck their hair. (Hair-sucking is just one of his quirks.) Similarly, each night, he would invite a different woman to plumb his pants in search of his magic scissors. "To get up onstage and have an excuse to flirt with the best-looking girl in the audience—what could be better?" It is by these words that he lives. And so it was that he found Claudia Schiffer, in just this manner, out in the darkness, on October 10, 1993. ("I spotted her!" he told me proudly.) She had come to his opening-night performance in Berlin, along with her parents. "The only thing I knew was that he was the great magician," she later recalled. "I mean, in Germany, not knowing about David Copperfield is like not knowing about Michael Jackson." ("Michael who?" Copperfield responded in his irrepressible way.) Fortunately, she had been only seven when the first of Copperfield's annual network specials debuted in America. He was twenty at that time, a gawky prodigy, who would need most of the seventeen intervening years to metamorphose into the winsome rogue that he is today. (Coppermaniacs began noticing the great transformation on the television specials sometime *after* his levitation across the Grand Canyon and *before* his escape from Alcatraz. Schiffer, meanwhile, would go on to become the Bardot of supermodeldom, the Guess? girl and Revlon girl nonpareil (her three-year Revlon deal is worth a record-setting $10 million), and the Monaco resident best known for resisting the ongoing marital advances of Prince Albert.

In Berlin, however, their lives would change forever. He plucked her from the crowd of fourteen hundred and predicted graffiti she sprayed onto a wall. He did not suck her hair, but drank her in otherwise. "It was her eyes," he reported afterward. "There was a connection, a comfortable feeling." She reciprocated: "I'm fascinated by his eyes," she told the German press. "They are so brown and warm. When he laughs, his whole face laughs." They attended a postshow gala together and danced slowly to a Lionel Richie tune, mouthing the portentous lyrics: "Hello, is it me you're looking for?" He later did table magic for her with French fries. "You know how you get vibes?" his father said, for he saw all of this occur. "The glow was in both their eyes. I told David, 'Hey, latch onto this feeling—hold tight. Don't let it go.' Even I was crazy about that girl!"

Two days later, the magician flew to Paris to watch the model model Chanel. Afterward, they dawdled in art galleries, lunched, dined, and began to know the inevitable. In no time, there appeared in his dressing room a framed Bruce Weber portrait of her, which accompanied him to every venue. He would never again perform magic without first gazing upon her. "He's had girls before, yes," one key Copperfield adviser told me in Florida, "but I've *never* seen a picture in his room before. I mean, *never!*"

Because they are not subtle personages, theirs cannot be a quiet romance. As with Crawford and Gere, they must represent more—embodying perhaps the death gasp of glamour itself. ("Why do you think he doesn't just say 'I am not gay'?" Copperfield asked me at one point, pondering the puzzle of Richard Gere; even he cannot resist celebrity speculation. "I mean, I would absolutely, positively, for sure say I wasn't.") Riding the elevator to his Orlando hotel room, he silently perused a faxed copy of the latest *Paris Match,* on whose cover he and Schiffer embraced in paparazzi pose. The cover line—CLAUDIA: *"CELUI QUE J'AI CHOISI."* "The man I have chosen," Copperfield translated in his soft nasal voice, seeming neither pleased nor violated. Now in their fourth month of courtship, and such news splashes about them are commonplace. (Not before or since he sent an Indiana college girl a truckload of flowers three years ago has his personal life attracted press of any kind.) In January, for instance, a buzz storm erupted when, as a gift to Schiffer, he paid a reported $2 million for the yacht *Honey Fitz,* on which JFK once dallied. "I like the idea that Marilyn might have slept on board with John," he told me. "I like setting myself among these ghosts."

Of course, Copperfield is a man for whom grand gestures come naturally. Not long ago, he hung upside down from a burning rope, wrapped in a straitjacket, ten stories above flaming metal spikes—just to overcome a fear of heights. That afternoon, in his hotel suite, I would witness still another marvel. First, he excused himself to take a surreptitious meeting in an adjoining room. When he returned, he could no longer focus on conversation. "I'm going to show you I trust you by letting you see something," he said. He handed me a small packet, inside of which was an item of majestic radiance, the size of a grape, impossibly perfect, and worth an epic sum. Unfortunately, he asked me to say nothing more about it, except that he planned to present it to Schiffer within days. In the meantime, he walked it over to the window to study it in the light and giddily poke at it. More than once, he asked, "Well, what do you think?"

He flies nervously. On jets, he is always wary. "I do a lot of praying," he confessed. He feels safer flying manually—onstage, without strings. Thus far, however, he has not managed to fly himself anywhere he really wanted to go. For this reason, he hired a Lear six-seater to get from Orlando to New York, where he would surprise Claudia. Earlier in the day, he had hatched his plan: The pair had been apart for two weeks and, although he was booked on a commercial flight the next morning, he could stand no further sacrifice. So minutes after his second show of the night, we sped to the airport. Out on the tarmac, pacing wildly, he called her from his omnipresent cellular phone and lied that he was about to go sign autographs for Floridians. "I'm creating an illusion," he told me. Upon landing at LaGuardia, he would call her again, to say good night, as is his small-hour custom, still pretending to be in Orlando. "Further misdirection," he explained. Meanwhile, an accomplice had hidden a spare key outside Schiffer's doorstep, with which Copperfield would burst into the model's boudoir. "We should still be on the phone when I make my entrance," he said, a man in full control of his craft. As the plane descended over Manhattan, I noticed that snow was falling, as it always does near the end of a Copperfield performance. "God did it," he said, sharing credit.

"I screamed so loud I almost had a heart attack," she confessed that night. "I had no clue!" Now reunited, they were intertwined in the backseat of a limousine cruising up Eighth Avenue on the way to dinner. Another woman, I suggested, might have called the cops on him. "This is not just any woman," he said. "This is *the* woman!" "Did you get that one on tape?" she asked, pointing to my recorder. This is how they are when they are together. All day, in fact, they had been nuzzling at a photo studio, her rightful domain. There he would bide his time by wandering regularly into her changing area to clutch any exposed flesh he encountered. Occasionally, they would transfer chewing gum between their mouths or practice illegal wrestling holds. At one point, he watched her conduct a telephone call in torrents of French. "I don't speak French," he informed bystanders, "but I kiss that way."

At dinner, they feasted on chicken fingers inside Planet Hollywood, where their arrival incited a stir. "We're not worthy, we're not worthy!" bleated one table of youths as Schiffer glided past them. ("I am the number-one babe of Wayne and Garth, you know," she later said pridefully.) As they sat ensconced beneath memorabilia from *The Wizard of Oz,* Copperfield seized the moment to explain to Claudia subtle distinctions between such short American entertainers as the Munchkins, Mickey Rooney, and the late Herve Villechaize. Suddenly, Schiffer's musician friend Peter Gabriel, with whom she was once photographed sunbathing topless, approached the table to pay a quick visit. Copperfield, who has set some of his finest illusions to Gabriel songs, greeted him warmly and professed his admiration. (A lesser man might have thrown a punch.) Afterward, to change the subject, I asked whether Schiffer now knew how Copperfield's tricks were done. Here his eyes flashed. "She knew how it was done *long* before I came along," he said, implying more, in the nicest way.

After midnight, they sipped sambuca in the lobby of the Royalton Hotel. They were, by now, fuzzy-headed, and would soon go upstairs to sleep hard before departing at dawn for the Caribbean. Copperfield had rented a private island for four days, and that is where he would bestow upon her the precious object he'd shown me. "What a day we had!" he said, overcome with his own good fortune and, possibly, the sambuca. "I mean, I feel really good right now. Here I am with an incredible person...." Schiffer rolled her eyes sweetly and yawned. "No, I'm very lucky," he went on. "I really am. Very. I mean, I don't want to wax romantic. I mean, I work my ass off for all this. But when I decide I'm gonna have fun, there's nobody like me in the world." Schiffer did not deny this; she had, in fact, cradled her head on the table and begun a light nap.

"Her answer was yes," he said, coyly neglecting to mention what the question was. Because resolutions are helpful, I had come to Las Vegas, where he was about to open a two-week stint at Caesars Palace. Just back from his vacation, and so much the tanner for it, he displayed the anxiousness of a man whose life was about to revise itself. "You're asking a magician to reveal his secrets!" he would often groan, pacing about his massive headquarters, itself a shrine to secrecy. Located in an old nut-and-bolt warehouse, Copperfield's roost is concealed behind a fake bra-and-girdle showroom replete with lingerie-clad mannequins and sales placards (e.g., WE FIX FLATS; WE SUPPORT ALL OUR CUSTOMERS; and SHOPLIFTERS WILL BE BUSTED). Access to his inner sanctum is gained by way of a sliding mirror that opens at the touch of a mannequin's left nipple. It is from here that he runs his empire, stores more than 250 illusions (the Death Saw, the Death Table, the Floating Ferrari), curates a priceless collection of historic magical artifacts (Houdini's Metamorphosis Trunk, Dante's Spirit Cabinet, Cardini's Tuxedo), and occasionally sleeps, burrowed deep within his customized bachelor digs. It is like the Batcave, only with less furniture and no kitchen. And soon, it now seemed, all of this could become joint property.

"So are we engaged?" Copperfield asked, after much stalling. "The answer is yes." Sparing the private details, he confirmed that his island mission had succeeded, his proposal happily accepted. "I've made several propositions to her over many months," he joked. "I mean, wouldn't *you?*"

This time, however, his aforementioned luck had prevailed. Now he was beaming, as well he should have been. "I gave her that secret thing, and she *loved* it," he said, predicting its imminent appearance on her left hand in all forthcoming paparazzi photographs. And it is here that all begins anew.

"Just let me say this now," promised a hopeful Penn Jillette. "There's a double-sawbuck in it from me if she changes her name to Claudia Schiffer Kotkin."

Postscript:

Frog v. Scorpion:

Feud of the Faxes

W hat's more exciting than a show business feud? This was my first and only. Now, with the full permission of the great illusionist himself, I share Copperfield's angry response to the preceding piece and my own point-by-point reply to him. I like to think of the following as a stark lesson in journalistic ethics, and in how certain jovial reassurances can be interpreted by a subject. Keep in mind that if you cannot tease your "friends," who then can you tease? Also, I include an additional epilogue written by Copperfield especially for this book.

March 18, 1994
Dear Bill:

I have just finished your *Esquire* article, the one which was to have been, in your repeated words, "the definitive portrait of David Copperfield." It was to be the piece that had never been done, the story of my career, with Claudia just brought in for "icing," to use your term.

I guess that story will have to wait.

The scorpion bites the frog carrying him on his back across the river because it is in his nature. I think I have some understanding of the press, and I have taken cheap shots before, and fully expect to take many more in the future. If I am writing you, it is not in your capacity as reporter, but in your capacity as, again to use your term, my friend. There are some things which I think should be said, if only to close the loop.

I always took your words "Trust me, I'm your friend, I'll protect you, this is a collaboration" at face value. The more time we spent together, and the more you told me "Trust me, I'm your friend, I'll protect you," the more I did just that.

I feel he bared his soul in earnest and have no reason to doubt him.

I consented to do this interview, where you joined my company and lived with us over several days, because you portrayed yourself repeatedly as my friend, someone to trust and confide in. You would turn your recorder off constantly, a visual sign confirming your verbal assurances that some portions were clearly off the record. I was, I will admit, excited by the project, excited to have an in-depth article about my career, excited to have this chance to meet a reporter who was sincere when he said "Trust me, I'm your friend, I'll protect you."

I will also admit, I wasn't quite prepared to learn that my soul was primarily about Pringles, diarrhea, trivia, nipples, and the importance of having a tan.

If you listen to the many hours of recordings of our meetings, you may concede that perhaps my soul includes one or two other—how shall I put it—weightier aspects than diarrhea (it was food poisoning, but diarrhea is such a more inspiring word). It's there on your tapes. Trust me. I'm your friend.

Sure, I may have mentioned an interest in TV show themes. Sure, trivia and other things may provide color and perhaps even balance, if there were anything else to balance it against.

I know how frustrating it is to have an editor cut out words, scenarios, paragraphs, and sections. But are editors now cutting out the last half of thoughts? For example, when I discussed at length the tradition and rather odd and certainly sexist magician's role of controlling women, I concluded with "That's why in my show I took magic and did more things to myself. I, not the girl, gets tied up in the cocoon; the girl goes through my chest in Interlude; it is I who gets sawed in half in the Death Saw. I am the one who gets impaired." Trust me, it's on your tape recorder. Alas, I read in *Esquire* that my words, my only words, are:

"Men enjoy seeing women controlled."

Pretty rough stuff, without the rest of my thought. I think I preferred Pringles.

You saw the show many times, and viewed most of my past television specials. We talked at length over many days about the structure of the show, and how I would go from the romantic visual of the magician and the beautiful partner, to my walking forward and cracking a joke, poking fun at myself, telling my audience that I don't take myself seriously. It really is there on your tapes. But, no less than astonished, I read in *Esquire* that I am quoted as saying:

"The structure of the show is me posing, looking really cool, and having girls wrapped around me."

Sounds pretty macho to me. But where is the rest of my sentence?

You spent entire days with me. You saw how 85 percent of my staff is composed of women who run my corporation, how I go out of my way to make sure that in my show, women volunteers get respect and admiration, at my expense in most cases. But I read your words:

His life would be spent wreaking out sweet revenge (on women).

Wow! That should endear me to my fans. I find more balance on the political pages of partisan magazines.

I guess I shouldn't dwell on the betrayal of confidences. (Don't call me a Vegas act, I ask my friend Bill Zehme. And my friend Bill Zehme doesn't call me a Vegas act. Instead he quotes me as asking him not to call me a Vegas act.) Nor should I linger on the new meaning you have given to the phrase "Trust me, I promise" (the Butchie's section comes to mind). Disappointment, while never welcome, is, I suppose, inevitable. There are others that have been wounded here, innocent bystanders, and I'd best concentrate on them.

As I mentioned earlier, this letter is being written to the person who represented himself as being my friend, not the reporter (otherwise I would have listed at length a number of other points, such as the alleged quote "I fly because there's a market for it," which I surely did not say in such an unqualified manner).

My job is deceiving people (here is a good example of the first half of a thought that would sound bad quoted out of context) but I start out by telling my audiences that I am a professional deceiver, an illusionist, and that they shouldn't believe anything they see, but that I'll make them believe anyway. It's a fair game. I don't tell them "Trust me."

Anyway, you got me. I believed you when you said the article would be a "collaboration." Your pen hand was quicker than my trusting eye. "Trust me, I'm your friend, I'll protect you" turns out to have been a perfect misdirection. As I read the article I could almost hear the word "Gotcha!"

But I am curious: When you listen to your recordings, and hear yourself say, "Trust me, I'm your friend, I'll protect you," what do you think?

Sincerely,
David Copperfield

March 27, 1994
Dear David:

First of all, you are mistaken. By now, you may know that no harm can or will come of your reputation through my writing. But I will do my best to answer your stunning and misbegotten ire.

If I wanted to betray you, I could have and would have, but I did not. It is not what I do. If anything, what I did do was reposition you a bit: I made you male-friendly, for a male-oriented audience. I'm afraid you have structured the presentation of your image so meticulously, veiled your world with such tony mystique, that you might have obscured some of your humanity along the way. I saw your humanity and pulled it up to the surface. I believe I did so amusingly, respectfully, never unkindly. I feel I compromised you not one iota. I know I betrayed your trust not once. Never once.

I was given thirty-five hundred words to tell a tellable tale. I was deprived of sufficient room to construct a full-bodied serious profile of your life. Even if there had been space to do so, however, I doubt that I could have pleased you entirely. You lose sight of something here: You and I are entertainers—not deceivers. Simply, we are stylists, but with different styles. Just as you are known for what you do, I am known—or so I'm told—for being a humorous impressionist of popular culture. We both deal in whimsy; we both take it seriously. My work has never been considered mean-spirited. If anything, it is playful. It teases the subject, the reader, the writer, and the culture all at once. I am not the person to write a sober treatise on the equal-opportunity ethics and romantic choreography of your illusions. Furthermore, *Esquire* is no place for such soulful appraisals.

Know this: I did not come to profile a master illusionist; I came to profile a man, albeit one who happens to be a master illusionist.

You allege much wrongdoing on my part. You say I trivialized you, but one man's trivia is another man's meat. That you admire the packaging of canned potato chips suggests you admire precision and order. That you attribute your career endurance to the image you affect onstage suggests you are shrewd. That you said—and you did—that you fly because there is a market for it suggests you understand the dreams of the marketplace. That you can hum any forgotten theme song suggests that you possess a steel-trap mind. That you came down with a news-making case of the trots suggests you possess actual human intestines.

I remember the many times I challenged your oft-quoted stance that you became a magician in order to get girls. You insisted that was indeed fact—which most men, in particular, would certainly find relatable—and that fact then became the comic conceit of the profile. (All of my profiles hinge on a very real comic conceit, or overarching premise, but you must know this if you know my work.) The quote in which you explain the "sexist" role of the magician—the domination and trust stuff—spilled from your mouth seventeen years ago in an interview with the *Chicago Tribune*. In that piece, you were not portrayed taking exception to it, but instead you seemed fascinated by it. If you have spent the intervening years trying to reinvent history, so be it.

And, moreover, Dave, so what? These are not bad things. You are a magician, not an elected official. Nowhere do I suggest that you are anything but innovative. Even so, all of this was presented by me in a gentle, funny fashion. I've yet to speak with a woman reader who was offended. And I have spoken to many, in a wide cross section. Nor has anyone bristled at the three *very* mild Butchie's slogans I chose to record. As you know, there were many far more lurid. And, as I assured you, I would not print those. I did not. I wonder how much of your 85 percent female staff avert their eyes when reporting to work there. It is amazing that they have not overturned the mannequins and set the showroom aflame. They must have, what, a sense of *humor*?

Nothing you said off the record appeared on the record, I assure you. No subject has ever been more aware of when the tape recorder is running and when it is not. You miss nothing, nor did I wish for you to. (Often you did the turning on and turning off for me.) Nowhere in your letter do you bristle about the handling of the Claudia situation. And that, of course, was your chief concern during all of our dealings. And that, of course, was the topic over which I assured you protection. I hear that your camp generally likes the way Claudia comes off in the piece. You candidly explained to me the nature of your sensitivity over the relationship. You paced about my Caesars room, confiding the delicacies involved. I promised to present your private business coyly and discreetly and respectfully. And, of course, I did just that. You worried about exploitation of the relationship; I neglected to even mention the *Entertainment Tonight* crew that followed your every movement in New York. I spared everyone that less than reticent spectacle. I restricted my observations to moments that approximated a more natural reality. I did that, David, to protect you.

In the end, despite your reaction, I suspect that this profile will do you more good than harm. I know how these things work. Another writer might have actually tried to rough you up. I chose to render your passionate persona with a light touch; you weren't prepared for the wry treatment. Still, readers won't know that. They'll just think you're an interesting guy, a guy who swears he doesn't take himself too seriously. Call that misdirection if you like, but all the same, I do wish you well.

B. Z.

Whether my response quelled his anxiety, I never heard. A couple of years later, I was hired to do a weekly irreverent entertainment segment in Chicago on a freewheeling news program called *Fox Thing in the Morning*. One week, I thought it would be amusing to unveil the blueprints for the David Copperfield theme restaurant being planned to go up in Times Square (as it turned out, the restaurant never materialized). In the course of my report, in which I displayed publicity materials for the restaurant, I spoke of our "show business feud" and often repeated the words "David Copperfield hates my guts." Copperfield apparently got hold of the tape and immediately called me from somewhere on the road. "I do not hate your guts," he told me, and said that he was concerned about my thinking so. He told me that he and Claudia—with whom he would later part ways—had watched my report and thought it was very funny, and also said that he might have initially overreacted to the *Esquire* piece. He came to Chicago shortly thereafter and invited me to bring my girlfriend and my daughter to see his show. I almost suspected this to be some kind of misdirection so that he could at last wreak revenge. But we went anyway.

Because he is aware of every detail involved in his show, including the seat locations of certain guests, he found me right away and playfully slapped the back of my head while running through the auditorium doing magic things. When later selecting an audience member to participate in his graffiti-guessing illusion (the same one for which Claudia Schiffer was first pulled onto his stage and into his life), he immediately grabbed my girlfriend, who is, blessedly, a woman of great game spirit. She went up and spray-painted her graffiti, which he had already predicted and sealed in an envelope. He is good that way. After the show, he indicated that our feud was now over, gave me a warm hug, then proceeded to throttle my neck. He did not kill me, I can only believe, because he was my friend and, yes, I trusted him.

NOTE TO THE READER FROM (MY FRIEND) DAVID COPPERFIELD:

Reading it now, nearly eight years later, Bill's *Esquire* profile strikes me as the humorous piece he intended. And, yes, I probably overreacted in my letter.

"At the time, I didn't realize Bill was a humorist. Like most of the world, I had no idea who the fuck he was. It still perplexes me that he calls our pen-pal relationship his 'first show business feud.' As far as I can tell, only one of us is *in* show business.

"Besides, the signs that Bill couldn't be trusted were there early on. I just chose to ignore them. Like the time he told Claudia that, in France, he's considered to be 'Leo Tolstoy—only funny.' Or the time he begged me to let him cuddle Claudia's laundry.

"But grudges hurt the grudger more than the grudgee. Which is why I've long since forgiven Bill and, to borrow a phrase from Woody Allen, think of him as a brother—David Greenglass.

"Time passes, Bill does his job, I do mine, and we share a mutual respect. Still, I can understand why he waited to put pen to paper about his pal and hero Frank Sinatra until Ol' Blue Eyes was old and infirm: It's bad to have your legs broken. Especially by a close friend."

Part Five:

BIG **TALKERS**

Regis Philbin * Howard Stern *
Geraldo Rivera

Even five years before the debut of *Who Wants to Be a Million-aire*, the ubiquitousness of Regis Philbin begged scrutiny and celebration. As a result, my life would never be the same. Sub-sequently I helped him write two books (he made me) and thus now un-derstand him as few others might dare. Actually, Regis is simply the most decent and human show business personage I have ever encoun-tered. He is merely the real thing, and I am proud to have become a small part of his extended media family. Meanwhile, he naturally bris-tled at *Esquire*'s cover line for this piece: "The Unlikely Cult of Regis Philbin." His preference: "The Hippest Man in America." Hey, you ar-gue with him.

Regis Philbin
Is Only One Man!

Esquire, June 1994

He is, of course, out of control. And that is how he must be. Aggravation is art form in his hands. Annoyance stokes him, sends him forth, gives him purpose. Ruffled, he becomes electric, full of play and possibility. There is magnificence in his every irritation, and he knows this. Thus, he takes umbrage wherever it is available. Regis Francis Xavier Philbin is a small man enlarged by indignation, and each day he grows larger. Personally, I see him as a colossus, but then I have probably spent more time with him than you have.

Regis Philbin cannot be ignored. People tried for years, but it was no use. He defies inattention, much like a mad dog. His life has known many obstacles, to be sure, but without these obstacles he would not be who he is today. Today this is who he is: *"I am the king!"* he will tell anyone, very loudly, and there is empirical evidence to bear him out. At sixty, after thirty-three years of broadcast survival, he has found his moment! Suddenly, there is respect where there was once derision. Also, there are ratings, as he would fervidly show me each morning, sifting printouts for his jumbo numbers like a coot prospector. Among collegians and coffee klatches alone, he is omnipotent. The fact is, never has a man who loves to be liked been liked and loved more: "He's just about the best there is at what he does," says a deeply earnest David Letterman, who recently threatened to instate Philbin as host of the coveted hour following his own mighty *Late Show*. "It must be odd to be his age and be at the top of your game," says Letterman, awestruck. "He just wears me out." ("Dave's adopted me or something," shrugs an incredulous but grateful Philbin, whose ubiquitous Letterman cameos bespeak his hipness.) But it does not end there. *Washington Post* TV critic Tom Shales not long ago offered only two words of advice for the novice Conan O'Brien: "Watch Regis," he sternly wrote, wielding the keen example of "Philbin's ability to make entertainment out of nothing, to bound onto the air day after day, always personable and amusing." Likewise, Dana Carvey, who demonstrated the importance of being Regis with his fine *Saturday Night Live* impersonation, cannot suppress his profound admiration. "Regis embodies comedy in the classic form!" he says eagerly. "He's the Put-Upon Guy, the guy who always gets the bad seat at the roast and isn't afraid to tell you about it. He has no pretense! He's totally honest on the air, and if you're totally honest, how are you not cool?"

Regis Philbin is only one man. There is only so much he can do. Certainly he cannot be everywhere at once. "Everyone wants a piece of me!" he likes to say, exasperated, as he likes to be. Still, each day that he lives is another day he must give. In return, he asks for little, and in return, that is exactly what he gets. As he rushes into his studio every weekday morning, seconds before airtime, he draws a deep breath and announces, "It's another wave coming over my head!" Beleaguered with responsibility, he must summon superhuman doses of adrenaline to meet demands heaped upon him from all sides. He must, first of all, parry on camera with his excellent partner and foil, Kathie Lee Gifford, herself the unrelenting sun which the Philbin cloud must necessarily diffuse. (*"I had to shield my eyes,"* wrote Regis of their first meeting in his memorable essay "Where Would You Be Without Me?" which was published as the foreword to Gifford's autobiography.) Next, as the hour that comprises *Live With Regis & Kathie Lee* unfolds, he must lead the interrogation of celebrity guests, an activity known to sap life force from the steeliest mortals. Undiminished, he moves on, availing his schedule to the inevitable clamor for his unique services: Perhaps his friend Lou Holtz, head coach of Notre Dame's Fighting Irish, will require a quick boost of confidence. "Lou needs me!" he is fond of blurting. "Lou! Lou! Lou! Lou!" he will then chant, even when no one is listening. Or perhaps his friend Bobby

De Niro will want him to deliver another small but rousing performance in an otherwise dreary movie. (Their work together in *Night and the City* leapt off the screen.) Or perhaps the Letterman writers will need to infuse that night's program with a fresh jolt of Regis. Whatever the task, he will rise to it and still have room for concert appearances, cookbook signings, charity benefits, film premieres, Broadway galas, medical appointments, and dinner with his family. And, all the while, no matter the circumstance, he will work the phones (doing all his own dialing) with special brio, keeping in constant touch with friends, acquaintances, and the general state of the world in which he mercifully dwells.

I came to know of the Philbin telephone prowess very quickly. To properly assess the broad scope of his life, I would not leave him alone. Naturally, he complained about this. When I wouldn't relent, he called my mother to complain. "He won't leave me alone!" he told her. He also called his wife. "I can't get rid of him!" he complained. He called many people, complaining. "Jesus Christ, HE'S DRIVING ME CRAZY!" he told them all. Then he would hang up and beam gleefully and say to me, "Now who else can we call? This is fun."

Like a juggernaut, his impact sprawls across the American landscape. Thus, to satisfy his vast minions, he must regularly jet around the nation, bringing with him wherever he goes his effervescent irritability and, very often, his young executive producer, the one called Gelman. Gelman, as Philbin loyalists know well, is a dominant source of annoyance for the great broadcaster. Gelman is thirty-two, unflappable, born with a first name (Michael) never acknowledged by Philbin, and can be seen withstanding daily admonishments from him on the sidelines of *Live*. Behind the bluster, of course, there is something approximating paternal love, so much so that when Philbin was about to undergo emergency heart surgery last year, his lingering concern beyond the welfare of his family was simply this: "I thought, *My gosh, who's gonna finish raising Gelman?*"

They were together in Milwaukee when I first entered their crackling orbit. They had come, on a cold Saturday night, to perform their highly entertaining nightclub act (technically, Gelman warms the crowd; Philbin entertains) for two thousand discerning heartlanders. Immediately upon their arrival at the grand Riverside Theater, the first offense of the evening presented itself: "Oh Christ, *they misspelled my name!*" Indeed, the marquee heralded the appearance of REGIS PHILBN. "Can you *believe* this?" said the offended one, pleased and perturbed all at once. He was, by now, ensconced in his small, spartan dressing room, where

Gelman stood before a mirror modeling comedy wigs. "Gelman should be in another room," Regis told me, "*but he's made himself at home in here*—SO WHAT AM I GONNA DO?" (The Philbin cadence, it must be noted, invariably swells as final punctuation nears.) He stepped behind his bathroom door to urinate while singing "You Make Me Feel So Young," which would be his opening number that night. (His own special lyrics: "Hey, lady, are you lookin' at me? My name is Regis Philbin— I made a star out of Kathie Lee!") Donning his crisp tuxedo, he explained, "You will find over the next several days very few of the usual star trappings around me. I'm a *real person*!" Even so, he cannot escape outsize adoration. Now, for instance, a stagehand rushed in with his fan mail: one letter. "Look at the mail pouring in!" he grumbled. "WHEN ARE THEY GONNA LEAVE ME ALONE! WHAT THE HELL DO THEY ALL WANT FROM ME?"

Because he is a professional, he knew exactly what they wanted and, of course, he delivered. From the outset, pandemonium gripped the auditorium and would not let go. That night, men cheered and women swooned. He sang and bristled and regaled and held back nothing. He accepted native gifts of cheese ties and cheese hats and wore them with aplomb. "What a reception!" he said with majestic sarcasm. He invited many women onto the stage to irritate him. He noodled clunkily at the piano ("You're gonna *love* this!"). For a stirring climax, he defeated a strapping twenty-year-old student in a push-up contest (by craftily swiping a hand from beneath his challenger as they approached the count of twenty-six). Afterward, he received a small group of dignitaries in a cramped room backstage, where men told him of their heart ailments and Indian cuisine was served. "What a night we're having!" he exclaimed. "It doesn't get any crazier than this!" He then repaired to the lobby, with Gelman in tow, to autograph copies of his new exercise video (*Regis Philbin: My Personal Workout*) and accept further platitudes. An hour later, he made his getaway, toting valise and garment bag, through a back alley where a sedan idled amid a gaggle of female devotees. "LOOK AT THESE GROUPIES!" he said mirthfully. "*They're still here in the shadows!*" Then, more quietly: "You're waiting for Gelman, aren't you?" Later, I would learn that Gelman painted Beertown crimson that night. Regis, on the other hand, tossed alone in his hotel bed, worn to pulp and strung out on too much Coca-Cola.

•   •   •

On Oscar night in New York, it is good for a king to be seen, even if he is extremely tired. Although he toiled for most of his career on the West Coast, it is New York that seethes in his Bronx-bred blood. New York is where Regis Philbin belongs, where he broadcasts, and also where he lives, which helps cut down on commuting time. Here, he is a man of the masses, approachable to all, at home on pavement and pay phone, in cafeterias and fetid cabs. Still, he must move among the swells when necessary, and this was just such an occasion. After flying all day from San Francisco, where he'd emceed a trade show for record merchants, he had returned in time to pop over to the Oscar-watching party hosted by Joan Rivers and Blaine Trump at Elaine's Restaurant. (It is this sort of function that gives him something to talk about on the air the next morning.) Because his wife, the wise and glamorous Joy Philbin, was indisposed (tending to the launch of her own decorating program, *Haven*), he asked me to pick him up and accompany him. Because rain had depleted the city's taxi supply, I gave a foreign guy forty bucks to ferry us over in his stretch-limousine-for-hire. Because Regis Philbin hates extravagance, he yelled at me for much of the short ride. "You're embarrassing me!" he said, deeply chagrined. "I'm getting very nervous here!"

At Elaine's, Gelman waited. Also present were Liza Minnelli, Jason Robards, Richard Chamberlain, former mayor David Dinkins, Ashford and Simpson, and other assorted cognoscenti, all milling about large television screens no one watched much. "I can't hear a damned thing, Gelman," said Philbin above the ruckus. Not a man to work a room that is not his own, he politely sipped a tonic and lime and waited for dinner that did not come. Since he hadn't eaten anything all day, he grew restless. To pass time, he entertained tablemates with his impersonation of Cary Grant looking for a waiter to bring dinner that would not come: "I say! Where's my *wait-tah*?" When this did not work, he finally stormed the kitchen. "Come on, chef!" he said, thrilling the cook staff into submission. "I'M STARVING!" Shortly thereafter, heaps of greens and pasta landed before him, and he ate and was happy, except for the fact that he was jet-lagged and couldn't hear any of the Oscar presentations because of the goddamned noise and ultimately was sorry he'd even come. "Never again," he told me before he bolted, which he did before dessert. "I'm slowin' down. I'm outta control! No more parties for me!" He said this and almost meant it and then cabbed home.

Each morning he rises at seven-thirty, a scant ninety minutes before he overtakes the American airwaves. Once out of his cozy Park Avenue apartment, he travels across town, arriving no sooner than eight-thirty at his office, five floors above the WABC-TV studios, seven blocks from the hospital where he sprang from his mother's womb. "I am like the elephant who has come home to die," he often says. His office betrays him as a man who forgets nothing and discards less. Strewn everywhere is stuff, much of it relating to Notre Dame (his beloved alma mater), Perry Como (his beloved idol), and his own endless career. His career has been fueled on pure instinct. His method is uncomplicated: He avoids speaking to Gifford anytime before or after a broadcast. "It plays better that way," he says simply. He has no writers and writes nothing for himself to say on air. Rather, he spews from the top of his head, citing headlines and personal travail and dyspepsia and somehow making it funny. Because of this (and the sulfurous flint that is Gifford), the first twenty minutes of *Live*—the extemporaneous, two-headed Host Chat—has been regarded as perhaps television's truest sheer human comedy. As such, the man is the material, and has been since 1961 when he climbed onto his first talk-show stool in San Diego and began talking about nothing in particular. ("I, for one, couldn't be more impressed," Jerry Seinfeld has said of Philbin and Gifford, acknowledging their exemplary work in the field of Nothing, his own specialty. "You can't do less than they do and make a living.") The Philbin rationale: "I really had no tools to fall back on," he says, explaining the birth of his style. "I wasn't a comedian, didn't know any jokes—still don't know any jokes, really. I wasn't a singer. So all I could do was be myself and do what I did as a kid on the street corner. And I was a scream on a street corner."

A Man and His Ratings, as pertaining to one Tuesday in March (a performance piece):

Regis: [*in his office*] All right, gimme the big number!
Gelman: We got a 7.4 rating with a 28 share!
Regis: That's big! Now, give me what *they've* got.
Gelman: [*scanning local Nielsens*] Our competition: *American Journal* and *Hard Copy*, both of which cost about ten times more to produce than our show? A 6 share! We're almost five times bigger!
Regis: [*sings loudly*] *"Hey, it's spring again!"* Okay, now give me Dave.
Gelman: Aw, poor Dave. Seven-three—he's a tenth of a point behind us.
Regis: Please!

Gelman: As a matter of fact, Regis—

Regis: Yes, Gelman?

Gelman: You had the highest share yesterday of any show at *any* time on *any* network! Oh my God!

Regis: [*sings, performing twist*] *"It's spring aaagain! Gelman's on the wing aaagain!"* [*pause*] You mean, we even beat Oprah? Five-hundred-million-dollar Oprah?

Gelman: Her share is 21, ours is 28!

Regis: We're the BIGGEST! STOMPING, CRUSHING, MOVING, GOING! We're a RUNAWAY BEER TRUCK OUTTA CONTROL!!! [*more singing and fade*]

Philbinalia and other findings: He loves his feet. He removed his shoes and socks to show them to me. "Look at those fabulous arches!" he said. "Smooth as silk! No long gnarled toes, not a bunion, not a callus! They're just naturally beautiful!" He once showed his kidney stones on television, but only after they'd been removed. He possesses a fear of actress Bea Arthur. "Formidable woman!" he told me, shuddering. "Terrified to get close to her." Madonna has felt his biceps. "Tell me the truth," he said to her at the time. "Am I an attractive man or not?" (She said yes.) In Woody Allen's film *Everything You Always Wanted to Know About Sex,* he played celebrity panelist Regis Philbin on the mock game show *What's My Perversion?* On his own show, he recently admitted to having gone nine months without sex. He was murdered in a *Perry Mason* movie. Cindy Crawford has felt his biceps and taken workouts with him at the gym they both frequent. ("He likes to look at himself in the mirror while he does those bicep curls," she told me.) He gave Richard Simmons and Robin Leach their first television exposures on *A.M. Los Angeles,* and has never apologized. Richard Nixon once played the Notre Dame fight song on the piano for him in San Diego. Interviewing Bobby De Niro about their unforgettable three-minute scene in *Night and the City,* he asked, "Did I make you better than you were?" ("You did, absolutely," De Niro assured him.) He is the opposite of handy around the house and has forgotten how to make coffee, formerly his lone culinary skill. He snores in variety. ("The worst one is the *gurgle,*" his wife told me. "When it stops, you think he's going to die.") To get someone's attention, he will inexplicably shout the word *gazzah*!—which, to date, has no known meaning. When playing tennis, he likes to be addressed as Net Man. Before *Live* debuted in syndication six years ago, his only other national talk-vehicles, *That Regis Philbin Show* for Westinghouse (1964) and *Regis Philbin* for NBC (1981), lasted thirteen weeks and five months, respectively. (Both shows forced writers upon him.) His first real fame befell him as the-overzealous-sidekick-with-the-dumb-name on the increasingly legendary *Joey Bishop Show* (1967–69). He walked off the show during the first year, partly because he felt responsible for low ratings and and partly because Bishop privately suggested it would be an interesting thing for him to do. He returned a week later, upon public demand. "All's well that ends well," Bishop told America. Not long thereafter, Bishop wrote liner notes for Philbin's one record album, *It's Time For Regis!* (now available on CD), promising "For a man his age, he sings great." The two men have not spoken in several years and Philbin cannot say he knows why.

Letterman needed him. He had known it for a week, and now it was time to render his assistance. Tonight he would be the comic culmination of a segment called "New Medical Products," bursting into the Ed Sullivan Theater the moment Dave activated the revolutionary Regis Alert Bracelet ("Guaranteed to cut medical response time in half!"). Since his own angioplasty last year, he has become an inadvertent icon for the cardio-afflicted, a role he accepts with reticence. He is private about pain, having withstood inordinate sums of it. On the day of the show's taping, he shared much of it with me as we rode back from Monmouth, New Jersey, where he had greeted hundreds of women at a Macy's charity reception. ("I've had *five* bypasses, and look at me!" one woman eagerly told him.) Beyond the dismal career valleys, there was a misbegotten first marriage in California that never should have been but was. It produced two children: a daughter, Amy, now thirty-three, a musician whose work can be heard on her father's exercise video; and a son, Danny, who is a twenty-seven-year-old political scientist and who was born with missing vertebrae and no muscles in his legs. The life of Dan Philbin, while triumphant, has been a long, complicated ordeal of surgeries (the legs were eventually lost) and ongoing rehabilitation. "He's my hero in life," his father told me, emphatic and emotional. "For him to overcome all this disability, to graduate college, to work on his master's program—he's just dynamite, a remarkable kid. Now he's got a permanent job coming up. But it's been a *grind*. I remember for one year straight he was in the orthopedic hospital and I'd go see him every day. I tell you, anytime he goes back into the hospital, it's like a knife in my heart. I wish it were me, not him." He has felt the pain anyway, but never publicly spoken of it, certainly not on television, fearing the obsessive pity of viewers. "Dan doesn't want it, and I don't either," he said pridefully. His friends, nevertheless, report of his devastation when the *National Enquirer* ran a story painting him as an uncaring father. Howard Stern worsened matters by mounting a Danny Philbin Radiothon. ("That was the worst time," confirms Gifford, still appalled. "It was the cruelest, nastiest, most dishonest story. And then to make fun of it! You could burn in hell for that.") "Howard Stern is probably a nice guy," said Regis, visibly frustrated, as we approached the Ed Sullivan Theater. "But I'm not gonna go on the radio with him and defend myself. I mean, who would it help?"

"CAN A GUY GET HIS FLY ZIPPED UP?" Outside the theater a mob had descended on the car; in the backseat, a loud human prop was hastily climbing into better pants (a professional courtesy). "All right, yes—*Regis Philbin is changing his pants!*" he announced to the throng hovering curbside. Meanwhile, youths hanging out of a passing school bus spied him and began chanting, "REEGE! REEGE!" "That's right," he hollered. "I'm here to save Letterman's ass one more time!" Upstairs he waited for makeup and informed fellow guest Plácido Domingo of his recent singing conquest in Milwaukee. "You sing?" said the great tenor. "What?" replied Philbin. "You think you're the only thing around? *Come on!*" *Late Show* staffers then briefed him on the intricacies of his surprise cameo ("You want me to run up and down the aisles like a moron, right?"). Head writer Rob Burnett assured him, "You know what we call you around here? Two words: Show Saver." "SHOW SAVER!" repeated Philbin, embracing the notion. (Indeed, for use as a future bit, Letterman himself would burst in on *Live With Regis & Kathie Lee* the following morning, bearing tokens of loose meat and wilted flowers, saying "I'm so sorry to interrupt this rehearsal! W-w-where's Oprah?")

Once stationed in the lobby, he paced anxiously behind the doors through which he would soon explode, hurling his exercise tapes at stunned audience members. As Letterman's muffled voice resonated from within, Philbin provided searing insight from without: *"Listen . . . the audience is dying down! He always does two bits too many. . . . Show Saver's gonna have to gear up! Gonna have to get out there and win one for Dave! . . . He's beginning to flounder. . . . They're giving him intellectual nods of recognition now . . . Dave's voice getting higher! Panic setting in! I've been there, I know. . . ."* Then, Letterman boomed: "And *finally*—oh boy, and not a minute too soon—*finally* . . ." And finally, the Regis Alert Bracelet was triggered, as was Regis, who tore through the auditorium to strains of "The Sabre Dance," inciting havoc, dispensing videos, getting mauled. *Did you see that!* he said, crashing back into the lobby, only slightly winded. "I GOT MUGGED! They grabbed the tapes right outta my hands! I RAN FOR MY LIFE! The hell with it! Six hundred and sixteen bucks to do *this*?! It ain't worth it!" And he was very happy indeed.

For the rest of that night, he seemed almost subdued, and I like to think it was because every ounce of his Herculean stamina had been sucked clean by the unslakable mistress that is our culture. He, on the other hand, said it had more to do with missing a nap. But he also said, "You know what they say: If you stop, you're dead." When that time comes, he has made it known, his ashes are to be scattered over Notre Dame. "I think it appeals to his economic side," Joy Philbin later told me, chuckling. They have been married for twenty-four years, have raised two college-age daughters, Joanna and Jennifer, and have continued to laugh. After the Letterman episode, she joined us for what would be another typical Philbin night in New York, beginning with a Harry Winston cocktail party (ten minutes), then a private screening (*Jimmy Hollywood*), then dinner (Italian). Joy brought along directions. "Regis doesn't always know where he's going," she said, gently needling, but at the same time hitting smack upon his peculiar genius. "It's a character flaw," she said, "but nothing I can't live with." Later, at the screening room, I watched them sit—not incongruously—within a constellation whose number included Minnelli and Scorsese and Pesci and De Niro, who, being De Niro, slipped in just as the lights dimmed and out just before they brightened. "Where's Bobby?" said Regis, craning his neck while the final credits rolled. "He left, didn't he? He always does that." He shrugged and yawned and rose and took no offense. It was their city, after all, and they knew how to find each other.

Here was a quandary: To promote his autobiographical film, *Private Parts,* Howard Stern was at this moment oversaturating all media—of which he remains king, of course. Since seemingly everyone else was writing Stern pieces, I faced a special writing challenge. My solution was to bring his lovely, long-suffering wife into the fold and to focus only on how that remarkable marriage had thus far survived. Perhaps what follows helps to somewhat explain why the couple separated three years later.

The Howard Stern
Marriage Manual

Esquire, April 1997

In that most vexing realm of matrimony, the heroic are few. The knowledgeable are fewer. Each day, wedlock means less to participants everywhere. Fatigued, unsatisfied, they flee, seeking bliss unattainable. Desperate, gullible, they flock to false prophets who fob off faddish theorems. (I ask you: Mars? Venus? Who actually marries on those cold, distant orbs? Nobody I know.) Yet, amid this futile thrash, there long ago arose one voice of reason, of tangible truth, of *durable experience.* He was a renegade, yes; one whose methods shocked so as to awaken a numbed, hapless pupildom. Summarily dismissed, as are all fresh visionaries, he persisted. He opened his own marriage to public inspection, bemoaning its tiny injuries, the kind that accrue and erode connubial love. "My wife," he would say, "won't let me do her." Or: "Everybody is getting laid but me." Bravely, he tested marital boundaries, often implementing naked lesbians in his work. Indeed, his laboratory would be populated by harlots and starlets and others whose every orifice knew no unimagined violation. Never did he stray or even touch all that much; instead, he *verbalized* all misconduct, broadcast it over airwaves regulated by our freethinking government. With each torrid case study, he demystified the baser human urges that lure men toward alimony payments. As if to declare "I will show you what you are missing, for I am missing it, too, and perhaps all that we are missing is disease and debt and much therapy. And also fun." He did this, and does so still, for you and for me and for many million dollars a year. But, arguably, he does it mostly for love of his wife, without which he knows he is nothing.

Naturally, I speak of Howard Stern, the misunderstood oracle, the devoted Long Island husband, and perhaps the finest man I have ever encountered. Faithfully married to the same woman for nineteen years, he has remarkable hair—long, dark, thick, lovely sheen—as well as a luminous complexion and three daughters (aged fourteen, ten, and four). Also, he stands six foot five and masturbates with his right hand (which he also employs for firm handshakes). It is no secret that he believes masturbation saves marriages, his own especially. As he wrote in his first groundbreaking manifesto, *Private Parts,* now a major motion picture: "It's the greatest single source of sexual satisfaction I have. I can get myself off in three seconds." Because of his arduous schedule—he must wake before dawn to begin the daily toil of speaking aloud—he likes to perform self-gratification most weeknights as a means to induce sleep. He does this in bed when his wife and children are downstairs.

Stern had not yet ejaculated on the day of our long-anticipated first meeting. He wore his hair in a bun and later down on his shoulders. Gaining physical access to his person understandably required months of negotiation, endless telephone wrangling with protectors, and finally the designation of a secret rendezvous place: the Italian restaurant Vizio, in Roslyn Heights, New York, located minutes from his home, whose hallowed but unpretentious premises are known only to intimates and to Richard Simmons (not welcome back after misbehavior with cucumbers at poolside). Our assignation was set for early afternoon, when the restaurant is closed and thus clear of Stern sycophants, who might wish to have sex with him or shake his right hand. (A man cannot traffic in taboo, even constructively, as he does, without stirring the loins of lower intellects.) Here he was delivered by his loyal driver Ronnie, the only man who can glimpse Stern in meditation, which he does, full lotus, in the backseat of his vehicle en route to and from Manhattan, where his microphone awaits and spends him each morning.

"Did you meditate?" asked the good wife Alison upon her husband's arrival on this day. (I had insisted upon her presence.) "Uh-huh," he replied, kissing her warmly, his arm curled around her sylphlike waist. Then he said to no one in particular, "I don't have any underwear on now." His retinue of stylists, present as well, exchanged glances whose meaning I could not discern. To his wife, he said brightly, "Hey, Alison, you're all dolled up!" And she said, "Yeah, honey!" Two nights earlier, the Sterns had had sexual intercourse, the details of which will follow, and I sensed their pheromones still hanging thick about them. (Moreover, buoyed by some heartfelt revelations I was to elicit during this summit, their ensuing physical relations would increase exponentially!) Eyeing his missus appreciatively, Stern announced, "I gotta get her interviewed every day!"

What, then, of Alison Stern, age forty-three (like Stern himself), postmodern housewife and mother, whose full-throated voice is sometimes heard during her husband's radio communications, via telephone, instructing him to grow up and stop lying about what transpires in their boudoir? The question comes up incessantly. The answer is this: She is very nice. Her laugh comes easily. In conversation, when you say something with which she agrees, she will say, *"Right . . . right. . . ."* Twice, like that. But this woman is no pushover, and that is why her marriage succeeds. If her husband must exaggerate truth in order to relate to his troubled minions, she is truth personified, brooking no guff and, at the same time, setting new standards in affording marital leeway. "Clearly, she's the boss, huh," asserts the beautiful actress Mary McCormack, who, as it happens, portrays Alison Stern on-screen in the current film release *Private Parts,* considered by many to be one man's love letter to his wife, featuring lesbians. "That was the way I played her," says McCormack. "I think she's totally in charge." (From his February fourth radio broadcast—Stern: "The only thing wrong with the film is Alison looks too much like a hero." Alison, phoning from home: "I *am* the hero.")

Without doubt, it is his mate's good-natured mettle that has allowed Stern to become the influential figure that he is today. Thus, I felt it would be illuminating to see the two of them alone together in relaxed surroundings, with hair-and-makeup people also in attendance, plus a photographer, the photographer's two assistants, and a small, bored restaurant staff. In this casual crucible, I would mine the minutiae of their exemplary private dynamic. I would ask questions about bedroom politics, secret spite, and personal hair care. What emerged was an inspirational portrait, something akin to the Howard and Alison Stern Marriage Manual, describable only as a glorious testament to enduring love and grim resignation. "It's true," Stern would tell me. "The world is filled with temptation, yet we are here and still together. Of course, it could fall apart tomorrow. It's not a done deal. She could throw me out any day now."

LIMITATIONS ARE LIMITLESS!

"Don't assume that it's easy living with me," he said next. She nodded, then elaborated, "It's not easy living with him." Her voice bore no malice. It is a fundamental acceptance: No man is easy, nor is any woman, and once this can be acknowledged, wedded life beholds great adventure. Excited by that possibility, Stern set out to create a marriage that would be remembered for its epic daring and sexual frustration. The rewards were plentiful. In time, Hollywood called. The Stern relationship now merited cinematic celebration. Stern himself would star in the male lead and perform love scenes with a woman who was not his wife, but played her, so infidelity was at last technically permissible. What could be more perfect! Moreover, his real-life wife could only thrill to such glamorization, as would any civilian, and her gratitude would manifest itself in new and surprising ways. For he insisted that it would be so:

"Ohhhhh, yes, let me tell you, there's gonna be some big changes around my house!" he declared for my benefit. "First of all, she'll be shackled to the bed every night. That's what movie stars do!"

Here, even Alison Stern brightened, adding with only minimal irony: "I'll be greeting him with nothing on under my bathrobe."

"By the way, we'll also be joining Scientology," he continued. "Oh, yeah—me, Cruise, Travolta. As soon as you get into the stratosphere, you gotta be a Scientologist. I'm a little confused, though. I think you have to pray to a test tube. Anyway," he concluded, "every married couple should have a movie made about them. It really helps!"

BE VAIN IN LOVE!

As we spoke, Stern sat at a table where makeup was being applied to his gaunt countenance. He is, after all, a man who likes to look good for his woman, a lesson in itself. "She's got natural beauty," he said of his wife. "But when you got a face like mine, you gotta be worked on. Makes a big difference." Convinced of his ungainliness, he prefers to obscure his God-given features with dark glasses and long hair, a measure he prescribes for men similarly afflicted. It is, however, his coif that concerns him most. When I asked how his miraculous tresses are maintained, his wife rolled her adoring eyes and said, "Do you have all day?" (In part, much deep conditioning is involved, administered by professionals, followed by the rigorous and repeated twirl of a curling iron.)

But this vainglory made him a complete man. Indeed, were it not for his hair, there would be no Alison in his life, and this is why: Caught in the rain on his way to a party in 1974, young Stern, then a Boston University junior, panicked that his proud mane was being badly drenched. "I decided I needed a blow-dryer," he would later significantly write in his memoirs. Finding himself in the neighborhood of an old female friend, he barged into her apartment in search of hot air. On his way to the bathroom, he spied his future sweetly loitering in the kitchen: "She was just my type—real cute, great thin body." The coed Alison Berns rebuffed Stern's awkward advances only slightly—and only after his hair was dry—but, within days, consented to appear in his student film project, in which she was seen meditating on a rock. (He wooed her with cinema from the start!) On their subsequent first date, they saw the movie *Lenny,* the story of the revered and reviled comic Lenny Bruce, which, although they could not know this, foretold the tumultuous life that loomed before them. Then he got her drunk on Blue Nun wine, which got him to third base, which got them to where they are today, more or less.

MARRY TWO PEOPLE!

Epiphanies in marriage surface without warning, and on this day one swam sharply to the light while the two Sterns were exchanging ideas before me. As a paradigm of good partner dialogue, I will attempt to recapture their intrinsic rhythm herewith. (Note his deft tactic of softening her urgency with self-deprecatory remarks. Men, try this at home!)

Her:	I just came to an interesting revelation—
Him:	Just looking at me now?
Her:	No, recently—that—
Him:	—I'm a filthy, dirty bastard?
Her:	—that I've been married to him for almost twenty years—
Him:	—and she's sick of it.
Her:	—but there's a third person in our marriage.
Him:	Who is that?
Her:	The guy on the radio. I've got no problems with the guy sitting here in this restaurant—
Him:	That's what you think. I just passed gas.
Her:	—but this third person I'm not crazy about.

True, the person one marries is not necessarily the person one ever knows absolutely. People change; they grow; they have large-breasted strippers occasionally sit on their laps at the office. It is part of the wonder of life. Indeed, the public Stern and the private Stern are legendarily reputed to be quite different, although the physical resemblance is uncanny. But does this mean that one Stern is any less real than the other? Hardly. (It is, after all, the public Stern who pays for his wife's personal trainer.) Robin Quivers, the bright woman who assists Stern in his work, attests: "Yes, there *are* two Howard Sterns. In fact, one of the funniest things Alison ever said to me was *'I have no idea who he is when he's on the air!'* She had come by to visit one day and couldn't recognize the man she saw. It's one thing to hear him on the radio, but then to *see him do it...* She doesn't *see* that every day; she doesn't deal with that person! She kept asking me 'Who *is* that?' "

Of course, who among us is not two or more people, depending upon our levels of psychosis? Still, it is understandable that Alison Stern waited this long to acknowledge her second husband, the colorful one so fascinated by C-cups and sadomasochism, so willing to give voice to our universal id. Such profound acceptance does not come overnight. Some may think, however, that evidence was in place fifteen years ago, after she miscarried the fetus of their child; he worked through his grief over Washington, D.C., airwaves by postulating "My stupid wife had to have a miscarriage! It's all her fault!" Unfortunately, it was the private Stern who thereafter had to sleep on the couch for days. (Postscript: Because he is wise enough to know that there is no mistake from which a marriage cannot ultimately benefit, he wastes no time with unnecessary contrition. "Let me tell you something, Alison," I heard him lecture her. "It was a good thing I did that! It gave the movie great dramatic scenes!" She quietly signaled her agreement with a firm shove to his rib cage.)

SPEND LESS TIME TOGETHER!

Healthful marriage requires ample breathing room, and Stern makes every effort to honor his wife thusly: "I leave her alone for a couple of days and then she comes to appreciate the great man that I am." Deprivation, he feels, only prolongs wedlock. As he told me, "The reason this lasts is that we don't see each other at night." To wit: Due to the unforgiving demands of his profession, the Sterns have separate bedtimes, thus ensuring separate lifestyles. (Also, they keep separate dressing areas, but share a bathroom. "We *wanted* separate bathrooms," she blurted to me. He shrugged: "Hey, the family that craps together. . . .") According to ritual, she tucks him in by eight and does not retire herself until eleven. "I love my nights!" she offered, perhaps a bit too enthusiastically. He said, "As far as I know, she could be doing anything." The hiss of his white-noise machine beside him muffles all traces of her merry nocturnes, but not her snoring. "It's an issue for me," he told me later. (Alison insists that she doesn't snore.) His solution: "I put a pillow over her mouth. No, I don't recommend that. You'll end up in jail. I just wake her up and say, 'Listen, honey, shut up! You're snoring like a guy! I can't take it. I gotta sleep. You gotta leave the room.' Then we start whining at one another until somebody drifts off again."

They elect to meet only on Saturday nights. "Those are date nights," he explained. "I strip down to my bikini underwear and pose for her." Because he cannot leave his home for fear of mass adulation, their interludes are confined to his basement lair, where most of his waking hours are spent in cognitive reverie and watching TV (a one-hundred-inch AMX touch screen!). "My dungeon," he calls it proudly. "I sit there and control the universe." This private refuge, whose door is electronically fortified with two double locks, is also where he composed his two best-selling autobiographical texts and where he conducted experiments in Prodigy cybersex, the details of which appear in the second Stern memoir, *Miss America.* "I did it only for the enlightenment of humanity," he told me as his wife looked on. "Otherwise, I would never do that. Why would a man jerk off in front of a computer? That's sick."

Understandably, the subject is a delicate one: He boasted in print of reaching repeated climaxes with his on-line partners ("cybersluts," in his lighthearted parlance), but denied it to his wife. "Alison doesn't go for that kind of stuff," he said, turning to her. "Honey," he asked, "do you think it was cheating or not?" She said tentatively, "Well, I don't believe that part [the cyberorgasms] was true." He said, "Of course it wasn't, darling!" He then leaned out of her view and, nodding vigorously at me, silently mouthed the words, *"It was true! It was true!"* He seemed very happy.

ACCEPT HIS OTHER WOMEN!

"I can't play the jealous wife anymore," she said. Her conviction, along with his fine belches, resonated throughout the room. "I can't, I can't!"

she repeated a little urgently. "I feel that I can trust him." Stern gently patted her forearm and added, "Isn't that what Mary Jo Buttafuoco said?" But his fidelity is, of course, a matter of record. "All I'm doin' is *looking* at naked women," he would tell me later. "And I'm being *honest* about it. I'm not doin' anything to 'em. There are guys who go to work, and they're fucking their secretary and twenty of their clients and everyone else, but you would never know about it. I'm probably the only guy *behavin'* himself!" Or, as Alison Stern wisely noted, "When he stops talking about these women—then I'll be concerned."

MARRY A THERAPIST!

So, when they fight, they fight about the petty annoyances. Like his flatulence. (Him, proudly: "I am noxious!" Her: "You can tell a mile away.") Or her habit of leaving closet lights burning ("Makes me nuts, costs money!") or milk and chicken languishing out on the countertops ("All kindsa fuckin' salmonella!"). "Oh, I'm a nag!" he confessed, bravely owning perhaps his worst quality. Fortunately for all, Alison Stern is trained in psychiatric social work, having earned her master's at Columbia. "I'm her biggest case," he said mournfully. Under her aegis, their arguments explode and die quickly. Rather than attack, they express hurt. No grudges are held. Each episode is resolved.

Until, of course, it recurs: Most famously, the ugliest Stern imbroglios revolve around his peculiar diet ("I only eat like five things!") and the occasional lack of a specific food item. Most recently, there were no Cheerios, for which hell was loosed upon the household.

Her: He hadn't eaten Cheerios for over a month.
Him: But you gotta be prepared! Buy nine hundred boxes! Give me a fuckin' break!
Her: Our kids were in tears.
Him: It's good for them! They should learn life sucks!

HUMILIATE EACH OTHER!

What did he say when I asked the secret to getting what he wants from his spouse? I will tell you. After a considerable pause, he said: "How the fuck would I know?" Then he said, "Make a lot of money." His excellent jest notwithstanding, he teaches us to be direct, to be vocal, and, failing that, to beg. I watched him cuddle his mate for the benefit of photographic commemoration. He pulled her close and simply stated, "Look at me like you love me, honey." She chuckled sweetly and wryly said, "Oh, that's so hard to do." And she did what he asked. It was just that easy. "Very beautiful, Al," he said. "The woman loves me!" Soon after, he turned quite serious, startling all present, except for maybe the busboys, who could not understand him, and said, "Alison is my best friend. I just know that out of anyone in this universe, there's a person here who would never do anything hurtful to me or attack me. She is the one I trust. That's why I will never cheat. Plus the germs." Alison blushed beatifically. (Still touched days later, she asked him on the air to repeat this proclamation; he declined. "I don't want to look weak in front of my audience," he hedged. "Besides, there was a writer there. I had to say it.")

Of course, few things are more attractive than insecurity in an important man. Perhaps that is why he suddenly reached forward and plucked a thin breadstick from a container on the table before him. "This is what I actually look like," he said, brandishing the snack with great lament. His meaning was clear: his fabled dearth of manhood, his compromised appendage, his genetic misfortune. You know. Seen only by his wife (he will stand at no urinal), it is his private leveler, reminding him, and us, that he is no better than other men and many children. "I'm hung like this breadstick," he informed me. "You're not that long," Alison asserted softly. "Okay, I'll be more realistic," he said, breaking off an inch and a half. "How's that? I'm hung like a needle. Evidently, it doesn't matter to her."

And that is the good news. "Sex has been wonderful lately," he actually said next, an admission he'd never before uttered in public. "She believes she's in bed with a movie star. And I think I've gotten better. When we first met, I used to hold out for like thirty seconds; now I can go two, three minutes!" She said, "More like fifteen, twenty." He beamed. "Well, I didn't want to brag. But I don't get enough, I don't get enough."

To evince this point, he described their interlude of two nights before: He had just returned home from the West Coast and was feeling pent-up. "I tell Alison, 'I want to have sex.' And she was like 'Ohhh, ohhhh, I thought we'd have it tomorrow night... I'm in my sweatpants; I have a cold.' I say, 'No, no, no, let's have it tonight! I really need to release now!' We go back and forth for an hour, to the point where she *hates* me. Finally, she says okay. Then I say, 'Ahh, forget it! You don't really want to have sex.' She says, *'I hate you!'* But now she *has* to have sex with me, because I've humiliated her! Worked perfectly! And I was good, too."

Alison Stern did not quibble here. She just studied her husband for a few long moments and said finally, "Well, you know, hate is very close to love." Few men could know this better.

This piece was orchestrated to be a fish-out-of-water romp, in which I profiled the brash, histrionic Geraldo Rivera amid the tranquil remove of a winter family vacation. The action occurred mere months after his notorious on-camera scuffle with skinheads wherein Geraldo's nose was busted by a flying chair. We converged at the swanky Stein Erickson Lodge in Park City, Utah, where the Riveras and company had come to ski. Let me confess: I don't ski, then or now; I'm too tall a galoot, at six foot five, to endure the damage ensured by altitude and sheer velocity. And yet I felt a journalistic responsibility to seize the opportunity to ride the ski lift (i.e., flying chairs!) with my subject. So I rode with Geraldo to the tops of mountains, where I then bribed resort employees to drive me back down to the bottom in their snowmobiles. Then I would wait for Geraldo to ski down so that we could ride up again and again. Admittedly, this was the apogee of wussiness, but, hey, I broke no bones in the process. And, more important, my inexperience on the slopes led to the incident that began this profile, for which how could I not be grateful? I was especially pleased by the serendipitous cameo appearance of Steven Spielberg in the piece—a strange summit meeting captured forever. Also, while Geraldo proclaimed below that his days as a sexual rogue were behind him, he would years later revert to old ways and thus unravel his marriage to C. C. Dyer.

Mr. Rivera

Takes a Holiday

Excerpted from *Playboy*, May 1989

Chairs: We see them every day. Often we sit on them. Sometimes we have them reupholstered. Occasionally, we even find coins under their cushions. Lately, however, the common chair has emerged as a heinous weapon, an instrument of death. Fiendish lunatics now use chairs to bludgeon human skulls! In hellish rituals, chairs are hurled at the heads of innocent victims, rendering them helpless or—worse—lifeless. Chairs: Are we sitting ducks? Or ducking seats? That's the focus of the next three paragraphs.

Geraldo, unlike me, knew the chair was coming. For him, it was something implicit: Grass grows, babies cry, chairs fly. He got his indoctrination last fall, nailed by one of those chrome-and-leather numbers while scuffling with Nazis on television. I got mine a few months later in, of all places, the mountains of Utah. Geraldo was there, too. Amazingly, we were actually standing together, only millimeters apart, when the flying chair struck me. Geraldo escaped injury but missed none of the irony. "Now you know how it feels," he said, laughing ruefully.

This flying chair did not flatten my nose, however, as was Geraldo's experience. Rather, I took a glancing blow to the back of the head. I was merely shaken; virtually no pursuant cosmetic surgery was required. Still,

I was forced to wonder: Had I not been standing within chair range of Geraldo, would I have been hit in the first place? Was proximity my undoing? Didn't that chair, in all likelihood, have Geraldo's name on it?

Or perhaps it was just a coincidence. After all, at the time of the incident, the two of us were paired at the foot of a snowy slope, waiting for a ski lift. True, I'd never ridden a lift before and had no idea that the gondola chair scoops up its passengers from behind with such, well, *insistence*. Nevertheless, I can still feel the sharp crease on my cranium. Geraldo, keen to the resonance of the airborne chair, instantly recognized poetry in the moment, for he suggested to me on the spot, "There's your lead."

Of course, I would be naïve to discount his professional wisdom. Geraldo Rivera has a nose for drama.

This story takes place some two thousand miles from New York City, as the chair flies. Our subject has temporarily abdicated his natural element—the angry, corrupt, virulent streets of said cosmopolis—and deposited himself on a pristine white canvas: Park City, Utah. Mormon country. An altitudinous moral high ground where decency prevails and the skiing is swell. Here, with no societal evils for him to expose and no critical scorn to confront, a man can *breathe*. He may well be the most mocked and detested man in contemporary popular culture, but here, in these benevolent bluffs, he is simply a man. Albeit a man with free time and fabulous accommodations.

Geraldo Rivera on holiday is nothing like Geraldo Rivera on television, where he tends to be so, um, *zealous*. There, he scorches around the edges. "I have a higher temperature than most people," he will reason. "I think hot, I write hot, I am hot," he will say. "I'm not afraid to be zesty." Indeed, in his reporting and interviewing technique, he postures like a matador, a slippery taunt artist, arrogant, confident, full of extraneous flourish. He flaunts his hubris as though it were a bejeweled cape. If he's riled—and he is frequently riled—his machismo plumps like a frankfurter.

But here, disconnected from his arena, he deflates. His inner fires diminish to a cozy flicker. The strut and swagger slacken. The shrill, italicized vocal intonation—a journalistic carnival bark that owes deeply to Walter Winchell—winds down and husks up. His eyes actually twinkle. Self-irony burbles out from a secret reservoir and a winsome Latin charm issues forth. His nearest stab at investigatory behavior is asking a hostess how he might locate a toothpick. (So astonishingly nimble is he with a toothpick, by the way, that he can manage to drink, whistle, and even kiss while clenching one in his teeth.) Were it not for the mustache, he might be Ricardo Montalban.

This Geraldo, the hidden Geraldo, even embraces clean family living. Freed of his duties baiting scoundrels, mutants, sad sacks, and sex fiends, he surrounds himself with loved ones. (*Yes, Geraldo has loved ones!*) Those present with him here in the peaks of Utah include his wife, C. C. Dyer, who, in addition to being the fourth Mrs. Rivera, works as a staff producer on her husband's talk show; his nine-year-old son (by his third marriage), Gabriel, who lives in Los Angeles with his mother; Geraldo's close friend, the comedian Cheech Marin; Cheech's wife, Patty; and the Marins' toddler son, Joey. Fortified by their company, Geraldo finds repose. Geraldo finds peace. Geraldo finds his way to the nearest bartender.

"Give Geraldo a couple of gin and tonics and he'll loosen right up," his wife had advised when extending the invitation for me to spy along on this winter frolic. Forthright, ebullient, and redheaded, she told me, "People see only his bravado, never his passive side. He's a different man off-camera, and *no one* knows this. I mean, I was shocked when I met Morton Downey Jr. and discovered what a nice guy he is. It was so pleasing to know that this abrasive monster on television is, in reality, a sweet, simple, thoughtful, generous guy."

Geraldo likes Geraldo jokes.

While he has never been a guest on *The Tonight Show* or *Late Night With David Letterman,* rarely a week passes that he is not mentioned in one or the other program's opening monologue. Comedians subsist on him. They revel in his searing self-seriousness, his penchant for lurid sensationalism. He belongs to an exalted pantheon of ridicule, firmly ensconced in the rarefied company of Tammy Bakker and Dan Quayle. Following Geraldo's recent network probe of devil worship, there was Jay Leno, asking "Do you believe Satan stooped so low that he appeared on the *same show* as Geraldo Rivera?" Letterman presented a Top Ten list of potential Geraldo specials, among whose entries were: (10) *Live From Elvis's Grave With a Shovel,* (8) *Staking Out the Keebler Elves,* (5) *Former Nazis Who Work at the Gap,* (2) *Geraldo and the Dancing Chipmunks,* and (1) *Raising Raymond Burr.*

I ask Geraldo to cite his favorite japes, while sharing a ski lift (flying chair) with him and his wife. "I think Leno's had the funniest stuff," he says magnanimously. "He came up with the new Geraldo Home Game. It was a life-size cutout of me, and to score points you had to throw a chair at it. He missed the first time he tried."

"I like Johnny Carson's line," says C. C., piping up. " 'Have you heard? There's now a *second-chair* theory.' "

Geraldo says, "Leno had a funny one when it was announced that my brother Craig, who works on my show, was leaving to be an on-camera reporter on another show. He said, 'Wouldn't it be funny if Geraldo turned out to be the *conservative* one in the family?' "

"These barbs never sting?" I ask. Geraldo shrugs manfully. "Sometimes his feelings are hurt," C. C. confides, "but usually the jokes are so funny, you have to laugh."

Geraldo then recalls a momentous summit meeting: While attending the fiftieth birthday party of showbiz impresario Jerry Weintraub not long ago, Geraldo found himself face-to-face with Johnny Carson. "He came up to us, right, honey?" he says, looking to his wife for confirmation. Fraught with import, he continues. "He just put his arm around C. C. and said to her, 'Please don't let anything ever happen to this man. If you do, I'll be out of material.' "

Here Geraldo cannot help but bare his dentition and beam with pride.

Cheech perpetrated what was perhaps the first Geraldo parody on record. Literally on record: On a Cheech and Chong comedy album from the mid-seventies, there is a cut titled "Wake Up, America," in which an intrepid reporter named Horrendo Revolver (curiously portrayed by Cheech affecting a belabored lisp) barges into a blaxploitation recording session, seeking to shut it down. Foiled in his effort, he is somehow enlisted as a shoobeedooing backup singer. It is a humbling portrait—Geraldo, undone—that loopily portended his notorious professional belly flop years later: the fruitless excavation of Al Capone's secret vaults in Chicago. Geraldo sang that time, too. Slinking off the air in the dank, bulldozed basement of Scarface's decrepit lair, he weakly warbled the refrain of the old Sinatra tune "Chicago."

Geraldo does not deny his showmanship. Explaining his unlikely alliance with Cheech, he blurts, "There aren't that many of us brown guys in show business." He is referring to Cheech's Mexican-American heritage and his own Puerto Rican descent. But he implies something larger: Both of them are performers—one a tragedian, the other a fool, theatrically speaking. (Occasionally, one may even actually cross into the other's province, but why name names?) They've known each other more than fifteen years—since the days of Geraldo's short-lived ABC-TV talk show *Good Night America,* on which Cheech and Chong were guests. They've traveled the globe together. Their ex-wives used the same divorce attorney. Cheech's son was conceived on Geraldo's couch.

Cheech, on Geraldo: "He has an intense edge and I have a laid-back edge. We complement each other."

Geraldo, on Cheech: "I like hanging around with him, because he tells me what's hip and I wouldn't know otherwise."

But even beyond the Cheech connection, Geraldo's recent resume is bound inextricably to Hollywood. He left ABC News—his professional petri dish—in a snit stemming partly from the suppression of an incendiary *20/20* report on Marilyn Monroe's death (it wasn't even Geraldo's piece; such are the selfless principles of this man). Contract talks at NBC News, where he hoped to hire on next, unraveled when Geraldo reportedly asked for the inclusion of a clause permitting him to appear in movies. While he soon after found his present niche in the syndication market, film offers were, in fact, tendered, including one for the role of a homicidal hairdresser in *The Morning After,* which starred Jane Fonda. Geraldo opted to pass.

"He can't act worth a damn," says Cheech.

"The only thing I'd ever do," says Geraldo, "would be one of Cheech's movies."

"Yeah," says Cheech, grinning. "He's gonna star in my new movie, *Prison Rape.* A thousand convicts and Geraldo."

"I'm very big in prisons," says Geraldo.

It is doubtful that Geraldo has ever killed a man. Which isn't to suggest that he has never been tempted. For instance, he sputters at the mention of the Joel Steinberg–Hedda Nussbaum case, in which Steinberg was being tried for the murder of his adopted daughter in New York. "He's a total slimeball," Geraldo inveighs. "He should die tomorrow and I should be his executioner."

Retribution, as a concept, makes Geraldo lick his chops. "If you challenge me, I'll fucking kill you," he likes to hypothesize. "I'll fight you bare-knuckled, I'll fight you knife to knife, I'll fight you gun to gun." I asked him if he actually packs heat. "I'll never tell what I make for a living or whether I'm armed," he replies cagily. "But let me say that I am very comfortable with firearms."

(As for knives, C. C. was once quoted as saying that in Geraldo's secret vault, if he had one, there would be a "quart of Cuervo tequila, a switchblade, and a Johnny Mathis tape.")

Fisticuffs are more his style. He has brawled in saloons and boxed in Madison Square Garden (for charity), and, when savoring details of such square-offs, he delights in spraying around corny forties' pug lingo, such as "I was *raining blows* down on his head and body." He is a forty-five-year-old punk, always ready to rumble. Dukes up, he twitted at evil genius Charles Manson during their televised tête-à-tête last spring. "Charlie, you mass-murderin' dog!" Geraldo sneered. "I could take you!" He still grieves that Manson didn't accept the bait: "It would have been impossible to lose. *What*—he's gonna jump on me? Charlie Manson's gonna jump on me?"

The day the chair flew on his talk show (its topic: "Teen Hatemongers"), one skin-headed panelist persisted in calling Geraldo "Jerry." Geraldo seethed. "That's your *name,* isn't it?" the skinhead demanded.

"No, it's *not,*" Geraldo softly replied, resting a leaden paw on the hatemonger's shoulder. "And I would really recommend you don't push me too far." It was a moment of macho frisson, a flash of the essential Geraldo, scarily telegraphing his urge to surge. The fracas that erupted later (incited by racial slurs between panel guests) was merely anticlimax. Still, even after the program had been tabled and Geraldo had been chaired, his bluster prevailed. "I promise," he said, caressing his busted nose, "it was the only time that Nazi-thug-pig was able to land a blow."

"This whole macho trip troubles me," he is now saying, reconsidering his soul in the mountain air. "It's this pride, this unswerving commitment, a rigidity that I don't appreciate in myself. To live your life constantly at war...I really should mellow out a little. Here I have all this money now and all this future, but if someone challenged me in a bar and said, 'Your mother wears Army boots,' I would fight him. It's just the way I grew up dealing with problem solving. Direct action. And I'm not a violent person. I mean, I don't hit women or children."

I ask Citizen Rivera to reveal his Rosebud.

"For me," he replied, "wouldn't that be Noseblood?"

Open his psyche, however, and you will find pulp. As a boy, he suckled on Saturday afternoon serials. Visions of swashbuckling danced in his head. "I was a hero waiting to happen," he is fond of saying, an allusion to his dichotomous pedigree: His father, Cruz Rivera, left Bayamón, Puerto Rico, in 1937 and settled in New York, where he married Lily

Friedman of Newark. They never prospered (Cruz drudged as a kitchen laborer), but their five children were bequeathed an ethnic-fizz bloodline. "I come from two violently different cultures," Geraldo says. "I can remember one schoolyard fight where I was simultaneously called a dirty Jew and a lousy spic. I mean, that's tough."

It was a chromosomal curse that would later pay off. Being half-Jewish, he theorizes, embedded in him congenital compassion and outrage at human suffering. Being half-Latin gave him the overheated brio to spring to the rescue, to kick some ass, if provoked. He merely took his cues from cliff-hanger plots and practiced when no one was looking: "I remember going out into my backyard and pretending I was Flash Gordon in a spaceship, triumphing over evil. Everything was fantasy and heroes. But you've gotta understand—I lived in Long Island, which is noplace. I mean, the horizon was the edge of the table."

His comic-book dreams solidified when he entered Brooklyn Law School at the age of twenty-three. "Geraldo was born then in every sense," says Geraldo weightily. "That was the beginning of my life." There, while earning his degree, he spit-polished the righteous indignation he would eventually brandish as a crusading local TV reporter at WABC in New York and, later, as a network correspondent. Up from the streets himself, he covered the streets with an instinctive aplomb. Like an emotional howitzer, he trampled the hallowed rules of objective coolness. On-camera, he harangued in the face of injustice and he wept in the presence of plight. He wept a lot. "The toughest man, in my view," he asserts, "is someone unafraid to be womanlike."

Action, however, was his forte. Hunting down scoop, he went—and still goes—plain gonzo: clambering over rooftops, crawling through windows, hurdling walls, ambushing reluctant interviewees, dodging bullets, wearying dopey disguises ("I'm the one in the red bandanna," he memorably informed viewers during footage of a drug raid in one of his later syndicated specials). His reports crackled, sometimes excessively, but crackled nonetheless. By the time his star was in the ascendant at ABC News, armloads of Emmys (and one Peabody) stocked his trove.

"You may hate it," he says of his method, "but you have to know that I don't turn it on. It's not an act." Indeed, he has even made crime fighting his hobby. More than once, he has thwarted purse snatchers on New York streets. He regularly walks his dog in Central Park after midnight, sniffing for hoodlums. "I'm out there like a frigate on patrol," he acknowledges. He rails at any junkie in his path (*"Aren't you fucking embarrassed? Look at you, you goddamned junkie!"*) and is the scourge of the crack hustlers who congregate at pay phones outside his Times Square studio. "I just pull them away from the phones, throw them against the wall, pat 'em down, frisk 'em, and kick 'em in the ass," he says, laughing. "It's a citizen's harassment. I scream at them, *'Don't you have any fucking self-respect?'* I am outraged by it all.

"One day I'm gonna get killed, and it'll be by some fourteen-year-old crack addict with his mother's kitchen knife," he concludes, smiling, clearly charmed by the notion. "What a way to go, though."

"Hey, Spielberg's coming over," Cheech tells Geraldo and C. C.

The Riveras have been sipping hot glogg before a crackling fire in the lobby of the lodge, recovering from a fine day's schussing. (Cheech's wife is off getting a massage.) At Cheech's insistence, Steven Spielberg and his wife, Amy Irving, who also happen to be staying at the lodge, approach and pull up chairs. Pleasantries are exchanged. Then Geraldo, who had never met the Spielbergs previously, mentions that he spotted Amy not long ago in New York at the Russian Tea Room.

"I bet that was the day my purse got stolen there," she says, prompting a quorum on Manhattan peril. While making a film in town last year, it seems, she encountered rampant surliness. Her husband even hired a security detail to protect her.

Spielberg confesses, "Hey, *I* got real nervous just getting out of the car and walking a block to where they were shooting."

Geraldo, undoing the top buttons of his flannel shirt, shares a tale of his own. Climbing into a cab with C. C. outside the *New York Times* building last summer, he says, "I saw in the rearview mirror this fucking bum all of a sudden running behind us—"

"I thought it was a street psycho," C. C. interjects.

"Here was this long-haired freak," Geraldo continues, "with a huge beard and flowing braids, a real sixties throwback. He jumps up onto the *trunk*...and it's *him*." He points to Cheech.

Cheech smiles.

"He was in costume, making a movie about hippies," says Geraldo. "It's a good thing I didn't have my gun. I might have used it."

Cheech stops smiling.

Further movie talk ensues. Spielberg suggests that Geraldo should devote one of his shows to a movie theme. Geraldo blanches. "That's kind of out of character for me," he says. "But who knows? I definitely want to change a little. Lighten up some."

"The show of yours I liked the most," Spielberg tells him, "was the Mafia show. Very informative show."

"Sons of Scarface," says Geraldo pridefully. "You know, after it aired, the Mob was after me. They fucked up my car, sent threats, had some of their goombahs come rough up my doorman."

"Really?" says Spielberg, impressed. "We sit out there in TV-land and have no idea what you have to go through in real life."

Geraldo opens his shirt completely, exposing his thermal underwear. He tells Spielberg he cried while watching *E.T.* He inquires about the next Indiana Jones film. (Geraldo considers Indiana Jones a kindred spirit, but he doesn't tell Spielberg that.) Suddenly, it seems, the most important man in Hollywood and the man who invented tabloid television have found an easy rapport. They swap skiing stories, and Geraldo mentions breaking some ribs in a wipeout last year.

"Did you find it difficult to catch your breath?" Spielberg asks, concerned.

"Catch my breath?" Geraldo huffs. "I couldn't even make love!"

Before the fireside chat breaks up, his flannel shirt is gone altogether and he is wearing only a T-shirt. All the others have kept on sweaters.

Scene from a marriage, on love and death (*actual dialogue*):

C. C.:   I find murder fascinating.
Geraldo: It's the ultimate selfishness.
C. C.:   Murder? I think *adultery* is the ultimate selfishness.
Geraldo: No. It's murder.
C. C.:   Adultery.
Geraldo: Murder.

Confessions of a reformed lecher:

"Until now, I was never faithful to any wife or girlfriend. The greatest thrill of my life was finding a new pussy. You know, just finding out what it felt like, who she was and what the circumstances would be. It was an addiction. I took tremendous joy in sampling the variety of bodies and minds and attitudes. It's a marvelous adventure, a conquest. There came a time when it wasn't even *my* conquest any longer: It was *theirs*. They were attracted to my fame. 'Cause, let's face it, there are a lot more better-looking guys. On a scale of a hundred, I'd give myself a sixty, a sixty-five. So, ultimately, I'm not sure who was fucking whom, as the disco song goes. It was the rock-'n'-roll phenomenon: I was being used so that they could go tell their friends about it afterward. It was like being in a candy store. I mean, I've had thousands of women, literally *thousands*. It's *gaudy*. But figure it out for yourself: If you have a different woman every couple of days, and you do it for years running, it just adds up. I'm forty-five. I'm old. I've been around. I've done every pussy. Even during my courtship with C. C. and all through our engagement, I was wildly unfaithful. But there finally just came a time when it was either lose her or lose the lifestyle. And losing her just wasn't worth it. There's no looking back. I really feel I'm married forever now. My wife totally satisfies me sexually. She's my partner in life. I'm not tempted to go searching elsewhere. At all."

I ask C. C. what frightens Geraldo.

"Going bald," she replies. "And lingering death. He wants to die in action." Bluntly put, what frightens Geraldo is aging. Like a matinee idol dipping a toe into his middle years, he clings to his vainglory. He is a man unafraid to preen, to luxuriate in his virility. He is forever lovingly stroking his mustache. He labors over his physique, which he likes to display in razor-cut clothes or in hardly any clothes at all. (Backstage at his television studio, he inevitably greets staff and visitors bare-chested.) His wife tolerantly—bemusedly—tells friends, "He fantasizes that he will always be able to run with the bulls and swim with the whales." (He has done both for *20/20* assignments.)

"One thing I never want to be is physically weak," he tells me, tugging on a beer. "I have seen people like Walter Cronkite go from giant to feeble, relatively speaking. I never want to be frail. I never want someone else to defend me. I have a mortal fear of embarrassment or humiliation. At the same time, I have an absolute arrogance about mortality. I don't fear death at all."

Do you fear fear? I ask.

"I don't think that a brave person is a person who is not afraid," he says thoughtfully. "If you have a hero-martyr complex, as I do, you don't show fear—you thrive on it. Jesus, I'm afraid a *lot* of the time. For instance, I was really spooked after *Sons of Scarface* aired, when the Mafia guys were after me, sending threats. Even now, before drifting off to sleep at night, I imagine every possible worst-case scenario and play out my reaction to it. Crazy scenarios, like seven guys in ninja suits coming at me and sixteen goombahs with shotguns and armies of skinheads. I think, *How am I gonna blow my way out of this? And who do I take out first?*"

He gives a robust laugh.

"See, I'm not fated to turn and run," he says. "They'll never get me in the back. Unless they sneak up behind me."

After dinner one night, the Riveras repair to the Marins' suite to watch a movie on tape. The VCR starts up and the two families hunker down onto couches and armchairs around the television. The movie is *A Christmas Story*, a fairly recent yarn set in the forties about the yuletide high jinks of a wholesome midwestern family. Geraldo is instantly befuddled. "Is this movie colorized?" he asks, helpless. "When was it made? Is that supposed to be Ronald Reagan narrating?" Soon his eyelids grow heavy and he moves from the couch onto the floor, where he sprawls and quickly dozes off.

"Get your dad a pillow," Cheech tells Gabriel.

Gabriel retrieves one, creeps up behind his father, and, crouching near his head, stealthily attempts to slip the pillow into place. Geraldo, perhaps dreaming of ninjas, flinches suddenly and almost bolts upright, then sees the situation for what it is.

"Oh, thanks, Gabe," he says groggily.

He burrows into the pillow and sleeps through the rest of the movie, never stirring.

Part Six:

NIGHTBOYS

Johnny Carson * David Letterman * Jay Leno *
And All Matters Late Night

Here begins my life with Dave and Jay, two very unusual men. In this chapter, I cover the late-night war—*their* late-night war—from the front lines and from the trenches, starting out in peacetime, then marching into full combat and beyond. (I was there for all of it.) Primarily, it is a personal, chronological twenty-year excavation of two sets of hearts and minds, a careful examination of these two friends-turned-rivals, David Letterman and Jay Leno. I think of them, respectively, as the Olympian half-brothers Hercules and Hermes, with careers spawned (one way or another) by a Zeus named Johnny Carson. Indeed, the godlike presence of Carson hovers on nearly every page, because he and his immaculate *Tonight Show* would forever represent the gold standard in late-night talk-comedy television broadcasting; it would be Carson's shimmering kingdom that later became a bloody battleground for this pair of chuckling warriors. Over two decades, I would get to know Letterman and Leno as intimately as any journalist who had ever entered their orbits—if not just a little bit better. Also, I would feel an affection for each, still unparalleled in the realm of all my subjects. Their very disparate psyches fascinated me from the start—Letterman's quicksilver mind has no match that I have encountered anywhere; Leno, on the other hand, lives and breathes comedy twenty-four hours a day—and that is where my focus dwells through all of the writing collected here.

The journey starts with the following: *NBC-TV's Late Night With David Letterman* debuted on February 2, 1982, and I went to visit the thirty-five-year-old host for the first time the following summer. I happened to share a surreal connection with Letterman: Not only were we both sons of florists, but his father and my grandfather, also a florist, had been close friends. The resulting profile—a document now most humbling to both subject and writer, I promise—appeared in *Success: The Magazine for Achievers*, which indicates that early publicity of any sort is better than none, even for Letterman. (He kindly sent me many complimentary flat *Late Night* sponges upon its publication.) Thus was established a relationship that would become much more meaningful ten years hence, by which time Letterman's career had reached its most dramatic crossroads and I had found a larger national forum in which to chronicle his drama. This piece also represents the birth of my relationship with Leno, then a premier stand-up comic and favorite Letterman guest. Without question, their rollicking rapport on-camera catapulted Leno to new fame. *Late Night,* meanwhile, was Letterman's second enterprise at NBC, following the fast demise of his award-winning morning program two summers before. This excerpt, which means to foreshadow all pursuant war coverage, finds a circumspect young Letterman unable to enjoy his recently achieved fortunate station in life. Some things, as you will see, would never fully change.

Young Dave in Short Pants

Excerpted from "Stranger in the Night,"
Success, December 1982

The problem is fear. Letterman, a realist, suspects evil underfoot. He thinks the ax may fall at any time. "Our last experience here at NBC was so awful," he acknowledges woefully, "that I keep expecting it to be like that now, which it's not. I'm guilty of anticipating trouble that does not develop. When you get right down to it," he says, brightening, "we're trying to fill up four hours a week. I mean, it's just American TV. It doesn't have to be perfect. We'll be back the next night."

So far, *Late Night* has done well enough in the ratings—slightly eclipsing those of Tom Snyder's *Tomorrow Show,* which occupied the same time slot for eight years—and the audience seems to be younger and more willing to throw money around, which translates into more advertisers. Critics, meanwhile, have been uniformly appreciative of Letterman's likable manner, his cut-to-the-quick humor, and the innovative spirit the staff has shown in utilizing the medium. One night, for example, the host walked out behind a minicam and viewers at home were able to see the show through his eyes. On the other hand, *Late Night*'s breathlessly manic pacing and Letterman's rough-edged interviewing technique in the early going drew some fire. As Steve Allen notes: "Occasionally, he's sort of operating up on another little level. He's not always communicating on the same level as the guest. I think he'll probably get past that stage, because he certainly has the talent."

But these quibbles are minor. The show doesn't pretend to be high-gloss showbiz shimmer; it's a spontaneous-feeling gabcom. The fun is in the bumps and jolts. Even Letterman fairly flinches at the notion of being a polished performer: "I think of myself as being in broadcasting and not in show business," he claims with a proud smile. "I can't see myself singing in Vegas. I don't think that's gonna happen."

"There's no hypocrisy in what he does," Jay Leno elaborates. "What you see is what's there. I think he tends to lead his life exactly the same way he behaves on television. He's not at all phony. He has the amazing ability to be a professional performer who reacts to situations in a way which corresponds with how people at home probably would."

One recent night, Letterman agreed to stay late at the office and discuss his life, his ambitions, and his future. He would have rather talked about the Dodgers. He is not his favorite subject. It was all luck, he swears. Yes, there were heartaches, obstacles, frustrations, but at least he never had to struggle in a job he really hated. He never had to do any heavy lifting, which he feels makes it all especially worthwhile. His instincts steered him toward a specific career path, and he never stopped.

"I don't consider myself a success," he contends, fidgeting with a baseball. "What I'd like is for this show to stay on long enough to become just a pattern of American television. If we're still on the air in five years, then I'll think of it as a success. The reason Carson has been on the air for twenty years is not because he does a *great* show every night. He has his great shows and he has his awful shows, like everybody else. But the reason *The Tonight Show* succeeds is because people like *him*. They don't really turn the show on to see whoever Johnny has as guests. They turn on the show to see Johnny." He pauses, then demurely mumbles, "Hopefully, that will happen here."

"The only thing I have learned through all of this is, if there's something that you want to do, there's a pretty good chance you'll be able to do it. And I never used to feel that way. It wasn't until I left Indianapolis and just sort of stepped off the edge of the curb that I realized you can accomplish almost anything you want to. There was really no risk, in my case. It was an imaginary risk. I didn't have that attitude until I took it. I always wondered why I couldn't get another job. And then when I just left and found myself succeeding by the definitions of my peers, I realized that *Jeez, if you want to do something, then you can certainly do it by just goin' to work on it.* That was a real revelation for me."

He reaches for a white walking hat and pulls it on snugly. He throws a large shoulder bag over his T-shirt, snaps off the lights, and moves toward the fourteenth-floor elevators. Suddenly, he realizes that he's forgotten to mention one other important goal in his life.

"I have an ongoing project," he says eagerly as we enter the elevator. "I would like to be able—in one fell swoop, in one visit to a clothing store—to purchase all the pants that I'll need for the rest of my life. That's what I'm working on now. And I thought I had it. I thought the pants I would buy for life would be Levi's—thirty-two waist, thirty-two length. But now, after buying about ten pairs of those pants, I discovered that the length is off. So now I don't know if it's thirty-three or thirty-four. I'm right in the middle of this quandary. But as soon as I make the decision on the length, I'll go to a store and buy all the pants I'll need for the rest of my life. Yep, I'm pretty excited."

And, with that, he descends into the New York night and briskly walks east on 50th Street. Nobody notices him.

A few years prior to writing the following profile, I had flown with Leno to a college engagement in Iowa, so as to conduct a "20 Questions" interview for *Playboy*. I had stayed in touch with him since the Letterman piece appeared in *Success* magazine—an occasion for which Leno would mercilessly tease Letterman on Letterman's program. Then, in 1988, *Playboy* asked me to write a lengthy examination of Leno, whose star was now in full ascension—he had recently become the sole substitute host for Carson on *The Tonight Show*. The ensuing piece, in its original published form, began with the ironic, audacious words: "You ask me of Leno. I will tell you everything." While that was largely true, there would be so much more to know within the next five years. For one thing, Jerrold H. Kushnick, identified here as Leno's manager, was in fact only half of the comic's management team. Kushnick's wife, Helen Gorman Kushnick, claimed to have actually discovered Leno and would very soon step forth to propel the Leno career to great triumph while alienating almost everyone in her path. My only in-person encounter with her occurred during the reporting of this piece: She burst into Leno's *Tonight Show* dressing room one day, flinging at him papers that needed signing. I still recall how the air in the room continued to crackle long after she left.

Being Leno Is Not Hard

Excerpted from "A Stand-Up Kind of Guy," *Playboy*, July 1988

LENO DOES THE IMPOSSIBLE

A booking quirk! An amazing feat! On the same night Leno is to guest-host *The Tonight Show*, he must fly afterward to Las Vegas and perform twice on the stage of Caesars Palace, then immediately return to Los Angeles in order to host *The Tonight Show* again the following night. A most formidable show business accomplishment, this. A comedian's Holy Grail. Leno, though, being Leno, is, um, *embarrassed* by the prospect. "It's so stupid," he whinnies, as he is wont to do, in his bemused Lenoesque fashion. "I feel like Sammy Davis Jr. *Hey!* I'm gonna fly off to Caesars, *hey*! Very funny, isn't it? Very stupid."

I find Leno, on this significant day, in his *Tonight Show* dressing room, in backstage Burbank, sprawled on a couch. He is wearing jeans and ratty shit-kicking boots. This is all Leno ever wears, unless he happens to be onstage or on-camera, in which case he adorns himself in oversized shiny blazers and thin Day-Glo ties—cartoon Leno clothes. Technicolor comedy props. He greets me, brandishing one of the two outmoded telephones at his disposal. "Dial phones!" he bleats incredulously. "Isn't this hysterical?" Leno finds amusement anywhere.

Fred De Cordova, the septuagenarian executive producer of the program, glides in. Lank and elegant, with an Acapulcan tan, he has come by to check up on his charge.

De Cordova:	Young man!
Leno:	[*snapping to attention*] Yessir.
De Cordova:	Have you read your notes for tonight?
Leno:	[*unconvincingly*] Yessir, all set!
De Cordova:	Now, look me in the eye and say that!
Leno:	Oh, the *notes*! Uh, yeah, yeah. Got a little busy in here today, boss. Didn't have much of a chance to look at 'em. Uh, I think they, uh, they . . . *fell behind the couch*! That's what happened!

Leno has difficulty taking such show business minutiae seriously. He substitutes for Carson, the absentee despot, more than fifty times a year, a responsibility he calls "the easiest day job I've ever had." On these occasions, he noses his motorcycle into the great man's parking spot (the one nearest the door) and, three hours later, mission accomplished, he takes a powder.

After De Cordova's exit, Leno rehearses his monologue, which he alone writes, reading it from the cue cards. "I spoke with my stockbroker yesterday," he recites. "I said, 'Waiter!' " He does six more minutes of new material, then goes into makeup and emerges, made up. He performs the monologue for five hundred members of the studio audience and, to fill out the hour, yammers with couch occupants Marilu Henner, Fred Dryer, Anita Pointer, and the little kid from *Family Ties*. He then returns to his dressing room and again changes garments as the producers give an appreciative postmortem. Seconds later, he flees for Las Vegas.

Leno takes the wheel of his manager's Mercedes-Benz while his manager, Jerrold H. Kushnick, a large solicitous white-haired man whom Leno calls Kush, piles into the passenger seat for the ride to the Burbank airport. The *Tonight Show* taping ended at six-thirty; the Las Vegas flight departs at seven. Leno, for whom speed is primary, hurtles us through the maw of traffic, weaving and careening. "What are you doing?" Kush complains, clutching the dash. "Just because the light is green doesn't mean you can go ninety!"

Leno shrugs innocently and, in a detached manner, reviews his television performance, lingering only—and rather rhapsodically—over an ad-lib he perpetrated while interviewing the *Family Ties* kid. Supposedly an alphabet whiz, the kid agreed to have Leno test him with flash cards. When Leno flashed a *Z*, however, the kid identified it as an *N*. Leno, smelling opportunity, instantly turned the card on its side, transforming the *Z* to an *N*—to hoots of audience approval. "I must admit," Leno says, chuckling, "I was very proud of that stupid ad-lib." That is the closest he ever comes to self-congratulation. In fact, he will reenact the *Z/N* incident nearly a dozen times before the evening ends.

VIVA LENO VEGAS!

A thick layer of Burbank Pan-Cake still coats the magnificent anvil-like Leno mug as we board the plane. There has been no time to swab it off after the show. "This is embarrassing," he says self-consciously. "People think you walk around with makeup on all the time. They think, *Oh, look at that asshole!*" He does resemble an orange mime. Which reminds me of the time Marcel Marceau grabbed Leno's amazing jaw—true story—and enviously exclaimed, *"Wonderful face for the theater!"* Leno is doubtful about that, an instinct colored, perhaps, by early warnings from casting directors who fretted that his looks would frighten children. Children, however, are mesmerized by Leno; they are uncommonly fond of his commercials for tortilla chips. On this flight, in fact, a small boy presents him with a novelty airlines badge. Leno immediately pins it on, beaming goonily. He then burrows into the stack of motorcycle magazines he carries with him at all times.

He first played Vegas a decade ago. Opened for Tom Jones. He stopped playing Vegas shortly thereafter. By choice. "I didn't want to come back until I could at least headline," he says. "I don't mean that in a snobby way. But I'd rather go to little weeny places where people come to see *you*." So he played little weeny places—clubs and such—a new one almost every night, across the map. He traveled, he slew, the legend of Leno grew: Two-and-a-half-hour sets! Two, three shows a night! More than three hundred dates a year! The Bruce Springsteen of Comedy! The hardest-working white man in show business!

"I always feel goofy riding in a limo," says Leno, who, as it happens, is riding in a limo. It offends his gnawing Everyman sensibility. "Besides, people are disappointed when they see it's only me." The car, provided by Caesars Palace, purrs through the dry night, shuttling Leno to his eight-thirty curtain. He will have not quite fifteen minutes to spare, which for Leno is a surfeit of time. "Got plenty of time!" he sunnily asserts. Unlike most stand-up comedians (and all other two-legged mammals), Leno requires no backstage periods for torturous self-psyching before facing an audience. Flop sweat is anathema to him. He knows no fear.

Where else but Vegas can you see what now looms on the horizon? There on the Caesars Palace marquee... there, depicted by thousands of dancing fluorescent bulbs, billions of watts... it's *Leno's face*! Impossibly magnified and illuminated, the goony, retro–Stan Laurel grin blazes against the black desert sky. The lighted Leno macromandible alone is approximately the size of three parallel-parked school buses. I cannot help recalling Leno's frequent self-description: "I look like a big doofus guy."

This is the final night of a weeklong engagement during which Leno has shared his bill with the musical mother-daughter country duo the Judds. "I like to go on first," he says, answering the question I was about to ask. "Comedy should always go first." The car nuzzles into a loading dock behind the hotel kitchen. He must perform two one-hour sets, a task Leno will find as demanding as swallowing. "Playing Vegas is very easy," he says. "It's like your greatest hits." He snatches up his two ever-present travel bags (garment and duffel), which he permits no one to carry for him (an Everyman prerogative), and plunges into the hotel catacombs hollering "Bus Riley's back in town!"

LENO'S GREATEST HITS

We all have our favorites. Chestnuts such as Leno's dichotomy of the sexes: "All men laugh at the Three Stooges and all women think they're shitheads." And his response to Nancy Reagan's being given a humanitarian award: "I'm glad she beat out that conniving bitch Mother Teresa." On the preponderance of evil twins on series television: "My favorite was the *Knight Rider* episode where Michael Knight was forced to do battle with his evil twin. I knew it was his real twin, because this guy couldn't act either." On National Condom Week: "Boy, there's a parade you don't want to miss!" On the welcome return of full-figured women: "Ever make love to a skinny girl? You always get strange problems. [*in a girlish voice*] *'My back broke.'*" On Stallone and Schwarzenegger: "They've opened up the acting profession to a lot of people who couldn't get into it when speech was a major requirement." On sticky endearments: "I live in Hollywood, where you have all those dramatic types who introduce themselves, 'Hi, I'm Susan and this is my *lover*, Bob.' *My lover?* Shut up! Why don't you just lie down and do it for us right now!"

I could go on forever, but, hey, what did you pay to get in here, anyway?

JUST A MATERIAL GUY

The Leno canon is prodigious, a bottomless inventory of PG-rated irony and bombast, and it has made him a millionaire. He lives to make fun of, to identify, absurdity. For that, he is revered and well loved. His comic brethren line up to touch the hem of his tattered jeans. They seek out his advice and encouragement, which he delights in dispensing, usually during informal summit meetings that he hosts in his home late at night, in the blue-cathode glow of his wide-screen Mitsubishi television. Father Comedy, they call him. He presides over a Eucharist of popcorn and Doritos, wielding the remote control like a scepter. And, with his knee jangling uncontrollably (his only pronounced tic), he pontificates.

"I used to call them the Sermons on the Mount," says comedian Kevin Rooney, a close Leno confidant. "He gets a big kick out of doing this. It's usually midnight or one o'clock, and Mavis [the good Leno wife] has gone to sleep. He will sit on his couch and we'll all be on the other couches—Larry Miller, Jerry Seinfeld, Dennis Miller, myself. You have to watch *The Tonight Show* and *Letterman,* those are your school sort of technique things. Then Leno will fly around the cable dial, all one hundred stations, at a blinding speed. It's a psychotic experience. Just as you start to look at something, he's moved on to something else. If there's not a joke there or something interesting to make fun of, it's gone. *Click!*"

Seinfeld adds, "One great Leno line is 'Props—the enemy of wit.' And whenever we're watching someone do a shot on *Carson* or *Letterman,* he's always snapping his fingers and going *'Jokes! Jokes! Jokes!'* Because that's his philosophy: You've got to have a steady rhythm of jokes that you can snap your fingers to. It's not so much that you understand the lyrics, but it's got to be good to dance to. Ultimately," Seinfeld says, "he wants everyone to do exactly as he does—only less well."

I beg Leno to impart his comedic theories. "All that counts are the jokes," he says. "You're only as good as the jokes you tell," he says. "Give us the good jokes," he says. "What Letterman likes, what Johnny likes, what I like are jokes," he says, adding, "I like people who do *jokes.*"

Now, let me see if I've got this straight.

"I never want to have a hook or be known for anything other than new jokes," he says. "I always liked Robert Klein, because he never had a gimmick; everybody else had an oddball character or an expression or a catchphrase. Whenever a bit didn't work out, they'd go to the catch-phrase, which is okay. But to me, Klein always had just material. He was never the man from space or the wacky guy or the Jewish guy from the mountains or whatever it may have been. He was always just a guy. And he was funny."

EVIL TWIN–ISM IS NO JOKE

I am standing in Leno's Vegas dressing room, reading his mail. He has just stepped out the door to do his eleven-thirty set. The letter in my hand, scrawled on loose-leaf paper, is from a fan who, no doubt with jovial intention, chose to sign off with the mock warning "Stay on the look out for your evil twin (a.k.a. scheming look-alike)!" The television in the dressing room suddenly blares with the *Tonight Show* theme music, followed by Doc Severinsen's voice-over announcing the scheduled guests. At the same time, I hear the Caesars Circus Maximus showroom emcee rattling off a list of upcoming events. Then, in surreal synchrony, Doc and the Caesars emcee—matching syllable for syllable—introduce Leno. On the TV, Leno lopes out through the Burbank curtains. Twenty feet away from me, Leno lopes out through the Vegas curtains. The two Lenos begin to speak at the same time. A couple of stagehands, sensing the utter peculiarity of the moment, wander in and stand with me in front of the TV.

"This is amazing," says one.

"How can he be in two places at once?" says the other. I look at the fan letter and say nothing.

WHAT LENO REMEMBERS

Leno remembers everything he has done that has gotten a reaction, by which he means a *positive* reaction, by which he means jokes that have worked. "I mean, that's what comedy is," he says. He remembers the first joke he ever told onstage, at the Bitter End in New York, early in his collegiate years (he attended Emerson in Boston, studying speech, because the final was oral). This is the joke: At his dormitory, you could have girls in your room, and liquor in your room, and drugs in your room; there was only one thing you couldn't have in your room, and that was a hot plate. "Hey," he says now, "I was only in the business a *week*."

Leno remembers driving to New York twenty-four times before

"getting on" at the Original Improvisation, a stand-up Valhalla. That was a frenetic period, during which he would attend morning classes at Emerson, then slog away afternoons doing odd jobs for a Boston Rolls-Royce/Mercedes-Benz dealership. He was known for pulling up at the Improv in a different Rolls each night. After graduation, he set out on a dues-paying odyssey of East Coast strip clubs and college gigs and laffeterias. Comedians working the Boston Playboy Club—Billy Crystal, Richard Lewis, Freddie Prinze—often crashed in Leno's apartment, a hovel whose most distinctive feature was the gaping hole left in the wall after Prinze punctured it with three hundred rounds of live ammunition. Then, in 1975, after watching a weak stand-up shot on *The Tonight Show*, Leno screwed up his courage and flew to L.A. the next morning. That first night, he got on at the Comedy Store and afterward slept fitfully on the club's back stairs. He stayed on in L.A. and soon befriended Letterman of Indianapolis, himself a migrant stand-up. Together, they championed an attitude of rarefied sarcasm that would much later define an era in American comedy.

One evening, however, the great Carson dropped by the L.A. Improv and, after watching Leno work, lectured to him. Leno remembers, "He said, 'You're a funny young man, but you're not ready for my show. You need more jokes to be on TV. You can't just go up there and do attitude stuff.' He was real straightforward and helpful. I said, 'Thanks a lot.' Then I went outside and egged his car."

I, ROBOCOMIC

There is no way of knowing whether he does this for my benefit, but while we are waiting to board our 1 A.M. return flight to Los Angeles, Leno begins to limp exaggeratedly around the gate area. Lugging his right leg like a stump, he hobbles up to an attendant, tells her something, then rejoins me where I sit guarding his bags. "I told her I've got a bad leg," he says, grinning. "We can preboard now."

Leno will go to any extreme to secure overhead storage bins. It is his obsession. Leno lives on planes, though he has only recently learned to sleep on them. Tonight, however, he reads and chats and shows me an item in *Newsweek* about George Bush visiting Baby Jessica after her dramatic rescue from the Texas well. "This is what America is," Bush is quoted as saying, referring to the valiant effort. Leno chortles. *"Like the Swiss would let her die!"* He spies me scanning an itinerary of his bookings. "Can I see that? Oh, Christ." He sighs. "I've got so much stuff to do, don't I?" He seems tired, for the first time all night. "It's almost scary to look at this."

His itineraries are notorious not only for their sheer congestion but for their nonsensical routing. In a typical five-day period, he will serpentine from New Hampshire to Toronto to Orlando to Santa Clara to Atlanta. He thinks nothing of playing San Juan one night, Atlantic City the next. Honolulu today, Cleveland tomorrow. Whenever I try to commiserate with him, however, he grows defensive. "It's not *hard*," he says soberly. "Anybody making money in show business has no right to complain." Which he never does. He boasts, instead, of never having gone a week without performing. Last summer, while making the yet unreleased cop movie *Collision Course* in Detroit, he would charter flights out at night in order to fulfill concert dates and stay fresh. On infrequent nights off, he works out at comedy clubs. He has never taken a vacation—he relaxes poorly. In his lifetime, he has consumed one beer, an experience he disliked and chose never to repeat. (Rum cake reduces him to stupefaction.)

"He loves the iron-man attitude," says Kevin Rooney. "He'd be happy if he could do comedy as an eight-hour workday. He likes being a journeyman. Besides, he doesn't do normal stuff like have a cup of coffee or a cigarette or a beer. His impulses are not human ones."

Jerry Seinfeld says, "He doesn't eat like humans, he doesn't sleep or work like humans, he doesn't think like humans. I'm sure if you caught him at some unguarded moment, you would see a panel fall open on his chest to reveal wires and electrodes. He is Robocomic."

LENO IN LOVE

Perhaps you saw it. The cover line on last year's second-lowest-selling issue of *People* magazine facetiously declared Leno, pictured with a smirk, "THE SEXIEST MAN ALIVE." But don't laugh too abruptly: Leno understands women.

I sat with him one night in Chicago as he counseled a friend racked with marital problems. Leno, in order to make a point, peppered him with leading questions: "How is she wearing her hair? When was the last time she changed it? What color are her fucking eyes? When was the last time you *talked* to her—really talked? When was the last time you took her flowers? Took her to the movies? Went out to dinner? You're being selfish! Hey, I'm not one of those I-love-you kind of guys. Nobody's home less than me. But you have to show interest. Tell her you've been selfish! Talk with her tonight. If not tonight, you'll never do it."

"You know what's interesting?" Leno later confided in me. "I've lived with five women in my life and every one was born on the same date." That's not true, I said. "Yes it is. Not the same year, but the same twenty-four-hour period. September fifth and sixth." That's incredible, I say. "Not really," he said. "I'm one of those people who accept things exactly as they appear to be. And I just seem to be attracted to a certain type. I've always like women who are my opposite."

Mavis Nicholson (long raven hair and hazel eyes, born September fifth) is a tolerant woman, raised in the San Fernando Valley, the daughter of a character actor. She is a writer of children's books and, at one time, comedy routines and is fond of English literature and European travel (she takes her mother along). Whenever possible, she accompanies her peripatetic husband of eight years, who is, by all accounts, famously devoted to her. "Let me tell you something," says Kushnick. "He and I have been together fifteen years, during which time I have called him all over America, at every conceivable intrusive hour, and the only woman who has ever answered the phone is Mrs. Leno. That says something." He adds, "And I'll tell you one thing I love dearly about Mavis: She doesn't spend money."

The couple met twelve years ago, during her comedy-writing phase. An Improv habitué, she was immediately captivated by the Leno style and by the authority he exerted over his peers. "He seemed to be in charge of the rest of them whenever he spoke," says Mavis, who is one year Leno's senior. "When I met him, he wore this snap-brim scoop-ace-reporter-type hat, always a jeans shirt, a black leather vest, a mother-of-pearl belt buckle, and tiny wire-rimmed glasses. I would go into Improv and see his hat and the smoke from his pipe, drifting above the heads of everyone else in the room." She pauses, and then, as if to explain herself, adds conspiratorially, "I have a tremendous passion for men with blue eyes, black hair, and large jaws."

AT HOME WITH THE LENOS

Here is the pecking order, as it has been suggested to me, of Leno's most profound pleasures in life: (1) his comedy; (2) his wife; (3) his motorcycles (eighteen of them at last count, mostly Harleys and English antiques); and (4) his cars (two Lamborghinis, a Jaguar, a Mercedes, a 427 Cobra, and a cavernous '55 Buick Roadmaster reputed to be his first California residence). Most of those things can be found, at various turns, on the leafy, sun-dappled grounds of Leno manor, an ersatz English country house, all stone and beams, perched above a Beverly Hills ravine, just around the bend from Jack Lemmon's place. It manages somehow to be both unpretentious and baronial. Still, Leno, a Hollywood Hills dweller until last September, is uncomfortable with the pristine rites of Beverly. He will, for instance, wave and hoot at every gardener he spots landscaping the neighborhood.

On the evening following the Las Vegas jaunt, I ride home with Leno after he completes his second straight day of Burbank hosting chores. He pilots the low-slung thunderous Cobra convertible through the mountains, along the snaky corridors of Mulholland Drive (his favorite L.A. driving experience), and, goosing the accelerator, he appears contented. "Ya know," he says happily, "a man can *breathe* up here!" As we reach the electronic gate to his property, he begins to imitate a pack of howling Dobermans. *"Rooof, roooof, rooooof! Release the dogs; release the dogs!"* Opening the front door of the house, he calls up the staircase, "Hi home, I'm honey! *Mave!*"

He heads for the garage, leaving Mavis to explain her quixotic husband. She speaks of his epic unflappability, his lack of temper and jealousy and greed, his patience when colleagues got ahead sooner and his indebtedness to Letterman, who generously has called himself a poor man's Leno and whose show loosed Lenomania upon the land.

When Leno reappears, he is smoking his pipe, humming the theme to *Entertainment Tonight,* and toting a slab of index cards. "Time to try out some jokes," he announces, and plucks samples from the deck, testing them for *Tonight Show* durability. He begins, "A lot of high schools are banning Budweiser's Spuds MacKenzie T-shirts. I guess they want to discourage kids from drinking... out of the toilet."

Mavis listens, her comments ranging from "That's great!" to "I dunno" to "I'm sick of Bork jokes."

After he exhausts the material, I try to lure him into basking ever so slightly in his success. The effect is akin to dousing a vampire with sunshine: Leno, I say, you are a big-deal guy now! A designated Carson replacement! Movies! Prime-time specials! And that itinerary! How great does it feel? He shifts uneasily. He grows edgy. He winces. "I guess," he says finally, "there's a quiet satisfaction I get out of it." He then nervously amends himself. "When I'm dead and buried, then we'll look at the record." Clearly, he is befuddled. "I really try not to take an *interest* in my own career," he says. "I like to do the work. I just like to come up with jokes and tell 'em." But, I press him, would it be so bad to take credit and enjoy yourself? Pain creases his face. "I kind of live in my own little world here," he tells me. "And I do enjoy myself a great deal." He then quickly excuses himself and lunges for the garage.

THE MEANING OF LENO

Leno does not say this, but his friend Jerry Seinfeld does: "You have to realize that success is the great poison of stand-up comedy, because it takes away the hunger and it takes away the fight you need to make your shows good every night. You need to go out there feeling you've got something to prove to these people. Once you feel you've proved it, the entire foundation of your act is gone. Leno knows that, and that is why he won't admit to success. He has to kind of not look at it, like Lot's wife averting her eyes from Sodom and Gomorrah.

"His philosophy is, There's no such thing as a comedy star," says Seinfeld. "Once you think you're a star, you're no comedian. A comedian is someone like us. A star is somebody like Cary Grant or Robert De Niro. We don't know who they are; we don't really want to know. But a comedian has got to be somebody I *do* know and I can relate to. So a comedy star, in effect, is a contradiction in terms."

Leno once told me that his two all-time favorite movies were *A Face in the Crowd* and *Sullivan's Travels,* both of which happen to be deft moralistic fables about comedians. I have studied them and suspect they speak volumes about his fears and his beliefs. Elia Kazan's *A Face in the Crowd* is a chilling cautionary tale based on a Budd Schulberg story. It chronicles the meteoric rise of a cornpone comic named Lonesome Rhodes (played by a lean Andy Griffith), a charismatic scoundrel who, feeding on the power of television, is consumed by fulsome megalomania. In the end, he is found out and left with nothing and no one. Leno says, "That was the only time in my life that I've seen a comedian portrayed on screen where I really believed he was funny and yet a prick."

It is, however, *Sullivan's Travels,* a forties' Preston Sturges yarn, that seems to more closely reflect the Leno we have come to love. In it, we meet John Sullivan (Joel McCrea), the wealthy Hollywood director of such tonic comedies as *Ants in Your Plants of 1939* and *So Long, Sarong.* Predictably, he decides to make a doleful film about the downtrodden, and in the name of research, he masquerades as a tramp. He barely escapes the conceit with his life and wisely beats a hasty retreat to the good old funny stuff, a better man for it. "There's a lot to be said for making people laugh," Sullivan concludes, sounding just a little familiar. "Did you know that's all some people have? It isn't much—but it's better than nothing in this cockeyed caravan. . . . Boy!"

"I love that movie," says Leno. "Isn't that a wonderful movie?"

Johnny Carson rarely gave interviews. I begged for months before he departed *The Tonight Show*. As the end of his reign drew near, I was permitted the fairly unprecedented opportunity to hang around his Burbank studio and offices, so as to make sense of our imminent collective national grief. This short piece feels sadder with each passing year; he's still gone and nothing will ever be the same. Leno, meanwhile, through maneuvering most suspect (i.e., Helen Kushnick), had been named Carson's successor a year before and would take over the King's program on Monday, May 25, 1992, three nights after Johnny had left the building. Although no media was invited, I did attend the final Carson taping, thanks to some friends who happened to be the publicists of bandleader Doc Severinsen. When the broadcast had ended and the cameras were turned off, Johnny stood onstage with his eyes glistening, because no one had stopped applauding. He stood there for quite a while before disappearing behind his curtain one last time.

Johnny Calls It a Night

Rolling Stone, May 1992

The King is just a man. Evidence: On a Leno night long ago, Leno himself led me behind the Desk and pointed to the floor. "Look at this," he said, like a bemused archaeologist. Speckling the carpet all around the Chair was a vast sea of black holes. "Cigarette burns," said Leno appreciatively. They were the King's, of course. This was where so many of the Great Man's unfiltered Pall Malls had gone to die, neglected or forgotten. Change being inevitable (and coldhearted), that carpet is now gone—and soon enough, alas, so too will be the King.

These are dark days in Comedy. Carson is going, and we hardly knew him, which is how he liked it. On May 22 (officially Comedy's Darkest Day and his 4,530th night), he will cease to do what it is he has done that no one else could do as well. Expect no maudlin Final Interviews from him; whatever he must say he will say on *The Tonight Show*, where he has kept to himself for thirty years. ("I will not even talk to *myself* without an appointment," he once noted.) Carson, we accept, is the most public of private men, and vice versa, and that is only part of his peculiar genius for longevity. He's even private where others are concerned: The day Madonna wed Sean Penn at the Malibu house next to his own, Carson took to the beach with a broomstick and, for the benefit of the buzzing helicopter press, grandly etched in the sand FUCK YOU.

"You carried this network," Letterman said to him on-air the day Carson told NBC it was over. "Oh, I don't think so," said Carson (who comedically begat Letterman, who begat Leno, who inherits the throne). "We were just here," Carson added gently. Indeed, more than any other man, he was here ("HEEEEEEERE's Johnny!"), and like no other man, he was the night. Little wonder he knows more about astronomy—the science of the night—than mere dabblers. "What made you a star?" he was once asked. "I started out in the gaseous state," he replied, "and then I cooled." He was only half-joking: He burned cool so as not to burn out. At sixty-six, he is as cool as ever. Of Burbank's commemorative new Johnny Carson Park, he has announced, "The warm water in the drinking fountain will now be cool and aloof."

Because, for once, he will not Be Right Back, there is room for sentiment. After Carnac the Magnificent made his last appearance, the King took home his bejeweled turban, permitting himself a lone keepsake. (Art Fern's pointer and the Fork in the Road have gone to his writers; the Desk awaits interest from the Smithsonian.) With his drawbridge lowered, he squirms less at mawkish farewells from those who crease his couch. "I'll miss you, too," he even admitted to his finest foil, contentious actor Charles Grodin. *Tonight* co–executive producer Peter Lassally observes: "There's a part of him that's relieved, but that's only a small part. There's another part that's sad. I mean, his life is changing dramatically. When you're used to thirty years of people cheering you every day and then that stops—I think that would be a *terrible* feeling. All of a sudden you're just another person."

You did not know that: The King smells good. He walks in a cloud of spiced cologne that trails him like a small entourage. Backstage, he walks into makeup, where Ed McMahon has not yet vacated the chair. "Oh, am I early?" he says hoarsely, his tone suggesting that Ed would do well to remove himself, which he does. Half-dressed, standing in the mirror, here is Johnny, considering dentition and wattle; he closes the door to take his touch-up unscrutinized. He has a largeness for a man who is not large; "a magnified leprechaun" is how Kenneth Tynan saw him in his famous *New Yorker* profile. Certainly Carson eyes twinkle better than other eyes—and never more so than when watching a comic do stand-up fifteen feet from the Desk. (His eyes have said everything he never could, always directly into the camera, his great silent partner.) Off-camera, Carson watches comics with absolute glee, eyes wide, mouth agape, a luminous face poised to laugh. And no laugh will ever mean more than his.

I mentioned Carson's Face to Steven Wright, moments after his last turn with the King. "To hear Johnny Carson laugh, it's very inspiring, you know?" says the comic, insecure in his dressing room. "It's a great feeling...my absolute fantasy-come-true. I don't think it's hit me that I'm not gonna ever do another one with him." And so it begins to hit him, just as *Tonight Show* coproducer Jim McCawley pops in and reports, "He liked your stuff very much tonight." Wright: "He did?" McCawley: "He's down in his office quoting your lines." Wright: "So he really liked it?" This could be any night after Carson, except that it is one of the last nights.

"He has been the best with comedians, the best there is," says Albert Brooks. "What separates him is that he is very generous. When you were on a roll, he never stopped you, yet he always got his share of laughs." As Woody Allen once put it, "He loves it when you score, and he's witty enough to score himself." Simply, Carson fortified his monarchy by embracing the Comedy of others—a wildly unnatural act among comedians. "Never compete with them," he explained throughout his reign. "The better they are, the better the show is."

A realistic King, he has kept two artifacts at his feet behind the Desk all these years: a rubber chicken, now decrepit, symbolizing Comedy, and a wooden arrow, left over from a bad Custer sketch, symbolizing Failure. While no life-form fails funnier than Carson, he knows that now he must be going. "I don't envision sitting there in my sixties," he told *Rolling Stone* thirteen years ago, when he was fifty-three. "I think that would be wrong." As we are bound to discover, not as wrong as Carson not sitting there at all. He gave good stuff.

David Letterman gladly toiled for a decade in the hour after Carson's *Tonight Show*, ostensibly earning the right to take over whenever Johnny chose to retire—a move that would have made for a just and logical transition of power. Devastated by Leno's appointment, he had immediately hired omnipotent superagent Michael Ovitz to secure offers from competing networks and also to force NBC to rethink its commitment to Leno. I sat with Letterman for many hours on the early January day when NBC executives met in Florida to decide whether to unseat Leno—already six months into the job—and grudgingly give Dave *The Tonight Show* once and for all. It was arguably the most nerve-racking moment of his life up to that point. (And of Leno's, too, for that matter.) By the end of the day, the network did, in fact, agree to offer him the show. He would be able to step in when Leno's contract expired several months later. Letterman opted not to take the job he wanted most, finally convinced that it would not be Johnny Carson's show he was inheriting but Leno's. (Carson himself helped persuade him of this in a telephone exchange conducted a few days after this interview.) Reproduced within are essential passages

from our conversation—plus some previously unseen chunks of dialogue—that would inform all Lettermanology thereafter. His unbridled
honesty was especially heartfelt—and hilarious—on that day. I called
him the following week, once fate had been sealed, and asked him
what sort of headline should accompany his *Rolling Stone* cover photo.
He said, "How about: 'Can This Man Rebuild the Soviet Union?'"

Letterman Waits for the Call

Excerpted from the *Rolling Stone* Interview, January 1993

... Here is Dave, true broadcaster, unbound. He entered this, the Year of Dave, asleep in Barbados, in denial. Back in New York, he is now bearded and beset. He presides at the seat of Worldwide Pants, as he calls his television empire—itself the spoils over which a historic battle between two networks is being waged (the very day this conversation takes place!). When the smoke clears, NBC, having employed Dave for eleven years as host of *Late Night With David Letterman,* will lose him to CBS, which promises him an eleven-thirty time slot and a reported salary of $14 million a year. The Carson throne—*The Tonight Show* and its coveted time slot—will remain in Jay Leno's possession. Blood will spill, men will weep, and lives will change forever. "None of it could be more silly," Dave is saying pensively, fielding all bulletins from the front. Rose, his faithful assistant (played by former dancer Laurie Diamond), reports, "They're looking for a picture of you hosting your show for *Business Week.*" Dave: "I don't do a show for *Business Week.*" Rose: "I tried to explain that." Dave: "Well, maybe I do. Check the assignment board." It is during this uncertain time that he cheerfully submits to the long and merciless debriefing that follows. ...

How are you sleeping at night during these heady times?

By and large, I sleep fitfully. And when I wake up the sheets are drenched in perspiration. But the experts believe it's just a lack of amino acids. So we're trying to correct that with the cigars.

Aren't those Cuban contraband?

[*cups his cigar away from view*] Uh, these are White Owls! You can get these anywhere!

I heard you only smoked Cubans.

You got the wrong guy. You don't know what the hell you're talking about! Call the IRS. I pay my taxes.

Have you spoken to Johnny Carson lately?

Not too long ago, Peter Lassally, who came to our show as an executive producer after doing the same for Johnny, told a newspaper that Carson used to come in to work at two each afternoon and that I was coming in at ten. And so Carson read this and started calling my office at ten that day. I didn't get in till like eleven-thirty, and as soon as I got on the phone with him, he was screaming and howling: "Oh, get in at ten, huh? Where ya been? Car trouble?" It was very funny. The last time I saw him, which was at the Emmy dinner, he just seemed great and happy. He's really getting a kick out of everybody else's troubles.

Are you any more comfortable in your relationship with him than you once were?

I'm more comfortable now that he doesn't have a show. That part of his life is over, so I can maybe relax a little bit and try to have a more honest human exchange with him. For a whole generation, he kind of established the model of how cool guys behaved. I just had so much respect for him that, right or wrong, it was an inhibitor for me.

On the air, he was always inviting you to come over to play tennis with him. Ever go?

Yeah, I did it because he had asked me and asked me, and I finally said to myself, *This is a living legend—you're stupid if you don't screw up the courage to go!* He just thinks, *Well, I'm a guy, you're a guy—let's have lunch.* And I thought, *Jeez, no, Johnny—I can't!* [*sighs*] But I finally went over to play tennis with him.

And?

He beat me. He's very good. He can stand in one place, never break a sweat, and run your pants off. And so he beat me. But in my defense, how can you just go to Johnny's house? First of all, his house is like a goddamn Olympic venue. Johnny's court is like a stadium where they have the Davis Cup trials. He's got this state-of-the-art tennis surface—something NASA developed when they went to Neptune, and now Johnny's got it on his court. I couldn't relax, so the whole experience was unnerving. And his wife was very nice to me. But there wasn't a second during that experience I didn't fully expect to just kind of turn abruptly and destroy a six-thousand-dollar lamp or vase. I just felt, *Something's going to go wrong, like I'm going to kill Johnny's wife with the ball machine.* "How could you have killed his wife with the ball machine?!" It's just like I'm too big, I'm too dumb, I'm too clumsy.

Is it true that for years you wouldn't watch his show?

It was always too depressing to me. I know what it takes to just get something on tape. Hosting this show, I always feel like "Man, I'm struggling, I'm like a drowning man in quicksand!" And then you turn on Johnny's show and say, [*beaten*] "Oh, it's fuckin' Johnny!" He's just easy, cool, funny. He looks good, he's got babes hanging on him, he's saying witty things and making fun of Ed. And it's just like *"How can it be that easy?!"* It so intimidated me that I couldn't watch it. But I guess like everybody else I watched him pretty much every night during the last month or so.

How did your own Johnny grief manifest itself?

I can remember watching that last show and just being woefully depressed. . . . Every time he threw it to a commercial, I just felt he was slipping away. It was sort of like a doctor telling you "Well, we've looked at the X rays and your legs are perfectly healthy, but we're still going to amputate them." You think, *Whaaa?* Why is he going?

But, as with most aspects of his career—there's no mistaking it—he did this retiring thing at the right time, the right way. I mean, he even did *that* properly. And I look at the mess I'm in now and I think, [*as Dumb Guy*] *What the hell am I gonna do now!* I have no clue. But Carson just figures it out and carries it off with great skill, grace, and aplomb.

One week before he retired, you went on The Tonight Show *and attempted to soothe America's apprehensions about his departure. It was almost heroic.*

Well, that's my job. [*chuckles*] But for me, that was an easier task, because in the back of my mind, just before going through the curtain, I realized that I'm never doing this again. That was always the most difficult thing, because if you go out there and you piss Johnny off or you kill his wife with the ball machine, then every part of your dream collapses in on you. But this time I knew, even if I killed Johnny's wife with the ball machine, he's gone. I'll never have to go through this again. So I was able to psychologically push that burden aside.

At the end of that show, you said to him, "Thanks for my career."

I knew at the time it might have sounded flip, but it's certainly the case. He's the only reason I'm here. The truth of it is, there have been a lot of people in my life who have been very helpful to me and have really done me favors and helped me in ways I'll never be able to repay. But if there's one person to whom I owe the most, it has to be him. Without question. It just would not have turned out this way.

By the way, when Bob Hope came out onto the panel that same night, did you get the feeling that he wasn't fully aware that Johnny was leaving?

[*laughs*] See, if you consider ways to end up very successful careers, Bob Hope *could* have done a similar version of what Carson did—kind of step aside. I watched a lot of his early films over the holidays on AMC and, Jesus, talk about a guy who was sharp and on the money and appealing and fresh and charismatic. Then I saw his *Bob Hope Kodak All-American Football Team Christmas Special* with Eva Gabor—and it was tough to watch. If it had been a funeral, you would've preferred the coffin be closed. It was sad. I mean, can he be gratified by that?

If you'd gotten The Tonight Show, *would you have dared—as did Leno—to go on the Monday following Carson's final Friday? Isn't that a no-win scenario?* [*Note: In his first* Tonight Show *broadcast, Leno was ordered by his famous manager/executive producer Helen Kushnick to not mention Carson or his astonishing finale even once. Leno obeyed her, most misbegottenly.*]

No, if the circumstances had been different—by which I mean, *if they'd given me the job!* [*laughs*]—sure, I would have done it. This is not to demean what Jay accomplished, but were it I that night, it would have been handled much differently. Because you can't just turn off over one weekend that six-month period of genuine emotion and interest and care and concern that had been generated and perceived and enjoyed. You *have* to address that, and I would have done it. Now, you could be criticized for trying to make yourself look good by kissing up to Johnny. But there was so much positive feeling about this man and the show that was the symbol of his life that it would have been hard to make too big a mistake there. Though a daunting task, I'm confident that we would have done a really nice job for that first show. Now I'm not saying the rest of the week would have been anything. It would have sped downhill immediately.

Life at NBC turned especially ugly before the holidays. On the air, you referred to it as "The Happy Network."

That last day it just seemed like the sky had opened up. There was all this friction—and it had little to do with me, I thought. Even if Johnny were still hosting *The Tonight Show,* I'd do myself a great disservice if I didn't explore other possibilities after ten, eleven years in one spot. The thing that's made it so dramatic is the situation with *The Tonight Show* and my alleged bitterness. But I *was* disappointed that I didn't get the show. I would have loved to try to follow Carson.

If you had aggressively campaigned for the job—which Jay reportedly did with NBC big shots—do you think things might have turned out differently?

Well, in regard to *The Tonight Show,* when Johnny was still there, it would have hurt *my* feelings if he'd thought that I was politicking for his job. I owed so much to him that I was not going to be guilty of any kind of supposed breach of that loyalty. I mean, Carson was still sitting up and taking solid food; who am I to be sidling up and saying "Oh, by the way, Johnny, when you do step down—and we're not saying you're close, you understand—let's grease it for me to step in." Who could be that presumptuous? So what I did was take every opportunity, if asked, to go on record as saying yes, I would like to be considered for the job. I wasn't comfortable with anything more than that. Because in essence what I would be saying was "John, the clock is ticking, it's time to go."

This is you, on the record, six years ago in the New York Times: *"In the back of my mind, if I weren't asked someday to do it, I'd feel kind of sad. Yet, doing it—that's my worst nightmare. That I'd be foolish enough to take the Carson position if offered me, that I'd die a miserable death in that time slot, and meanwhile NBC had given my old show to someone who was quite happy to keep doing it. Maybe the prudent thing would be to let some other poor bastard walk into the fray for several months and* then *try doing the show."*

[*chuckles*] Those are *wise* words, children. That was a wise, wise man speaking years ago. . . . Well, those were honest expressions. I stand by that.

Have you spoken to Jay amid all this stuff?

I speak to Jay now with the same regularity that I always have spoken to Jay. Which is not much. There's no ill will personally. If I felt I was deprived of something that was rightfully mine, if I had fantasies about being hoodwinked, or misled—then there might be ill will. I'm not the kind of person that wants to see somebody else fail on television. I don't have any active animosity toward anybody. Whatever the future holds, I'm in pretty good shape. So, no, I'm not upset with NBC, I'm not upset with [network president] Warren Littlefield, I'm not upset with Jay.

I guess a case could be made that maybe George Bush is upset with Bill

Clinton, because George didn't get the job and Bill Clinton did. So what? Who among us hasn't endured disappointment in our life? But for me to be upset with Jay, you would have to suppose that he found a way to do something hurtful and awful to me by being hired as the host of *The Tonight Show.* And I would guess that you could look long and hard and not find evidence of that.

Your relationship with him has great ironic overtones, in that you've credited him with being among your primary comic inspirations.

Oh, without question. As he's probably been for a whole batch of other guys who came after me. He was the best—and still is—as far as stand-up comedians go. His attitude, as applied to contemporary culture, was always the sharpest and the most satisfying to experience.

On the flip side, he's said repeatedly that he wouldn't be where he is if you hadn't given him a showcase on Late Night.

Well, he's being gracious, because he did as much for us as we did for him—maybe more. He could have accomplished for himself what he did here on any other show. But for us, like I said earlier, to find a regular guest who could always come out and who really could deliver, jeez, that was money in the bank. He did us a great service.

The Talk Show Wars were first made a gruesome spectacle when NBC fired Leno's irascible manager/executive producer, Helen Kushnick. Did you ever feel the effects of her hardball tactics?

It was mostly just something in the air that we'd rather have done without. We were closely tied to it because we're back-to-back on the same network and booking a lot of the same guests. But it was more of a nuisance in theory than in reality. I'm glad that part of things has passed, because you want as few annoyances in your life as possible. On the other hand, she was just trying to do the best job she could possibly do for Jay and for the show. People operate in different ways.

She was your manager at one point, wasn't she?

Yeah, years ago. For a couple of years. A finite period.

She's reportedly been known to take credit for securing your morning show deal at NBC.

Mmmm. We had parted company long before my relationship with NBC.

To do your present bidding, you hired CAA superagent Michael Ovitz, the most powerful man in all of show business, a formidable man who's universally feared. Do you think you could take him?

[*laughs*] Maybe. Not in any kind of martial arts discipline, but maybe straight fisticuffs. I don't know. I have nothing but positive things to say about this guy. He lives up to all his advance billing. I'm very comfortable with our association—that is, until he starts squeezing me for commissions. Then there's going to be trouble.

You're not a fan of change, are you?
I certainly recognize the importance of change in the context of the show. Probably the most stringent ongoing self-criticism I can make is that we don't do enough new things on a regular basis. And I would take all the responsibility for that. Ultimately, the biggest roadblock to getting a lot of new stuff on the air would be me. I guess that's the difference between me being thirty-five and forty-five.

So you're a pretty discerning judge of material?
Who are we kidding—I'm a maniacal asshole.

Some of your former writers are working on The Larry Sanders Show, *a great neurotic satire of talk-show life. Does this suggest that you are the real Larry Sanders?*
Every time I watch that show I think—*Hey, wait a minute! That's me!* But I don't know if it really is me or if they have the talk-show machine so well assessed that it looks like me. I've seen four episodes and during almost every one I think, *Boy, didn't that happen here once?* They've all had an eerie effect on me. In the one I saw most recently, Larry and his girlfriend were fighting, and she was threatening to go back home to Chicago—

Déjà vu there?
No, that one didn't ring true. Had it been Cleveland, then maybe—but Chicago? No.

You're famously brutal about your own performance. For instance, your recent session with Walter Cronkite—while genial to the naked eye—left you greatly unhinged.
I really felt like I had screwed that up, because I was just overwhelmed by the guy. He sits down and you think, *Oh my God, it's Walter Cronkite!* So I just yammered all over him and just fumbled it.

Your postshow drill, then, is to come back to your office and review the tape, dwelling on the mishaps?
I have my own little ritual, yeah. But I should. If you've got men on base and you can't drive them in, how come you're getting major league money? That's the point. At this stage, I ought to be able to do a better job. I just felt that not only did I let the show down—I let Walter Cronkite down and I let myself down. And it shouldn't have been.

But do you also recognize that you're being awfully hard on yourself—

No! No! Why let yourself off the hook? If I fucked it up, I fucked it up. So, obviously you come back the next day and try it again. Fortunately, we had Marv Albert on and got right to his blooper reel. Smooth sailing! So I was able to rally the next night.

And feel better about yourself?

Yeah. Sure. I don't choke every night.

Do you buy the notion that awkward TV is good TV?

Yeah, if it doesn't involve *you*—absolutely.

To a certain degree, if a guest brings out visible discomfort in you, it's actually kind of entertaining.

I've heard people tell me that many, many, many times. And I guess if you provide yourself the luxury of some distance and a little objectivity, that couldn't be more accurate. But at the time, you just think the studio is filling up with room temperature saliva.

Pee-wee Herman was that type of catalyst. You introduced him to the mainstream, but then he disappeared from the show altogether.

Something about a Florida movie theater, I think. Did you hear anything about that?

Before all that. Was he banished?

No, Pee-wee Herman was always great for us. There was a very small falling out—I think it had something to do with *The Arsenio Hall Show*. I don't know whether it was him or us or both of us.

Would you have him back?

Oh, yeah, absolutely. You know who I really miss? There's a song on the new R.E.M. CD that I listened to like six times before I finally realized, *Holy shit, this is about Andy Kaufman!* Andy would orchestrate and rehearse each of his appearances for maximum impact. And when the impact worked, good or bad, he would savor it. If we could have one guest like Andy—to me that's worth six months of new material. Steve Martin also does it for us. He always has lots of things he wants to do, and he's so concerned about detail. He comes on and actually performs. There's nobody else like that now.

The night Sonny & Cher reunited on your show, you spoke of the futility of mixing business and romantic partnerships. You were alluding, I guess, to your relationship with Merrill Markoe, with whom you created this show.

Right, right. One night I think maybe Merrill and I will get back together on the show and do a couple of songs. I'm still very fond of her, and she's one of these people to whom I owe a great debt. She's one of the smartest people I've ever known in my life. I mean, we haven't had a good idea since she left. Sadly, I haven't talked to her in years. This is so silly, but in the time that has elapsed, Merrill's mother died, and I never knew about it. Two more years go by and her dog Stan dies. So I sent her a note of condolence over the death of Stan—completely ignorant of the fact that her mother had passed away. I somberly wrote, "I now take pen in hand"—and she must have thought, *Yeah, but what about my mother? She's been dead for a year and a half, and you never said anything!* But with Stan, word came to us that he'd been left in the care of a neighborhood kid and somehow ate an entire ham. Oh God. [*chuckles*] And it just killed him. Too much ham.

As I recall, your dog Bob was on the West Coast with Merrill when he died. That must have been a tough night for you to get through the show.

Yep, yep. At the time, Merrill and I were estranged and not getting along. But it was one of those deals where Bob was terribly ill. After many misdiagnoses, it turned out he was ridden with cancer. He had eaten a Presto log and, as a result, the vet told Merrill that his lungs were covered with tumors. But they give off a nicely colored flame when burned—very festive for the holidays. So she called one Tuesday afternoon and said the vet thought we should put him to sleep. I said, if we could wait, I'd be off the following week and would come out. But the vet said we couldn't wait. So they put him to sleep right there, which was—it was sad. . . . But I can't—I'm not sure I would have been much good had I been there.

For the last four years, you've been involved with a mystery woman. Does she enjoy her anonymity?

[*laughs, embarrassed*] Well, no, her name is Regina Lasko. Of the Ohio Laskos. When I met her she was equipment manager for the Rangers. Marv Albert introduced us one night between periods. She was leaning on the Zamboni, and I knew then my life would never be the same. [Note: Ms. Lasko, a former *Late Night* staffer, was at this point a production manager for *Saturday Night Live*.]

Are there liabilities to being in a relationship with you? Any conceivable downside?

Do the words *moody drunk* mean anything to you?

How tough is it to get the woman in your life to share your great passion for going to big-time auto racing speedways?

If you suggest a trip to Italy and mention, "Oh, by the way, while we're there we may spend an afternoon at Manza"—that should take the edge off. But, in reality, the one and only time I was at Manza was 1987. Back then, I was with Merrill and we'd planned this trip to Italy, part of which included tickets for us to go see the Italian Grand Prix. I can remember one of the biggest fights of my life in the hotel in Milan—"I'm not going!" "Merrill, you've got to—are you going to sit here in the hotel?" "I'm not going!" I remember driving alone in my rented car out to Manza, while Merrill was back arm-wrestling bellhops. It was a horrible fight.

Do those lingering hugs you lately give to fabulous-babe guests cause any trouble at home?

You know, almost everything I do represents trouble at home. The truth of it is, as I get older, I'm actually getting away with far less. That's why if an opportunity presents itself at work, I feel like I have an obligation to exploit it. But some of them are genuine. I remember with Goldie Hawn, I'd always wanted to do that, so here she is, why not?

You could say you're doing it for the guys at home.

Believe me, I ain't doin' it for you at home.

Are you feeling pressure to get yourself hitched?

Well, you know, I've had that kind of pressure for as long as I can remember. In fact, the only one who didn't pressure me was the woman I was actually married to. And I think she was greatly relieved when we were no longer married.

I don't know, it seems like I've spent way too much time in my life concentrating on just one thing—the work. And the older I get, it now seems like maybe that was not necessarily *the* thing to spend all my time on. Because after almost eleven years, it's not like we've got it figured out. I think to myself, *We're doing something wrong, we've misplaced part of the instructions, because after all this time it's still hard and you would think at this stage of things it would be easier.* I don't think Carson ever went home with his stomach in knots because Sharon Stone was in tears.

Sharon Stone went home in tears?

In fairness to me, Howard Stern made her cry in the greenroom—it wasn't me. What a baby.

During the campaign, Bill Clinton appeared on your program, telephonically, and went on to become president. Correlation or coincidence?

He had no clue to the damage he was doing there. He knew what he was doing by appearing on *The Arsenio Hall Show*—but if he'd known what he was doing in our case, he would've had nothing to do with us.

You supplied him with the campaign slogan, "We don't have a clue, but we don't have a Quayle."

It's so embarrassing to me. I can remember early on—right after Clinton did the *60 Minutes* thing—I was talking to Tom Shales, and off the record, he asked, "What do you think of Clinton?" I said, "The guy's a pretender. He doesn't have a chance in hell. This guy, he's not a president." Two days later this shows up in the *Washington Post*—my assessment of candidate Clinton, where I just completely write him off as a loser without fiber. [*laughs*] And now he's the *pars-dent*. So I know I'm going to pay for this. I know something ugly will happen and he'll be behind it. Some huge tax audit or he'll start nosing around my domestic staff.

You've got a domestic staff? Do you have a houseboy?

Don't we all?

What about your housewoman—that is, Margaret Ray, the disturbed woman who kept breaking into your home in Connecticut. Were you ever genuinely frightened by her?

Yeah, it was cool—and I say *cool* only because it's now over and done with. But there were two hilarious scares in particular. One time we had come back from vacation and pulled up to the house around two in the morning. There was an immediate sense of something not being right. Things had been moved in a way that you would never move your own belongings. In the kitchen, there was a sinkful of dirty dishes. So I realized that somebody was in the house. We got out and called the police from the car phone. And then we pulled around in front of the house and watched—it was odd—the police going room to room turning on lights. They finally found her asleep in bed and bounced her.

The incident that was most frightening came a week later. It was one o'clock on a Sunday morning and we had just gone to bed. For some reason, I thought I smelled smoke in the bedroom, which is not a good sign. So I sat up in bed and at the end of the hallway I could determine the silhouette of the woman standing there. That scared me. It scared me for a second and then I realized, *Oh, I know what this is, there's no trouble.* I rolled over and I called the New Canaan police.

Another time I heard that you gave her a half hour to get away.

Yeah. She was on the property and wanted a glass of water, and I went in to get her one—well, first I said, "Finish raking the yard, then I'll get your damn water." So I went inside and called the police. But then I thought, *She's never threatened me, it's not like I have children that she's terrorizing, it's not like I'm finding dead raccoons in my disposal.* I just felt like "Wait a minute, this is lopsided." So I went back out and I said, "Margaret, I've phoned the police, you better get out of here." And she—not *went* nuts, she *is* nuts—she started shrieking, and then took off and the police picked her up.

So there was never any threat of bodily harm?

No, never. There was a time when I felt frustrated and annoyed by it. But I never really felt I was the victim—this woman is the victim. She's had a very sad life. She's got like six or eight kids, and is estranged from them all. No one seems willing to help her. We gave her many, many benefits of the doubt. Finally she went to jail for about a year, and got out last fall. I don't think we'll hear from her again.

And all along her fantasy was that she was your wife?

Oh, no, that part's true. Oh God, we were married, what, eight, ten years. A beautiful woman.

Explain why it's important to you to be on television at eleven-thirty.

I'm too old to be on at twelve-thirty. There's nobody watching at twelve-thirty—just guys on Death Row who haven't lost their TV privileges. No one's watching. I'm too tired to watch—not tired of being *on* at twelve-thirty, because I'm lucky to have had a job for this long in television. It's all I've ever really wanted to do. I just feel that in order to extend my career, my public life, I've got to make this change.

You've often said that you couldn't very well do this *show*—Late Night—*at eleven-thirty.*

Maybe you could. I think people spend too much time addressing that issue. Give us a time period and we'll do a show that we're happy with that's also palatable for the time period. Automatically, there are things that we would change if we were on at eleven-thirty, although the changes may not be that dramatic.

What's the most obvious change you'd make?

The only thing I can think of—and we've discussed this with consultants—is for me to go with the jet-black Wayne Newton hair and the pencil-thin mustache. And I'd oil it back. So if we ever get to eleven-thirty, that'll be the first thing to look for.

On the first day outside parties were permitted to start bidding for your services, you opened your monologue by announcing "I feel like a million bucks!" Just how does a million bucks feel?

Beats me. I'm just kind of tickled by the phrase.

You're saying you've yet to feel like a million bucks during any of this?

No, no, I'm embarrassed by all the attention.

So what kind of dollar value would you place on how you feel right now?

I feel like a million bucks.

CBS's *Late Show With David Letterman* debuted on August 30, 1993, and instantly began trouncing Leno's *Tonight Show* in ratings and in critical regard. It was a triumph of will and talent; some sort of justice, it seemed, had been served at last. More than a year into his newfound reign, and now that a larger audience had discovered him in the more accessible time slot, Letterman's inimitable quirks stirred deeper curiosity throughout the land. Because the preceding *Rolling Stone* interview had somehow greatly pleased all in Lettermanland, five months later his producers asked me to conduct another long freewheeling session with him before cameras, pieces of which were cut into network promotional spots for the new show. Thus, I had a rather privileged vantage point to explain all that was explainable to date. I will say, however, that I may have explained a bit too much; Letterman all but gave up talking to media within a couple of years. His producers, while ever friendly with me, suggested this profile might have convinced him to clam up.

Inside the Mind of Letterman:
Enter If You Dare

Esquire, December 1994

Inside Letterman's skull, you will find Letterman's brain, which holds captive Letterman's psyche, squirming, dark, and exquisite. This is no place for trespassers. It is a protected place, where the brave and the bold know not to tread. Even Letterman keeps his distance. Long ago, it is said, a couple of trained professionals tried to gain entry and were never heard from again. Like any man of substance, Letterman is hard to know. If he knows himself, he knows only enough to wish he knew less. I have known him for a dozen years, spoken with him during hours grave and triumphant, acquainted myself with the infrastructure of his world, seen his hot-sauce collection. I have watched him become the most powerful man in all of television and derive enjoyment from almost no aspect of it, save perhaps the good seats at Indy. "I have my own private struggle," he will admit, persevering under punishing physical conditions, declining any promise of balm or respite. He must be so encumbered so as to be Letterman. "Very strange," observed the wise Carson when recently asked to ponder the miracle. "Lot of churning going on inside David there." That Letterman has now become Carson, which is to say become omnipotent, only bedevils him further. He will not bask, so instead he wallows. To reign, he must first and always deny himself, deny satisfaction, deny everything. And yet if he did not reign, he would perish. He cannot win even though he has won. That is Letterman.

I have been inside. I have gone there in increments, over long periods, each time retreating hastily, before harm could come. I am the friendly inquisitor, who pokes him gently and buffets with apology, performing painless extractions. We get on fine. There is shared history: His father and my grandfather, both gentlemen florists, both long dead, tippled together and made much hell at regional FTD board meetings. My mother called his father "Uncle Joe" and remembers his father's visits to Chicago from Indianapolis as pure ruckus, full of noise and nonsense. It is a slender bond, but one too odd to ignore. So I dip in and dip out, tormenting him as mildly as he can stand, then leave before he summons the urge to slap me. "Why, you son of a bitch!" he grumbled to me last spring during a chance meeting backstage at *Live With Regis & Kathie Lee*. (He had come over to wreak havoc.) "You've ruined my career more than once!" Whereupon he circled me, hunched like a wrestler, then wordlessly walked away. Such is our special rapport.

Of course, no human walks faster than Letterman, and this is essential to understanding him, if there is any understanding him. His gait is long because his patience is not. He barrels forth, an unstoppable force who presumes to waste the time of no one living. He possesses no such arrogance. Likewise, his mind is so fleet and dexterous and artful in private conversation that I am convinced no equal exists, certainly not among entertainers, itself a fraternity to which he would rather die than pledge himself. Still, his quickness does not make pointed talk any easier for him. He has always thought he was boring me senseless during any given exchange—or, at least, pretended as much. "Oh, it was a huge waste of time!" he said recently, recalling several extraordinary hours I spent debriefing him last year, all filmed for CBS promotional spots, that heralded the arrival of his *Late Show*. "For *you* it was, I mean," he added. "I felt badly for you. I kept thinking, *This poor man...*"

According to legend, he feels bad always, except for the one hour per weekday he broadcasts, during which time he is adrenaline personified. On TV, he is alive with rush. "Way too much coffee," he says woefully. "But if it weren't for the coffee, I'd have no identifiable personality whatsoever. So that's what we have here." (Also, he is known to consume preshow allotments of fresh pineapple and Hershey's chocolate to enhance the buzz.) "He's basically the same guy up until show time," says coexecutive producer Robert "Morty" Morton. "Then he assumes a different personality for that hour, but afterward he's right back again." Afterward, he repairs to his twelfth-floor office, where he studies the show tape and systematically divests himself of whatever hubris that got him through the last hour. "If a show sucks, it's me," he has long said, fully sure he has never given a performance that didn't at least partially suck. He once told me, "I can never walk out of there thinking *Oh my God, we're a hit! Everyone loves us!* I've never experienced that." Nevertheless, he is a hit and everyone loves him. From his Emmy acceptance speech upon receiving this year's award for outstanding variety, comedy, or music series: "Well, I don't need to tell you folks—there's been a *huge mistake*! Ha ha!" Then: "I have very little to do with the show. Every day, about five, after my manicure, I put on a suit and go to work."

Outtake from interview conducted June 1993, in a stark West Side film facility, recorded by CBS (Letterman and I sat at opposite ends of a long table):

Q: How would you explain your work to foreigners?
A: Well, first of all, I wouldn't be hanging around foreigners. You know that. I'm xenophobic. [*chuckles*] I'm the guy running the TV show. Not really a host. Anybody who has ever seen me work knows that. Anybody who has been a guest in my home knows that. And, by the way, there have been very few guests in my home. Especially foreign guests. I don't know. You're the guy on the show who has the best wardrobe, so people in the audience at least know where to look. Everything falls into place after that. There is very little skill involved with it. You just have to smile when things really aren't that funny. And when things are sort of funny, then you have to laugh like crazy. I'll be doing a lot of that here today with you. That's about it. Everything else is done in the control room.

He is a nervous king, for which he cannot be blamed. There he stood, next in line for eleven years, too polite to grease his own ascension. He had been prince and future king since the night of his first audience with monarch Carson, had even been allowed to sit on the throne, in substitute capacity, sooner than any other mortal—after a mere three stand-up shots. (His first *Tonight Show* appearance remains, in his appraisal, the last time he actually felt good about himself—sixteen years ago.) It was Carson who then, in 1982, permanently installed Letterman in the empire of late-night TV, gave him the hour affixed to his own, so that they could rule in tandem. Everything was in place. Until the palace coup: Leno, greatest jester in the land, who did not initially amuse Carson, but always amused Letterman, consorted with dark forces to nuzzle and sway network cabinet ministers ("NBC pinheads," in the dour parlance of Letterman). In short order—a feverish blur to this day—the network had nudged Carson aside and, without royal consent, enthroned Leno as host of *The Tonight Show*. Carson retired to Malibu, shaking his head, appalled but unsurprised. Letterman, who saw it all coming, nevertheless fell into fits of incredulity and extreme self-loathing. Blindly, honorably, his allegiance had belonged only to Carson, never to the network, for which he was punished, if but for a moment. Elsewhere, he was quickly promised the moon, so he took the moon, at CBS, and instantly owned the night. At once, *The Tonight Show* was reduced to shambles, a hollow residence unfit for a king. Letterman's *Late Show* gleamed and ruled. He was now a man in control, like Carson. Don Rickles came on one night and grumbled, "Gotta go. I'm due at Jay Leno's house for dinner later." Said Letterman: "I'm sure you'll enjoy the peace and quiet." (The exchange was excised from the broadcast; Letterman is nothing if not a benevolent king.) Leno, for his part, essayed contrition: "Dave's story is the great American story," he said. "You work for a place. You're unappreciated there. You leave. Your boss tries to get you back. You tell him to stick it. Then you go across the street and build a bigger business."

On the January day NBC executives huddled in Florida to decide whether to dump Leno or lose Letterman, I spent the afternoon in his *Late Night* office at Rockefeller Center. He was just back from Barbados and looked numb and wore a beard. We had been talking about relationships with women—about his own inadequacies therein—and disappointment in general. Also present were two women he trusts implicitly and relies on always: his executive assistant, Laurie Diamond, and associate producer, Barbara Gaines. They prop him as few others can and are never far away should he sink into mire. He was saying, "My sister told me something a couple weeks ago that I'm trying to apply to my life, which is: Don't have any expectations of anybody and you'll never be disappointed. But, you know, it doesn't work. But then that makes it sound like I'm the most giving, most understanding, best buy on the shelf. And I know that's not true. I'm no day at the beach, let's just say that. Right, kids?"

"I couldn't disagree more," said Gaines.

"You are too the best buy on the shelf!" said Diamond.

"Um-hmm," said Letterman, unfooled.

Always he drives himself, fueled by demons. He is known for his drive as well as for his driving. Like Leno, he is a car guy; both men keep hangars full of classic junk at southern California airports (Leno's collection is in Burbank; Letterman's is in Santa Monica, although he almost never gets out there anymore). But unlike Leno, who is happiest monkeying under the hood, Letterman just takes the wheel and drives—from which all metaphor springs. For his daily commute to midtown from New Canaan, Connecticut, he pilots his all-wheel-drive turbocharged red Dodge Stealth, occasionally achieving velocities that paralyze radar guns. Still, the trip never takes less than an hour, usually much longer, forcing him onto the road before nine each morning, rarely getting him home before ten each night. He keeps a downtown Manhattan loft, in TriBeCa, but never uses it, although his longtime girlfriend Regina Lasko spends most of her week there. The road, he feels, is his salvation, pending speed traps. (When stripped of his license a few years ago, he nearly lost the will to live.) "I think that car is his little womb," attests Morty, glad for any decompression his star can find. "I like to get outta town," explains Letterman. "Driving home at night is not such a bad thing. It's a good way to sort of let stuff go a little. I don't like leaving the office, but when I do, by the time I get home the circuit breakers have been reset, you know?"

Before leaving the office each night, after having chastised himself for gaffes imperceptible, he will likely apologize to any staff members he encounters on the way out. "Good night, Dave," they will say. "I'll be better tomorrow," he will reply. Conscience notwithstanding, he travels light, wallet in back pocket, yellow envelope of joke submissions in hand. Once home, he immerses himself for hours in BBC Radio, which serves both to distract and to shape his worldview. "Oh, it *booms* in," he says excitedly. "The short-wave radio's a wonderful thing, a gift from God. And the BBC—they are just *relentless*. They put everything in perspective for you, and you realize why you shouldn't be too worried about too much of anything. I've become addicted to it." He watches no late-night television, gets to bed by one, sleeps five hours a night, sleeps hard. "What I don't do is sleep much, but when I'm out, I'm out."

He is forty-seven, which seems inconceivable, especially to him. He has lately, however, begun to concede the battle, frequently ending conversations with young staff members by blurting "I don't know—*I'm a fifty-year-old man!* How am I supposed to know what you guys like?" It is his neck where mortality besets him most. "I got a bad neck," he says, often on the air, although he asks for no sympathy. He will not speak on the record about his neck. Suffice it to say, he is never not in acute agony, but is also unwilling to pursue corrective measures. If hugged around the neck, he brays like a mule. He lives in abject fear of headlocks. He would rather touch than be touched, although he enjoys nothing more than a woman's touch. Women in his audience regularly ask to kiss his forehead. "The answer to that question," he says, is "Of course, under any circumstances, absolutely, yes!" (Days before we last spoke, alas, one woman had made the mistake of collaring him. "I've been seeing birds ever since," he told me grimly.) I once asked him what a guest on his show should never do. "Number one: Don't frisk me," he said. "Don't hurt me physically. Don't get anywhere near my neck. And don't call me Regis." (Actually, for the record, he reveres Regis Philbin, whom he calls "the most entertaining man on television. . . . If I could be half of what he is, I wouldn't have a care in the world.")

Still, he goes not at all gently into middle age. He is a fellow who loves the rock 'n' roll, loves it loud, loves his Springsteen and Seger, Petty and Zevon, Counting Crows and Nine Inch Nails. He was riveted to Woodstock broadcasts last summer. His office stereo pumps only the hard-rock sounds of WNEW-FM. He prefers music to stoke him, never to soothe. (Under no circumstances does he wish to be soothed.) In diametric opposition to his idol Carson, whose idol was Buddy Rich, Letterman hates jazz, regards it "sleepy." (Within the Ed Sullivan Theater, bandleader Paul Shaffer is forbidden to play that which could be construed as esoteric.) He does, however, fancy bright classical music, is awed by conductor Sir Georg Solti ("In his realm, that's as big as it gets!"), and is rendered limp by the Puccini aria "Nessun Dorma," which he longs to have performed on his show. To his dismay, both Pavarotti and Domingo refused him when they appeared. "Oh, they can do it, for God's sake!" says Letterman, disgusted. "If you're a tenor, *that's what you do!*"

His happiest moments are the moments he is not himself. Most days, he yearns to be somebody else, and on many days he actually is. His credit for the recent film *Cabin Boy,* in which he winningly portrayed the part of "Old Salt in Fishing Village," listed him as Earl Hofert. ("Listen, do yourself a favor," he lectured Chris Elliott on-screen. "Don't let 'em give ya any of that flank steak bullshit! *Try the London broil!* Pamper yourself!") On the phone, he likes to assume disparate identities and expects nothing less from his inner circle of friends, among them comedians Jeff Altman and John Witherspoon and actress Bonnie Hunt. One evening last year, after a show, he took a call on his private line, overheard as follows: "Hello? Hi, Joe! It's Joe Frazier calling. Yeah, Joe, how are you? No, I don't need to buy any hats, Joe. [*long pause*] Oh, all right, I'll take some disco hats. [*pause*] Marvis? Sure. Marvis Frazier is going to be delivering some disco hats from Joe. Are you still workin' with the Knockouts, Joe? [*pause*] Yeah, I know, you were packin' 'em in back then, weren't you, Joe? Yeah, *The Mike Douglas Show,* sure, I remember...." (This was just another typical roundelay with Witherspoon.)

Pure bliss, for Letterman, is committing crank calls on phone-in programs, his guise obscured and never dropped. (Not surprisingly, he is a huge fan of the prankster Jerky Boys.) On both Tom Snyder's old ABC Radio show and his recent CNBC show, he would become various rural morons, seamless in their stupidity, always diverting the subject at hand. In stultifying detail, he would discourse on the new line of Miatas or the bylaws of Kiwanis, Moose, and Elks clubs or share random snacking tips or compliment on-air guests upon work they'd never done. Snyder indulged him as perhaps no other host would have: "Larry King will never put up with me," says Letterman. "By the time you explain to Larry that you want to talk about sunspots and what they're doing to Bill Clinton, you're gone." He prizes the memory of his first Snyder call, before Snyder began catching on to him: "When I got off the phone, I just couldn't sleep, I was so exhilarated by the experience!"

Perhaps his most significant performance in this genre came last February, the night Snyder's CNBC guest was *New York Times* television reporter Bill Carter, promoting his book *The Late Shift,* which dissected matters Leno-Letterman. (Although Letterman availed himself to Carter in the book's reporting, he refused to read it; passages, however, were eventually read aloud to him. "It kinda made him queasy," says Laurie Diamond.) On this night, he was the first caller on the line, a husky-voiced trucker named Don from Kokomo, Indiana. Excerpts:

Tom: How are you tonight?
Don: I'm drivin', man. I'm on 465, it circles Indianapolis, it's a access road—and I got the cruise control hooked up, I'm doin' ninety-five miles an hour, and I got the lights off. How're you doin', buddy?
Tom: I'm okay, buddy, how're you?
Don: I'm in sand and gravel.... When the sand and gravel comes in,

they gotta have a man tell ya what's sand, what's gravel. That's
me.

Tom: In other words, you pick the sand from the gravel?

Don: Well, not actually *pick* it. I have a trained eye. We ain't talkin'
about cotton.... Say, whatever happened to that Doc
McMahon? Remember him on that Johnny Carson?

Tom: No no no no, *Ed* McMahon.

Don: Is he *dead*?... Hey, Tom, I'm callin' to wish you a happy anniversary.

Tom: Okay, Don, thanks a million. Watch that speed now, Don.

Don: Huh?

Tom: Don't drive so fast.

Don: Yeah, well, hey, look—I don't tell you how to run your little
show!

Tom: [*laughs*] But you will.

Months later, Dave told me that his lone goal in making the call,
which went on interminably, was to keep Carter from talking about him,
and his professional travails, for as long as possible. "I just didn't want to
hear them talking about that bullshit," he said, as pleased with himself as
I've ever seen.

Deprivation is a leitmotif to his existence. He likes to imagine he cannot
have that which he clearly could. Not so long ago, he stood on the deck
of co–executive producer Peter Lassally's beautiful Malibu beach home,
staring off into the Pacific. "I wish I could have something like this," he
said wistfully. "Dave," said Lassally, "you *can*." Luxury embarrasses him;
he prefers to believe himself undeserving. That he reportedly earns between $10 and $14 million per year does not register at all. In his mind,
he dwells but a heartbeat away from failure and ruin. His office in the Ed
Sullivan Theater building is large and stark and spartan, nothing on the
walls, shelves barren except for two Formula One race-car models and
twenty-one bottles of hot sauce ("I loves the hot sauce," he likes to say).
He allows in his midst no memorabilia or reminders of triumph. Says
Diamond, whose outer wall is permitted just one photo of her boss, only
because he's disguised as Santa Claus: "He still has that thing—'If this all
tanks, if they get sick of me, I don't want to have to pack up anything; I'm
just gonna put my wallet in my back pocket and walk.'"

I recently asked him how he likes to indulge himself. "I'm not in-
dulging myself—that's the thing," he said. To stay preternaturally thin, he

consumes one meal a day—always pasta on show days, to carbo-load. He hasn't touched alcohol in a decade (when he guzzles vodka on TV, the bottles contain only water). Lately, he has even sworn off his beloved cigars, although he keeps a handsome humidor full of Cuban Cohibas behind his desk and hundreds more at home. "I desperately miss them," he confesses, full of regret. "It just got to be insane. I'd have a cigar first thing in the morning, have one driving to work, have one in the office, have one after lunch, have one before the show, have one during the show, have one after the show, have one driving home, have one before I went to bed. And I loved it. I loved how they smelled, loved how they tasted, I just loved everything about them. And I was making everybody sick. But, man, I'm telling you something—it's a pleasure I'll go back to one day."

While few mortals have penetrated his Connecticut fortress (not counting deranged stalker Margaret Ray), it too is said to be simple and unremarkable, a big barn of a house, free of clutter. Each year, on his birthday and on Christmas, head writer Rob Burnett sneaks up to deposit massive quantities of condiments in Letterman's driveway (for it is only with condiments that Letterman will luxuriate). If caught, Burnett will be invited inside to taste spoonfuls of hot sauce, a ritual of endurance that bonds the two men. "I go right up to the Batcave," Burnett acknowledges. "And whenever I'm done at his house, he always hypnotizes me before I leave, so I can't remember how to get there again." He reports that he has seen no signs of extravagance on the premises, except for Letterman's automobile collection. "That," he says, "and, of course, the mink coats."

"I don't think women get over him," says Laurie Diamond, who regularly fields calls from ex-inamoratas resurfacing to reconnect. "They're married to somebody else now and are still dying to talk to him," she says. With women, of course, Letterman is mercury, quick to slip away, forever dispossessing his appeal. Besides house-breaker Margaret Ray, up to fifty other women are known to think he talks directly to them through the television. Many skulk around the theater, one of whom managed once to throw Letterman up against a wall for a long kiss. Likewise, actresses and models—Ellen Barkin, Vendella, Sarah Jessica Parker, and Julia Roberts, among them—will flirt recklessly with him on-camera, getting nowhere. "It's just silliness," he says crankily. "It's like professional wrestling. I mean, how nuts would you have to be to get involved with an actress or a model?" In general, he distrusts glamour, tends to be unnerved by women in makeup, and finds himself drawn only to unadorned wholesomeness and fierce brainpower. "There is something very appealing about smart women, intelligent women," he once told me. "And you could see the problem there: If they're smart enough for me to be interested, then they're not going to have anything to do with me. But I like somebody who is really, really smart. It just helps me overall in trying to turn the gaze from inward to outward."

Those who know him best speculate that he could, on any given Monday, show up for work having quietly married girlfriend Regina Lasko over the weekend. It has yet to happen, having happened only once, long ago, back in Indiana, when he took himself a college bride named Michelle Cook for a term of seven years. "For what I put her through," he has said, "I should burn in hell for the rest of my life." Lasko, whose profile is kept so low as to be invisible, is said to be warm, devoted, bright, and patient, now in her fifth year of involvement with Letterman. They met when she worked at *Late Night,* after which she became a production manager for *Saturday Night Live,* before quitting altogether last year. ("She has her hands full just taking care of him," says Diamond, chuckling.) Prior to Lasko, there was Merrill Markoe, the woman who arguably created Letterman, who was *Late Night*'s first head writer, who withstood his life for more than a decade and survived to write obliquely about it on occasion. From her just-published book of essays, *How to Be Hap-Hap-Happy Like Me,* Markoe warns women to avoid men who walk fast: "I mean walking half a block ahead of you, no matter how fast you walk, and never slowing down to accommodate you. An informal poll I have been taking for a number of years has convinced me that these fast-walking guys also have terrible tempers and commitment problems."

Before her October *Late Show* appearance to promote the book, Markoe and Letterman hadn't spoken for six years. "I'm actually looking forward to it," he told me a few weeks earlier. "We've exchanged some letters, just casualness, casu—I almost said *casualties,* but that's not right. I mean, looking back at the end of that relationship—it was so unpleasant and mostly my fault. You know, I don't know how to do things with women. She was so good and so smart and just so decent. So I feel like, if there's anything I can ever do for her, I would do it nine times. I just don't know how to behave, you know? I don't know how you break up with people."

There sits Harry Joe Letterman, one of seventeen men at a long table, gray men in suits fixed with boutonnieres, in a photograph my mother gave me. (My grandfather is one of the men.) It is a thirty-year-old picture taken at an FTD meeting in Michigan. Bespectacled Hoosier florist

H. Joe Letterman, as he was known, looks at once dignified and sweetly goofy, about ready to cut loose. "Look at these guys!" his son was saying, studying the picture and chortling. "Don't they look like the old steel and coal robber barons? He loved going to Detroit for this stuff. Oh, he was a big talker! What he was not so good at was actually running the store. But this stuff was his lifeblood, you know?" We were, for the moment, holed up in a conference room above the Ed Sullivan Theater, where he now runs the store. And he was recalling the annual summer fishing excursions he and his father made to a local reservoir: "We did it right up till the time he died," he said. "It wasn't really a ritual. In those days he was drinking heavily and I was drinking heavily, so it always seemed like a good excuse to go out and get drunk while you were fishing. We used it for that pretense. I mean, how could you live with yourself, going to a tavern with your dad to get shit-faced? So our actual purpose for fishing was to go get loaded. I mean, we never caught a fish. I mean, *nothin'*. Not ever."

The widow of H. Joe Letterman has, meanwhile, made much of her sunset years, having recently earned great acclaim as a Winter Olympics network correspondent. (During the two weeks of her satellite-fed *Late Show* reports from Norway, her son had never appeared more professionally rattled.) The former Dorothy Letterman, mother of two daughters and one son, grandmother of four, is now the wife of a decorated World War II glider-pilot named Hans. Her son gave her away—"so to speak," he says—ten years ago, back home in Indianapolis. As with many complex men, his mother is largely the reason he is who he is. "It wasn't until my dad died that I realized my mother is the least demonstrative person in the world," Letterman has said. Never certain what she thought of him, he always assumed the worst, manufacturing a persona to match. "For a long time she told her friends that I was in prison," he said last year, reprising a favorite projection. "It was easier for her to deal with that ignominy than saying 'Well, he's hosting a TV show.'" In particular, he has held close the memory of her reaction to his woeful high-school record: "At one point, my grades were so awful that she wanted to enroll me in a trade school," he says. "Dad had less of an interest in it than Mom. It was just that she was very concerned about my lack of academic accomplishment. But, I tell you, it doesn't seem to bother her now when she gets that fifty-dollar check every week."

Carson had waited an hour before Letterman showed up at Granita. It was the night before the Emmys and Letterman was hosting a party for his staff, as he does every September, at Wolfgang Puck's seaside restaurant. Carson had come, an invited guest, to demonstrate his great fondness for Letterman. A couple of years earlier, Carson had turned up at the event and signed for the tab. "I think he was under the impression the dinner was just me and Peter and Morty and our dates," says Letterman. "So he said, 'I'll take care of it.' And it turned out to be eighty people and it cost him twelve grand!" This time, however, Carson and his wife, Alex, were to be treated in kind. After all, it had been a year in which Carson made three cameo appearances on *Late Show,* something he has yet to do even once for Leno's *Tonight Show,* the implications of which are thunderous. (For Letterman, there was no greater thrill than visiting Carson in his dressing room the night of his memorable walk-on last May. "In all those years I did *The Tonight Show,* I have these memories of Carson coming by my dressing room before the show to say hello and wish me well," he says. "You couldn't believe how cool that was. And so to be able to go up and see him in his dressing room at *my show*—I mean, the full-circle nature of that was maybe more meaningful than I can explain.")

But now Letterman was late, having spent the afternoon at a racing school out in Ventura. And Carson waited. And Carson does not wait. But he didn't mind waiting. And when Letterman arrived, wild and windblown, the two men fell into easy conversation, a phenomenon to which neither are especially prone. And when a woman approached the table and commented on Letterman's height, Carson sparked and twinkled and murmured, Carson-like, "Oh, he's a *large* man!" And he kept going: "Oh, he's *enormous.* That's one *big* guy." And he did not stop: "God, he's practically a *freak.* Stand up and let us see how big you are!" And Letterman, feeling bigger than usual, which is not all that big, paid for dinner.

Most probably he came late because he did not want to believe Carson was there, much less believe what it meant. In his mind, however, Carson is always there, right there—looming gracefully, representing life unachievable. Carson wore power well, wore it effortlessly. "You know," says Letterman, "he's never gonna be on television again. And he shouldn't. He doesn't need to go on television. He's got nothing to prove. I mean, thirty years! And he really seems contented now, he's getting no less enjoyment out of his life." Letterman cannot fathom such contentment for himself: "I can't imagine myself operating at a different level of activity," he says pensively. "I can't imagine that. I hope to hell that I could, but..." He shrugs and says, "You know, you run fast, you smell bad." E!

Entertainment Television, which now broadcasts Letterman's old *Late Night* shows, regularly airs a promo where he says, "It's not so much a television show as a nightly desperate plea for help!" Laurie Diamond tells me, "Whenever I see that I think, *He's just telling us the truth here.* At that desk, he's working out this angst that most of us work out on the couch."

Every night before the show, he is led by Barbara Gaines through the catacombs of the Ed Sullivan Theater, up to the stage. On the way, he will toss a football over a pipe, a ritual that indicates whether he will do well or fail, depending upon trajectory of the ball. He takes torment wherever he can find it. One night, Madonna tormented him and he prevailed, but thought he had failed and let down a nation. Only now, a half-year later, has he relented: "She made me uncomfortable for about twelve minutes," he says, "but, good Lord, we got *huge* attention for it." (He is less sure of his reconciliation appearance with her at the MTV Awards: "It may have been ill-conceived, but at the very least, it made for a lovely photo.") Still, the first thing he does each morning is scour the overnight ratings, surveying his kingdom, taking nothing for granted. One week in September, for the first time ever, early numbers suggested he was being beaten by Leno, whose *Tonight Show* was emanating from Las Vegas. During that week, on a night when his studio audience was particularly lackluster, he grew morose. At a commercial break, he looked helplessly at Morty and said, "This is an audience who's watching somebody that lost." In the end, of course, he won the week, but his panic was palpable.

I visited him after his final show that week, a fine romp of a broadcast featuring Sylvester Stallone and Public Enemy. That night I spoke with a man ajangle, still operating under the notion that his world had collapsed, that he was a loser, after all. He was warm and funny, but also antsy and couldn't wait to get home. Shortly thereafter, he learned that his winning streak had gone unbroken. The following Friday night, we spoke again, this time on the telephone. To purge doubt, it had been a week in which he pushed himself harder than ever and won handily. Before coming to the phone, he had endured a photo session, an activity he despises. (For optimum results, Gaines will sometimes stand nearby and chant, "Happy Dave! Happy Dave!") "Oh, I'm exhausted!" he said, getting on the line. We talked for a while about his passion for old British films, for Myrna Loy, for tales of unrequited love. He told me of how the original versions of *Goodbye, Mr. Chips* and *The Ghost and Mrs. Muir* reduce him to tears. "Those'll just drop ya in a minute," he said. After ten minutes, however, his tone plummeted. I broached the subject of anxiety.

"The anxiety in me is now starting to build to unbelievable proportions," he said irritably. "This has been such a long, grueling week for me.

I've just had my picture taken and now *I'm still talkin' to you* . . . and you, *of all people,* must know by now that *I have nothin' to say*! Let me ask you a question: Does it sound like I'm hangin' up?"

Actually, it did for a second, but he recovered and was able to laugh a little. And then he hung up. Fortunately, Monday would come again in a few days and he would have an hour to feel better.

The winds had begun to shift for Leno. By the time this piece was published, his ratings—already on the rise—had finally overtaken Letterman's. Years would pass before Letterman won even a single night of combat again. This profile would be Leno's first and only true public mea culpa in matters of late-night skullduggery; it was not a particularly heroic portrait. He told me afterward, "At least it's not another one of those Nice Guy pieces." I was surprised that he asked me months later to help him write his comic memoir, *Leading With My Chin*. But, then again, after years of friendly conversation, I knew most of his favorite personal stories, perhaps better than he himself did. Some of them, in certain instances, were actually true.

Leno Lives!

Esquire, October 1995

What, then, of Leno? Is he man or machine? Is he good or evil? Theories abound, yet none satisfy. There is nothing simple about Leno, although he would argue otherwise. He dislikes emotions and claims to possess none. He has learned to question pain, so as to distract himself from ever feeling any. When bad things happen to him, he will shrug and actually forget them. In this way, he has erased much of his life story. Long ago, he literally erased every tape of his first four months of *Tonight Show*s, declaring that they will never be seen again. "They don't exist," he says firmly. "Never happened." Conversely, he has been known to reinvent other key moments of his life, adding fine comic embellishment. (Rule one: Never mistake a comedian's anecdote for fact.) Yet, where others are concerned, he tirelessly quests for truth. "What do you hear?" he asks everyone he knows before asking anything else. "Got any good gossip?" he says. Information seals off his heart, if not his decency. Inscrutable and impervious, Leno cannot be surprised. He cannot be hurt. Also, Jay Leno cannot be stopped.

Leno lives to be misjudged. "I may look dumb," he will say, "but, you know, I am Italian. We can't be underestimated." Indeed, according to legend, he was last at everything before he became first. He thrills to be counted out, knowing fully well he never can be. Born when his mother was forty-one, he has ever since turned up when he was not supposed to. It was in this manner, three years ago, that he became the host of *The Tonight Show*. ("The biggest gig in the world," he would call it, in deference to the man he replaced.) For him to get the job, bad blood spilled everywhere, and he has been working nightly to remove the stains. He has not succeeded entirely, nor has he finished dabbing. Leno must make nice or die trying.

"By this time, I was supposed to be long gone," he says. But he is still here, better than he was, not as good as someone else, dependable all the same. "I'm not surprised Jay didn't go away," says David Letterman, who knows Leno like a brother, albeit one who does not speak to the other. It has come to this, although it was not supposed to.

Let me tell you of the Leno I know. In most of the thirteen years I've known him, I never doubted him. More than once, we took to the road, where he thrived in clubs and where I would study his technique. In comedy, no greater technician lives. He practiced every day. He dispensed jokes in all pockets of the nation, fulfilling 250 gigs a year, minimum. "Life is a marathon, not a sprint, and you just work hard," he always said, and so he did, more than any other comic. On planes, in hotel rooms, on the phone, I listened to him and learned his beliefs. He was affable and kind, but also pointed and judgmental. There was much in the world he did not like, and his opinions singed. He spoke of famous people he considered idiotic. He questioned the work of other comedians. He speculated about the personal habits of actresses he had interviewed on television. "It's so stupid," he would say—usually justifiably—about practically everything. But what offended him most was unpleasantness of any sort. He saw no call for it, ever. In Los Angeles, we would ride in his magnificent roadsters, and he would take me to his home and to the set of *The Tonight Show*—this during his early tenure as sole substitute host. He led me behind the desk and pointed out Johnny Carson's cigarette burns in the carpet. He found this funny, as he finds all human foibles. "So stupid," he said, and giggled in his whinnying Lenoesque fashion.

He had two managers then, a married couple, and I knew only the man. His name was Jerry Kushnick, and Leno called him Kush. Kush was a large, old-time showbiz guy, full of breeze and bluster. If Leno was on-camera delivering his monologue, Kush stood just off-camera, laughing and applauding loudly, even before the audience could respond. The two men had a mock-cantankerous rapport. If, say, there was a booking screwup, Leno would tease Kush, and Kush would tease back. "It's not my fault!" Leno would protest. And Kush would answer, "*Nothing* is *ever* your fault!" And that was true. Leno never placed himself in any situation where fault could find him. (That is why managers exist.) Repeatedly, Kush told me with awe and relish, "Jay Leno has no dark underbelly. If anyone would know it, I would." The world of Leno, he said, was predominantly about two things only: being funny and fixing cars and motorcycles.

Kush died shortly after I last saw him. On his deathbed, he exacted from Leno promises that soon propelled Leno to astonishing heights and then into utter abyss. Among his last requests, Kush made Leno pledge to stand by his widow, Helen, and have her continue to guide the Leno career. Helen Gorman Kushnick had, in fact, discovered Leno and had always steered his professional course, letting her husband handle daily minutiae. But now Kush was dead, and she steered with new and desperate vengeance. By all accounts, Helen was volatile and abrasive and impossible, which made her the opposite of Leno, giving great pause to all who knew him. In the name of Leno, she began to trample everyone in his path.

I called him at home one day five years ago. He was in his garage, as he usually is on his rare days off. At the time, I was helping to compile a tony coffee-table book celebrating comedy heroes—Hope, Carson, Letterman, Pryor, Martin, Seinfeld, Newhart, Rickles, the entire pantheon of Leno peers and predecessors all included. But now, I'd suddenly learned, Leno had withdrawn his participation from the project, and that made no sense. So I called to see if there was some misunderstanding. Friendly as ever, unconvincing as never before, Leno told me his belief that comedians weren't supposed to be in books. "Too pretentious," he said. "Plus, I don't want any record of my career after I'm gone. No evidence lying around." But, I reminded him, even Johnny and Dave were happily on board—the implications of which were obvious. He remained mysteriously unmoved, so we chatted amiably about other things and hung up. (Thus, Leno omitted himself from coffee-table posterity.)

The next day, Helen Kushnick called me and began to scream and never stopped screaming. "How dare you call Jay behind my back!" she thundered. "You have ruined your relationship with Jay Leno! You will have no access to him! You can never call him at home again!" She went on like this without drawing breath. My receiver vibrated with her hysteria. I offered apologies and confessed to be mystified. She did not care. So I immediately called Leno at home, again, and told him that I hadn't meant to offend him and that his manager had just decimated me and that I was terribly confused. He seemed not to hear what I was telling him and instead said, merrily and emphatically, "There's no problem. Everything's fine. Call me anytime. You've got the home number. Keep in touch." But, of course, I never called him again.

At that moment, I had begun to doubt Leno. Then I recalled an odd revelation he often advanced: that he fell into trances whenever he performed his stand-up act, that he was so proficient at his work that he could somehow put himself to "sleep" while telling his jokes. I wondered if he was now living entirely in a trance. Something didn't add up. Something was off. Leno did not seem to be Leno anymore.

Next, the world heard that Leno would succeed Carson. The news came quickly, stunning Carson (who had not been consulted) and crushing Letterman (who had rightfully earned the job). But never mind that now. Leno shakily took the throne and continued not to be his old self. His early shows, overseen by Helen Kushnick, were uniformly awful, bearing no resemblance to his apt stints as a substitute. Then Helen was gone, fired, banished. Leno kept on making awkward television, although not as bad as before and, once in a while, not too bad at all. Last February, at a broadcasting museum tribute to Tom Snyder, I met Debbie Vickers, the talented woman who replaced Helen Kushnick as *Tonight Show* executive producer, and I told her of how my long alliance with Leno had ended. She listened knowingly. The next night, shortly before midnight, my phone rang and it was Leno, sounding not unlike the old Leno, the Leno I knew before he seemingly lost control of his life. He spoke to me for an hour and before hanging up said, "You've still got the home number, right? Call anytime."

Look at him now! See the change! The first redemption of Leno is nearing completion. I have come late to the purge. It has been ongoing since September of 1992, dating from the moment Helen Kushnick was ripped from his side. The patient improves daily. Toughened by turmoil and tragedy, he is—at age forty-five—finally manful, something he never before needed to be. It is now possible to watch him do his work and not wince. And his ratings, while never small, grow more formidable, giving great chase to the Letterman *Late Show,* which has been overtaken just twice in two years of week-to-week battle with Leno. The first time came only last July, the result of actor Hugh Grant's electing to honor a long-standing commitment to appear on *The Tonight Show*—by happenstance, his first public outing following his arrest in a car with prostitute Divine

Brown. Leno won that one on sheer luck. (His opening question to Grant, however, restored him further: *"What the hell were you thinking?"*) At last, Leno had tasted triumph, a forgotten sensation. It seemed to be time. By then, he had already apologized to just about everyone he ever knew. He shouldered blame—with stoic grace—for wrongs he either ignorantly permitted or shrewdly sanctioned. (He swears only to the former.) Helen Kushnick left Leno holding the bag, and so he has held it, if a bit incredulously. "It was an odd situation to suddenly be made out to be this asshole," he says now, as he said to me on the phone that February midnight. "I was perceived as the bad guy, and I never understood where that came from. What the hell did I do?"

But, of course, it is what he did not do. He did not stop the madness. He averted his gaze from the danger, because that is what he does. "A classic case of closing your eyes to what's going on around you," he acknowledges. (*Sleep! Sleep!*) That, however, may be too simplistic an alibi. Helen Kushnick held fierce, unnatural sway over the Leno psyche. Her life had known profound horror—the death of a three-year-old son and a bout with breast cancer. It was not without cause, then, that she may have seen the world as an evil place and believed that survival required no small measures. She told Leno that no one could be trusted and that only she could protect him. It did not occur to him to doubt her, much less question her motives. "Fine, fine," he would mutter numbly, distractedly, then go back to his garage.

After all, she got him results, got him *The Tonight Show,* no less. To do so, she had busted network balls with sledgehammer ultimatums, preemptive strikes. To expedite Leno's ascension—but without his assent—she fabricated a story and had it planted, in February 1991, on page one of the *New York Post.* The headline: "THERE GOES JOHNNY; NBC LOOKING TO DUMP CARSON FOR JAY LENO." Carson was humiliated, and, because no three-decade sovereign need suffer tiny fools, he announced his retirement without warning three months later—if only to humiliate his network in kind. (Sly as ever, before dropping the bomb at an affiliates meeting in Carnegie Hall, he told all gathered, "I like Jay Leno.... He is very concerned about my health. In fact, he insisted that I jog through Central Park—about midnight tonight.") But Carson knew all and told Leno so, who denied all. (He should have suspected but chose not to.) And, while continuing duty as substitute host during Carson's final year, Leno was never again invited to be Johnny's guest on the panel. Helen fumed over this. (At one Leno staff meeting that year, which Leno did not attend, she reportedly began to chant *"Die,*

Johnny Carson, die!") Nor did Carson make mention of Leno in his farewell hour—which should have been about no one but Carson anyway. But this, too, enraged Helen, who forbade Leno from mentioning Carson upon his live debut the following Monday night. Mavis Leno urged her husband otherwise, as did all of his confidants, but Leno obeyed his manager, and it looked appalling. (Leno, an ungracious upstart! How could it be?) As that broadcast concluded, Helen Kushnick was heard to exclaim off-camera, "Fuck you, Johnny Carson!"

For the next four months, rampage ensued. Helen implemented thug tactics in booking guests, verbally assaulted anyone who challenged her, and, in so doing, gave rise to the notion that Leno might be far from the nice guy he otherwise aggressively portrayed. Old Leno cronies fell away. Fellow hosts Arsenio Hall and Dennis Miller denounced him and renounced his friendship. Leno played mystified. He asked Helen about the darkening buzz, and she would scream, "Go write your fucking jokes! I'll handle the business!" So he let her until NBC no longer let him let her. They called it an intervention. He did not understand, but it was pounded into his head. Finally exposed, she confessed: "I've been serving you steak dinners for the last eighteen years. I just haven't bothered showing you how I slaughtered the cow." And then it was over.

"Let's get the porterhouse for four," Leno suggests. "It'll be funny." His blue Leno eyes twinkle. His fine wife, Mavis, groans. On a summer Saturday night, we three have come to Ruth's Chris Steak House in Beverly Hills. I have horned in on Leno date night, the only night of the week the couple eats together. To compete with Letterman, Leno keeps gruesome hours, not at all unhappily. Each weekday morning, he is at work in Burbank by nine and never home again before nine at night. Then, by midnight, his friend *Tonight Show* writer Jimmy Brogan, himself a veteran comedian, arrives at the hillside Leno manse, and for a few hours more the two men winnow much of the next Leno monologue, lone jewel in the replacement crown. (Because it is his one great strength, he has inflated his monologue from its original six minutes to a swollen fourteen and padded it whenever possible with staged comedic video clips.) He subsists on four hours of sleep per night. Out of fifty-two weeks, he gets four weeks off, during which time he is miserable. "I hate those weeks off," he tells me. "If it was up to me, we'd have two production teams, let them alternate, and just do the show every night. To me, a week's vacation just means you're now a week behind. Sooner or later, the other people who do these shows—not Dave necessarily—are going to want to do something else. They'll want to go on a vacation or go out to dinner or get laid and, when they stop, I'll be there and just keep going."

Such is the life gently withstood by Mavis Nicholson Leno, dark beauty, wise partner. The Leno wife of fifteen years has been conditioned to cohabit with a human blur. She sees him when she sees him, but always sees him clearly. Former writer, amateur numerologist, passionate reader of great literature, capable of fire, she is his balance. "He's absolutely the best-natured person I've ever known, and also the most level," she told me years ago. "When we first moved in together, I kept waiting for the pain-in-the-ass stuff that always emerges when you live with somebody. And it never happened." There is a sweet patience to her adoration. I watch her stroke the iron-gray Leno forelock as he speaks. I watch her laugh as he pounces ravenously upon the vast platter of steaks that lands before us. (To venture anywhere between Leno and his food is to risk losing a limb.) "Honey!" she scolds, but he has already set the legendary jaw in masticating motion. It is not a pretty sight. Through the mighty mouthful, he calls for ketchup and chews onward. Mavis points out, "Jay is oblivious when meat is in front of his face."

Leno oblivion, of course, is a perilous state. It once nearly destroyed him. So I wonder, in the grim matter of Helen Kushnick, what did he know and when did he know it? "Some things I knew, some things I didn't know," he says. And he sighs profoundly. "But the things I did know were always presented to me as her response to some conspiracy or other. It was always 'We gotta screw them first, 'cause they want to screw you! They're gonna walk all over you!' With her, every action called for an overreaction. I knew in my gut that it was the wrong thing to do. All these people were allegedly against me—and, of course, they weren't at all! I was ashamed of myself that I let it happen. But it's my fault. It was my watch. If you're the captain of the ship, you go down with it."

What is known now helps no one especially. Now Helen Kushnick has moved to New York, where she is said to be ill, and chooses not to comment. Leno has not spoken to her since the time of her dismissal. (Shortly afterward, she appeared on *Donahue*, airing her grievances. "It's always the same story," she said. "Every time a woman gets into a position of some kind of authority where they're not wanted, they're considered crazy, hysterical, a nut.") The shame she brought him manifests itself now as cold dispassion. "I look at that whole relationship as like a bad two weeks out of my life," he says. "Never happened." Through selective amnesia, he obscures and detaches from his own ferocious ambition. Leno is no dupe but plays one to imperfection. Of Helen Kushnick's late hus-

band, the blustery Kush, he says, "I don't remember much about him."
Of the couple, he says, "It was bad cop, worse cop. I would give it all up
to have never met either of them. I would! I would give up this job in a
second. Because it cost me way too much." I ask him about not mentioning Carson on his first official *Tonight Show.* "That was the biggest mistake of my entire life," he says with palpable woe. "Don't forget, we
weren't on tape for those first two weeks. We were broadcasting live. And
in my mind, if I had said something about Johnny on live TV, I thought
she would have gone nuts and started screamin' at me on the air. I
thought, *Oh jeez, let me just get through this.* But I didn't enjoy it. After
that show, I didn't say, 'Hey, let's have a party!' I remember saying to myself, *Why aren't I enjoying this? Why isn't this fun? Why don't I care anymore?*
And I thought, *Is this what it's gonna be for the next twenty years?*

"I consider my first night to be the day she left. I've told NBC if ever
we do an anniversary show, we'll do it in September, not in May. The first
three months of shows were practice shows, as far as I'm concerned.
They'll never be seen again by anyone."

Let us now ponder the emotional life of Leno, a topic charged with much
controversial discourse. One industry observer describes Leno thusly:
"No interests, no feelings, no soul." Executive producer Debbie Vickers
tells me, not without concern, "He's very afraid of feelings." I mention to
Dennis Miller the famed Leno method of shutting himself down. *"Oh!"*
he exclaims. "Like Tor Johnson! Nobody knows Leno's back-story. I don't,
and I was a decent friend of his. Somewhere along the way he got hung
from a tree by the football team with a massive wedgie—and he went inward." Jerry Seinfeld notes, "He holds it all in check. At this point, he's
almost like an automobile part. But he's always been that way." Unlike
Letterman, whose torment is transparent, Leno is opaque, a slab of comedy marble. "I have an expression," he says proudly. *"Think like a man,
smile like a woman.* And that's how I get through life. Most people don't
know how I feel on most subjects. I don't have a temper. I don't get depressed."

When news came that HBO would make a movie of *The Late Shift,*
television reporter Bill Carter's detailed book about the Leno-Letterman
saga, Leno fretted over who would play him. (Kathy Bates will be Helen
Kushnick.) "You cast a comedian, right?" he asked director Betty
Thomas. "No," she said, "we cast an actor." Leno moaned. "Ohhhh, is he
gonna *emote?*" he said. "Because, you know, *I don't emote.*" Daniel Roe-
buck, the actor who will be Leno, assures me, "I've been trying to temper

my performance by not emoting. I keep thinking that's how Jay would want it. I'm like furniture."

More than once, however, the facade has cracked. On the day NBC first sternly suggested that Helen had to go, Jimmy Brogan found Leno in his dressing room crying. When his mother died two years ago, Leno called Brogan from the airplane while flying home to Boston. "He could barely talk," Brogan recalls. "He was in tears the whole conversation." Upon his return to the air, Leno sat at his desk and spoke briefly, and movingly, of her passing. "I count among my friends people like Jerry Seinfeld, George Carlin, Johnny Carson, David Letterman, Carol Burnett," he said, eyes misting. "But, you know, none of them could make me laugh the way she did. I really did lose the best friend I ever had." (If one can believe a story that circulated later, he was heard to sigh deeply during the next commercial break and sadly say to himself, "Not bad for a robot.")

After his father died last year, he again faced the camera directly—which he does not do easily—and delivered a beautiful eight-minute eulogy. It was not only his finest broadcast moment, but perhaps among the most riveting talk-show moments ever televised. Never had Leno been more pure. (It was the kind of display Letterman would not dream of attempting.) Voice atremble, he began, "This is a little tricky. I lost my dad last week. It was pretty rough. Losing two parents in one year is a pretty tricky thing to take." Further along, he said, "When I hear that expression—*it's lonely at the top*—I never knew what it meant. I had no idea. Because at every point along the way, they were there for me to talk to. . . . My dad would call and say, 'You just fight the good fight, son!'" Here, he exhaled a gale of grief. "You know, it really is lonely at the top. You have no idea. But . . . we'll fight the good fight, Pop."

Good boy to the end, Leno lost all innocence upon losing his parents. Always, he made sure to make them proud. They gave him pedigree and example. His Italian father taught him to be outgoing, relentless. His Scottish mother taught him to be unemotional, analytical. "I like my mix," he says. But his father had a hot head, whereas Leno's stifled anger emerges only in response to phone-company inefficiency and bad driving. In *The Late Shift*, there will be a reenactment of an instance when Leno tried to silence a screaming Kushnick by shattering a Hirschfeld portrait of himself on her desk. ("I should have hit her on the head with it," he says now.) But he claims he wasn't angry. And, moments later he was with Brogan, who recalls, "He couldn't have been calmer. He said, 'I was just trying to get her attention.'" Even in January of 1993, when NBC briefly considered turning *The Tonight Show* over to Letterman to keep him from bolting to another network, Leno barely bristled. The testiest he got in public was the monologue joke: "Welcome to NBC, which stands for Never Believe your Contract." ("If I had lost this job while my parents were alive—that would have killed me," he says, relieved to this day. "I never got fired from a job in my life.")

All the king's men gathered but once, in black tie, to entertain the king. A photograph exists, taken long ago on the occasion of a Carson anniversary special, and Leno prizes it. There he is, with Johnny, with Dave, with Garry Shandling (who, upon abdicating his substitute-hosting role, further cleared Leno's way). Captured for eternity, their body language portends history: Carson points to Letterman, Leno looks on respectfully, Shandling looks elsewhere. "Try getting that picture together again," says Leno, a tad ruefully. I tell him that a framed enlargement now hangs outside Carson's office in Santa Monica. "I didn't know that," he says, surprised. He has yet to drop by, for obvious reasons. But he has worked to make repairs. They met again, in the aftermath, backstage at an American Teachers Awards ceremony, and Carson gave him a welcoming smile. "He was wonderful," says Leno. "We spoke for a long time. He was very gracious. He would certainly be well within his rights to never speak to me again if he didn't want to. I understand that. Obviously, he favors Dave. He and Dave were friends long before I came along. He's done things on Dave's show. But everybody has their favorites. That's fine. I'm thrilled that the man is civil to me."

The loss of Letterman in his life, however, disappoints Leno more than losing to him in the ratings. They seemed like a package from the start. It was through Letterman that America learned of Leno, whose attitude he revered. They found each other, in the beginning, at the Comedy Store, the bearded Hoosier and the eastern Elvis, the gap and the jaw. Once Letterman was canonized by Carson and given his own *Late Night* hour after *The Tonight Show,* he let Leno loose in near-monthly guest shots. Seated beside his cohort, Leno was never more alive. "So, what's your beef, Jay?" Letterman prodded him each time. And Leno would thrash with ironic majesty. "There's no question that nobody helped Jay more than Dave," Mavis Leno told me a half-dozen years ago, well before anyone could guess at fate. Leno himself credited Letterman always. "He's the only reason I'm here today," he says. On *The Tonight Show,* minutes prior to Letterman's final *Late Night* broadcast, Leno stressed, "Whatever you read in the paper, Dave and I are friends." That same night, he used a schoolroom blackboard as a comedy prop and on that blackboard, in the unmistakable Leno scrawl, were the words DAVE RULES! Leno called no attention to this on the air, but the sentiment resonated, if only in chalk.

But it was Leno who got what Letterman wanted. Leno wanted it, too. In 1992, he gave the quote, "I wanted *The Tonight Show.* I admit that. And after five years [of filling in for Carson], I think I deserved it." Of course, Letterman had already been toiling in the wings for a decade, but had refused to articulate his dream. He did not wish to crowd Carson, his idol. So he kept to himself, as always, whereas Leno did not, as always. Just as his father sold insurance door-to-door, Leno crossed the country doing stand-up and shaking hands with local NBC executives. He told *Time,* "My attitude was to go out and rig the numbers." He meant nothing presumptuous by it, he claims. "To go out and actually meet the customers who buy your product just seems like sound business to me." But he also says, "When the show was offered to me, I distinctly asked, 'Doesn't David want this?' And I was told by NBC, 'He has expressed no interest in it. We like the way it works now.' I said okay; I'm not going to go to Dave and say, 'Do you want this?' I was ready to sit home and wait and wait for whatever Johnny wanted. Of course, Johnny was not even consulted, which I didn't understand. Why wouldn't you ask him? That made no sense to me."

Letterman, for his part, does not speak ill of Leno, never has. In the corridors of his CBS *Late Show,* however, Leno is sometimes referred to as Evil Jay, for the scheming look-alike character he plays in *Tonight Show* sketches. Letterman writers grumble about bits of thievery, but Letterman will not. Ever the quirky diplomat, he tells the press that he has never seen the Leno show because he wouldn't want to be influenced by his competition. "That's true," one of his minions tells me. "I guarantee Dave has never watched—but that's probably because he still can't believe it's not his show." Last July, Letterman nevertheless announced to an assembly of TV critics, "What we're doing now—started about a week ago—we're supplying most of our guests with hookers and just hoping they get arrested." It is well known that both he and Leno cannot begin their day without scouring the overnight ratings, memorizing every decimal point. (Leno likes to note that at least he always wins big in Los Angeles and Chicago.) "Why don't they just strap on guns and go do it?" says Debbie Vickers, rolling her eyes. But Leno loves his pummelings, finds them invigorating. "The fact that Dave works hard makes me like him more," he says. "I hate whiny people who can't take the race and quit. I say, 'Fine, kick me in the ass! Make me work even harder.'" So goes war.

On a recent Sunday night, I ride home with him after he has tested monologue jokes at the Comedy and Magic Club in Hermosa Beach. It is a weekly Leno ritual. ("Why did I sign this stupid contract nine years ago?" he said, taking the stage. "Seemed like a great idea back in '86! Seventy-five bucks every Sunday! *Whoa!*") We tool along in one of his thirty rare automobiles, an experimental all-wheel-drive Cyclone pickup, and the Letterman name comes up, as it will. "I would love to talk cars with Dave sometime," Leno says, sounding to me like a man who misses the only other man who could ever understand him. "He knows cars and has some really good ones," he says. "It's just awkward now. I did call him a couple years ago to ask him about a Daytona Ferrari and we talked a little bit about cars. . . ." His voice trails off. "You know, I would love to have the opportunity to make Dave laugh again," he says. "And vice versa." He guns his engine. We head for the hills. "But now it's just so odd," he says. And it wasn't supposed to be.

T he Final Chapter:
You walk around knowing what you know about a couple of peculiar fellows and, frankly, you assume—hope, even—that you'll never have to write about them again. After all, they have thrashed forth in a static battle continuum all their own for years now. You have never stopped observing them, of course—because, alas, you know too much not to do so.

After completing work on his book in 1996, I had spoken with Leno not much at all—he had his show to do, and I had other subjects to pursue and books of my own to write. Letterman, meanwhile, had altogether stopped speaking with media people in early 1997, although he was most cordial, in his awkward way, when I bumped into him late that same year at the "21" Club in New York. He and his executive assistant, Laurie Diamond, were sneaking into the wine cellar—his preferred sequestered dining nook—to have a private meal with Mr. and Mrs. Don Rickles. (Letterman will not eat in the presence of public, especially in Manhattan.)

Anyway, both hosts had become well-worn staples in the popular culture landscape, so much so that their unending late-night war came to mean little to anyone but themselves. And then mortality tapped Letterman on the sternum—in the form of a sudden quintuple bypass. *Esquire* editor Mark Warren suggested that it might be time for me to revisit the fray about which I knew too much. *Late Show* executive producer Rob Burnett—who had managed to forgive me for bookmaking with Leno—threw open the portals of Worldwide Pants and Letterman's world in general so that I could come reassess the shaken state of *The Late Show*. Despite several entreaties from me, Letterman himself kept mum, recuperating in silence. I decided to make this piece a full disclosure of all that I knew to be quintessentially true about Letterman and, therefore, about Leno. I knew I would scorch some earth in the process. In the aftermath, Letterman, typically, did not react; Leno, typically, did. My phone rang seconds after he finished reading the piece. He was displeased and surprised that I had not called him for comment during the reporting. I explained that, if I had done so, he couldn't have told me anything I hadn't known all along.

Leno would continue to win in his ratings war, which consoles him as nothing else can. Letterman, meanwhile, would continue to tease his rival. Memorably, on an October 2000 night, after he had thoughtfully eulogized the great early *Tonight Show* host Steve Allen on-camera, he affected the Leno whinny and chastised himself, "Where were the jokes in there? I talked for five minutes and didn't tell a joke! No jokes!" (His Leno impersonations then began occurring almost weekly; months later, Leno finally acknowledged the parodies to a reporter: "When Dave does me, that's *funny*!")

As for the further evolution of Letterman: After the cataclysmic terrorist attacks of September 11, 2001, it was he who heroically led all of late-night television back onto the air the following week with the most dramatic broadcast of his career. (Indeed, he was widely credited for leading all of entertainment itself back into the national consciousness.) Appearing on September 17, as devastated as the rest of the American populace, he cathartically embodied every conceivable emotion raised by the attack. Noting that the terrorists were "zealots fueled by religious fervor," he implored, "If you live to be one thousand years old, *will that make any goddamn sense?*" An NBC late-night executive spoke anonymously to the *New York Times* afterward, confessing "Everybody looked to Dave for the way to do this," meaning return to the airwaves. "If there's a Johnny out there today, it's Dave." Weeks later, once American troops began to liberate oppressed cities in Afghanistan, Letterman was back to his pointedly teasing ways: "These people have gone ten years without television," he said in one monologue. "So right now, people are turning on the TV and thinking *Oh, Leno is guest-hosting for Carson.*" And so it continues.

Daveheart: A Resurrection—
The Whole Ugly Epic Story
of an American Giant Explained

Esquire, May 2000

And then, quite suddenly, there was a man down. And he was the big man who had first lost everything and then won it all back before he began to lose again and he never stopped losing (at least, as per stats and tallies) and now he was down and nothing was right. At *Late Show* headquarters that morning, executive producer Rob Burnett got word first and shared sparingly throughout the upper ranks. "This is just between us," he told producer Barbara Gaines, "but Dave is actually having surgery right now." And she would later report, "I remember going 'What?! What?!' I got, like, teary. I wasn't understanding it. Everyone here was like that. We were all kind of walking around bumping into walls." Then, as speculation filtered beyond the portals, a confidential conversation was held between Burnett and the opposition, Leno himself, although there would be conflicting reports as to who called whom. However, most sources—including some close to *The Late Show*—indicate that it was Burnett who reached out to Leno, as both a courtesy and a preemptive strike. As one mole would reveal, "The fear was that Jay would seize the news of Dave's emergency and, as usual, grab the spotlight for himself by playing his Nice Guy role, the concerned so-called friend. Like, you can almost see him jumping at the chance to do an hour of Dave reminiscences with Larry King." (There has always been more Leno animus in the *Late Show* camp than the other way around.) Anyway, Leno said nothing of his fallen rival on the air that night or anywhere else. By then, of course, the rest of us had also learned, quite suddenly, that the big man's heart was wrecked, that it had been about to give out and needed fixing and was, in fact, already fixed by the time we learned that he was gone from the front lines and breathing through tubes and resting uncomfortably.

And, while he was missing (more than once spotted restlessly walking hospital corridors at four in the morning buying M&M's and chocolate bars from vending machines), something akin to nostalgic love for him grew all anew. Without him, the balance was wrong, and we remembered his honor and also his candor—he was always the one who told us, but fast, the unvarnished truth! In this alarming fashion, he reminded many people—primarily the few million people who had stopped paying attention—that he actually did have a heart.

I always knew that he had one. Truth be told, he hides it badly. He likes to think that he obscures it with stoicism and bravado and barbed wire. More than not, he has been ashamed of its presence. "Oh, I'm a huge emotional ninny!" he has often told me—with great chagrin—during the many years he has told me things. I remember him telling me about how he watched Johnny Carson's final broadcast eight years ago and how bereft it made him feel—"Every time he would throw it to a commercial, I just felt him slipping away forever because he wasn't ever going to be doing that anymore. I don't know that I'll ever be able to express the way that that just tore up my heart." He also said, "Maybe this tells you more of the wrong kind of thing about me than I would like." Anyway, I will tell you that someone else told me that he told another person that there were tears in his eyes the night he watched Johnny go. And, afterward, he couldn't sleep. "I was up the whole night," he said. "The sadness lasted for weeks."

His dead father—H. Joe Letterman—has been staring at him in the mirror for the better part of the last decade. Every damned day, his father has been right there, living life all over again inside the face of the only son he ever had, David Michael, the famous television broadcaster. Genes recreated the countenance almost exactly enough so as to startle—platypus mouth, berm chin, thatched brow, skyward forehead, goofy hair (but of course). Middle age rightfully cinched the replication—abetted by interesting eyewear. "I have pictures of him in the house," Dave has said. "I look at him and see myself." I gave him one such photograph eighteen years ago when we first met in his old fourteenth-floor office at 30 Rockefeller Center. He was thirty-five and beginning his seventh month on NBC as the host of *Late Night With David Letterman* and his guests on the program taped earlier that evening had been test pilot Chuck Yeager and the raving downtown performance artist Brother Theodore, who always spit during delivery of harangues. ("I don't know—*who* would go to see that?" said Dave. "Would *you*?") Anyway, this picture I gave him had belonged to my grandfather, who was a good friend of H. Joe Letterman's by dint of fraternity among florists—both ran flower shops, Letterman's in Indianapolis and my grandfather's in Chicago—and there they were, in this picture, at some regional FTD board meeting looking smart and important with a bunch of other guys, all of them elected committee officials, making congress in their noble lot of pushing perishable merchandise. ("I can remember leaving poinsettias on people's porches when I helped out with deliveries at Christmastime," Dave once told me. "And, of course, within an hour, they'd be frozen rock hard.") By all accounts, his father was the kind of man they used to call a stitch, a card, a cutup. "He was the circus. He was the show. When he walked through the room, the lamps would rattle," his son likes to say. Then and ever since, whenever we looked at a picture of his father (well, I can think of three occasions), he laughed a small wistful laugh, bittersweet and bemused—and you knew there had been much unfinished business between father and son when father departed this mortal plane in 1973, at age fifty-seven, by way of massive coronary, keeling over right there in Letterman Flowers at Fifty-sixth and Keystone, dead and gone just like that, at which point local weatherman Dave was twenty-seven and was rendered profoundly woebegone, also just like that. He has said simply, "His death was horrible for me. Just horrible. It was awful." What is rarely noted, however, is the occurrence of Joe Letterman's first heart attack, which came at age thirty-six and which pitched a grim cloud onto the life horizon of young Dave Letterman, who later recalled, "When he got over it, in the back of my mind was this fear that it could happen again."

Fear has never left the back of his mind, I will tell you. Because, along with his father's face, he had always suspected—no, he was always *convinced*—that inside of his lank thorax there beat his workaholic father's selfsame genetically cursed, fatally flawed, big and fragile rumpus-loving heart. It's no wonder, then, that the vaunted Most Powerful Man in American Broadcasting—the brightest and quickest and funniest TV

Boy ever to crack wise in the history of late-night talk television (and maybe all of television itself, period)—had somehow, within a few years, transmogrified himself into one uniquely strange and jumpy bastard.

"Why is Dave making all those faces?" Leno would say to me. "Why is Dave always shouting? Something *odd* there." I will tell you that there was *concern* in the Leno voice whenever he said such things, this beginning five years ago. "I don't get what the problem is," he would say. But, of course, no small part of the problem has been Leno himself. To write about Letterman is to also write about Leno, and vice versa, which I have done in equal fashion for this magazine and other ones ever since their careers took wing—and which lately seems increasingly unfair to both parties, but possibly more unfair to Letterman. (They have become— maybe always were—entirely different animals, never mind their job descriptions.) But, per back-story and per one large episode of show business dramaturgy, James Douglas Muir Leno, the pride of Andover, Massachusetts, is unavoidably and inextricably bound to the great, epic Letterman saga. Here, from unused transcripts, is Letterman back in 1982—when America knew not what to fully make of this newfangled sort of humor he was peddling ("rarefied sarcasm," he pronounced then)—telling me how he first found his attitudinal chops: "Well, you go to the Comedy Store night after night and you see these people, like yourself, floundering to develop an identity. In any kind of work—even in writing or in art—you go through a process where you imitate somebody else's stuff to help your own evolve. And one night I saw a guy named Jay Leno onstage, who was a comic from Boston and New York. When I saw him, I just thought I might as well go home. Because his attitude and his style were so crystallized and so right on the money and he had such good observations. I mean, his entire life and existence seemed to be a setup and then he would provide the perfect punch line. I thought, *Jeez, that's the way it ought to be done.* So I really started patterning my material after him."

Naturally, I then called Leno—accessibility, of course, has forever been his special province—who happily returned the compliments, which I included in a cover-story profile of Letterman for a motivational magazine called *Success* (hey, you start wherever you can), and, upon its publication, there was Leno carrying a copy out onto the *Late Night* set so as to mortify Letterman (*"Give me that!"*). "Did you all see this?" Leno barreled forth, unstoppable even then. "This is the December issue of *Success* magazine! *Just coincidentally*"—and here he brandished a mocked-up cover of his own—"... *I-I-I-I-I* happen to be on the December issue of *SUPER-Success* magazine! See the headline? 'JAY LENO: THE BEST COME-DIAN IN THE WORLD!' As you can see, it's a little glossier, better stories, more features... it's a little *better* magazine!" And Letterman was at once relieved and entertained—"So apparently you're doing pretty well then?"—because no *Late Night* guest amused him or understood him as did Leno.

Even so, as with the nonsense above, competition has lurked in their sub-text always. Theirs was never a genuine friendship (Leno's frequent con-tention) so much as friendly professional peerage; they have never once broken bread socially, not even as Young Turk comics. (Letterman, of course, has never been known for his social forays. After his heart was fixed, he recounted to viewers his vow of renewal: "I thought, *That's it—I'm changing my entire lifestyle!* Then it occurred to me, *I don't have a lifestyle.*") At present, the two men have not spoken in eight years, the last time being on the air; it is an awkward standoff, both unsettling and proud—Letterman prefers it this way, Leno does not. (He would love to call but fears the rejection that might greet any such attempt.) Letterman has told certain intimates that ever since their early club tenure, he has been leery of Leno's consummate politicking. According to one, "Dave says that even when Jay was a nobody, he wanted to destroy everyone else." Nevertheless, Letterman arguably made Leno a somebody by in-stalling him in regular *Late Night* guest rotation—where Leno always shone and killed—at a time when *The Tonight Show* had no remote inter-est in Leno. The fact that Leno later took part in the now-infamous NBC palace coup whereupon Johnny Carson's majestic *Tonight Show* was sur-rendered to him, after Letterman had logged eleven exemplary years in the adjoining hour to rightfully earn the position (as was Carson's wish)—well, truthfully, Letterman was surprised not in the least, merely humiliated.

The Leno I know—and I know him very well—is many things, in-cluding savvy and talented, but he is nothing if not a warhorse. Life, for him, is a contest and a tote board; he breathes largely to compete (even though he is a guy with no sports acumen whatsoever). Which is to say, he lives to keep tabs on Letterman, with every fiber of his being bent on outmuscling and outdistancing him. ("Jay is forever destined to be Salieri, trying to improve upon a delicate Mozart concerto by adding a banjo and a kazoo," one Letterman acolyte confided to me long ago.) "I've always been the underdog," Leno informed me in the summer of

1995, and on several occasions before and after—but at that moment he had begun to prevail in the ratings for the first time since Letterman debuted his triumphant CBS *Late Show* twenty-two months earlier. By that autumn, Leno would only prevail and then prevail for years to come, but taking nothing for granted and never averting his gaze from Letterman. It is an obsession rooted in deep respect, I believe, but also rooted in gnawing insecurity over his own good fortune. "Dave makes me work harder," he would say, the implication of which has always been that Letterman's wry genius ever looms at his doorstep to intimidate and spook. "I'm not as good," he said not long after he began winning, "but I'll stick with it."

I saw a great deal of Leno in 1996, when he approached me to put together his anecdotal life-on-the-road memoir, *Leading With My Chin*—he knew I knew him very well—which more than one reviewer had wanted to be the true confessions of the scheming jokesmith who cuckolded David Letterman's dreams. (*That* book will never happen.) So we talked for many hours over many months, whether on the phone or in hotels or at his Beverly Hills home, where he dials up his satellite dish like clockwork each weeknight to visit the opposition on Eastern Standard Broadcast Time. "Let's see what Dave's doing," he would say, then assess Letterman's jokes (most often favorably) and also his mental state and deskside manner with guests (more often not): *"I wish he wouldn't make those loud noises! Isn't it odd? What's he doing? Do people like this?"* As Leno has said always, "In any business, you've gotta pay attention to what's going on across the street." To that end, I am told that powerful entertainment publicists claim to be well accustomed to receiving a personal Leno condolence call on mornings after he senses that any of their star clients have experienced a rough-edged *Late Show* turn. ("Jay rushes to the rescue and promises the moon," says one.) As such, he is tireless on his night watch and unapologetic about his methods. "It's all part of the game," he would say, quite merrily, to me and to anyone else. ("I didn't know there was a *'game'* involved in this," Letterman grumpily told *Vanity Fair* that same year.) Anyway, for what it's worth, I will tell you that Leno initially preferred another title for his book. He had very much wanted to call it *A Good Dog Will Run Till His Heart Explodes*. "It's an old hunting expression I heard and always liked," he explained. It gave the publisher the creeps.

Numbers crushed the Letterman heart, I'm thinking. They got in there and burrowed and amassed misery and confirmed self-doubt and gummed the arteries that genes had already impaired. His father gave him the example by which he has lived—which is that your life is a daily struggle to stay afloat and you cannot stop struggling because that is how business is done, and if you don't believe it, look at the receipts, look at the invoices, look at the buckets of gladiolus dying on the shelf. (Dave sees himself as his own perishable merchandise.) "Life is like swimming the English Channel," he once told me. "Just because you're greased up and on the shore doesn't mean you won't be taken out by a 'cuda." Of course, neither of us knew what that meant exactly—he is gifted that way—but I am sure he was implying that imminent doom is never far afield, especially if you are him. Therefore, he worried throughout *The Late Show*'s initial reign in the ratings, basking in nary a single ray of glow, and then found familiar woeful validation when finally taken out by Leno. As ever, he blamed himself—as ever, unjustifiably, because he was never not good and was usually very remarkably good and most every critic alive attested that he was never less than superior to Leno (not that Leno wasn't making some noble strides) and what had really happened was that his network, which was number one in prime time when he came aboard, collapsed underneath him (loss of NFL telecasts, loss of major affiliate stations, loss of younger viewers, loss of strong lead-in programming) and what had also happened was that those of us who always loved him did not abandon him but found ourselves living these complicated sort of upwardly mobile and/or child-spawning lives which require time away from television screens late at night but if we were going to watch anyone we would probably watch him unless there was something really good on cable. Furthermore, his work as Oscar host earlier in the year—which some observers marked as the moment everything turned—wasn't all that horrible, really; he erred most by presuming that trademark bits (a spinning dog, a filmed piece with New York cabdrivers) would play amid the pomp of Hollywood's greatest pageant of self-regard. (Remember: Carson never wore Carnac's turban on Oscar night. Then again, shortly before the broadcast, a cantankerous Dave reportedly threatened to not wear a tuxedo, which would have been even worse.)

But the point is that he blamed himself into toxic disconsolation. Whereas Leno is a pragmatic competitor, Letterman is an irrational one. Like all true artists, he competes only with himself and his own legacy. A few months into the ratings plunge, he told Bill Carter of the *New York Times* and author of the Letterman-Leno NBC-atrocity primer *The Late Shift*, "It's too bad we had such a large dose of success in the beginning. Because, you know, that's addictive. Now all of a sudden, we're shopping at the Price Club, pal."

At which point—*haah-heeeeeeeeeeee!*—a sprocket loosened somewhere inside of him. Never capable of lying on the air (thus making him the purest of broadcasters), he could no longer suppress that which chewed holes in his heart. The face now twisted, the eyes now spun, he brayed, he keened, he yelped and puffed and churned—here, then, was a man imploding but loudly and, well, *weirdly.* He had become a coot. "It was unpleasant to watch," says a *Late Show* insider. "He looked angry and miserable, which of course he was." As Tom Shales then wrote in the *Washington Post,* "The decline in ratings is apparently enough to drive him visibly crazy.... David Letterman has become the Captain Queeg of late-night TV. He'll launch a search for missing strawberries any minute now." (Even Johnny Carson was mystified at this turn of temperament, often using the term *self-destruct* with friends while sadly shaking his head.) Moreover, as the mania enlarged so too did the program itself, swelling disproportionately—a deliberate and misguided response to Leno's big carny ruckus of a *Tonight Show.* Letterman's nimble wit, which never waned, was now drowned by a nightly circus cacophony that all but pried the lid off the Ed Sullivan Theater. "Don't forget that Dave is a born studio performer," says one former associate. "Then, as the ship started sinking, he felt obliged to become a showman and a stage performer to correspond with his Broadway marquee. Comedically, he lost his way, and it cost him dearly." Rob Burnett, the former *Late Show* head writer who became executive producer four years ago amid the grim clangor, confesses, "For a while there, we did let the theater run the show. Sometimes we felt like it was more energy than funny and we got sick of it. But that was an unhappy period for Dave and for us. And, yes, some of that spilled onto the air." But he adds, most significantly, "Ultimately, maybe we lost sight of the foregone reality here, which is this: At the end of the day, when you look back on the creative landscape of television and who did what, Dave is not gonna be remembered for his ratings, you know? There's no one like him and there's no one who's ever gonna be like him." Of course, if Letterman had heard Burnett talking about him like that, he would have fired him in a heartbeat.

Anyway, in late 1997, they decided to make the most of their precipitous fall from grace. NBC had just posted an enormous billboard high atop a building in Times Square festooned with the smirking mug of Leno, declaring him #1 IN LATE NIGHT! The sheer gloat of it was not subtle—it merely screamed right across Dave's front yard. Letterman and Burnett stared at the sign for a long time one day from Dave's office window. "You know what we have to do?" Letterman said. "We have to put up our own billboard. Let's just do it." Within weeks, an even larger billboard appeared in Times Square, very near the Leno one. It pictured

Dave waving goofily at all of New York and was accompanied by the prideful boast: #3 IN LATE NIGHT! (ABC's *Nightline* had, by then, secured second place.) Burnett now laughs. "That was a great call to CBS! I told them what we wanted and that it would cost fifty thousand dollars and they were like '... *WHAT?!?!?'* "

In desperate times long past, Carson—Letterman's professional father—imparted to him this simple shimmering directive in talk-show Zen: "It's all about the guy sitting behind the desk." The guy behind the desk, Carson implied, must presume to carry the calm mantle of authority, but must always do so with the likable Everyman touch. All else—guests, music, lighting, set—would never be anything more than gravy. And so, heeding that lesson with renewed conviction, Letterman wore his authority with aplomb on August 30 of 1993 as he strode forth across the freshly lacquered *Late Show* stage for his first-ever eleven-thirty broadcast. He walked out confidence-coated, a sixteen-million-dollar man, buoyed by media buzz and promotional hype and universal goodwill. Also, he was vulnerable, and thus more human than at any time in memory—the fact that he had been sneakily screwed out of Carson's throne was lost on no one. (It is Dave, not Leno, who was always the true underdog of late night.) But I will tell you that he had no expectation of trouncing the venerable institution that was *The Tonight Show*—Leno or not—certainly never so soon and so soundly and for so long. "Even CBS presented it to us as an impossibility long before we hit the air," says Burnett. "The only tragedy of those first two years was that it made the expectation of winning all too possible."

Jitters and uncertainty, therefore, were already endemic in the hushed (and always tense) corridors of Letterman's Worldwide Pants empire months prior to his big debut. One afternoon late that spring, I was summoned to a West Side studio facility to perform an extensive and rather unusual on-camera interrogation of Letterman from which CBS would splice out dozens of promo spots that aired throughout the summer, heralding the imminent march of *Late Show.* My charge was to somehow extract glimpses of Dave-the-Human-Being with whatever oddball questions I could cook up and, whenever possible, to try to showcase him as "female-friendly" (so as to help lure women toward his built-in core demographic of young men). He arrived walking fast and looking deeply embarrassed—which, I will tell you, is how he arrives anywhere—and he immediately took me aside. "Are we payin' you enough dough for this bullshit?" he asked, quite concerned and apologetic about the whole thing. "Because if we're not, just tell me and I'll make sure we do. Because I appreciate you puttin' up with this crap." I assured him everything was fine, then he was instructed to put on a T-shirt under a crisp navy blazer (Everyman meets Authority, natch) and he sat at the end of a long board-room table, where he smoked Cuban cigars and drank quarts of black coffee to fortify spontaneity. He took all bait I threw him and dexterously traversed, usually at dizzying length, such topics as bagging groceries ("the only honest work a man can do") and hobbies ("I'm a ball-lightning maven!") and how to emulate his hairstyle ("Fly to Phoenix and rent a convertible and just drive for a day") and life wisdom gleaned from his sister (" *When you go to the bathroom, close the door* ' ") and the vagaries of love ("I think it was George Bernard Shaw who said, 'You can't start it like a car, you can't stop it with a gun' ") and the prospect of having children ("I know that my kids are just going to be impossible and hateful and spiteful—you don't suppose that's part of my DNA, do you?"). The interview lasted hours—and it was a spectacle to behold, equal parts comic and revelatory. At one point I asked what sort of man could stand a chance with him in a fight. And with a glint in his eye, he replied, "Certainly no mortal man."

That is the Letterman I like to remember—feisty and confident and human and wise—a man in rebirth, ready to conquer a new world (and/or time slot). That is the Letterman who, in the last two years, began to gradually reemerge from the padded bog, as evidenced by *The Late Show*'s two consecutive Emmy awards in the category of outstanding variety, comedy, or music series. (Dave stopped attending the ceremony years ago but still flies out to California just to host a party for his staff the night before, always at Wolfgang Puck's Granita.) Somewhere along the way, the circus tent folded and the screaming muted and the fright-face soft-ened and he became his show again—"We realized that the one weapon we have that no one else has is Dave," says Burnett. "That show we were doing was not an effective use of him. We thought it was time to just let Dave be Dave, to let him be the guy behind the desk and not the ring-master. We thought: *Let's just try to do a show we enjoy again.* Because we didn't get into this for ratings." But the ratings did rise, just a little, just enough—and then came the visit from the First Lady this past January 12 and the ratings were the best in six years and decimated Leno as in nights of yore. (He began the interview with her as no one else could have— "Are you nervous?" he asked. HC: "Just a little." DL: "Yeah, me too.")

The next morning, a Thursday, he ran his regular six miles near his

Connecticut home (at present, he has two there, for variety; eighty-eight relatively new acres in Bedford and his longtime residence in New Canaan) and, that night, he taped two shows—the second of which would air on Friday, January 14. And, of course, it was during that second taping that he spilled his guts to guest Regis Philbin and nervously confessed that his heart was in trouble and begged Regis's counsel, right there on the air, because Regis had received angioplasty years ago ("You're kinda my role model here") and Dave was scheduled for an angiogram the following morning and his fear was palpable ("Were you scared? You're out like a mackerel, right?") because, as per him, he feared only the worst, which was not angioplasty ("the balloon kinda thing") but heart bypass surgery ("It's open Daddy's rib cage! *I don't want that!*"). And this was really the first anyone on his staff had heard of it—and they know most everything. And then Friday morning, when he reported to the Cornell Medical Center at New York Presbyterian Hospital, the front-page headline of the *Daily News* blared "DAVE'S HEART SCARE" (which he never saw) even though all he was going in for was your basic unpleasant goddamned angiogram. Few people knew, however, that two years earlier he had taken his first angiogram, which turned up traces of coronary-artery disease for which he took daily meds, or that now, only a week before, he had flunked a new stress test. So—being the (almost) fifty-three-year-old son of his dead father—he agreed again to let the doctors shoot dye through a groin catheter ("very close to your deal," as he put it) and on up into his cardiocircuitry to see what might be going on in there. But he knew anyway. "I had a feeling I wasn't gonna be lucky on this one," he said later. "I kind of had a hunch."

All that happened next happened as a blur and it would feel like the longest day of his life (and of the lives of his *Late Show* stalwarts as well) and also like a fever-dream of muffled voices and hidden faces and vague unknowingness and no small fear. By eight that morning, the test was already completed and he was looking at his angiogram films with his personal physician, Louis Aronne, who has treated him since the NBC years, and his cardiologist, Martin Post, and also his girlfriend of eleven years, Regina Lasko, and they all saw the obstructed plumbing. "He had a blockage in his left main artery, which feeds the heart," Dr. Aronne told me. "If that artery gets clogged, then there's no blood going to the heart, which is exactly the kind of situation that can lead to a heart attack, when somebody just keels over. Do you want to hear that you need multiple coronary artery grafts? No. But we told him we gotta do this and let's get it going here right away." Dave took the news with typical nervous stoicism—"I think mentally he was very prepared for it," says Aronne.

"He's a very educated medical consumer. He asks the right questions." Dr. Post had meanwhile guessed a week earlier that the bypass was a foregone conclusion and had asked the hospital's chief cardiosurgeon, O. Wayne Isom (who performed the celebrity bypasses of Larry King, Walter Cronkite, and former *Tonight Show* host Jack Paar), to hold open an operating room for Dave. (Isom balked at Post's suggestion, believing it premature, then ended up canceling another patient's less dire elective surgery after seeing Letterman's angiogram results. "He had the kind of problem you can't wait on," Isom told me.) At eight-thirty, as prearranged, Dave called Burnett at the office to tell him that the bypass was going to happen—"He sounded calm and as matter-of-fact as you can be at a time like that," Burnett recounts. "He sounded like himself, but businesslike. I said, 'Good luck and we'll talk on the other side.'"

He is back and there is wire wrapped around his sternum to hold his rib cage together and he is missing two long saphenous veins, one from each leg, pieces of which are now grafted into his coronary arteries in five places. Like no mortal man, he had faced down his own mortality and come back five weeks to the day that he was rebuilt. And immediately there seemed about him an air of liberation and authority and refocused sense of self; it reminded more than a few people of the Dave Letterman who had been freed from the quagmire of NBC seven years before, eager again to be his own man unbound. Rob Burnett noticed a new calm in him that morning, Friday, February 18—and it was *late* morning when Letterman arrived in the office, amid a snow blizzard. (The old routine had him in before nine and rarely out by ten at night, ajangle throughout.) "He didn't seem nervous to me, honestly," Burnett told me. "He wasn't obsessing over or questioning the material. He wasn't making us rewrite things a thousand times. I think he knew the show had very little to do with us and had everything to do with him." That which had been expunged from his heart—the residual gunk of genetic embattlement—now seemed missing from his psyche as well. He itched to display his improvement. *"Man,"* he said to Paul Shaffer in the makeup room, "I haven't done this in *five weeks*!" Paul said, *"Dave,* that's not very long for somebody who's had quintuple bypass." But the void of his absence felt eternal to him, and to the nation, and to those who worked for him. (Three of those lost weeks were filled, quite remarkably, with programs called *Late Show Backstage* wherein such stars as Julia Roberts, Steve Martin, Robin Williams, Bruce Willis, and Mike Myers regaled stand-in hosts Shaffer, Philbin, Charles Grodin, and Toms Snyder and Arnold with happy reminiscences about previous *Late Show* appearances. Dave, however, watched none of the *Backstage* shows, as the whole idea made him queasy. "You know," he told Shaffer in a telephone conversation before any of the retrospective shows were taped, "people talking about me and me not being there, like I'm dead—it kinda gives me the creeps." He had even instructed Burnett: "Just make sure people don't compliment me. Make sure they're making fun of me.")

Unannounced, on the Wednesday before his return, he had briefly dropped into the office to regain bearings of his kingdom. Producer Maria Pope spotted him striding along the eleventh-floor hallway. "I was like '*Oh, my God!* You're *here!*' Without thinking, I jumped up and raced to hug him. And what I heard was 'UHHHHHHH! MY STERNUMIIII' He was joking, of course, and then I realized, *Dave is back!*" He asked her to walk him down to his car and said, "You know, I might be feeling *too* good. They might've overdone it. I think there's *too much* blood flowin' through my heart. I'm thinkin' of having 'em go back in and close down a couple arteries, you know?" She tells me, "Down at the car, I told him how much we missed him and how much we love him and he expressed the same and kissed my hand and said, 'Thank you for everything.'"

On his night of triumphant return, there was new empowerment in his performance. He was at once mature and graceful and personally fearless—qualities most Carsonesque which he had never quite permitted himself before. Four moments during the broadcast resonated, in particular, as unprecedented mileposts in Lettermanology: (1) He broke down. And he let us see it. After his sincere and hilarious introduction to the stage of his "Medical All-Stars"—the six doctors and two nurses who oversaw his operation and recovery—he faced the camera from his desk and said, "So it was five weeks ago today that these men and women right here saved my life...." And he choked on the word *life* and raised his glasses with thumb and forefinger to dam his spilling tear ducts. And we learned: Dave loves his life. He *really* loves his life. Who knew? (2) The hug. He has always hugged awkwardly or comically. (His friend Tom Dreesen, the comedian, tells me that Dave's second greatest fear in life, next to bodily injury, has been the threat of receiving or giving a hug, especially a *sincere* one.) But after walking down the line of doctors onstage, he stopped at the end and wrapped his arms around nurse Ana Williams—"Ana and I fell in love and we spent every night together after the surgery," he had said moments earlier—and held her tight and kept holding her tight and sort of swayed back and forth in the hug and audibly whispered to her, "Everything all right?" And we learned: Dave can love people. He can *appreciate* people with all of his refurbished heart. (3) The girlfriend. He has spoken of Regina Lasko in interviews, of course, if sparingly, but has never on the air indicated that there was such a person in his life. ("It's a Peter Pan thing," one former staffer says.) But during his desk chat with Regis "The Last Man to See Me Alive" Philbin, he said, "The worst part of [bypass recovery] is being driven around. You can't drive for, like, the first three weeks. . . . The girlfriend loved it. She *loved* driving me around. *'Well, I've got you right where I want you now!'* " And we learned: Dave has a *life.* He has more than a television show; he has a relationship with a woman who also has a life with *him.* There are three dimensions to him, after all. (4) The ugliest ugly truth. During his opening remarks, he explained the following: "Bypass *surgery*—it's when doctors create new blood flow to your heart. A *bypass* is what happened to me when I didn't get *The Tonight Show*! It's a whole different thing." It was a joke, yes, but it was something more. We learned that he had found perspective.

In that shining moment, he seemed to have finally extricated himself from the picayune puniness that is Late Night Television War and to know what we know—which is that he is larger and better than it. He has always been Johnny to Leno's Merv—and Johnny, by the way, *never* regarded Merv as competition, even when they worked at the same hour of night. ("I hear *Merv* is doing another one of his little *theme* shows tonight," the King used to tease and twinkle, thereby separating apples from kumquats, not that there is anything wrong with kumquats.) Until this heroic night, Letterman had never acknowledged on the air the existence of Leno's *Tonight Show.* The closest he'd ever come was a 1997 broadcast during which guest Eleanor Mondale mentioned that she had recently interviewed Leno on her cable show. "Nice man, is he?" Letterman asked. "What's Jay doin' now?"

Because Jay is ever aware of what Dave is doing, I will tell you that he saw Dave's fifth postbypass broadcast, Wednesday, March 1, on which—due to scheduling conflicts—his guest, the Republican presidential candidate George W. Bush, could appear only via satellite from St. Louis. This, of course, rankled Letterman, who for months on the show had been fond of calling Bush "a colossal boob." So, at the close of their awkward satellite exchange (during which Bush did little to alter Letterman's initial appraisal), Dave tried cajoling him into appearing as an on-set guest the following Monday. Bush averred that he would be in California. Dave looked over to Burnett afterward and said, "He'll be on the Jay Leno show Monday night, is that what he's doing? That's where he'll be?"

Burnett said yes. To which Letterman edgily responded, "*There's* a real summit meeting!" Whereupon the audience whooped and Paul Shaffer marveled at the brio: "It's *true* what they say—you don't give a damn anymore!" (An executive who knows both hosts pointed out, "It was unheard of! Notice that he didn't say *The Tonight Show*—he called it the *Jay Leno show*. In Dave's mind, *The Tonight Show* ended with Johnny.") And four nights later, which was Sunday night, there was Leno bounding onstage to collect his trophy for Best Talk Show during Fox's broadcast of the TV GUIDE Awards, and he was clutching his chest as he did so. "Ohh," he said darkly, "I almost had a heart attack when I heard I won!" And before he left the stage, he made sure to add "We have to go home and write Bush jokes because he's on tomorrow!" And this was his return volley of sorts, I guess, because to my friend Leno it will always be a contest. But I know that he was stung; Letterman used to jab him all the time back at the old place when Leno sat in the chair beside Letterman's desk, largely because Leno usually used to jab him first. But that was before everything else happened and before Letterman's desk moved so far beyond Leno's proximity.

Anyway, somebody told me that Tom Snyder gave Leno a call to congratulate him on the nice job he had done with George W. the next night. And I guess they got around to talking about Letterman and Letterman's heart and Letterman's little poke at Leno. And Leno kept saying that he just didn't get why Dave had said what he said. "It's been *eight years!*" he complained. "Can't he just let this go?" But, in fact, Letterman did let it go. It had been stuck in his heart for the longest time. But lately things have never been more clear.

Oh, God. If anything, consider the next piece as a palate-cleansing sorbet to all previous Sturm und Drang. An *Esquire* editor named Randy Rothenberg suggested this foolish experiment, knowing my peculiar foothold in the realm of late-night television. Following the spirit of George Plimpton, master of experiential journalism, I attempted to participate in the lost art of "sidekicking"—as in pretending to be Ed McMahon on a real talk show. Unlike Plimpton, however, I consented to try this largely because no actual physical expenditure, or unpleasant bruising, would be attendant.

I had twice substituted for Greg Kinnear as guest host of his *Later* program on NBC the year before—my guests were Sandra Bernhard and millionaire/presidential aspirant Steve Forbes, both of whom accepted my apologies most gracefully at the time, thank you. (Hosting is another story altogether. Nevertheless, as did Bette Midler with Johnny Carson on his penultimate show, Miss Bernhard lovingly serenaded me on air, because I made her do so. It was Burt Bacharach and beautiful.) I never wrote about the hosting experience (and barely spoke of it) until this story came about. What transpired here, however, was even more harrowing. For the record, in aftermath: Charles Grodin, the host who had let me sidekick, largely objected to the published story because I casually mentioned his hairpiece in the text. On camera, he later asked his producer: "Is this a hairpiece?" His producer said no, of course it wasn't, no, not at all. (Mm-hmm.) Regis Philbin would also somewhat regret having participated in this exercise, since he regularly dines with Grodin in Connecticut. Conan O'Brien sidekick Andy Richter, meanwhile, seemed especially touched by the final dyspeptic paragraph and sent me an antique cocktail mixer with a note that read: "Practice, practice, practice."

Paper Sidekick

When we started this show in 1962, the total population of
the earth was three billion one hundred million people. This
summer it is five billion five hundred million people—a net increase of two billion four hundred million people, which
should give us some pause. The more amazing statistic is that
half of those two billion four hundred million people will soon
have their own late-night TV shows.
      —Johnny Carson, in his final broadcast, May 22, 1992

Esquire, June 1997

Even I have hosted. The Kinnear boy had a movie to make and they were
letting anyone substitute-host, so they called me and I hosted *Later* on
NBC. The day after I hosted, I met the King, who knew what I had
done. That is why he is King, even in retirement. I had dropped by his
plush Santa Monica office suite, where friends of mine work, and heard
his voice issue along a corridor: "I understand there's a new late-night
talk-show host in the building." So I stood before Johnny Carson, an im-
postor before majesty, humbled beyond human reckoning. But his eyes
twinkled warmly and he asked with genuine interest, "Did you enjoy it?"
I do not recall my exact response, but I believe much stammering occurred, kind of like when I hosted.

    Did I enjoy it? I am still uncertain. It is a very frenetic thing, hosting:
Producers parade through your day, giving notes, making program
changes until show time, during the taped blur of which they give more
notes and make more changes. Feigning impossible calm on camera, you
must engage and delight guests while juggling topics of inquiry and
watching for time cues from nervous guys waving cards and fingers. Afterward, you wipe away orange makeup, apologize to network executives,

and quake with surplus adrenaline unexpended. And then there are the stains. It calls to mind one early episode of HBO's fictional *Larry Sanders Show* when the estimable sidekick Hank Kingsley was forced to stand in for his host, who had suddenly been felled by poisoned yogurt. Valiantly, Hank muddled through, then crumpled into a heap once it was over. "Man, I'm *tired*!" he said. "Now I know why Larry is so fucked up!" Even the sage Jack Paar, on that famous night when he walked off his own *Tonight Show,* weepily postulated: "There must be a better way to make a living than this." Alas, he could not find one and returned until he could host no more, repairing finally to Connecticut, where he recovers to this day, thirty-five years hence.

To host, I will tell you, is to court cataclysm. It is high-wire business, best suited to the highly wired and the tightly wound, then televised so as to amplify all possible humiliation and to also just plain entertain. Hosting only further complicates the complicated life. So I ask: Who needs this kind of headache? For the sole purpose of journalistic endeavor, I must answer: Not me. That is why I decided to become a TV sidekick.

Whereas a host must spin, a sidekick must be steadfast. Whereas a host must control, a sidekick must relax. Hosts strap their wild synapses into rigid ergonomic chairs and await incoming missiles of doom. Sidekicks get couches on which to plump and sprawl, from which to cushion disaster and think about dinner plans. Without doing much of anything, they serve and protect the poor bastard running the show. It is all about just being there for somebody. Does life behold any gesture more beautiful than this? Plus, the pay is tremendous! On his Final Night, there was Johnny Carson nodding toward the large fellow to the right of the Desk, stating his debt plainly: "Ed has been a rock for thirty years, sitting over here next to me."

To sit like a nearby rock! That is sidekicking, my friends. And you are all my friends, for I am a sidekick, like the great Ed McMahon, who is merely Gibraltar, friend to all and possibly even to Johnny. "Hi-yo!" Ed would say and, now, so too do I, although I am still unclear as to what *hi-yo* actually means. (Something about rounding up horse wagons, I think. Maybe Budweiser Clydesdales? Hmm.) Nevertheless, Ed has taught me well, for I sought out his epic wisdom and golden reminiscences. (Me: "When do you laugh?" Him: "When something is funny." Me: "Right, right.") Indeed, my quest for such intrinsic knowledge led me to the most towering fonts of experience: Hugh Downs, who genially bestrode the Paar couch; Regis Philbin, whose fame blossomed as Joey

Bishop's most earnest foil; Jeffrey Tambor, the actor who becomes "Hey, Now!" Hank Kingsley for Larry Sanders who is Garry Shandling; and, significantly, the last of—and perhaps best of—the breed, postmodernist Andy Richter, who flanks and anchors Conan O'Brien and redefines the role to which I aspire and he never did. "I'm not sure this is something anyone would really *want* to do," he told me from the start a tad hedgingly. Eventually, his point would caress my psyche like the reaper's bony claws. Hi-yo.

But first, I needed a host who needed me. It is, alas, a time of megalomania and insecurity among our hosts, an ungenerous era when only bandleaders are permitted to share spotlight and faux-kick, no matter that they have better things to do. Like make music. At present, only two bona fide sidekicks work in America and one of them isn't actually real. Desolate couches cry out for steerage. Hosts have never looked lonelier or more lost. They crane their necks hideously, unnaturally, in search of support, only to make do with the wavering attention of a distant tunesmith. They are tragic figures. I wanted to work for just such a host, one whose every on-camera twitch and pause represented desperation and woe, one who seemed to sorely need a pal—and, preferably, one who could only be seen on cable. (Hey, I didn't need the world watching this experiment blow up in my face.)

So I went after Charles Grodin. One of our finest comic actors, he had sunk into a maudlin quagmire as host of his own nightly CNBC show. There, of late, he mostly dodders gloomily. The trial of O. J. Simpson seemingly killed Grodin's sense of play, turned him into society's Great Lamenter or, put simply, a mope. Often, he stares mournfully into the recesses of his studio for catatonic moments on end, as would a man in need of a defibrillator. What fun is that? I wished only to lighten his load, to buoy his hangdog spirit, to bring back the wry and mirthful Chuck Grodin who once so gamely tormented Carson and Letterman.

I faxed my heartfelt proposition to his home and waited. When we later spoke on the phone, he sounded pre-Simpsonian-funny again. He did twenty rollicking minutes just on back pain. But he fretted over my selfless offer: "You know, I can't—it'll totally look like I'm doing...like you're sitting beside me so I can get a nice piece in *Esquire*," he said. "I mean, the only way this could conceivably work would be for me to spend the hour attacking you for insulting me with this offer. If you want to do *that*..." He chuckled at the idea. "I mean," he said, "I would be *thrilled* if I could get Charles Grodin to offend *me*."

But of course: All hosts must demean their sidekicks. Already our rapport was well in place.

Lessons began on floor nine of 30 Rockefeller Center, Midtown Manhattan. Here was Conan wandering into Andy's office, a smoky, untidy nook whose doorplate reads TELLY SAVALAS. (Just next door, the host's placard announces occupancy by C. CONUS CONEWORTHY, THE RICHEST MAN IN TOWN.) Both men loom tall, although Andy was slumped at his desk, atop of which a fragrant candle flickered. "Give me back my Silly Putty," he groaned at Conan, who ignored him and informed me, "I created the character of Andy Richter. When I found him, he was a blank slate."

"Give me my putty!" Andy repeated. Whereupon Conan lectured him, while gesturing toward me: "Remember, when he asks you something, just nod like we told you. Then wait three seconds and repeat what he said in a knowing way."

"Right," said Andy. Conan stepped out of the room. "He's a dick," said Andy, moving to slam the door, which he did just as Conan turned to reenter. "Asshole!" said Conan, muffled through wood. I never saw any putty.

What I saw was love. It is the kind of love few men could understand, unless they have a sidekick or are one. Said actor Alec Baldwin of the O'Brien-Richter electrolyte during one *Late Night* appearance: "You guys do seem like disengaged lovers. There's a lot of subtext." To which the brave host confessed: "It's a sexual tension." On another night, Conan told guest Larry King: "On this show, Andy is a star. I *love* him." King: "You love him? Why don't you two kiss each other?" (There is good reason why Larry King works alone.)

A proper sidekick will engender such love. Andy Richter, thirty and mordantly cherubic, is nothing if not lovable. I think I love him, but then we have shared much vodka. (Blessedly, as Big Ed has taught us, sidekicks are guys who know how to drink. Indeed, on the fourth O'Brien *Late Night* show ever to air, Ed himself appeared, whereupon Andy challenged the master to a beer-guzzling contest called Quarters. Who could not help but admire this boy's hubris?) That Conan O'Brien can publicly display couchward affection only confirms that he is the right host for a lost generation, that he is not too proud to express need of fraternity. Moreover, if he has Andy there for him, shouldn't we be there for him as well?

More than three years after his rocky start on NBC and much critical thrashing, Conan today is thriving, his ratings good, his spirit and contract renewed. He offered me this salient explanation: "Having Andy creates the subliminal perception, *Well, how bad can this guy be? He's got one friend.* The crime is less heinous if you've got someone else there helping you who looks sane. Like you have an accomplice."

I turned now to the first such accomplice who mattered: Hugh Downs, who forged this craft amid frenzy and looked sane best. From 1957 to 1962, he was there for Jack Paar, broadcast dramatist nonpareil, whose writhing emotions ripped through television screens. Paar bled and Downs mopped. Paar cried and Downs comforted. "It was like riding a bronco," Downs recalled, not unaffectionately, when I phoned him at his ABC-TV lair, where he presides as coanchor of the newsmagazine *20/20.* "Every night you didn't know what was going to happen and it always did." Before Downs, sidekicking was an ephemeral thing, an ensemble art spread amongst a broadcast family of oddballs taking turns at support. Jack Benny, whom Ed McMahon cites as the key Carson influence, had his antic regulars—as did Steve Allen on the first *Tonight Show,* as did Paar for that matter. But Paar also had Hugh Downs, his announcer (as every classical sidekick would thereafter be, up until Andy Richter), who hovered on the outskirts, bursting with keen knowledge, which Paar prized. "If you ask Hugh what time it is, he'll tell you how the watch works," the host often joshed. Indeed, Paar asked many things of Downs, not least of which was eventually to sit beside the desk, where no announcer had sat before! (Paar! Father of the Form!)

"He had this idea," Downs said, laying the Stone Tablet before me. "He'd call me over and I'd sit in the chair and when the first guest came in, I'd greet the guest along with him and move down to the couch and keep moving down throughout the night. That is still done, and nobody's improved on it." (As Ed would later tell me, "I always knew when I hit the end of the couch, the show was over." Yes! The sidekick's curb feeler!)

So there sat Downs, the Columbus of Couch, charting territory unexplored, wondering what to do with himself. Some nights, he did nothing: "I'd go home and think, *God, I'm just not earning my keep.* Then I learned that it wasn't important that I be in there trying to make a big contribution every time." He learned that proximity was all, that proximity bonded men plenty. This, of course, was both the rapture and the pity of the role. But many a night (and more than anyone else, even a youth named Carson), he filled in for Paar, including the historic night Paar took his on-air powder—the Great Walk-Off—triggered by network censorship of his legendary water-closet joke from the night before. And Downs was the only person he told ahead of time that he was leaving.

"The surprise to me was that he left at the *beginning* of the show!" he said, still amazed. But, true to his host, Downs plowed on with the program and becalmed a nation stunned. "I'll tell you, it was probably the hottest spotlight I was ever in, before or since."

I went off to annoy my friend Regis Philbin, something I have done countless times since I profiled him three years ago in this magazine. He is most fun when annoyed. As the announcer for ABC-TV's *Joey Bishop Show* (1967–69), however, he never bristled on camera. Rather, he was Regis carefree: freshly into his thirties, a hurricane of pep gusting into the sleepy sails of his low-key host. *Enthusing* was his racket. For the annals, he is the only sidekick ever to become a giant among talk hosts. But his work as Bishop's knight nevertheless remains unforgettable. It was the one time more energy stirred from the couch than from the desk.

He has kept but a few old show tapes and I had asked to watch one with him—thus the annoyance. "The sidekick is a relic of the talk-show business!" he moaned, as he will, leading me into an edit bay at *Live With Regis & Kathie Lee* headquarters. The tape was dated June 11, 1968, just one month before Regis walked off the show, à la Paar, crushed by rumors that the network felt he hurt ratings. (He was back the next week, embarrassed, but more beloved than ever. "I slipped on my second-banana peel," he admitted three decades later.) Now, on the monitor, he saw himself, a man-child with complexion aglow, voice of cotton, hollering (even then), "And now, ladies and gentlemen, *it's time for Joey*!"

We watched Bishop lope out, peering through drooped eyelids, and begin: "That's what I like, folks, a sitting ovation." In lieu of telling his usual joke or two (never more), he asked that people stop sending him cakes. Then he teased young Philbin about his recent record album, *It's Time for Regis!* (Sidekicks, alas, have sung in their spare time, McMahon and Hank Kingsley among them.) At which point, Regis rushed over from the wings, all afire, with a topic for Bishop to traverse: "Time to dip into the mailbag!" ("Every night I had to come up with something different," he told me now, shaking his head. "Joey never knew what it would be. Didn't *want* to know! He would just counterpunch, his specialty. But if it didn't pay off or wasn't cute, it was my fault.") After this, Regis performed his regular surreal task of trying to excite Bishop about the guest lineup: "What a show I've got for you! The funniest man alive, one of your dearest pals—Buddy Hackett is here!"

"Feeding him was my job," he said, shutting off the tape. "But you had to know your place. You couldn't be funnier than him. It was important to me that he get his laughs. On the other hand, the perception of me was that of an inconsequential, trivial kind of guy. It was a tightrope act."

To prepare for my role, I became Andy Richter's off-camera sidekick for many days. I knew my place and tried not to be funnier than him. Also I fed him, and his wife, actress-writer Sarah Thyre, at their favorite French-Alsatian restaurant. We consumed many exotic potions and I prompted him to recount amusing anecdotes. Like his triumphant first meeting with Conan, at Junior's Deli in West Los Angeles: Andy ordered borscht, whose sheer purpleness amazed the nascent host, and also a misshapen knish. "It had a knob on top of it," he recalled, "and when the waitress set it down, I said, 'Man, check that out! It looks like a fuckin' tit!' That was the big icebreaker." Eventually, he was unafraid to climb in and out of his show clothes in front of me. When he aired his life concerns, I listened with empathy and, in certain such moments, if he was wearing a shirt, my hand fell easily on his shoulder.

For instance, he told me of his ambivalence over becoming what he is now: "When I heard the word *sidekick,* I thought, *I don't know....* It kind of implies *lackey.*"

Perhaps in another man's grasp it does, but Richter is not simply another man. Well, he sort of is, but anyway: Ingrained with farm boy innocence (Yorkville, Illinois), spit-polished by improvisational stagecraft in Chicago, he is a monument of gentle self-assuredness—happily contrasting to the jangles of O'Brien. ("I have like a sugar energy; I'm manic," Conan told me. "Andy always seemed more at peace with himself, just very centered.") Words tumble out of Richter unhurriedly, economically, and almost always they are funny, detonating like magic bullets. A random exchange: "Let me ask you something, Andy," said Conan, at desk. "What do we always try to do on this late-night program?" Andy, stroking chin: "Uh ... skim money out of petty cash?"

Hired as a writer, he was not asked to write so much as to just be around. During lighting tests on Bob Costas's old *Later* set, he played O'Brien's guest, and luminous alchemy emerged. His fate was sealed. Then he was given rein to mock couch-bound boredom. Unprecedented! A regular feature aimed an isolated camera on him suffering through

Conan's guest chats, sneaking cigarettes, reading the paper, playing catch. He sidekicked live from an aerial blimp over Manhattan. He invaded the Miss America Pageant, where he confounded contestants by demanding they find their home states on a map. And he spoofed the sidekick's need for "outside projects," making idiotic music videos, playing Elizabeth Taylor in a TV movie, and so on. Moreover, he became chief comic counsel to his host. Just before each show, he helps Conan pick and order the monologue jokes. ("He has really made me a big partner in this process, which he didn't have to do.") More of a team than their predecessors, they are each often asked in public where the other guy is.

Conan told me, "People want to believe that when the show's over, we get on a bicycle-built-for-two, ride it back to our house, I get in the top bunk, he gets in the bottom bunk, we put on our sleeping caps, and begin synchronized Three Stooges snoring. And maybe that's the way it should be. I've got to talk to Andy's wife about this."

My triumphant first meeting with my host! At a holiday party in the sky-rise home of Regis and Joy Philbin, there stood Chuck Grodin, hunkered in a corner with Tony Bennett. He saw me coming. His eyes widened in mock terror. (Well, it *looked* mock.) He put down his champagne glass and made a move to bolt. Just like Larry Sanders does when he sees Hank Kingsley! Our chemistry was that instantaneous. I tried not to be funnier than him. Pain creasing his face, he told me that our night would be scheduled as long as Regis agreed to be his guest. "But there should be lawyers on the set, too," he said worriedly.

Poolside, Los Angeles, betrunked actor Jeffrey Tambor, who is not a side-kick but plays one, spoke of the occupation: "The guy's got the best job in the world! I mean, his job is literally sixty minutes long. That's it!" He meant the character "Hey, Now!" Hank Kingsley, his bungling alter ego on Garry Shandling's fine true-life fiction, *The Larry Sanders Show.* But he may as well have meant me. My sixty minutes neared, and who better to take advice from than another pretender, albeit a professional one with Emmy nominations. Hank, as essayed perfectly by Tambor, is a man of quiet desperation and acute simplicity. Also, he is a former cruise director. How he coined his catchphrase: "I said, 'Hey,' then I said, 'Now.' Then I just sort of put 'em together!" Both tolerated and besmirched by his host, Hank lives obliviously and loves his couch. Among the pointers I cribbed from Tambor on the Kingsley style: "It is written that he is subservient, you know. . . . The key to the character is that he's vulnerable. . . . He's always happy. . . . He's a total professional, a very good announcer, but as a man, he's a total amateur . . . I don't think he's stupid, but that might just be me." I asked him what essential talent I should hone before my debut. "Listen . . . ," he said. "I am," I said. "Listen, listen . . . ," he said. "Yes, sir, go ahead," I said. "No, no, *listen*!" he repeated. "That's it! Just listen! And don't push. And react naturally. And try to be in the moment. And listen."

The prophecy came from on high: "I don't know . . . Grodin could put it in another dimension. You'll get that caustic stuff he does. He's very strange. But if you've made a deal, you've made a deal." I did not listen. Even though the one who warned me was the one who knows like no other: Ed McMahon, monolith and sole deity of upholstery. To be near him is to feel your own power magnified exponentially. If he is there, you are better, especially if he is ordering the wine. Just as Ed pressed fingertips together and bowed each night to a spotlit Nebraskan, I had come to Beverly Hills to pay him worship. At age seventy-four, he is ageless; no longer bearish of torso, he remains eternally Big, as does the Laugh that rumbles up from the caverns of his vessel and has made him millions.

I found him at home, itself Big, in his office, sort of small, whose walls and shelves bulged with Carsonia and McMahonia and mementos from Budweiser (for which he has voiced three decades of commercials). "See my pewter Clydesdales back there?" he said proudly. "There are only three of those in the world!" Piled before him was three thousand dollars in cash, large increments of which he was stuffing into holiday envelopes. "Gratuities," he explained. Weeks later, we met for lunch at the Polo Lounge, where he commands the coveted corner booth by the bar—"I've been sitting at this table for thirtysomething years"—and where he is revered by the staff. "I'm gonna write a new Bible," I heard a veteran waiter tell him, "and you're gonna be the master subject!" (Gratuities, natch.)

How it got to be like this: As per legend, they came together, host and announcer, on the game show *Who Do You Trust?* in October 1958, never to part until the King's elegant abdication. Just days before their first *Tonight Show* (October 1, 1962), however, the announcer wondered: "What the hell am I gonna do to be distinctive? I gotta do something!" He focused on the introduction. Whereas Hugh Downs had simply intoned, "Here's Jack!" McMahon would *elongate*: "*Heeeeeeeeeeeerre's* Johnny!" ("Instead of the *r*, I did it with the *e*. I knew it was right, be-

cause everybody picked up on it the next day.") *Hi-yo!* meanwhile, was
suggested by a producer, although Ed torqued that as well. "You have to
say it with a lot of *o*'s. You know, *Hi-yoooooooooooohh!*" We practiced together for a while. And it was he who decided that Carnac the Magnificent's hermetically sealed envelopes be kept in a mayonnaise jar on Funk
& Wagnall's porch since noon today. "*Funk* is funny, you know," he said.
"Words with *k* are funny." He claims, however, to have never said "You
are correct, sir!" On the other hand: "I may have said '*Yes!*' The *yes* was
very emphatic. But then my role was to supply punctuation."

And, as with all sidekicks before or since, he clung fast to the rules of
self-denial and modulated intercourse. "You have to be in there when
you're needed, but way the hell out when you're not needed," he instructed, the final authority. "Instinct is everything about the job. And
you have microseconds to make your choice." So infallible were his instincts that a singular 1965 misstep torments him even now: "Carson was
reading a news item about how mosquitoes will gravitate to the most passionate people. Without thinking, I slapped my arm and said, 'Ah!
There's another one!' Big, big laugh. But I get this look from Carson,
those steely-blues, you know? Then he pulls from behind the desk this giant prop can of insect repellent and said, 'Well, there's five hundred dollars shot!' He was going to spray himself, but I very innocently stole his
joke. My joke was better, but I felt terrible."

I would feel worse. What transpired March 19 over CNBC airwaves
should best be left to hazed memory. Unfortunately, it was videotaped,
and I have watched the debacle repeatedly. It happened in Fort Lee, New
Jersey, from whence the *Charles Grodin* program emanates. Weeks earlier,
my host had sprung his plan upon me: For a good portion of the show, I
would be sequestered in the backstage greenroom with a camera trained
on me, practicing sidekick craft—laughing, nodding, punctuating, feeding, listening. (Alone?) Then, from the studio, Grodin would cut over to
me, assessing whether my skill was worthy. "Somehow, toward the end,"
he promised, "we get you out there. See, that way it turns into a piece of
entertainment."

"He doesn't get it!" Regis said astutely, as we rode to Fort Lee on show
day. "The point of a second banana is that he is there *always,* at his man's
beck and call!" (Grodin *did* want me there the afternoon before, ironically, when he wasn't around. At his behest, I had pretaped my greenroom
buffoonery, improvising variations of subservience: "Yes!" "You are right!"
"And how are you, sir?" "That's terrific!" It didn't feel very good.) Instead

of me, it would be Regis who flanked Grodin when the show began. "Ughhh, I gotta talk to him for *an hour*?" Philbin merrily groused upon learning this. "I guess the O. J. thing is over, and now I gotta pay for it!" Meanwhile, I spent the first thirty-five minutes of the program nowhere near my host. I sat by a monitor in the makeup room and watched him talk about me.

To encapsulate: Maundering into his camera, Grodin opened: "The devil tried to buy my soul about two months ago—the devil, under the name of Bill Zehme." It was that bad. It got worse. "This guy really tried to corrupt my morals," he told Regis and viewership alike. "He said he would like to be my sidekick on this show. And, as a result, I could have a wonderful piece written about me in *Esquire*. That's what I call selling your soul." Valiantly, Regis leapt to my defense, explaining the integrity of this reportorial exercise and how Grodin was mistaken and should feel honored. He also said: "I have seen your new ratings at eleven o'clock. You *need* Zehme and you need *Esquire*! In second-banana tradition, he should be sitting here right now." They sparred for several more minutes; then Grodin said, "I want to see what kind of sidekick he would be. Let's see what he's doing now." The director cued up a sliver of my greenroom tape. There I laughed and toadied like a fool in soliloquy. Moments later, he did it again, and then again. "Oh, please!" Regis finally begged. "I think he's ready to come out!"

For the fourth segment, I emerged and was seated off-camera among a handful of Grodin's staff members. "We want to get you acclimated to the studio," he said a bit patronizingly. Then he asked me to laugh, which I did, pitifully, because it was my job. "Wait!" he interrupted. "I didn't say anything funny yet." (Tell me about it.) He further usurped time, forcing Regis to address videotaped (mind-numbing) questions from random people in the street. I was asked to laugh twice more, and did so, supportively, though without conviction, I fear. Responding to a gun-control question, Grodin asked me if I had a gun. "Not on me," I said, for which he looked relieved. Then: "After this break, we're gonna bring up the sidekick."

Eleven minutes remained. During the commercials, I took the chair beside Regis, across from Grodin, who consulted his pocket mirror and arranged his hairpiece. Just before we returned to the air, he told me to look at Regis, which I did, obediently, as the camera relit. He asked Regis why he liked Donald Duck, to which Regis said, among other things, "He didn't get enough attention." Grodin, to me: "Bill, do you find that interesting?" Me, to Regis: "Very interesting. Is that because Donald is a lot like you?" Regis, to me: "See, you don't understand. Second bananas

don't interview." I nodded. (Quite nicely, I thought.) Grodin then repeated his question, so I could try it again. This time I gave a small
chuckle. "That's a little better," said Grodin. "Thanks," I said. During the
next question, I laughed inappropriately once, was chastised, then
laughed with precision, and was complimented. Regis suggested I ask
Grodin why he had no sidekick. "Well," I said, "I think it's apparent now,
isn't it?" Then I told Grodin that I was his friend, as a sidekick must be,
and he said, "Why are you still talking?"

At last, surprise guest Ed McMahon weighed in, via satellite from
California: "Well, I'll give you the appraisal here in Burbank," he said,
meaning my debut work. "It's kinda less than exhilarating." He told me,
"You're so sure of what you do as yourself, you're not getting yourself into
the *role*. You haven't been in when needed, you haven't been out when not
needed. You haven't done anything!" Added Regis, "And, when needed,
be a little more subservient." Then Ed told the mosquito story and we all
laughed and the show ended and Grodin said, "I think that worked
pretty well."

That night, I met Andy Richter after his show finished taping. He took
me to the Rainbow Room atop Rockefeller Center, where we drank many
martinis and I regaled him with my sidekicking experience. As we
slouched at the bar, he asked with genuine interest, "Did you enjoy it?"
The martinis, I believe, expedited the vomiting, which came a few hours
later.

Part Seven:

AND IN CONCLUSION

The New Existential Crisis of Celebrity Journalism
(Plus Heather Graham!)

Between mid-1997 and the end of 1999—during which time I completed two books—I had written only one profile (of Hugh Hefner) for *Esquire*. Editors David Granger and Mark Warren demonstrated great patience during my absence, and so I was inclined to happily acquiesce to any assignment when they beckoned me back to the fold. I was, however, still reeling from the recent maddening experience of writing a biography about the ephemeral comic con artist Andy Kaufman. Therefore, I had told Mark to be gentle with me. "Nothing huge," I begged. The magazine's solution was Heather Graham. I further begged: "Please, don't."

While Heather Graham is a very lovely young woman, I have never been keen on profiling the latest flavors in Hollywood, for two reasons: (1) They usually haven't lived enough life to quite understand themselves yet, and (2) their publicists tend to overcontrol them. Moreover, because I had been away from the Hollywood celebrity beat for a while, I dreaded the sorry state in which I knew I would find it. Over the years, access to famous profile-subjects had generally dwindled to one or two cursory impersonal chat sessions, usually on neutral-ground locations, like restaurants and hotel rooms. Most of the work I had done, on the other hand, emerged out of reasonably longer periods, during which I would dip in and out of subjects' lives and observe them being themselves in semirealistic human circumstances. Only with that freedom can artful writers begin to work with palettes of bolder, richer color and thus render better portraits. Such days of worthwhile color had begun fading fast by the mid-nineties, as publicists gained more influence over the media. By 2000, those days were over altogether, especially in the realm of the attractive ingenue (and, for that matter, any actress under forty). So, quite rightly, I worried about Heather Graham.

After much whining, I went ahead and performed my duties anyway. Upon publication of the piece—which blatantly responded to, and quirkily exposed, the aforementioned concerns—media critic Peter Carlson wrote the following in *The Washington Post*: "Bill Zehme has lost it. He has cracked. He has snapped. And now he's going public, spilling the sordid secrets of his tawdry trade. Zehme writes celebrity profiles for *Esquire*. It's not a particularly lofty calling, but he's good at it. He possesses the key qualification for the job, which is the ability to become interested in—or at least to fake an interest in—the inner lives of bubble-headed celebrities. . . . But when *Esquire* assigned Zehme to write about Heather Graham, the busty blonde who played Felicity Shagwell in *Austin Powers: The Spy Who Shagged Me*, something in him snapped and he banged out a bizarre deconstruction of the whole celeb profile genre. And for some reason, *Esquire* has actually published it in the April issue. . . . Zehme is apparently so offended by [the current] trend [in which magazine covers feature semifamous young actresses wearing nearly nothing, as per *Maxim*] that he decided to expose the hidden backstage machinations behind celebrity cover stories. . . . Apparently, Zehme is going through some sort of existential crisis. Maybe his editors could help by assigning him to write a story about somebody who doesn't have a publicist."

Notes on the "New"
Celebrity Journalism

(Featuring Miss Heather Graham!)

Cleavage, baby! Or more precisely, *Maxim*. Circulation guys
all watch them in total envy, then lash editors to follow suit.
You do tits once, the numbers spike, and then you're fucked
for good—all anybody wants is tits. Probably we went too far
away from babes, until the Brits came and said enough p.c.—
let's have fun. Isn't it fun?

> —E-mail from a veteran magazine editor (not at *Esquire*)
> answering a magazine journalist's recent question,
> "What happened to this racket?"

I get so angry when I can't find a magazine that Heather
Graham has just appeared in. Why doesn't everyone agree
with me on this. I agree with Heather Graham on so many different matters. I wonder where Heather Graham shops for
clothes. Some people don't care much for Heather Graham
but I think that they are nuts! . . . I can't think of anyone more
beautiful than Heather Graham. Everyone should be grateful
to the parents of Heather Graham for bringing her into this
world. I can't say this any louder. I don't see why everyone
doesn't agree on this. . . .

> —From the website celebrity-fans.com/lylrrt.htm (essay entitled
> "Here's places to get what you want about Heather Graham")

Esquire, April 2000

Here in the new world of magazine making, it is a distinct pleasure to give you precisely what you want. It is a pleasure most distinct. For instance, the various persons who nowadays frequently appear on our covers without wearing very many clothes appear there for you and for people just like you. They know that you want them to appear there as much as we want them to, especially because you want them to. Often, these cover persons are photographed weeks before a writer is dispatched to divine their inner truths and tender secrets—that which becomes the nutmeat of the text (this) that accompanies photographs like the ones you may be noticing at present (those). Such was the case with myself and the beautiful Miss Heather Graham (her)—or Heather Joan Graham, as her parents named her on January 29, 1970, when she arrived in life, about which you are, or should be, extremely grateful. I did not personally know Heather Joan Graham, the talented movie actress, at the time these photographs were taken (for you)—another fellow was in charge of capturing her fine ephemerality via expensive camera equipment and artful conceptualization—but she would later tell me (once we began to know each other) that she had "fun" making the pictures. (She spoke enthusiastically of posing with a "towel" and "phallic-looking bottles" and "fat women" and "dwarves.") Heather, as she let me call her (although a few times I wryly called her "Baby" as only an older man might when he pretends to be sort of worldly, and, anyway, it seemed to make her laugh), is herself nothing if not a shimmering human embodiment of "fun"— which her publicist had assured editors of this magazine during negotiations that led to Heather's becoming our cover person (for you). I agree with her publicist on this. She is fun as well as five foot eight, blonde, inquisitive, unaffected, sweet, compassionate, full-breasted, openhearted, accommodating, spirited, worried that cell phones cause brain cancer, leery of tap water (more cancer), willing to make out with her boyfriend in public places, fond of yoga, and very thin. If certain people think otherwise or don't care about such qualities, they are quite probably nuts.

Here in the new world of celebrity appraisal, this is how things have been working: A writer is first permitted to meet a famous subject someplace other than the subject's home (intrusive, presumptuous), and then they Go Do Things together (or Create Events) so that the writer can observe the subject attempt to Approximate Reality, whereupon the writer can then write about these experiences as though they were, in fact, actual unchoreographed happenstance, so that the reader will gain visceral glimpses of revelatory behavioral traits, or candor, thus rich insight. If this sounds like fun, it is. Publicists and editors generally broker the details of such staged assignations between client and writer, so that the initial meeting will often feel like a blind date—albeit one set up by other people whose judgment (both parties pray) will be trustworthy. If this sounds exciting, it is. (Unless the circumstance brings together two heterosexual men, in which case it is what it is, nothing more, thank you very much.) For instance, after much scheduling and many telephone calls, it was decreed that Heather Graham would enter my life—and I hers—one bleak winter afternoon in Venice, California, at a restaurant called Hal's on Abbot Kinney Boulevard, an odd thoroughfare dotted with eclectic home-furnishing stores, where she reportedly wished to seek out objects for her house, but this turned out not to be true, but she hadn't been able to come up with anything else for us To Do. (Subjects, more often than not, decide on activities. Example: Sharon Stone once decided that she and I would receive massages together, then bake cookies. Another example: Johnny Depp once decided that he and I would climb the ruins of Harry Houdini's mansion so that we could be angrily chased off the premises.) "See," Heather confided to me, "I don't really need to shop for anything." She is just that honest, by the way. She then asked me if I needed to shop for anything ("Maybe you need to furnish someplace, huh?"), which I didn't, but I was touched that she had asked. (This, I soon understood, is part of her abundant charm; she is ever concerned about the needs of others; unlike many famous celebrities, she is unlike many famous celebrities; also, she is not too self-absorbed.) Anyway, she said: "My publicist was like 'Can you think of a concept of something to do?' And I'm like 'I don't really do things that are really that fun.' The ultimate fun is doing nothing. I like doing nothing with people I like—maybe just eating, hanging out, and talking." In no time flat, it seemed, we were having fun doing nothing much of anything at all whatsoever really. I noticed many men notice her doing this with me. If she noticed any of this noticing, however, I didn't notice it.

Here are some things you will now learn (in the text) about Heather Graham (partially based on research) and about the first hour I spent observing her (for you), including various comments she made during that time: At Hal's restaurant, she offered me a taste of her tuna, which was grilled ("I wonder if my ordering is too healthy"), but kept lustfully eyeing my turkey burger, of which she took several bites (at my own invitation). "Could I cut off a piece?" she asked, then announced after swallowing "This is much better than mine." We agreed that the special mayonnaise was the reason. In fact, I agreed with her on many different matters. "Aren't onions good?" she cheerfully asked at one point (re: turkey burger). Again, I agreed. Anecdote: Once, before engaging in a love scene with Mike Myers, the comic actor, for the popular 1999 film *Austin Powers: The Spy Who Shagged Me,* in which she portrayed the sprightly minx Felicity Shagwell, she ate some "really good tuna salad" made with a lot of onions and garlic that hung thick on her breath during the love scene, despite many spritzes of Binaca, causing Myers to utter amusing remarks to her off-camera. (He apparently compared that kissing experience to "shitting up a pine tree"—which she thought funny at the time, although I cannot say that I understand what he might have meant. By the way, in the 1998 film *Two Girls and a Guy,* she was also seen kissing the actor Robert Downey Jr. for a very long period during which they both utilized their tongues to prodigious effect before he seemed to burrow his face between her buttocks whereupon she made loud moaning sounds. She has not seen or spoken with Downey since he went to prison, in case you were wondering.) In case you wonder how she approached the role of pluckish Felicity Shagwell, who wielded guns and did other secret-agenty things, she told me this: "I pretended I was really confident." And then she laughed, as she will.

Here is where it would be good to ponder the laugh of Heather Graham, and other sounds she makes, in some sentences. The *New York Times* recently characterized her laugh this way: "She has a laugh that contrasts with her Breyers vanilla ice cream complexion, a flat, yet fluttery Phyllis Dillerish ah-ha-ha-ha-ha-ha." I do not agree with the *Times* on this. True, her skin is akin to some sort of dairy product (a pale kind; pick your brand); and yes, she has a "fluttery" demeanor (although I would call it *hyperblithe* or *hummingbirdesque* or maybe *preternaturally caffeinated,* but not in a bad way) which can produce dizzying loops of rapid-exchange conversation which follow no discernible path (as is common among all lively minds). But there is nothing "flat" about this deservedly flowering film star, including her laugh, which, I will agree, usually begins with an *ah,* but is then followed by something closer to *huh-huh-huh-huh-huh-huh-huh*—which is to say that the sound is not at all adenoidal, but rather guttural, thus more insinuating, conspiratorial, and, frankly, quite alluring. (Further, I can see no reason to bring the great Phyllis Diller into this equation, if you don't mind.) What should also be noted (here) is that her every utterance and response belies a yearning to *connect*. For instance, whenever someone else (me) said things to her, she would concurrently say *mm-hm-mm-hm-mm-hm* or else *right-right-right-right-right*. Moreover, her habitual reply to any question will be to ask three or four pointed questions of her own. (Indeed, so unslakable is her sense of curiosity that she will also frequently add a question mark to any statement of personal fact—such as "I wouldn't say that I have a bad temper? But I can get very angry? But I very, very rarely do it?") As a result, she tends to elicit more information than she dispenses—which, I am convinced, is not a calculated ploy, in that she is the opposite of reticent. What this does mean, however, is that she now possesses a fairly comprehensive knowledge of my life (how I survived divorce, how I met my girlfriend, how I indulge my daughter, etcetera), although I safely believe that she wouldn't use the information to harm me in any way.

Anyway: While most writers cleverly share elements of their own lives in order to prompt the same from interview subjects, and while I was flattered by her genuine semi-unwavering interest, it would now seem appropriate to unobtrusively shift focus back to the luster and insouciance that is Heather Graham, who was born in Milwaukee and raised in the Los Angeles suburb of Agoura Hills (from the age of nine, after having spent five years also being raised somewhere in Virginia, following Wisconsin); whose father is a retired FBI agent (who specialized in terrorism) (professionally); whose schoolteacher mother has written children's books; who no longer speaks to her mother or her father for reasons far too personal (for you) (and probably even for me) to fathom, although she has obliquely suggested (to several magazine writers who won't leave the topic alone) that her family's rigid and unyielding Irish Catholic piousness inflicted indeterminate damage upon her soul and psyche, wherein her pursuit of an acting career (in which blond girls sometimes have to take off their clothes on camera and/or pretend to do sexual things to gain attention) made her constantly feel that her parents constantly felt that she was not theirs—she felt that they felt that she had chosen to go straight to Hell, when all she really did was go to Hollywood, less than an hour from home. (Here is where the obvious ironic aside—re: Hollywood—would appear, but we will skip that. The larger point, I believe, is that her laugh is not flat.) Anyway, she told me this about the family-estrangement thing: "I'm sick of hearing myself talk about it." Also: "I mean, it's a really hard thing, you know?" Then we talked for a while about why she shouldn't have to talk about it any more ever again (unless in therapy), and we agreed that I agree with her on this matter.

•   •   •

Conventionally, when a cover subject has breasts, sly mention of such will be inserted (in text). Any belaboring of this, however, would be considered inelegant. But still.

It is It (as in the phenomenon, or moment, of) that now bears acknowledgment, although this (It) has already been made implicit by the fact that Heather Graham is the person wearing nothing more than a pink towel on the cover of this magazine (for you). It is generally subliminally telegraphed in that way. It was in the 1999 Hollywood-satire film *Bowfinger,* in which she played an opportunistic ingenue who had sex with everyone, that the scoundrel movie producer played by Steve Martin said this about It (and, ultimately, about the Heather Graham character): "*It* is a special quality. No matter what's going on, you cannot take your eyes off that person. Every word they say, every gesture—you're interested in!" It, many people thought, was meant to commence for her upon the release of the 1989 film *Drugstore Cowboy,* in which she was seen dead of a Dilaudid overdose on the floor of a seedy motel room. (So believable was she in death, perhaps, that we forgot she was still alive?) It did not truly begin to take wing for another eight years, however, when she became the peripatetic porn nymphet Rollergirl in the esteemed 1997 film *Boogie Nights,* in which she was seen naked (except for roller skates) while guilelessly posing the question "Are we going to fuck?" (As noted above, she excels in the art of inquiry.) Key roles in films like *Lost in Space* (which she found "boring") and others (see above) soon followed and now one (you) can find countless cyberclubs and websites that slavishly honor, and point up, her Itness (among them, Ohh, Heather; Heather Graham House of Worship; On the Heather Spot; Heather Graham Shag Pad; Abs of Steel: Heather Graham; and Undeniably Heather Graham). If you wonder what she thinks of this sort of on-line deification, she is conflicted. She told me that she logged on to one such site "like once, but it just freaked me out. It's flattering, but then you're like 'Wait till I do something really good and then you can [build these pages]'—you know what I mean?" (I believe I did, as the brackets indicate, but by this time I was well into my third hour with her and had grown fairly adept at knowing what she meant.) (We had meandered in and out of stores—"Do you want to go in here?"—and bought candles and looked at kitchen tiles and antique mirrors and things. When she walks, I noted, each foot seems uncertain where it will step next. Metaphor looms there, somewhere, probably, but not in a bad way.) "Usually," she said, "I hate [to watch] my work [in the movies in which I have appeared]." Certain people disagree with her on this. In something called *Stuff* magazine (whatever the hell that is), she has been declared the twenty-sixth Sexiest Woman in the World. That notwithstanding, she said, "It's still hard to get some jobs, though." And then, with much grace and self-effacement, she laughed. (Remember— *huh-huh*'s not *ha-ha*'s; okay?)

Certainly, undeniably, the reason for this opportunity to examine the wiles of Heather Graham (here) is that she will soon be seen (starring) as a willful new wife comically stalking the idiot husband who bolts from their marriage in the very likable forthcoming independent film *Committed*. (Her publicist agrees on this.) There is, by the way, no sex or even partial nudity in the movie, which seems intentional since no scenes call for such and since Heather Graham, as a diligent actress, is wisely trying to get away from the sex thing, since she has other excellent qualities (poise, gumption, fragility, interesting teeth, ability to kickbox). Inadvertently, I tested her in this regard: On our second afternoon together (the next day), we were driving around Hollywood (in whose Hills she lives) in her new Toyota 4Runner (which replaced her old one), and she asked, as she will, very gamely, "Should we Create another Event?" So I suggested the colorful notion—because someone had suggested it to me—of paying a visit to a rather dilapidated nearby strip club called Jumbo's Clown Room, to which, it turned out, she is no stranger. (She researched stripping there for some short she once made in which she stripped.) "My publicist would be so not into it, I know," she told me, however, a bit apologetically. "She doesn't want me to be doing things that are real, like, sexual? She feels like I already have done a lot of stuff like that? I think it'd be kind of fun. But if I told her, she'd be like [*makes mortified gasping sound*]!"

Of course, I could appreciate this point and that sound, as might her boyfriend of two years—the bright actor-writer-director Edward Burns— with whom she shares a birthday and her home and his New York apartment and whom she calls Eddie and who has said that the only good thing about Los Angeles is Heather Graham and who later told me (on the phone), "I wouldn't spend one minute here if it wasn't for her." He also said that her performance in the new film "feels, for me, closer to who Heather really is than anything she's played before. You can tell she's a sexy woman, but she's not playing the sexpot." (Their own sexual chemistry, meanwhile, is such that they are frequently spotted at parties or restaurants obliviously locked in passionate throes. Not long ago, the sister of a friend of mine saw them repair to the first-class lavatory of an

American Airlines jet for forty-five minutes. "You gotta live life, right?" Heather said to me, by way of explanation, and I could only agree.)

While searching for her next role—"You're like 'Where is that script that expresses *me*,' you know?"—she followed her boyfriend's lead and began writing a screenplay of her own, which deals with "very serious subject matter" that is "personal but not based on actual reality" and explores the quest of a woman "who's kind of trying to be happier and kind of achieves it in a way." Rather than show me pages, she described one scene: "This actually did happen to me, it was kind of funny, but I don't know, I think this is funny, you may not think it's funny. But I was going out with this guy and sort of after we had sex he asked me to help him do his taxes. He's like 'Will you help me organize my receipts? I need to organize them, and if you want to be my girlfriend, I need help in this.' And he basically gave me all the tax documents and receipts, but then I sort of realized that I really didn't want to."

I agreed on this being funny but kind of wished that we could have Created an Event at Jumbo's Clown Room, which also would have been funny. Instead, we went to a bookstore near her house, and she made me buy this book called *Full-Frontal: Male Nudity Video Guide,* which she thought was a funny thing for me To Do—probably not terribly unlike shitting up a pine tree, I suspect. I wonder if anyone will agree with me on this. Her sweater, meanwhile, was snug and pink. I forgot to ask where she bought it. About that (and much above), I'm sorry.

Acknowledgments

I now humbly give deepest acknowledgment to many of those brave editorial heroes who turned me loose in print and let me care too much about what I was trying to write. At *Esquire,* David Hirshey brought me in, where I proudly remain, and made me laugh hard always; also there were the great skills and heartening support of Mark Warren, David Granger, Michael Solomon, Ed Kosner, Bryan Mealer, Andy Ward, Ted Allen, Mike Sager, and Rachel Clarke. Earlier, at *Rolling Stone,* Bob Wallace served and protected like no other; then, of course, there was fearless leader Jann Wenner, and Peter Travers, Sid Holt, Bob Love, Lisa Henricksson, Jeffrey (The Pause) Ressner, David Wild, Tom Conroy, Robert Vare, David Handelman, Genelle Izumi, Shelley Cole, and Janie Matthews. At *Spy:* Graydon Carter, Kurt Andersen, and the perfect Susan Morrison. At *Vanity Fair* (my Maytag Repairman years, as the first and last Chicago correspondent): Tina Brown and Wayne Lawson. And, at *Playboy,* where I was first believed in, by my friend and magazine-racket mentor John Rezek: the great Arthur Kretchmer, the wise Stephen Randall, Jonathan (You Ask Me of Leno) Black—and, but of course, Hef. Aiding and abetting (and enduring), like magic, like crazy, like when it was very necessary: Chris (Dung-Hey) Calhoun of Sterling Lord Literistic, Mike Thomas, Sara Brant, Josh Schollmeyer, Tracy Barone,

David (Obi Wan) Rensin, Cameron Crowe, Chris Pallotto, Robert Shea, Robert Anderson, Tina Zimmel, Jacob Hoye, Peter and Alice Lassally, Regis and Joy Philbin, Clare Charles, Marcia Froelke Coburn, Paige Smoron, Phil Rosenthal, Helene Rubenstein, Ilene Rosenzweig, Rick Marin, R & D, and Robert F. Zehme and the gal he married and their remarkable daughter who is my sister. Also, certainly, I thank, and thank, my most beloved dancing girl, Lucy Ellen Zehme, and my most beloved art-mermaid Carrie (Without Whom I'm Nothing) Secrist. But please know that it was the generous and wondrous Zoë Rice at The Dial Press who made this book with me and who makes retrospective self-reconnaissance a pretty pleasant thing, after all. Who knew?